PRAISE F

OBJECTIVE TROY

"Scott Shane has done a masterful job of fleshing out the missing link in the evolution of Al Qaeda. The life of the American-born imam, Anwar al-Awlaki, serves as a cautionary tale about the conflict between Islam and the West, and about America's role in the Middle East. Years after his assassination by an American drone strike, Awlaki's voice continues to summon young Muslims to the fight."

—LAWRENCE WRIGHT

"Remarkable ... A dark and fascinating new book ... Shane's investigation into what he describes as the president's radicalization is one of the most thorough and level-headed that has been penned to date ... A crucial read."

—ARTHUR HOLLAND MICHEL, *BOOKFORUM*

"Scott Shane has written a bracing story about America's most notorious extra-judicial killing, the 2011 drone shot that took out the American-born terrorist preacher Anwar al-Alwaki. Here is by far the best reporting on the subject, from Alwaki's gradual evolution into a violent extremist to the Obama administration's internal struggles—moral and legal—over how to use the drone."

—MARK BOWDEN

"Mr. Shane performs a valuable service by stripping away many myths that surround Awlaki."

—MAX BOOT, *THE WALL STREET JOURNAL*

"No one has written a better book about Obama's war against terrorists. Shane is a superb reporter and a wonderful storyteller. I literally could not put this book down. It will join a short list of books that helps all of us to really understand the wars against terrorist groups that have defined US foreign policy since 9/11."

—PETER BERGEN

"A lucid and richly informed account.... Shane offers a detailed and convincing narrative."

—PAUL PILLAR, *THE NEW YORK TIMES BOOK REVIEW*

"Scott Shane has written a twenty-first-century morality tale about a president steeped in constitutional law and his hunt for a charismatic American terrorist—who just happens to be a 'skirt-chasing mullah.' But this murder mystery is alarmingly all true. The writing is riveting, the intelligence sources are impeccable, and the book is quietly elegant— *Objective Troy* is destined to become a classic text on both the Obama presidency and drone warfare."

—KAI BIRD

"[*Objective Troy*] delves deeply into a single life and still comes up with questions. This is perhaps its greatest service. It is an object lesson in the limits of the search for a root cause."

—DEBORAH PEARLSTEIN, *THE WASHINGTON POST*

"Scott Shane is unsurpassed in shedding clear light on America's darkest secrets, including the gripping human drama behind a drone strike that changed history. It's a story that had to be told, and must be read."

—JANE MAYER

"Remarkable . . . *Objective Troy* is a gripping read."

—BENJAMIN WITTES, *LAWFARE*

"A gripping, deeply reported tale of sex, religion, radicalization, and betrayal. In the telling, Shane reveals a strange truth: the key to understanding Awlaki's actions, and his fate, is recognizing how American his story is. . . . The reason we know as much as we do about the killing—and other drone strikes—is because of the efforts of reporters like Scott Shane. Read his book."

—NICK BAUMANN, *COMMONWEAL*

"The story [Shane] tells of Anwar al-Awlaki's life and death is deeply instructive, as is his account of Barack Obama's decision-making. Anyone interested in understanding the allure of radical Islam, and thinking about ways to counter it both on and off the battlefield, would do well to study this work."

—GABRIEL SCHOENFELD, *THE WEEKLY STANDARD*

OBJECTIVE TROY

ALSO BY SCOTT SHANE

DISMANTLING UTOPIA
How Information Ended the Soviet Union

OBJECTIVE TROY

A TERRORIST, A PRESIDENT, AND
THE RISE OF THE DRONE

SCOTT SHANE

TIM
DUGGAN
BOOKS

NEW YORK

Library of Congress Cataloging-in-Publication Data
is available upon request.

ISBN 978-0-8041-4031-7
eBook ISBN 978-0-8041-4030-0

Printed in the United States of America

Map by Robert Cronan/Lucidity Information Design, LLC
Cover design by Oliver Munday
Cover photograph by Tracy Woodward/*The Washington Post*

10 9 8 7 6 5 4 3 2 1

First Paperback Edition

For M, L, and N,

and, of course,

for F

CONTENTS

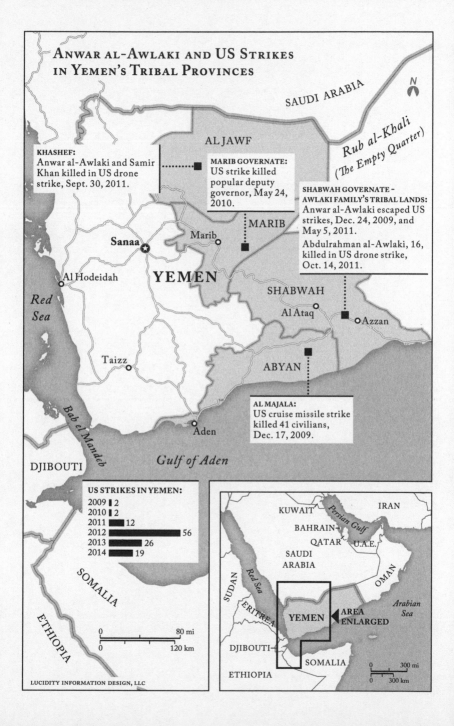

Anwar al-Awlaki and US Strikes in Yemen's Tribal Provinces

KHASHEF:
Anwar al-Awlaki and Samir Khan killed in US drone strike, Sept. 30, 2011.

MARIB GOVERNATE:
US strike killed popular deputy governor, May 24, 2010.

SHABWAH GOVERNATE - AWLAKI FAMILY'S TRIBAL LANDS:
Anwar al-Awlaki escaped US strikes, Dec. 24, 2009, and May 5, 2011.

Abdulrahman al-Awlaki, 16, killed in US drone strike, Oct. 14, 2011.

AL MAJALA:
US cruise missile strike killed 41 civilians, Dec. 17, 2009.

SAUDI ARABIA

AL JAWF

Rub al-Khali (The Empty Quarter)

MARIB

Sanaa

Marib

Al Hodeidah

YEMEN

Red Sea

SHABWAH

Al Ataq   Azzan

Taizz

ABYAN

Aden

Bab el Mandeb

Gulf of Aden

DJIBOUTI

US STRIKES IN YEMEN:
2009 | 2
2010 | 2
2011 | 12
2012 | 56
2013 | 26
2014 | 19

SOMALIA

ETHIOPIA

0   80 mi
0   120 km

KUWAIT   IRAN
BAHRAIN   Persian Gulf
QATAR   U.A.E.
SAUDI ARABIA   OMAN
SUDAN   Red Sea
ERITREA   YEMEN   Arabian Sea
AREA ENLARGED
DJIBOUTI
ETHIOPIA   SOMALIA

0   300 mi
0   300 km

I n the summer of 1984, Nasser al-Awlaki spotted a chance to take his growing family from Yemen on an extended visit to the United States, where he had spent nearly a dozen memorable years as a student and young professor. He grabbed it.

Dr. Awlaki applied for a grant from the Ford Foundation to attend a monthlong seminar at Stanford University on a cutting-edge topic, applications for the new machines called "microcomputers." His years as a graduate student in New Mexico and Nebraska in the 1960s had yielded a PhD in agricultural economics and an assistant professorship in Minnesota and prepared him for a distinguished career serving his country. He would serve as Yemen's agriculture minister, be named president of Sanaa University, and found another Yemeni university. Now he thought his children, especially the eldest, his thirteen-year-old son Anwar, were old enough to appreciate some of the wonders of American life.

Nasser al-Awlaki was a classic technocrat. Like generations of Muslims from the Middle East who had come to the United States for an education, he had found something more—an enticing openness, freedom from the straitjackets of tradition and authoritarian government, and, of course, a taste of economic abundance. Arriving as a Fulbright scholar in 1966, he had been dispatched to Lawrence, Kansas, for English-language training and was astonished to discover that he could have all the milk he could drink at the student cafeteria. After he began his studies at New Mexico State University, his host family in Las Cruces invited him to both their churches—the husband was Protestant and the wife Catholic. They fed him lamb and rice for Sunday dinner, figuring that menu might be familiar and comforting for a young man so far from his Arabian home.

"That was my introduction to America—good families and good people," he recalled, sitting with me in his spacious house in the Yemeni capital, Sanaa, nearly half a century later.

In the late 1970s, Nasser and his wife, Saleha, had brought home to Yemen warm memories of their American years. She took pride in baking an exotic dessert she had mastered while overseas: apple pie, a recipe from her Betty Crocker cookbook. He got up early many mornings to watch the softball interviews of politicians and celebrities on *Larry King Live*—live in Sanaa, too, via satellite.

On their way to the Stanford computer seminar in that summer of 1984, Nasser and Saleha and their four children stopped in New York City and bought a video camera, which was quickly commandeered by Anwar, their skinny, bookish teenager. "He was our cameraman for the whole trip," Nasser remembered. Anwar had been born in New Mexico when his father was a graduate student and spent his first seven years in the States, barely speaking Arabic when his parents moved the family back to Yemen. Now their oldest child proudly recorded weekend visits to Yosemite, Disneyland, and SeaWorld in San Diego. He accompanied his father to the Stanford seminar, too, growing fascinated with computers and their vast promise.

When the Awlaki family strolled the streets of Manhattan on the way west that idyllic summer, a lanky, brown-skinned young man a decade older than Anwar was walking the same crowded sidewalks. At twenty-two, Barack Obama was chafing a bit at his first postcollege job, researching and writing on business for a financial publisher and consulting firm, half-joking with his mother that he was "working for the enemy." Soon he would follow his idealistic instincts to the New York Public Interest Research Group, a branch of Ralph Nader's activist empire, and from there to his famous stint as a community organizer in Chicago.

Like Anwar al-Awlaki, Barack Obama had been born in the United States to a secular-minded foreign father of Muslim background who had come on scholarship to further his education. Like young Anwar, he had left the United States as a child and lived in a Muslim country. Obama stayed in Indonesia only from ages six to ten, clearly a visitor, while Anwar al-Awlaki lived in Yemen, surrounded by extended family, from seven to nineteen. When they returned to America, their unusual backgrounds and upbringings led to struggles for both men over allegiance and identity, with radically different outcomes. Obama would embrace America and ultimately vault to the pinnacle of power, his election as president in 2008 sending a message of empowerment and possibility that resonated with millions overseas, including the Awlaki family. Awlaki would briefly sample American fame, becoming a national media star as a sensible-sounding, even eloquent cleric after 9/11 when Obama was still an unknown. Later, he would gradually and then decisively reject America and finally devote himself to its destruction. The men would never meet, except virtually, clashing in the public battleground of ideas, where the cleric's mastery of the Internet would serve his jihadist cause, and violently, when Obama dispatched the drones that carried out Awlaki's execution.

Awlaki's death secured him a place in history: at least since the Civil War, he was the first American citizen to be hunted down and deliberately killed by his own government, on the basis of secret intelligence and without criminal charges or a chance to defend himself in court. Many Americans welcomed his demise, but its extraordinary circumstances, and the unsettling precedent it set, sparked a debate about law and principles that would go on for years.

When Nasser al-Awlaki brought his family to Ronald Reagan's America, "Islamic terrorism," a loaded phrase that would become a ubiquitous cliché after 9/11 and that Anwar al-Awlaki would do so much to seed in the English-speaking world, was already well known. In 1983, catastrophic bombings by Iran-backed militants had hit the American embassy and Marine barracks in Beirut, killing some 258 Americans. In September 1984, shortly after the Awlakis had headed home to Yemen, the Beirut embassy annex would be attacked, with twenty-four dead. But the US homeland—a word then rarely used, perhaps because for many Americans it carried an unseemly whiff of Nazism—still seemed safe from attack, protected by oceans from foreign enemies. The threat of such terrorism was distant and not so formidable. It had not yet remade the government, drained the federal budget, saturated popular culture, and overwhelmed all other associations of Islam.

This book grew from an obsession with three questions: Why did an American who spent many happy years in the United States, launched a strikingly successful career as a preacher, and tried on the role of bridge builder after the 9/11 attacks end up dedicating his final years to plotting the mass murder of his fellow Americans? How did a president and former professor of constitutional law, who ran against the excesses of George W. Bush's counterterrorism programs and vowed to forge a new relationship with the Muslim world, come to embrace so aggressively the targeted killing of suspected terrorists, sometimes with the emphasis on "suspected"? And what was the role of the technology that would link Obama and Awlaki, the armed drone, which was created to meet the challenge of terrorism, killed some very dangerous people, got oversold and overused, and further poisoned relations with Muslims worldwide?

As one of the many American reporters thrown into the maelstrom of terrorism and counterterrorism after 9/11, I wanted a deeper understanding of the disturbing arc of recent history. The life of Anwar al-Awlaki, who knew two of the future 9/11 hijackers at his San Diego mosque in the months before their plot unfolded, and who was killed a decade later after a high-tech, no-holds-barred manhunt, seemed to encompass the era. His story spanned four presidencies, raised in pointed ways the dangers of both terrorism and the reaction to it, and seemed emblematic of the defining conflict between America and an extreme school of Islam.

To the bafflement and alarm of many Americans, the bigoted and murderous ideology of Al Qaeda and its imitators, including the self-described Islamic State, has shown striking resilience. Militants who, like Awlaki, seem to offer mainly an anachronistic theocracy and a pedantic devotion to religious law, enforced with extreme violence, are still winning devotees and making headlines in Syria, Iraq, Pakistan, Afghanistan, Libya, Yemen, and elsewhere. In the United States and Europe, some of Awlaki's fervent admirers have followed his teachings with lethal effect, at the finish line of a road race in Boston and at an editorial meeting of an irreverent newspaper in Paris. His own unlikely evolution and influence offer a case study in a phenomenon that is still shaping world history and unsettling the West, which has long assumed that its own answers to existential and practical questions held universal appeal.

Two young children, a girl and a boy, solemn and silent, had opened the metal gate in the wall around the Awlakis' house and led me across a yard with toys scattered about and to the door, where their grandfather waited. With a start, I realized that they were Anwar's youngest children. When I visited Yemen, a land of haunting beauty and rich culture, it had descended into what seemed to be a semipermanent condition of violence and political chaos. There was news of fierce fighting near the Sanaa airport. A bomb had gone off in the middle of the previous night, followed by mortar fire. Visiting foreigners were being kidnapped regularly from the streets of Sanaa; their ransoms, if they survived, fattened the payroll of Al Qaeda. But inside Nasser al-Awlaki's home, with its crowded bookshelves, rich carpets, and memorabilia of academic life, a dignified quiet reigned. The little girl brought a tray with cups of tea for her grandfather and me.

Now, as we talked, the gentlemanly Dr. Awlaki, gray-bearded at sixty-seven, seemed bewildered by the tragedy that had overwhelmed his life. The country that had once so warmly embraced Nasser and his family had relentlessly hunted his son Anwar, incinerating him with a drone-fired missile, and then, in a cruel coda, had killed Anwar's own sixteen-year-old son, Abdulrahman al-Awlaki, who had no history of terrorism, in a second drone strike.

Even as he riveted the attention of Washington's vast secret bureaucracy, Anwar al-Awlaki was also part of a wrenching family drama, the rebellious son resisting the entreaties of his devoted father. Years earlier, as Anwar's growing militancy drew the attention of American and Yemeni authorities, Nasser had struggled to steer his son away from a career as an imam, nourishing the hope that he might still apply his talents and education to the overwhelming practical problems of Yemen. When that failed, he tried to talk Anwar out of his radical views, so antithetical to his own.

When none of that worked and Anwar's own plotting led the Obama administration to authorize his killing or capture, Nasser al-Awlaki went to court in America in 2010 to challenge the order on constitutional grounds. After all, he had long revered the American legal system, in particular its insistence on giving rights even to despised criminal suspects. It was the beginning of a long, anguished, and ultimately unsuccessful effort to get the United States to live up to the principles he still believed it stood for.

"I have no grudge toward the American people," Nasser al-Awlaki told a group of Americans who visited him after the drones had killed his son and grandson. He wrestled aloud with the contradictions that events had thrust upon him. "After all, I was an American product myself. All my education, all my thinking, my view of the world, you know—I developed it in America. I was so engulfed in the American way of life. I was so much attached to it. And after so many years, this thing happened to my son and my grandson. I never dreamed that one day America would do something against me— never. But that's what happened. So I just have to deal with it in a responsible way."

He could have responded, he said, "like any tribal people," with violence or protests. "No, I went to the American system of justice— that's what I did. I never raised a gun. I never asked anything to be done against America or American citizens or anything else. I would never dream of doing something like this, never. But I went to the American justice and law, and I hope that I will get accountability from the American justice system."

As we sat together early in 2014, discussing the troubled relationship between the United States and the Muslim world, Nasser al-Awlaki thought back to that golden California summer of 1984 and seized upon a passing moment that for him summoned up an earlier, happier time. At the car rental company in Palo Alto that summer, he recounted, he had explained sheepishly to the woman behind the desk that his old Minnesota driver's license had long since expired and that his current Yemeni license was in Arabic.

No problem, the woman said—just scribble down in English what the Yemeni license says, and I'll use that. And he did, and she did.

"That was the America I knew," he said, with a sigh. "Nobody was snooping on anybody. Nobody was stopping anybody."

His cup sat almost untouched on the low table between us, the tea grown cold. The light was fading over Sanaa's ancient tower-houses, and the call to prayer could be heard from a mosque a few blocks away.

Speaking of the deaths of his son and grandson at the hands of the country that had given him so much, he showed flashes of anger and exasperation, but mostly puzzlement and a deep, irremediable pain.

How could his family's life have taken such a turn? What had gone wrong? Who was to blame?

"I loved America," Nasser al-Awlaki said. He seemed to be near tears. Then, after a moment's silence: "I still love America, despite everything."

The Prophet beckoned with his hand towards Yemen and said, "Belief is there."

—HADITH
(saying of the Prophet Muhammad) No. 5670,
narrated by Abu Masud, seventh century

But what is one to say to an act of destructive ferocity so absurd as to be incomprehensible, inexplicable, almost unthinkable; in fact, mad?

—JOSEPH CONRAD,
The Secret Agent: A Simple Tale, 1907

Perfection of means and confusion of aims seem, in my opinion, to characterize our age.

—ALBERT EINSTEIN, 1941

PART ONE **2009–2010**

1

MERRY CHRISTMAS

Sheikh Anwar had instructed him to make sure the airliner was over American soil when he pushed the plunger on the syringe. With only sixty minutes left in the eight-and-a-half-hour flight from Amsterdam, Umar Farouk Abdulmutallab kept his eyes fixed on his video screen, tracking the location of the big Airbus as it moved across the map. Nearby, other passengers dozed and watched movies.

When the tiny image of the plane approached the American border, the twenty-three-year-old Nigerian squeezed past the American college student next to him and retrieved a small bag from his carry-on in the overhead compartment. Then he headed to the bathroom, where he made one last check on the equipment, performed a ritual washing, and doused himself with cologne to cover any chemical odor. He was a warrior now, one of the mujahideen. He'd soon be a *shaheed*, a martyr for Allah, only for Allah. America was his target, chosen for him in Yemen by Sheikh Anwar al-Awlaki.

It was America, after all, that was slaughtering Muslims in so many countries—Afghanistan, Pakistan, Iraq, Somalia, and now, of course, Yemen. It was to Yemen, the land that the Prophet Muhammad had once declared to be the home of true belief and wisdom, that Abdulmutallab had come a few months earlier in search of Sheikh Anwar, whom he knew from hours online listening to the cleric's calm, erudite lectures.

Over time, Abdulmutallab had found his way from Sanaa to Sheikh Anwar al-Awlaki's hideout in Shabwah province in the south. The sheikh had tested him and found him worthy of a martyrdom mission.

He had then sent him to Brother Ibrahim, the bomb maker, who had explained to him the technical details of pentaerythritoltetranitrate, the explosive known as PETN, and had fitted him with the strange undershorts that had the plastic bag sewn inside. Always the diligent student, Abdulmutallab had worn the underwear for three straight weeks, removing it only to shower, so that he could grow accustomed to it and make sure it was not noticeable to the people he encountered.

As the airliner descended toward Detroit, Abdulmutallab returned to his seat, mumbling to his seatmate that he did not feel well. He pulled the blanket over his head and groped for the syringe attached to the bag in his underwear. This was the moment he had trained for, for which he had given up an easy life as the son of a wealthy Nigerian banker.

Below his window seat over the wing, 19A, the dense Detroit suburbs of the Downriver area scrolled past and the jetliner banked toward Detroit Metro Airport. It was a land of infidels, obsessed with material things—he had seen it, in a visit to Houston for an Islamic conference the previous year. The Americans were at war with Allah and the believers. Perhaps this would make them think again.

He pushed the plunger home, as instructed, waiting for the chemicals to mix and explode.

. . .

In Washington, Michael Leiter, the director of the National Counterterrorism Center, had set aside the Christmas holiday for a mundane job. He was Jewish, and he had decided to take advantage of the rare morning off to perform an overdue household chore, painting his basement. Just before noon, his cell phone rang. It was Art Cummings, the FBI's executive assistant director for national security, with a heads-up: some kind of firecracker or incendiary device had gone off aboard an international flight into Detroit. The plane was about to land and the details were unclear. Leiter put away the paint and headed to his office in a warren of glass towers not far from CIA headquarters in northern Virginia.

. . .

In the darkened operations center at Creech Air Force Base in Indian Springs, Nevada, drone operators were changing shifts, joking and grumbling about having to spend the holidays patrolling Yemen from the sky. Three weeks earlier, the 432nd Air Expeditionary Wing Commander, writing on the base website, had offered commiseration, of a sort, to what he called "the RPA community," for remotely piloted aircraft. He knew, and they knew, that they lived in some strange psychological limbo, on the battlefield and away from the battlefield, living at home but never quite at home. "I know many of you missed Thanksgiving with your families," he wrote. "I also know many more of you will miss Christmas. But I ask you to step back and examine the environment in which we work. There are thousands of troops on the ground in harm's way. They missed Thanksgiving with their families also. Some of them won't see another Thanksgiving again." He signed it, but not with his name, in keeping with the blanket of secrecy draped over everything to do with drones at Creech. He was commander at the "Home of the Hunters," as it said on the sign at the gate. He signed it "Hunter 1."

In the last few weeks, the pilots and sensor operators running the drones over Yemen had been on high alert, with a flurry of intelligence suggesting that Al Qaeda in the Arabian Peninsula, the local branch of the terror network, was up to something. There had been two American strikes in Yemen, carried out not with drones but with cruise missiles and manned jets. The drone units at Creech that were assigned to Pakistan were carrying out their own strikes, firing missiles from unmanned Predator drones at a pace of about once a week. But the Yemen teams could only watch, circling above suspected militant camps in the tribal areas. Their drones were flown out of the little country of Djibouti in the Horn of Africa, a hop across the water from Yemen, and the Djibouti government had not yet permitted the United States to load missiles on its Predators.

The operators at Creech sat for hour after hour, mesmerized by the beige Yemeni landscape as it rolled beneath the drones. But on this Christmas Day their grinding routine was suddenly interrupted by alerts and instructions popping up on their computer screens. A plane had landed in Detroit after a fire of some kind, and there were indications that the incident might have links to Yemen. They were directed to step up patrols and look for any unusual activity. For now, however, they had to leave the shooting to others.

. . .

In their plush rented beachfront home in Hawaii, Barack and Michelle Obama were just starting their day, making last-minute checks on the Christmas presents for Malia, eleven, and Sasha, eight. The First Family had escaped Washington only the day before, delaying their vacation getaway to wait for what the wires were calling the Senate's "historic vote" to approve health care reform. Secret Service officers wearing unaccustomed leisure outfits were politely turning back early-bird beachgoers who hoped to catch a glimpse of the president. The Coast Guard patrolled part of Kailua Bay, cordoned off with yellow markers, to keep nosy sailors away.

The Associated Press had called it "Obama's aloha low-key holiday," and White House spokesman Bill Burton told the gaggle of reporters aboard Air Force One on the trip west that the holiday would be "an opportunity for the president to recharge his batteries." Obama had a message for the press, Burton said: "He would like for you to relax and to not anticipate any public announcements or news-making events." One reporter kidded back, "We've heard this lie before."

The Obamas were singing Christmas carols when a military aide interrupted and told the president that John Brennan, his counterterrorism adviser, who was staying nearby, was on the phone.

Barack Obama knew he had the responsibility to protect the American people, but the last thing he wanted his presidency to be remembered for was that phrase that had always rankled him, the "war on terror." You cannot wage war against a tactic, he would say, and he had no interest in becoming a sort of George W. Bush Jr. He had run against some Bush counterterrorism programs because he thought they had besmirched the name of the United States, and to no purpose: the "enhanced interrogation techniques," given that creepy name by CIA bureaucrats who insisted that torture was not torture; the "black sites" overseas where prisoners were held in secret, in violation of principles the United States had long upheld; the Guantanamo Bay prison that he believed had become a garish recruiting pitch for Al Qaeda. It was proving no easy task to undo such programs; he had banned torture and shut the black sites on his first day in office, but his Justice Department was still investigating torture and deaths in CIA detention, and Congress was blocking his plan to move the Guantanamo detainees to an empty prison in Illinois.

Perhaps Obama's most audacious foreign policy goal was to repair relations between the United States and the Muslim world. He believed the Bush administration had done grave and unnecessary damage with its counterterrorism policies and with the invasion of Iraq. To restore the American image in Islamic countries was not just a matter of idealism, Obama believed, but could have practical consequences, reducing the appeal of Al Qaeda and making the United States a more effective broker for peace between Israel and the Palestinians. He began his campaign for change with remarks to the Turkish parliament in April, declaring to applause that the United States was not, and never would be, at war with Islam. But it was in a long-awaited speech at Cairo University in the sixth month of his presidency that he pulled out all the stops in his attempt, as he put it, "to seek a new beginning between the United States and Muslims around the world."

No American president had ever given an address quite like this one. He wasn't the first president to offer an audience the traditional Muslim greeting, *As-salamu alaykum,* "Peace be upon you," but he was certainly the first to speak of the "generations of Muslims" in his father's family and of fond childhood memories of hearing the call to prayer in Indonesia. Obama quoted the Koran and paid lavish tribute to a long-ago time when Islamic science and learning had led the world, "paving the way for Europe's Renaissance and Enlightenment." Today, he said, a "small but potent minority of Muslims" carried out terrorist attacks, and the United States would continue to defend itself against them. But he also offered an unusual apology for the excesses in the American response to terror, including torture and the limbo for prisoners at Guantanamo. "Just as America can never tolerate violence by extremists," Obama said, "we must never alter our principles. 9/11 was an enormous trauma to our country. The fear and anger that it provoked was understandable, but in some cases, it led us to act contrary to our ideals."

In truth, while Obama felt it was critical to restore decent relations with Islamic countries, his most heartfelt ambitions lay in the domestic realm. He wanted to dig the economy out of the chasm into which it had fallen as he campaigned for office; to end the scandal that made the United States the only developed country where much of the population lacked health insurance; to reverse the trend of economic inequality that left not just the poor but the middle class struggling; to promote alternative energy and face squarely the dangers of climate change. These were among the problems that *The Onion* had memorably satirized after the election with the headline "Black Man Given Nation's Worst Job," but they were challenges the president relished. The national security stuff simply came with the territory, and the secure communications team and passel of security aides were along on his Christmas vacation, too, lest he forget.

Like every president, and every high-level appointee whose job brought him into the threat briefings, Obama woke every morning to a could-happen horror show, the myriad threats that seventeen American intelligence agencies "assessed with medium confidence," as their bloodless jargon put it, to be percolating in half a dozen countries. He often remarked to friends that only a president and his security aides could fully appreciate the crushing responsibility of keeping the country safe in the post-9/11 era, when the worst-case scenario was only too obvious. Bush had been surprised by 9/11, after he and his top aides had brushed aside the looming warning signs, but a grieving people had rallied to support him nonetheless. The next president would not have the excuse of surprise.

As it happened, 2009 had been the rockiest year on the domestic terrorism front in a long time—by some measures, the worst year since 9/11. If Obama felt his luck was rotten in that regard, he had good reason. Schemes had been uncovered to blow up the Federal Building in Springfield, Illinois, and synagogues in the Bronx; to shoot marines at their base in Quantico, Virginia; and to kill shoppers at malls in Boston. But those plots had been carefully monitored by the FBI and its informants—indeed, in some cases, the bureau's paid informants seemed to be the most eager conspirators. Not so the shooting in Little Rock in June of two soldiers at a military recruiting station by an American convert to Islam who had spent time in Yemen, a nasty surprise that had left one army private dead. Nor did the FBI discover until the last minute in August the plan of an Afghan-born man who had been a popular Manhattan coffee vendor,

Najibullah Zazi, to attack the New York subway with three suicide bombers wearing explosive-filled backpacks.

Then, the previous month, in early November, had come the deadliest terrorist attack on American soil since 9/11. At Fort Hood, Texas, an army major and psychiatrist, Nidal Hasan, had actually managed to carry out an attack, crying, "Allahu akbar!" before mowing down some fifty people, thirteen of whom died. Hasan's shooting spree, which followed months of signs that he was developing a lethal hostility to his fellow soldiers, had led to a lot of finger-pointing. Obama was grateful that George W. Bush had refrained from publicly criticizing him; the former president had said that his successor "deserves my silence." It was an especially gracious stance in light of the fact that Obama had effectively blamed his predecessor for the devastated economy and for betraying American values in the fight against terror. But congressional Republicans and conservative pundits, led by Bush's former vice president, Dick Cheney, had shown no such reticence. They had spent months advancing the notion that Obama was projecting weakness in the war on terror.

Cheney had accused Obama of "dithering" over whether to send additional troops to Afghanistan. When the Obama administration proposed a federal criminal trial in New York for Khalid Sheikh Mohammed, the main 9/11 plotter, Cheney said it would give "aid and comfort to the enemy," wording borrowed from the treason statute. After the Fort Hood shooting, he claimed that Obama was helping Al Qaeda by refusing to label the Fort Hood slaughter "terrorism." The "uncertainty" projected by Obama "feeds into sort of the basic al Qaeda strategy," Cheney told Sean Hannity of Fox News. "Remember the way al Qaeda operates and what their underlying plan is—if you kill enough Americans, you can change American policy." Obama refused to call terrorism by its name, the former vice president said, or to acknowledge that the country was at war.

In fact, it was a deliberate strategy on the part of Obama and his aides to hesitate before labeling some new act of violence as "terrorism," because they did not want to project a sense of panic that might play into the hands of Al Qaeda. And they were especially loath to link violent attacks explicitly to Islam. This was not because of some secret and mysterious affinity for Muslims, as the conspiracy theorists would have it, and not because of a politically correct sensitivity to hurting Muslims' feelings, though that was becoming a familiar Republican charge. The motivation for the linguistic tactic was more practical. To label terrorism or violence as "Islamic" or to call it "jihad" would be to confer a religious justification, a Koranic legitimacy, on acts of brutality that in the president's view had neither. A central aim of Obama's counterterrorism team was to separate the small number of Muslims who committed violence against innocents in the name of their religion from the great masses of Muslims who, they believed, decried such acts.

Those arguments made considerable sense, and they had been largely accepted by Bush, who had often emphasized that his condemnation of terrorism was not a denunciation of Islam. But in practice, when the media adopted the easy shorthand of "Islamic terrorism" and "jihadist," Obama's language could seem evasive, even obtuse. In his initial remarks on the Fort Hood attack, less than three hours after the shootings, Obama declared that "we don't yet know all the details" and called the assault "a horrific outburst of violence." The next day, a Friday, speaking in the Rose Garden, he urged "caution against jumping to conclusions." And in Saturday's weekly video and radio address, he said that "we cannot fully know what leads a man to do such a thing."

Well, Obama's critics on the right had no trouble at all determining what had led Hasan to start shooting. They pounced. "Unwilling to use the word 'terror,' let alone the phrase 'Islamist terror,' Obama warned us not to 'rush to judgment,'" sneered the conservative columnist Ralph Peters, a retired army lieutenant colonel, in the *New York Post* the day after Obama's radio address.

On Monday, four days after the attack, a new voice spoke with equal confidence about the Islamic motivation for the Fort Hood shooting spree, but with a starkly different attitude toward the attack. "Nidal Hassan Did the Right Thing," Anwar al-Awlaki wrote on his blog, using a slightly different transliteration of the shooter's name. Reporters covering the shooting had already learned that Nidal Hasan and his family had worshipped at Dar Al-Hijrah, the big mosque outside Washington, DC, where Anwar al-Awlaki had served as an imam in 2001 and 2002. Anonymous officials told the media that the government had intercepted e-mails between the cleric, now in Yemen, and Hasan. Now the journalists, myself among them, scrambling to learn more about this rebel American imam, were confronted by a quite chilling declaration from the man himself.

Like Obama's Republican critics, Awlaki had no difficulty in parsing the motive of "brother Nidal," even if he had a different assessment of its merits. "Nidal Hassan is a hero," began the post at anwar-alawlaki.com. Awlaki called him "a man of conscience" who could not bear taking part in "leading the war against terrorism which in reality is a war against Islam." In this war, Awlaki wrote, Hasan had chosen the righteous side: "Nidal opened fire on soldiers who were on their way to be deployed to Iraq and Afghanistan. How can there be any dispute about the virtue of what he has done?"

For those who had never heard of Anwar al-Awlaki—and that was nearly every American outside the security sector and a handful of journalists—the post was stunning. Awlaki's voice was something new, uniting an American idiom with wildly extreme jihadist views. His post was not a screed, it was a syllogism; he laid out his logic in easy steps. His casual tone suggested total confidence in the self-evident truth of his conclusions.

Under both Bush and Obama, Awlaki had already been an occasional subject of discussion at the White House. His writings and lectures, ubiquitous on the web, had turned up again and again on the laptops of the young men arrested in violent plots, not just in the United States but in Canada and Britain as well. Now he seemed to be connected, both before and after the fact, with the murderous shooting spree at Fort Hood. Awlaki's two e-mails to Hasan, it would turn out, had not addressed the army major's inquiries about a possible religious sanction for killing fellow American soldiers; the cleric might understandably have feared some kind of entrapment. But Awlaki's public endorsement of violence against Americans had become steadily more explicit, and he had specifically condemned as a "heartless beast" any Muslim soldier who would fight for an army against fellow Muslims.

For the first time, Obama's attention was focused on the name of a man who would be forever connected with his presidency. Anwar al-Awlaki was an American who knew the country's anxieties and vulnerabilities, and he was repeatedly reaching inside the United States with an insidious message. In the days after the Fort Hood shootings, Obama told aides that he was alarmed that Awlaki's message had penetrated the American military.

"The fact that he had an influence on a member of the United States Army—a field grade officer on top of that—was particularly vexing," recalled General James L. Jones, the retired marine then serving as Obama's national security adviser. "I think he was very interested in, obviously, trying to understand how a guy like Awlaki developed." As a politician, Obama had honed the skill of using speech to inspire voters and volunteers to act. But the notion that an Internet preacher might somehow have motivated the massacre in Texas seemed perplexing and disturbing. Awlaki's call for violence was reaching the vulnerable young sons of Muslim immigrant families and impressionable converts to Islam. Hasan, however, was nearing forty and had spent half his life in the army, first as an enlisted man and then in medical and psychiatric training at the taxpayers' expense.

Now, as it grew later on Christmas Day and Obama was briefed on the latest details from Detroit, Awlaki's name surfaced again. The bomb had flamed but not exploded, and passengers and flight attendants had jumped on Abdulmutallab to smother the fire. The intelligence agencies quickly found evidence that the young Nigerian arrested in Detroit had traveled to Yemen to find Awlaki. By the time Obama kept a planned appointment to stop by Christmas dinner at the nearby Kaneohe Marine Base, he had learned just how close the brush with disaster had been. He was beginning to grasp the dimensions of the failure of the nation's bulked-up, multilayered counterterrorism defenses, which had cost billions of dollars over the past eight years. A slight twenty-three-year-old with no experience in terrorist plotting or spy tradecraft, seemingly recruited for the mission by Awlaki, had penetrated airport security, the very part of the security system that had received the most attention after 9/11.

Worse, as agencies plugged Abdulmutallab's name into their vast databases, officials recognized with dread and dismay the pattern so familiar from 9/11: they had collected multiple, damning pieces of information about the perpetrator but had somehow failed to connect and act on them. And the key evidence came not from some shadowy informant or an ambiguous snippet of an intercepted call, but from Abdulmutallab's father, a wealthy and respected Nigerian banker. He had visited the American embassy in Abuja, the Nigerian capital, to warn officials that his son had embraced militant religious views, traveled to Yemen, and sent a good-bye text message from there. What more blatant warning could there be, and what more credible source? The name of the young Nigerian had gone into the biggest terrorist watchlist, the so-called TIDE database, but it had not been added to the no-fly list, nor had his visa to enter the United States been canceled. I spoke a few days after Christmas with Tom Kean, the former New Jersey governor, who as chairman of the national 9/11 Commission was only too familiar with terrorism tips lost in the bureaucracy. He sounded furious. The father's cry from the heart about his militant son should have awakened even the most jaded bureaucracy, he believed. For him, it was depressing déjà vu, another postmortem on agency failures. "It's totally frustrating," Kean said. "It's almost like the words being used to describe what went wrong are exactly the same."

The lives of the 290 people on board Northwest Flight 253 had been saved, not by the government's counterterrorism behemoth, but by flawed bomb design and alert passengers. And from the moment a shaken flight attendant first spoke to him, Abdulmutallab could not shut up about what he had been trying to do. He'd tried to detonate an "explosive device," he told her. He answered every question of the Customs and Border Protection agent who walked him off the plane, barefoot and wrapped in a blanket: he was with Al Qaeda, he'd obtained the bomb in Yemen, and his goal was "to bring the plane down over US soil." It was yet another refutation of the notion, put forth by defenders of the CIA's brutal interrogations, that committed jihadists would talk only if subjected to fear and pain. In fact, like Abdulmutallab, most ideologues loved to talk about what they were doing and why.

Taken to the University of Michigan hospital for treatment of the burns to his thigh and genitals, Abdulmutallab kept talking. He explained to a paramedic and a doctor how the syringe was supposed to detonate the bomb. He told a nurse that he was not depressed or suicidal—martyrdom was his goal. He told the FBI counterterrorism agents who had rushed to the hospital essentially the whole story, while obscuring real names: how he had gone to Yemen to find Al Qaeda; how he had been introduced to a man he called Abu Tarak;

how Abu Tarak had suggested the plan to blow up a plane; how Abu Tarak had introduced him to the Saudi bomb maker who had designed an explosive that would be undetectable to airport metal detectors; and how Abu Tarak had set two requirements for his mission—that he should choose an American plane and make sure it came down over American territory.

Then, after being taken away for treatment, he clammed up and was read his *Miranda* rights, a decision that Republicans later seized upon to amplify Cheney's complaint about the Obama administration: that it was treating terrorism not as war but as crime. In fact, Abdulmutallab had already said more than enough to implicate himself in attempted mass murder and to keep intelligence agencies busy for months. Counterterrorism analysts who had immersed themselves in Al Qaeda in the Arabian Peninsula, or AQAP, knew immediately who the Saudi bomb maker was: Ibrahim al-Asiri, who had dispatched his own brother the previous August to try to kill Saudi Arabia's counterterrorism chief. They also strongly suspected what intercepted calls and e-mails indicated and Abdulmutallab would later confirm: that much of what the Nigerian said about "Abu Tarak" was in fact about Anwar al-Awlaki. Awlaki was Sheikh Anwar, whose online eloquence had helped persuade Abdulmutallab to devote himself to violent jihad; whom he had come to Yemen to find; and who had coaxed him through all the preparations, including bomb training and the recording of a martyrdom video. AQAP would include a minute or so of Abdulmutallab's martyrdom message, spoken in stilted Arabic, in a web video with the title, perhaps overly optimistic, of *America and the Final Trap.*

W ith his cerebral approach to the hyperemotional realm of terrorism, Obama believed that the Bush administration had sometimes played into the terrorists' hands, magnifying the impact of terrorist plots by devoting breathless press conferences to them. Terrorists seek to provoke panic, his logic went—Why help them? It was partly for that reason that Obama kept to his vacation schedule on Christmas and in the next couple of days, as aides assured reporters he was "monitoring" the investigation.

That turned out to be a political misstep. Already by the morning of December 26, Republicans were filling the vacuum with the

Cheney narrative—the president is on vacation while the nation is at war. Representative Peter T. King, the pugnacious Long Island Republican whose own history as an avid supporter of the Irish Republican Army never discouraged him from calling others soft on terror, was as usual one of the loudest voices. But in this case King had a point. "This was an assault on the United States," he said on CNN, "and it is important at a time like this that the president of the United States or someone in the administration with stature step forward— whether it be the Vice President or the Secretary of Homeland Security, but basically, we see—there is no face of the administration on this issue."

Obama's aides fumed privately that the Republicans were helping Al Qaeda turn a failed attack into a success by playing up the close call and accusing the administration of weakness. "We, the United States' political and media culture, basically created a shit storm that turned it into a win for AQAP," an Obama aide told me. "Because suddenly you had every Republican on cable saying, 'This is the worst thing ever.'" The aide's complaint, however logical, was irrelevant. As Al Qaeda's leaders knew well, terrorism was not only about what happened but about how the American and global media reported it. If the administration chose not to put the president forward to frame the event, his political opponents would happily take his place.

Obama and his aides realized their tactical error, and the president went before the cameras on December 28 at the Marine base. He wore a suit but no tie and called out a jaunty "Hey, guys" to reporters and marines as he walked in, but he made sure to use the word *terrorist* in his opening sentence. He listed the steps his administration was taking to prevent a recurrence but also tried to put the failed attack in perspective. He urged Americans to be "confident" and not to turn Al Qaeda's failure into a victory. "An alert and courageous citizenry are far more resilient than an isolated extremist," he said.

By the day of the president's remarks, and an additional statement he made the next day, some television commentators were remarking on the "silence" from Dick Cheney—a thinly disguised invitation. The former vice president accepted it on December 30 with a brutal statement to Politico. Cheney, who had served as defense secretary before Obama had graduated from law school, used the failed bombing as only one count in a sweeping indictment of the freshman president.

"As I've watched the events of the last few days," Cheney wrote, "it is clear once again that President Obama is trying to pretend we are not at war. He seems to think if he has a low-key response to an attempt to blow up an airliner and kill hundreds of people, we won't be at war." Cheney piled on from there, complaining about the administration's preference for *Miranda* rights and criminal trials for terrorists. "He seems to think if he gets rid of the words, 'war on terror,' we won't be at war," Cheney wrote. "But we are at war and when President Obama pretends we aren't, it makes us less safe."

Dan Pfeiffer, the White House communications director, fired back on a White House blog, noting that Cheney had attacked only Obama and not the Al Qaeda plotters. He brushed off Cheney's claim that the president didn't realize the country was at war. "I don't think anyone realizes this very hard reality more than President Obama," he wrote. Had the White House been more geared up for bare-knuckle battles with its critics, Pfeiffer might have noted that the deputy leader of Al Qaeda in the Arabian Peninsula, Said Ali al-Shihri, had been released from Guantanamo Bay by the Bush administration in 2007 before cycling through a Saudi rehabilitation program and joining the terrorist group in Yemen.

But Cheney's pretending-we're-not-at-war critique actually showed how the political discourse had become detached from actual events. Throughout his first year as president, Obama had kept up the steady pace of CIA drone strikes in Pakistan that Bush had approved only in the last six months of his presidency. More significantly, Cheney's statement came just two weeks after Obama had expanded the new American policy of targeted killing to a second country, Yemen, where the only previous strike had taken place in 2002.

Far from being oblivious to the threat from AQAP, Obama had acted aggressively against the group, approving two strikes in the days before Abdulmutallab boarded Flight 253 in Amsterdam. In mid-December, the intelligence agencies had gotten wind of suicide bombers being dispatched from Yemen's tribal areas to the capital, Sanaa. With counterterrorism officials panicky and no armed drones permitted at the base in nearby Djibouti, Obama had approved a December 17 cruise missile strike on what intelligence analysts described as an Al Qaeda training camp in the southern province of Abyan.

That strike had killed as many as forty-one civilians, along with a number of militants, producing a political outcry in Yemen. Then on December 24 there was another American strike, targeting a house where AQAP leaders were believed to be meeting. Initial news reports that Anwar al-Awlaki was among the estimated thirty dead proved to be wrong. The opening salvos in Obama's campaign against AQAP in Yemen might be accused of many things—including poor intelligence about civilians in the target zone—but Cheney's repeated charge of "dithering" was not on the list.

On January 2, still in Honolulu, Obama used his weekly presidential address to counter his critics. In four minutes, speaking emphatically, he raced through the reports he had ordered up, the accountability he was demanding for the Christmas debacle, and the facts about the plot. He called it an "attempted act of terrorism" in his opening sentence and said it had been hatched in Yemen, which he called "a country grappling with crushing poverty and deadly insurgencies." Then he took aim at Cheney's repeated claim that Obama denied the country was at war. Recalling his vow to protect the country on Inauguration Day, he said: "On that day I also made it very clear: our nation is at war against a far-reaching network of violence and hatred, and that we will do whatever it takes to defeat them and defend our country, even as we uphold the values that have always distinguished America among nations." With that last phrase, he lobbed a brick back at the former vice president, who had presided over torture, rendition, and secret prisons.

But Obama did not mention the most obvious refutation of the Cheney critique—the two American strikes that he had approved in Yemen in December. The United States had agreed with Yemen's government not to reveal that its forces had carried out the strikes. The media had nonetheless immediately unearthed the American role, and the Yemeni public had no doubts about who had launched the missiles. But the president felt he had to honor the assurances of secrecy. It was not the last time that the Obama administration's insistence on maintaining silence about strikes that the entire world knew about would get in the way of a sensible discussion of American policies.

Obama's ruined Christmas, and his critics' raucous response, were in a sense to be expected. Every recent president had been ambushed by terrorist acts and the political freight they carried. Jimmy Carter's presidency had been upended by the seizure of the American embassy in Iran; Ronald Reagan's thrown off balance by the Beirut bombings of 1983; Bill Clinton's disrupted twice, by the first World Trade Center attack in 1993 and again by the bombing of two embassies in East Africa in 1998. Then there was the indelible image of Bush reading aloud *The Pet Goat* to Sarasota schoolchildren on the morning of 9/11 as an aide leaned over to whisper that a second plane had hit the World Trade Center. His presidency would be remade in ways unimaginable at that moment. The scale of the casualties on 9/11, of course, made it stand out. But the power of anti-American terrorism usually has less to do with body counts than with the brazen challenge it represents to a superpower's confidence and control. It is catnip for journalists and opposition politicians, who first suggest that the president must somehow be to blame for the attack and then taunt him with variations on the theme: Are you going to let them get away with this?

If that predictable pattern had not been obvious to the Obama White House before December 25, it was in the days that followed. Day after day, the media of a country of three hundred million people was dominated by an attack that had killed nobody and severely injured only one person: the attacker, whose genital burns struck many Americans as particularly just deserts for his crime. Then, on December 30, just as the White House was beginning to recover its balance, word came of a more lethal disaster in Afghanistan. A promising Jordanian source, a physician who dabbled in militancy and had told CIA officers that he had access to top Al Qaeda officials, turned out to be a double agent. He had blown himself up at the CIA base in Khost Province, Afghanistan, killing seven CIA officers and contractors and two others. Among the agency's main jobs at the Khost base was to collect intelligence to target drone strikes in nearby Pakistan. Though drones were valued for keeping Americans far from danger, Al Qaeda had found a way to strike back.

Each Tuesday, in the Situation Room in the White House basement, cabinet officers, military commanders, and intelligence agency chiefs would gather at the long table with the president, with others beamed in from overseas on the big video screens. These Terror

Tuesdays, as West Wing wags called them, were organized by John Brennan, Obama's top counterterrorism adviser, and usually included a review of reported threats and discussions of terrorists being targeted. Some participants, Secretary of State Hillary Rodham Clinton among them, thought the sessions were often too "tactical," too far down in the weeds of plots and targets for the attention of such high-ranking officials. Sometimes the president, aware of such grumbling, would broaden the discussion to cover the causes of radicalization and the adequacy of the broader strategy against Al Qaeda.

On January 5, back at the White House, Obama presided at the most highly charged counterterrorism meeting of his year-old presidency. His tone was somber, and the crowd of "principals," or agency chiefs, and assistants standing along the walls was bigger than usual. David Axelrod, the president's political guru, made a rare appearance at a security meeting, underscoring the broader implications for the presidency of the close call over Detroit.

When Obama got angry, aides said, he didn't scream and yell. Instead, his manner grew somber and his questions became more rapid-fire. This time he stopped just short of the obvious accusation—that those present, himself included, had failed the country. "I'm very disappointed," he said. "I'm really unhappy." He hardly had to spell out the obvious question: How was it possible, after eight years of colossal post-9/11 spending to build an impenetrable shield against terrorism, that a twenty-three-year-old Nigerian banker's son had nearly taken out an airliner over Detroit?

Different agency heads gave preliminary accounts of what they believed had gone wrong on their turf: Secretary of State Clinton spoke about Abdulmutallab's visa—missed in a review because his name had been misspelled in the computer system. Leon Panetta, the CIA director, spoke about why the agency had not fully shared the information it had from his father's visit to the embassy in Abuja. Michael Leiter, of the National Counterterrorism Center, discussed why nuggets of information about the young Nigerian dispersed among various agencies had never been put together. So went the grim round of self-criticism.

As a chastening thought experiment, Obama urged the assembled security grandees to imagine that the bomb had in fact exploded and the airliner had been destroyed, dwarfing every act of terrorism in the country since 9/11. For this crowd of terrorism specialists and political veterans, he didn't have to lay out all of the implications. Yes, 290 people would have been dead—289 plus the bomber. Yes, the air travel system would have been disrupted even more radically than it had been by the scare. Yes, the visceral public fear that had faded over eight years would return, and the feeling that Al Qaeda could strike at will would be resuscitated.

But that was not all. The Cheney critique would appear to be vindicated, and many Americans would accept it: For seven years after 9/11 Bush and Cheney had kept America safe (albeit after ignoring the warning signs before 9/11). Now Obama's feckless weakness had allowed the terrorists to strike again. It did not require a vivid imagination to play out the likely consequences. Obama would have faced huge political pressure to retaliate in Yemen, where he was loath to send American troops. "Part of his point was that the pressure on us would be to do a lot more in Yemen," said Ben Rhodes, deputy national security adviser. "Everything we were trying to do to scale back military involvement in the region would have been reversed." Obama's big ambitions on health coverage, immigration, and inequality would have been put aside, possibly forever. The president would have had to devote even more of his time to counterterrorism—and to defending the administration's record. He might easily have ended up a one-term president, tarred with a terrorism failure on his brief watch. To a degree that no one wanted to contemplate, the fate of Obama's presidency had been hanging in the balance when Abdulmutallab pushed that plunger.

That was looking back. Looking forward, the threat from Yemen, and the capabilities of AQAP, suddenly loomed much larger, eclipsing even the old core of Al Qaeda in Pakistan. The initial interview with Abdulmutallab, together with the intelligence dossiers from multiple agencies, pointed at two men. Ibrahim al-Asiri was the diabolically clever explosives expert whose experiments had already outclassed anything seen from Pakistan. And Anwar al-Awlaki, whose power to radicalize and recruit young English speakers had already set him apart as the most dangerous of influences, now appeared to have gone "operational," in agency lingo. It was evident, from intercepted communications, Abdulmutallab's still-incomplete testimony, and Awlaki's own pronouncements, that the cleric was now devoting his considerable talents and energy to plots against the United States.

As long as all Awlaki did was talk, the agencies had merely fretted about how to counter his message. Now he had placed himself in the director's seat in a major plot. If it were not for his American citizenship, he would automatically have joined Asiri and AQAP leaders on the government's kill-or-capture list—on which the "capture" option was proving to be largely theoretical. But Awlaki had not lost his constitutional rights when he began plotting with Al Qaeda. A legal analysis by the Justice Department, Obama said, was already under way. Somewhere in Yemen, meanwhile, a bespectacled cleric held uncomfortable sway over Americans' sense of security and Obama's control of his presidency.

They had been fortunate this time, Obama told his team. But they could not rely on bomb makers' mistakes. The Christmas episode, coming so soon after the slaughter at Fort Hood, had begun to persuade some analysts inside the FBI and CIA that the threat from Yemen of an attack on America might have outstripped the threat from Al Qaeda's old core in Pakistan. In AQAP, Obama faced a new mutation of the old enemy of 9/11, one that seemed to pose a double menace: stirring alienated Americans like Hasan to attack from inside the country, and dispatching foreign travelers like Abdulmutallab to bring lethal violence from afar. One name had surfaced in both cases, the name of a US citizen. At that January meeting, as he approached the end of his first year in office, Obama had an inkling of the legal and operational challenge he faced in confronting the complex threat that Awlaki posed.

A s the spies stepped up the hunt for Awlaki, the Obama administration's lawyers started in on their parallel project: If they located Awlaki, an American citizen facing no criminal charges, could they capture him? Could they kill him? By early 2010, American drones had already killed hundreds of people in the tribal area of Pakistan, but the answer to the US citizen question was far from self-evident. On the face of it, killing an American without first charging him with crimes and giving him a fair trial seemed problematic on several grounds. Awlaki had joined Al Qaeda, was publicly calling for the mass murder of Americans, and was actively plotting toward that goal. But did that mean he could simply be blown away on the president's orders?

Legal questions involving national security were generally hashed out by what was called "the lawyers' group"—the Obama-appointed general counsels of the Defense Department, the CIA, and the other intelligence agencies. They gathered for regular White House meetings with the National Security Council's legal adviser, Mary B. DeRosa, who had held the same job for a time under Clinton. When the executive branch faced an especially important and disputable legal question, however, it turned to the Justice Department's Office of Legal Counsel for a formal, written legal opinion. The OLC, a familiar abbreviation inside the government, had been quite obscure to the general public for most of its existence. But it had become known—indeed, notorious—in the middle of George W. Bush's presidency, when its legal opinions on torture became fodder for news stories and drew the opprobrium of many scholars. The main author of the most controversial opinions had been John C. Yoo, a young, conservative professor who went on leave from Berkeley's law school to serve in the Bush OLC. They were signed by Jay S. Bybee, the head of the office, whom Bush later named to a federal appeals court.

The classified 2002 opinions on torture found that a long list of interrogation methods proposed for use by the CIA on Al Qaeda suspects did not constitute torture and were lawful. Like other opinions crafted in the first years after 9/11 by John Yoo and his colleagues, the torture opinions were based on an expansive interpretation of presidential power. A president in wartime needed the freedom to do whatever it took to keep the country safe, and the Constitution gave him that sweeping power, Yoo believed. But anyone who did even an hour's research on waterboarding, the most extreme of the approved methods, found ample reason to question the Justice Department opinion. Waterboarding, in which a cloth was placed over a person's mouth and nose, and water was poured over it to produce a feeling of suffocation, had been a favored technique of torturers from the Inquisition to the Cambodian dictator Pol Pot. American military and civilian authorities had previously prosecuted its use as a crime. How could a legal opinion overcome that dark history?

Indeed, the torture opinions were withdrawn by Bybee's successor as head of the OLC, Jack Goldsmith, who found them poorly reasoned and far too sweeping. The memos were repudiated by Obama when he took office, along with all the other Bush-era legal opinions on interrogation. In the view of their critics, who were legion, the Bush torture memos had become an infamous example of dangerously sloppy and reckless legal advice.

Among the most outspoken of their critics were two law professors who had built their public reputations partly on their scathing analyses of the Yoo torture memos and other Bush-era OLC opinions on national security: David J. Barron and Martin S. Lederman. Barron had clerked for Justice John Paul Stevens of the Supreme Court and had joined the faculty at Harvard Law School. Lederman had worked as a litigator in Washington, taught at Georgetown, and become a hyperactive blogger on national security law. Both men had worked for the OLC in the Clinton administration, and both found the more extreme OLC opinions under Bush repellent. In 2008, in the midst of the presidential campaign, they collaborated on a two-part tour de force in the *Harvard Law Review* called "The Commander in Chief at the Lowest Ebb." It was a deeply scholarly analysis with little of the wit and acid of Lederman's blog posts. But for students of the battles over the Bush administration's legal opinions, it was a devastating attack on the overreach of the OLC in his first term.

After a march through presidential history from George Washington on, bolstered by hundreds of footnotes, Barron and Lederman portrayed the Bush presidency in the national security realm as essentially lawless. The Bush administration, they wrote, "claimed that the President could disregard an array of important statutes and treaties—from the Torture Act to the Habeas Act of 1867; from the Foreign Intelligence Surveillance Act even to the War Crimes Act; and more—if they happened to interfere with the manner in which he concluded the conflict against Al Qaeda should be prosecuted."

It was a harsh verdict, but one that coincided with the rhetoric that Obama was using on the campaign trail when the article was published. When he took office a few months later, he immediately appointed Barron and Lederman to the OLC, as the deputies to Dawn Johnsen, another Clinton OLC veteran and fierce Bush critic. When Johnsen's confirmation was blocked by congressional Republicans, Barron was left as the acting head of the office and Lederman as his deputy. After the Christmas airliner attack, as Awlaki's role in the plot became clear and the White House sought legal advice on whether he could be killed, the assignment went to none other than Barron and Lederman. The matter was urgent, the lawyers were told. If American intelligence suddenly got word of Awlaki's whereabouts, counterterrorism officials would not want to wait while Barron and Lederman polished up a learned treatise on targeted killing.

The turn of history was exquisitely ironic. The law professors who had once bathed in lavish praise from critics of President Bush on the left now were under scrutiny themselves. Torture and targeted killing were by no means equivalent: torture is always a heinous crime, while targeted killing can be legal under both domestic and international law. But the parallel was unmistakable nonetheless. The Bush administration had sought OLC approval to take extreme measures it claimed were justified by the dire threat of terrorism. Now the Obama administration was seeking legal approval for its own extreme measure in the face of the terrorist threat: hunting down and killing an American citizen, on the basis of secret intelligence, without charge or trial. The question went to the heart of the debates over presidential power, constitutional rights, American values, and government secrecy that had so bedeviled the Bush lawyers.

At the Justice Department, Barron and Lederman asked the intelligence agencies for every piece of evidence they had about Awlaki, what he had done and what he planned to do. Under conditions of the most extreme secrecy, they began their work.

2

YOU ARE STILL UNSAFE

From his shifting hideouts in Yemen's badlands, Anwar al-Awlaki had followed the tumultuous events of November, December, and January as best he could. With the Americans after him, he stayed on the move through the tribal provinces, mainly Shabwah province, where his family had deep roots. Sometimes he bedded down in a tent. He avoided phones and used the Internet only to send encrypted e-mails. Longer communications, including audio and video messages to his followers, he encrypted and saved to a flash drive, handing the tiny storage device to a trusted supporter, who would pass it to a string of couriers, who would deliver it to a trusted ally, often in Sanaa. It was agonizingly slow for a blogger who had grown accustomed to reaching his audience at the click of a mouse. But he wanted to stay alive.

After the American strike of December 24 destroyed a house where leaders of Al Qaeda in the Arabian Peninsula (AQAP) had met, Awlaki sent a friend an encrypted message expressing relief that he had escaped the missiles in time. "Phew. Maaaaaan—that was close," he wrote, showing off his command of American slang. Late on December 25, Yemen time, the news of another near miss, aboard the airliner above Detroit, was all over the shortwave radio channels that could reach even the remote hills where he was living. But neither the missiles that had missed him nor the failure of his young Nigerian fan to bring down the aircraft slowed him down. He was using a complicated set of coded messages to consult a militant in the United Kingdom who worked at Heathrow about how to get bombs past airport security. Most important, he was working on getting a new, long message out to his followers, one that would show he was still in business, express defiance to Obama, and rally support for jihad.

At the age of thirty-eight, Awlaki had rather suddenly emerged, in the view of a growing number of counterterrorism analysts inside the government, as the single most dangerous threat to the United States. He was an ambitious man who had followed a wandering path, considering or trying out several conventional career paths: engineer, American imam, post-9/11 peacemaker, Yemeni education professor, entrepreneur. But now he had found the fame he craved. For several years, his lectures and sermons had turned up repeatedly on the laptops of Western Muslims caught plotting violence in the name of jihad. With the Christmas airliner attack, he had moved decisively from preaching to acting, becoming the central figure in AQAP's efforts to target the United States.

Not so long before, a renegade cleric hiding out in the rugged tribal lands of Yemen would have been hard put to reach anyone beyond a handful of local villagers with his pronouncements. The idea that such a person in such a place could unnerve a superpower—or even get noticed by an American president—would have seemed preposterous.

But the twenty-first century had provided an electronic soapbox of extraordinary reach. Osama bin Laden had helped pioneer the use of the Internet to promote violent jihad, but his web performances were in Arabic and favored obscure poetry and high-flown rhetoric that sometimes bordered on the incomprehensible, especially to Western audiences. Even in 2010 he was still heard from on occasion, but his messages smacked of desperation, a plea that he was still relevant. A month after the Christmas airliner attack, long after the world knew that it had been planned and launched from Yemen, a message from Bin Laden implausibly claimed credit for the plot. Shortly after that, another quixotic message from Al Qaeda's founder lambasted America for its inaction on climate change, not previously a top jihadi priority, and called for a worldwide boycott of American businesses and of the dollar. Bin Laden's place in history was secure, but that was the point—his place was in history. In the years immediately after 9/11, the world had anxiously attended to his messages. But by decade's end he had the slightly pathetic sound of an aging pop star, well past his prime but still pretending to popularity.

By contrast, Anwar al-Awlaki, fourteen years younger, was the rising idol, preaching an ideology indistinguishable from Bin Laden's but in a refreshingly blunt, clear, and informal style. His usual choice of English limited his influence in the Arab world, but it gave him the same international appeal that made Apple and Toyota borderless brands. He addressed English-speaking Muslims in the West as an imam who knew from experience their lives and insecurities. The fact that he had been imprisoned for eighteen months in Yemen, and his notoriety in the American media after Fort Hood and the airliner attack, only burnished his appeal to followers. They believed he was speaking Islamic truth to infidel power.

So when Awlaki released a twelve-minute "Call to Jihad" in mid-March of 2010, he had the attention of the global media and plenty of young Western Muslims—not to mention a small army of American intelligence analysts. (A year earlier, in one of his most popular tracts, Awlaki had offered the sarcastic lament that "the only ones who are spending the money and time translating Jihad literature are the Western intelligence services." Unfortunately, he added, "They would not be willing to share it.") Recording his message in one of Al Qaeda's mud-brick safe houses in Shabwah's hills, to be dispatched via courier to sympathetic webmasters, he mounted an Internet podium not so inferior to that of the American president, and he knew how to use it. His audio message was excerpted on CNN and posted in full on jihadist forums, from which it spread virally across the web.

Awlaki had first recorded his inflammatory message on video, donning a green military camouflage jacket over traditional Yemeni garb—a signal that he, too, was at war. But the world's most powerful country was looking for him, and perhaps in an abundance of caution he sent out only an audio recording. The video version, which might have given the high-tech American hunters more clues to his location, would only come to light two years later.

The recording was a sinister rhetorical masterpiece. It was his fullest and clearest articulation so far of his advocacy of mass violence against the United States, a window on his political and religious appeal as he defied the American military and intelligence juggernaut now on his trail. To consider it in detail is to understand why this voice truly worried the White House.

As usual, Awlaki's argument was relentlessly logical, his tone cocky but conversational. He trumpeted the "operation" of "brother Umar Farouk"—his protégée Umar Farouk Abdulmutallab—gloating that an attack costing a few thousand dollars had penetrated a $40 billion counterterrorism shield. The power of his boast was that it was no extremist fantasy; it matched Obama's own chagrined conclusion about the near disaster. Still, Awlaki deftly turned what was, after all, a flubbed attack by Al Qaeda into a symbol of American impotence, aiming his sarcasm directly at Obama, whom he pilloried as an impotent successor to Bush:

> So if America failed to defeat the mujahedeen when it gave its president unlimited support, how can it win with Obama, who's on a short leash?
>
> If George W. Bush is remembered as being the president who got America stuck in Afghanistan and Iraq, it's looking like Obama wants to be remembered as the president who got America stuck in Yemen. Obama has already started his war on Yemen by the aerial bombings of Abyan and Shabwah.
>
> By doing that he has waged a publicity campaign for the mujahedeen in Yemen and within days accomplished for them the work of years. As the popularity of mujahedeen in Yemen skyrocketed the popularity of Obama in America is plummeting.

Awlaki knew exactly which American buttons to push. He knowingly echoed the Cheney critique, mocking Obama's "short leash" after the cowboy aggression of the Bush era. But he also seized upon the recent strikes in Yemen's tribal provinces of Abyan and Shabwah to show that Obama had not fundamentally changed the Bush policies, playing on the disappointed hopes of many Muslims in Obama's first year. And he played on American war weariness, stoking the justified fears of American officials that air strikes, especially when they were as botched as the December 17 cruise missile strike that had killed some forty-one civilians, could boost support for Al Qaeda.

Awlaki linked Al Qaeda's narrow ideological struggle and the atrocity of 9/11 to broader resentment of the American superpower. And though Abdulmutallab had told the FBI that the date of his fizzled bombing had been happenstance, not a deliberate choice, Awlaki exploited the particular resonance of the Christmas holiday:

> But America thought that it could threaten lives of others. Kill and invade, occupy and plunder, and conspire without bearing the consequences of its actions. 9/11 was the answer of the millions of people who suffered from American aggression.
>
> And since then America has not been safe and nine years after 9/11, nine years of spending, and nine years of beefing up security you are still unsafe even on the holiest and most sacred of days to you, Christmas Day.

He showed off his firsthand familiarity with American life, remembering what he called "the good old days" in the United States. "No one would bother asking you for an ID before boarding a plane," he said. "No long lines, no elaborate searches, no body scans, no sniffing dogs, no taking off your shoes and emptying your pockets. You were a nation at ease."

But ridiculing the American president and reveling in the shadow that Al Qaeda had cast over Americans' daily lives was only a sideshow—Awlaki indulging himself. His real goal in speaking out from his desert refuge, and the part that sent a shiver through counterterrorism agencies, was recruitment. Brave warriors like Abdulmutallab were taking on the most powerful of countries, he said, brazenly linking jihadist killers to the words of Jesus in the Beatitudes (which the Koran echoed in different language): "You have your B-52s, your Apaches, your Abrams and your Cruise missiles, and we have small arms and simple improvised explosive devices. But we have men who are dedicated and sincere, with hearts of lions, and blessed are the meek for they will inherit the world."

Awlaki's explicit pitch came at the end of his short address, when he addressed himself directly to "the Muslims in America." He had spent nineteen years in the United States, as a child, college student, and imam, and he had a visceral understanding of the competitive tugs of American liberties and of a rigid version of Islamic duty. In the place of loyalty to nation, he suggested, any observant Muslim must substitute loyalty to the *ummah*, the global community of

Muslims. That argument was the linchpin of Al Qaeda's appeal to the Muslim minority in Western countries. Having lived it, Awlaki understood it implicitly.

> How can your conscience allow you to live in peaceful coexistence with a nation that is responsible for the tyranny and crimes committed against your own brothers and sisters? How can you have your loyalty to a government that is leading the war against Islam and Muslims?
>
> The Muslim community in America has been witnessing a gradual erosion and decline in core Islamic principles, so today many of your scholars and Islamic organizations are openly approving of Muslims serving in the US Army to kill Muslims, joining the FBI to spy against Muslims, and are standing between you and your duty of jihad.

In other words, as George W. Bush had famously put it in his address to Congress nine days after 9/11, using a phrase that would be central to understanding Awlaki's evolution, "Either you are with us, or you are with the terrorists." Awlaki reversed Bush's meaning but made the same point to his core audience of young English-speaking Muslims: they had to decide which side they were on.

If Awlaki sounded implacably hostile toward the land of his birth, which he said had become "a nation of evil," the feeling was mutual. The December 24 strike in Shabwah, the southern tribal province where Awlaki was hiding on his family's and tribe's ancestral turf, had not technically targeted Awlaki; the legally approved targets were other leaders of Yemen's Al Qaeda branch. Privately, some American officials made clear that they would have been pleased had the cleric turned up dead.

On January 21, the Senate Foreign Relations Committee had called Awlaki "a direct threat to U.S. interests" in a report titled *Al Qaeda in Yemen and Somalia: A Ticking Time Bomb.* On February 3, Dennis Blair, the retired admiral serving as director of national intelligence, had said at a public House hearing that with "specific permission" strikes could target American citizens deemed to be a threat. He didn't name Awlaki, but he didn't have to. It was becoming conventional wisdom that Al Qaeda's branch in Yemen was now the most dangerous to the United States and that Awlaki now posed a greater threat than Osama bin Laden.

Many young Western Muslims were listening to messages like Awlaki's March 2010 "Call to Jihad," playing again and again his goading call for attacks, and some were inspired to plot violence. Others were traveling to Yemen, like Abdulmutallab, with the specific goal of seeking out Awlaki, their Internet hero, to volunteer for jihad.

Young people who came to Yemen looking for Sheikh Anwar, the title of veneration invariably used for him by now on jihadi forums, were heading into desolate and dangerous territory. Some months after AQAP announced its formation by Saudi and Yemeni militants in January 2009, Awlaki had departed his family's ancestral town of Al Saeed, located in a relatively verdant valley, and headed into the hills, initially occupying a modest house near an Al Qaeda training camp. The sprawling tribal governates were desperately poor: Shabwah, once a center of the ancient frankincense trade, in the south bordering the Arabian Sea; Marib, the home of the biblical Queen of Sheba, to its north; and Al Jawf, still farther north, stretching to the Saudi border. Estimates of unemployment, and they were the roughest of estimates, rose as high as 95 percent. Most income derived from payments sent from relatives working abroad in the wealthy Gulf states. The traditional Yemeni love of firearms, striking even by American standards, meant that disputes over water, business deals, or family honor sometimes turned bloody. ("They throw grenades at weddings, just for fun," said a former American military officer who saw it happen.) The national government in Sanaa, the capital, had little authority in the tribal areas, except through negotiation. When Ali Abdullah Saleh, Yemen's president for three decades, famously described his job as "dancing on the heads of snakes," he was talking in part about his ceaseless efforts to buy or rent with cash, weapons, and promises the loyalty of local tribal leaders who held the real power across much of his country.

Yemen, in older books often called Yaman or "the Yaman," literally means "country in the south." Three-fourths the size of Texas, it occupied the southernmost swath of the Arabian peninsula, sharing a long land border with Saudi Arabia to the north and a gorgeous coast along the Arabian Sea to the south, notable for the old imperial British port of Aden. In Roman times, Yemen had been known as Arabia Felix, or Fortunate Arabia, by some accounts a reference to the relative rainfall and greenery in the southwest part of the peninsula. But in recent decades that old title was preserved only on tourist posters, in the name of a local airline, and in ironic commentaries on the dispiriting state of national affairs. Yemen had about the same population as Saudi Arabia, twenty-six million, but the oil fields gave the average Saudi an income of $31,300. In Yemen, the per capita income was $2,500. Its poverty, ironically, had preserved its stunning ancient architecture; its mud-brick towers, most famously in Sanaa's old city, had not been razed for glass high-rises as in more affluent Arab capitals. But the modest Yemeni oil finds were running out, and more critically, so was the water. A secessionist movement had revived in the south, a Shiite group known as the Houthis was rebelling in the north, and AQAP was playing on all of these problems to lure young men to its ranks.

The jihadi recruiters had a colorful history on their side, too. Yemen was often described as "the ancestral home of Osama bin Laden," which Yemeni officials and scholars derided as a meaningless epithet, since Bin Laden's father had left Yemen as a boy to work as a porter in Jeddah and become a billionaire construction magnate. Al Qaeda's founder, they noted, had grown up in luxury in Saudi Arabia. But Yemen had other associations that gave it particular relevance for Al Qaeda. The country had a long history of jihadi movements, and Bin Laden had helped finance them in the late 1980s. In 1996, when Bin Laden was being pressured to leave Sudan, he told the London-based newspaper *Al-Quds al-Arabi* that "the choice is between Afghanistan and Yemen. Yemen's topography is mountainous, and its people are tribal, armed, and allow one to breathe clear air unblemished with humiliation." Though in the end he opted for Afghanistan, Bin Laden maintained an intense interest in Yemen and stayed in contact with militants there, especially his former secretary Nasser al-Wuhayshi, who had escaped from a Yemeni prison in 2006 and had formally announced the formation of AQAP under his leadership three years later.

Despite the occasional bombing and an old tradition of kidnapping, Yemen had long been popular with Westerners looking for an inexpensive place to learn Arabic. A subset of the language students, whether Muslim by heritage or converts to Islam, also were drawn into Islamic studies, and some of them made their way to Dammaj in Yemen's northwest to join an austere community of Salafis—devotees of a school of Islam dedicated to the ways and beliefs of the *salaf*, or early followers of Muhammad. A few of the devout wandered off to try to link up with AQAP.

Theo Padnos, an American writer who lived in Sanaa and spent time in Dammaj, memorably described the lure of Yemen for drifting or searching foreigners. Padnos noted that Abdulmutallab, the future underwear bomber, had lamented in an Islamic forum in 2005 his isolation and depression as a student in England. For such lost souls, he wrote, Yemen could seem like the solution to all of life's problems.

"The beauty of life in Yemen for someone like that is that it really can make them happy," Padnos wrote. "You wear the ancient robes. You memorize the ancient texts. The more you gain control over the Islamic mysteries, the stronger you feel. You don't physically triumph over anything, but there are times when the studying, the fasting and the support of one's brothers come together perfectly. At these moments you really do begin to feel the immanence of victory. Your loneliness and depression aren't bothering you anymore. You're on to bigger, more thrilling things."

In early 2010, chagrined at their failure to identify Abdulmutallab as a threat, counterterrorism officials scrambled to identify other Awlaki devotees who might have the necessary documents to be able to board planes to the United States. The American embassy in Canberra, Australia, sent a cable to Washington one month after the Christmas attack with the names of twenty-three Australian citizens or longtime residents who were "of security interest because they have either an historical or current association with Yemeni cleric Anwar al-Awlaki, or are based in Yemen or the surrounding region and may come into contact with al-Awlaki." The list came from Australian intelligence. In the cable, under a post-9/11 program with the curious name Visas Viper, the embassy proposed adding eleven of the people to the no-fly list and twelve to the "selectee" list, which would flag them for greater scrutiny at the airport. Of the twenty-three, six were women, targeted for special attention because, the cable said, "recent threat information suggests AQ Arabian Peninsula (AQAP) is looking to identify a female for a future attack."

The day the cable was sent from Canberra, a Senate report claimed that as many as three dozen American ex-convicts, who had converted to Islam in prison, had gone to Yemen to study Islam or Arabic and that some had subsequently "dropped off the radar." The FBI cast doubt on the eye-popping number. But such reports only heightened fears about Yemen and put more pressure on the Obama administration.

One case that illustrated why officials were so worried about the threat posed by Americans returning from Yemen was that of Abdulhakim Mujahid Muhammad, born Carlos Bledsoe. A troubled Muslim convert and Awlaki admirer from a middle-class African American family, Muhammad had dropped out of Tennessee State University and traveled to Yemen in 2007, seeking a more authentic experience of Islam. It is unclear whether he succeeded in meeting Awlaki, but he was eventually arrested by Yemeni authorities and deported to the United States in January 2009. He had already been infected with the notion that it was his duty to use violence to defend Islam from its supposed enemies. In June 2009, after experimenting with various ideas for attacks, Muhammad drove by a military recruiting station in Little Rock and opened fire with an SKS semi-automatic rifle, killing one soldier and wounding another. He was arrested, and three weeks after the failed Christmas bombing, with Al Qaeda's Yemen branch in the news, Muhammad wrote the judge from jail, saying he wanted to plead guilty. His letter captured the way a supposed religious imprimatur could lend grandiosity to what looked like a moronic and meaningless act of murder. "I don't wish to have a trial," he wrote. "I'm affiliated with Al Qaeda in the Arabian Peninsula." The attack, he told the judge, "is justified according to Islamic Laws and the Islamic Religion. Jihad—to fight those who wage war on Islam and Muslims." Muhammad would later be sentenced to life in prison.

Another American drawn to Awlaki and Yemen was a young martial arts black belt, Sharif Mobley. During his first trip to Yemen in 2008, he met with Awlaki. He returned to Sanaa in 2009 and was arrested by Yemeni authorities in a sweep of suspected militants after the Christmas attack; later he was charged with murder after killing a Yemeni guard in an attempt to escape. After his January arrest,

Mobley was visited in Yemeni custody by two American investigators, one saying he was from the FBI and the other from the Defense Department. The Americans had only one man on their minds, Mobley's lawyer said later.

"Awlaki," the agents said. "You help us find him and you'll go home."

I f it were not for the post-9/11 clampdown on access to the airspace above Washington, an hour's helicopter tour might have offered an instructive survey of the security archipelago that had been embarrassed by the Christmas attack and now was focused on hunting down Awlaki. This was the "intelligence community," a Mister Rogers term for agencies that often behaved more like hostile tribes, ready to do whatever it took to protect their turf. Under public fire after the exposure of the long list of flubs that had allowed Abdulmutallab to get on Northwest Flight 253, they were united only in their uneasy defensive crouch.

On the Virginia side of the Potomac River, there was the venerable CIA, whose officers in the Lagos embassy had met with Abdulmutallab's worried father. In a sparkling glass tower down the road was the National Counterterrorism Center, created after 9/11 with the sole purpose of pulling together threat information from different agencies—say, the several tidbits about the possible threat posed by the young Nigerian. In the same new Liberty Crossing complex was the Office of the Director of National Intelligence. The DNI's office was yet another layer added atop the sixteen intelligence agencies and subagencies—an eye-popping total that included some agencies whose existence few Americans suspected (who knew there was Coast Guard Intelligence?). The extra layer had been created explicitly to promote greater coordination and information sharing—to prevent just the kind of lapses that had occurred before December 25. From Liberty Crossing the tour might swing west past Dulles Airport to admire the famously plush headquarters of the National Reconnaissance Office, responsible for buying and launching spy satellites, whose construction using a hidden slush fund had set off a scandal in 1994. The budget-busting fleet of satellites designed and launched by the NRO were paying new attention to the desolate parts of Yemen where Abdulmutallab had met with Awlaki and gotten his training.

From here, in every direction, stretched the high-rise office suburbs where scores of spook contracting companies were thriving on the ballooning black budget.

Pivoting back toward the Potomac, our jaunt to spy on the spies would cross over the Pentagon, with its chastening 9/11 memorial, and into Washington, overflying the White House and the exasperated president. Just to the west would be the State Department, with its Bureau of Intelligence and Research, and to the east the FBI, its headquarters still embarrassingly bearing the name of J. Edgar Hoover as it struggled to remake itself as a sophisticated intelligence agency. The copter might circle above the temporary headquarters north of the White House of the Department of Homeland Security, cobbled together from twenty-two disparate departments and agencies in the post-9/11 intelligence reorganization, and then cross the Anacostia River to view the fancy complex of the Defense Intelligence Agency on the grounds of Joint Base Anacostia-Bolling. From there we might follow the Baltimore-Washington Parkway north a few miles to the spacious Fort Meade campus of the National Security Agency, whose more than thirty-five thousand eavesdroppers, linguists, codebreakers, and computer geeks made it the largest of the intelligence agencies. In early 2010, its files on Anwar al-Awlaki were growing by the hour.

And that would just about do it. Well, actually not. We would not have gotten a direct look at Air Force Intelligence, Army Intelligence, Marine Corps Intelligence, Navy Intelligence, the intelligence units at the Energy and Treasury Departments and the Drug Enforcement Administration—or the aforementioned Coast Guard Intelligence, one outpost that had managed to avoid criticism for the Christmas Day disaster.

Together, these agencies constituted a distinct kingdom, one with its own jargon and culture, all but invisible to the general public that was paying the bill. And the bill was considerable. The intelligence colossus was spending some $80 billion a year, dwarfing even peak Cold War spy budgets in real terms (though that was just an educated guess; until 2007, the government had actually refused to disclose total intelligence spending, making historical comparisons difficult). In 2010, the *Washington Post* shocked readers of its "Top Secret America" series with an estimate that 854,000 people held top-secret security clearances; but the following year official numbers were finally released, showing that in fact the real total was more than 1.4 million. And the number of people with any kind of security clearance, a large fraction of them contractors and not government employees, had passed 4 million and was still rising fast. This was the secret army of government experts, the long list of agencies and the cascade of tax dollars that existed to stop the Abdulmutallabs of the world, and that had failed.

Nothing motivated this far-flung empire like the ire of a president. In a quixotic effort to mimic the business world, the agencies spoke of the government officials who read and relied on their work as "customers." There was no customer nearly so important as the one in the Oval Office. Obama had repeatedly made clear his anger and frustration at Abdulmutallab's effortless penetration of the post-9/11 security bulwark on Christmas, calling it a "systemic failure" while still in Hawaii and declaring publicly after his January 5 meeting with security advisers that the agencies' performance was "not acceptable, and I will not tolerate it." The six-page summary of the White House review of the episode, pulled together by John Brennan, Obama's counterterrorism aide, and released to the media on January 7, 2010, was lacerating in its language: it used the word *failure* ten times and referred to "human errors," "systematic breakdowns," "shortcomings," and a "breakdown of accountability."

Some security officials were stung by the report, which they resented as expedient scapegoating by the White House. But more detached observers found the brutal language quite justified. The spy bureaucracy had seen its budget approximately double since 2001 and had become accustomed to presidential praise for its bravery and dedication. If Obama had any thoughts during his campaign about cutting back this secret empire, they had quickly fallen by the wayside. Like all presidents, he had quickly become dependent on the agencies. A rationalist who wanted to base his decisions on information, he had a voracious appetite for what they could serve up. After the near disaster, Obama had not chosen to fire anyone; characteristically, his approach focused on fixing the technical problems the AQAP plot had exposed rather than finding individuals to blame, which might have been more emotionally satisfying and politically protective.

In the months after Christmas, however, Obama began to get deeper into the weeds at intelligence briefings and the weekly terrorism meetings. He demanded that security officials describe not just specific threats but what each agency was doing about them. "After that, as president, it seemed like he felt in his gut the threat to the United States," said Michael Leiter, who as head of the National Counterterrorism Center might have made a handy scapegoat had the president been looking for one. "It meant a president who was more deeply engaged in the process of counterterrorism." Such presidential involvement, he said, was an "enormous hammer" that forced the agencies to be diligent and responsive. Ben Rhodes, a National Security Council aide, remembered the president forcefully and repeatedly making the point that the Christmas episode had exposed intolerable shortcomings in the security system. "He said, 'In the long run, as a country, we cannot be spending billions of dollars every time some scared twenty-three-year-old spends $10,000 and tries to attack a plane,'" Rhodes recalled. It was, of course, exactly the point Awlaki had made about what he called Al Qaeda's "war of attrition" against America.

To restore American confidence in the administration's ability to keep the country safe, Obama's aides knew, it would not suffice to wait and hope to foil the next attack launched by AQAP. They would have to go on the offensive in Yemen, stepping up the campaign to find and take out Al Qaeda plotters there. At the very top of the list was Anwar al-Awlaki.

Once upon a time, before 9/11, the mobilization of the entire American security apparatus to find one guy hiding out with a ragtag band of militants roaming the hills of Shabwah province might have seemed almost comic. It was as if some YouTube remix artist had taken the villains from *Gunfight at the O.K. Corral* and sent the ruthless techno-spy agencies of *The Bourne Identity* after them. But the Awlaki hunt was just another instance of what academics liked to call asymmetric warfare, posing a gang of terrorists against a superpower, and Americans had grown used to it in the age of Al Qaeda. The president gave the orders, and soon the agencies were competing to get scraps of intelligence about AQAP and Awlaki into the President's Daily Brief.

Every president since John F. Kennedy has had a personal, daily connection to the spy agencies, in the form of a top-secret binder delivered to the White House each morning at 6:30 a.m. The binder contains about a dozen articles, each up to four pages long, describing the most significant threats and scoops from the previous twenty-four hours. The President's Daily Brief, or PDB, as it is known around Washington, is the most exclusive daily newspaper on the planet, and agencies compete fiercely to get their items in. The binder is hand-delivered to a small number of top officials, including the vice president and secretary of state, and contains the spy agencies' greatest hits, including verbatim excerpts from the intercepted phone calls of world leaders and stunningly detailed satellite photos of terrorist training camps. If the president chooses, the written PDB comes along with personal briefings by top intelligence officials or specialized analysts to elaborate on its contents.

Presidents developed their own, idiosyncratic styles for handling intelligence briefings. Reagan, who found detailed briefings tedious, often delegated the daily CIA briefings and perusal of the PDB to his national security adviser, happy to get an oral summary later on. By contrast, George H. W. Bush, who had himself served as CIA director in the 1970s, read the PDB carefully but still sat down with CIA briefers each morning, often asking for additional raw intelligence. Bill Clinton had little patience for the oral briefings and famously shunned his own CIA chief, James Woolsey, but studied the written PDB. George W. Bush favored oral briefings and made sure they happened six days a week, especially after 9/11.

As Bush had learned, the PDB could become a political time bomb. He had been the recipient of perhaps the most famous item ever to appear in the PDB—the article headlined "Bin Laden Determined to Strike in US," which had appeared thirty-six days before the 9/11 attacks. When it was later declassified, it became Exhibit A for those who accused the Bush administration of being oblivious to the terrorist threat. That episode was not forgotten when Bush left office. When Rahm Emanuel, Obama's first chief of staff, saw a PDB item in 2009 that highlighted terrorist threats to the homeland, he accused the nonplussed director of intelligence, Dennis Blair, of setting up the Obama White House to face the blame if an attack occurred. Blair thought Emanuel's suspicion preposterous, the fevered imaginings of a pol who didn't understand how intelligence agencies worked.

Obama, the former *Harvard Law Review* editor, read the PDB each day before his discussion with the briefer—sometimes Blair, a retired admiral, sometimes one of Blair's deputies. As with other presidents, the session was a two-way street: Obama would ask for information beyond the brief, giving the agencies a sense of his concerns and preoccupations, and answers would often come back the same day.

The threat from Yemen was an increasing worry, and one that seemed uncannily connected to Obama's presidency: on the very day of his inauguration as president, January 20, 2009, Saudi and Yemeni militants had announced on jihadist web forums that they were uniting to form a new group called Tanzim Qa'idat al-Jihad fi Jazirat al-Arab, literally "the Base for Jihad in the Arabian Peninsula," which came to be called AQAP. The CIA veteran Obama had chosen as his counterterrorism adviser, John Brennan, was a former CIA station chief in Riyadh with a special interest in Saudi Arabia and its impoverished neighbor to the south. And through the first year of Obama's presidency, a rising number of PDB items focused on this troubled country that few Americans could find on a map.

Obama had plenty of help in trying to make sense of the flow of information from Yemen. The National Security Council, his in-house think tank, had grown steadily from a dozen people at its creation in 1947 to a formidable staff of about 240 by the time Obama took office, many of them young, bright, and shockingly inexperienced, as intelligence agency veterans were more than willing to complain. There was a "policy director" on the NSC staff for each major country and issue—sixteen directors for the Middle East alone, and an entire separate staff for terrorism. Yemen was judged to warrant its own director, and not because of its economic significance or diplomatic sway. By 6 a.m., each director would get a BlackBerry message listing the items in that day's PDB. If the list included an item on Yemen or AQAP, the Yemen director would scramble to write a half-page background blurb for senior NSC staff so that they would be well prepared in case the president zeroed in on the item later in the morning. All day long—and well into the night, since NSC staffers were routinely at their desks till 9 p.m. or later—reports from the agencies would flow into an intelligence file in each NSC staffer's Outlook e-mail account, tailored to match the employee's assignments and clearances. When things in Yemen heated up, as they did steadily in Obama's first year, the flow of intercepted communications, satellite photos, and topical analyses to NSC computers became a torrent.

B ack in November, as the first news reports linked Anwar to Nidal Hasan, the Fort Hood shooter, and as Anwar praised Hasan as a hero on his blog, Nasser al-Awlaki's phone had begun ringing. Reporters wanted to talk about his son. Dr. Awlaki said he hadn't had any contact with Anwar in eight months—but he nonetheless claimed to know about his activities and allegiances. "He has nothing to do with al-Qaida," the elder Awlaki said. "But he's a devout Muslim. He has never been involved in anything against anybody." It was a reflection less of scrupulous research than of a father's loyalty to his son. On December 24, as the false reports circulated that Anwar had been killed, Nasser spoke to a *Washington Post* reporter in Sanaa, his voice cracking. "If the American government helped in attacking one of [its own] citizens, this is illegal," the father said. "Nidal Hasan killed 13 people and he's going to get a trial. My son has killed nobody. He should face trial if he's done something wrong." Obama's election had thrilled Dr. Awlaki a year earlier, but now he personalized the case, knowing that only Obama could make a decision on such a matter. "If Obama wants to kill my son," he said, "this is wrong."

After Christmas, Nasser, who was already caring for Anwar's first wife and five children at his son's request, had watched the growing American hysteria about his eldest child with alarm and dismay. He didn't want to believe the things Obama administration officials and the media were saying about Anwar. He did not know whether to believe news reports that Abdulmutallab had implicated his son as an organizer of the airliner plot; the details would only be confirmed publicly in court documents two years later. On January 11, 2010, he agreed to speak to CNN reporter Paula Newton in Sanaa—though not on camera—and portrayed Anwar as a preacher who had expressed "controversial views" and was now "a wanted man" who was "cornered" and had no choice but to seek refuge with his tribe in the mountains. He did not know whether Anwar had met Abdulmutallab, he told Newton, but he did not think so. He was certain that his son was not a member of Al Qaeda, he said. Grasping for a way out of an impossible situation, Nasser al-Awlaki said he wanted to convince his son to talk to Yemeni and American officials and perhaps to surrender. But he complained that "they are not giving me time. They want to kill one of their own citizens. This is a legal issue that needs to be answered."

It was only one interview in what would become a years-long public fight by Nasser al-Awlaki to defend his son. But the elder Awlaki felt he was fighting not just for Anwar. He was calling on the United States to live by the moral and legal principles he believed it stood for, the idea of equal justice under the rigorous rule of law that had so impressed him as a young graduate student. In America, he had learned, a suspect was innocent until proven guilty. If Anwar had committed a crime, he said, let him face the charges in court.

But as Nasser al-Awlaki supported Anwar's family, defended his reputation, and scrambled to protect him from American missiles, Anwar offered no hint that he appreciated the help. All the evidence, in fact, was to the contrary. Anwar's public statements undermined his father's efforts to protect him. He praised Nidal Hasan's shooting spree at Fort Hood; he lauded Abdulmutallab, who he said had been his student; he wholeheartedly endorsed the mass murder of American civilians.

In another Internet statement in the spring of 2010, titled "Western Jihad Is Here to Stay," Awlaki showed off his easy fluency in Americana, quoting Donald Rumsfeld's famous memo as defense secretary that asked whether the United States was killing, capturing, or deterring more terrorists than the madrasas and radical clerics were producing. Awlaki asserted that despite huge expenditures the United States was losing the battle for hearts and minds. "The jihad movement has not only survived but is expanding," he said. "Jihad is becoming as American as apple pie and as British as afternoon tea."

Awlaki's gleeful phrasemaking brought to mind his mother's devotion to apple pie, the favorite Betty Crocker recipe she had brought home to Yemen from America. Now her son had turned it into a rhetorical weapon.

Nasser al-Awlaki said he did not believe Anwar had joined Al Qaeda, but since the Christmas attack all the evidence was going the other way. In May 2010, AQAP's leader Nasser al-Wuhayshi issued a statement embracing "the hero who strikes with righteousness, Sheikh Anwar al-Awlaki." Wuhayshi poured scorn on Obama, whom he mentioned seven times, and the American hunt for Awlaki. "Do not worry, oh Muslims, about the Sheikh," said the AQAP leader, "for he is in safe hands." Without expressly stating that Awlaki was part of Al Qaeda, Wuhayshi made it clear that theirs was a common cause and that AQAP would protect the cleric to the end.

A week later, the terrorist group's media arm released a lengthy video interview with Awlaki, who coolly dashed his father's hope of preserving his life by arranging his surrender. Senior Yemeni officials had raised such a possibility, saying they were talking to leaders of the Awaliq tribe in Shabwah about turning over the cleric to Yemeni authorities. But in the interview with AQAP's media unit, Al Malahem, Awlaki stated flatly that he would not turn himself in to either Yemeni or American authorities, declaring that "justice is not open for negotiation." He was trusting his fate to a loftier authority, he said.

"If the Americans want me, let them search for me," Awlaki said. "Allah is the best protector. If Allah, glorified and exalted be He, wants to rescue me from them, if they were to spend all what is on this earth, they won't be able to get to me. And if Allah predestined that my death be on their hands and the hands of their agents, then that would be my fate."

PART TWO   **1990–2002**

3

HE HAD A BEAUTIFUL TONGUE

For two Arab freshmen who had bonded during their first months at Colorado State, the trouble started, oddly enough, over the Super Bowl. Ghassan Khan, from Saudi Arabia, wanted to watch the Buffalo Bills face off against the New York Giants. Anwar al-Awlaki, from Yemen, objected.

"I told him, 'I want to watch the Super Bowl,'" Khan said. "He said it would be better even to stare at the wall than to watch. He didn't like the beer ads and the cheerleaders."

He watched despite Awlaki's protests, and it was a good game, Khan recalled: The Giants beat the Bills 20–19, the only Super Bowl to be decided by a single point. But Khan was bemused; his friend had been absurdly transformed over the monthlong Christmas break. Gone was the fun-loving character who had led him on various escapades in their first semester of college. In his place was a puritanical scold, a kid acting like a censorious old man, suddenly embracing a starkly conservative brand of Islam.

The two nineteen-year-olds had become fast friends after arriving in Fort Collins in the fall of 1990. They were both smokers and engineering students, the only two Arabic speakers in their stone-walled dormitory, and they connected while huddled outside with their cigarettes in the gathering autumn cold. There was a third Muslim in Allison Hall, a tall Indian student named Hozaifa, and the trio often hung out together, testing their new freedom in the time-honored style of college freshmen. For young men from conservative Muslim backgrounds, the liberties were especially heady.

None of the three was especially religious, and they went to parties and did some drinking. Because he looked older, Hozaifa was assigned to try to buy alcohol; Khan remembered that Anwar had urged Hozaifa to ask for a sweet coconut-flavored liquor, Malibu Rum, that Anwar said he had tried the summer before.

"Of the three of us, he was the fun guy," recalled Khan, now vice president of an investment bank in Riyadh. Anwar had an interest in politics and occasionally talked about the plight of the Palestinians. But he also had a hookah, or water pipe for smoking tobacco, and he was more comfortable than the other two talking to girls. One night at 2 a.m., Anwar, who had bought a car, suddenly said, "Let's go to Boulder!" Despite some grumbling from the others, the three teens made the hourlong drive and discovered—surprise!—that everything was closed. They found a twenty-four-hour Denny's, ate and hung around, and drove back to Fort Collins at 8 a.m., Khan said.

Khan and Awlaki grew so close that they decided to move off campus together for second semester, and they agreed to move into an apartment with an older Yemeni who had recently finished a master's degree in economics and knew Anwar's father. But because Khan headed home for the winter break, while Anwar stayed in Colorado, they were separated for several weeks. When Khan returned, he was stunned by what had happened to his roommate.

Awlaki, clean-shaven the first semester, had begun to grow a beard, often a clue to a Muslim man's growing religiosity. It turned out that he had fallen in with a group of Islamic proselytizers in Fort Collins from Tablighi Jamaat, which translates as "society for spreading the faith," a global movement encouraging piety and devotion. He had come under the particular influence of an older student from Egypt working on a master's in civil engineering who had the beard and somber style of a religious conservative.

And something else had happened during the break: on January 17, ten days before the Super Bowl, the United States had begun bombing Iraq in the opening air raids of Desert Storm. When Anwar saw CNN's Peter Arnett reporting live from Baghdad as the bombs began falling, he called his father at home in Sanaa, where it was 4 a.m., and woke him to tell him the news. Baghdad held special historical and symbolic significance for any Arab, Nasser al-Awlaki said, and his son's angry reaction to the bombing was the first time he had criticized the United States.

There was some irony in the fact that the student who had spent the holidays in Saudi Arabia had maintained his freewheeling American lifestyle, while the student who stayed in Colorado had embraced Islam. But the pattern of a Muslim visitor to the United States seeking solace in the clarity of religion when faced with the disorienting temptations and excesses of an American campus was well established. Khalid Sheikh Mohammed, the chief planner of the 9/11 attacks, had spent several years in North Carolina in the 1980s, earning an engineering degree at North Carolina A&T in Greensboro while spending his free time with the bearded religious students whom other Muslims on campus mocked as "the mullahs." The Egyptian scholar and Muslim Brotherhood leader known as the father of radical, anti-Western Islamism, Sayyid Qutb, had a famously allergic reaction to American materialism and sexual openness. While in the United States on a fellowship for teachers in 1948–49, Qutb (pronounced KOO-tub) spent time in New York, Washington, DC, California, and Greeley, Colorado, just a forty-minute drive from Fort Collins. It was a dry town of ten thousand people, known as "the city of churches," hardly Sodom or Gomorrah. Nothing captures Qutb's horror at what he considered American licentiousness better than his description of a church dance, of all things, overseen by a pastor: "The dance floor was lit with red and yellow and blue lights, and with a few white lamps. And they danced to the tunes of the gramophone, and the dance floor was replete with tapping feet, enticing legs, arms wrapped around waists, lips pressed to lips, and chests pressed to chests. The atmosphere was full of desire."

The atmosphere was not the only thing "full of desire," one is tempted to add, upon reading this 1951 Qutb essay, entitled "The America I Have Seen." And it gets worse, or perhaps better:

> The American girl is well acquainted with her body's seductive capacity. She knows it lies in the face, and in expressive eyes, and in thirsty lips. She knows seductiveness lies in the round breasts, the full buttocks, and in the shapely thighs, sleek legs and she shows

all this and does not hide it. She knows it lies in clothes: in bright colors that awaken primal sensations, and in designs that reveal the temptations of the body—and in American girls these are sometimes live, screaming temptations! Then she adds to all this the fetching laugh, the naked looks, and the bold moves, and she does not ignore this for one moment or forget it!

Qutb's reverie is by no means exclusive to Islam; there are plenty of analogical anecdotes in the history of Christian fundamentalism and Orthodox Judaism. But apart from its entertainment value, the essay sheds a fascinating light on Awlaki, for whom sex would become a dangerous trap and Qutb would become a critical influence.

The tension between Khan and his devout roommate grew, coming to a head not long after the Super Bowl confrontation. During one cold spell, Khan decided not to go to Friday prayers, a standard ritual even for many casually observant Muslims. Awlaki could not believe it. "He kept knocking on my door. I said, 'You go, I'm not going.' He said, 'What do you mean you're not going?'"

Awlaki told Khan he didn't want the television—Khan's television—turned on when he was home, a condition Khan grudgingly accepted. But one day a few weeks later, Awlaki came home to find Khan watching a movie on cable—nothing racy, Khan said, though he didn't remember which film. Awlaki flew into a rage. "He came into the living room and threw the TV on the floor and smashed it," Khan recalled. Khan told Awlaki, "This isn't working," and moved out. After that, when they met on campus, Awlaki was polite but unrepentant.

"He didn't apologize—not at all," Khan said. "I saw him a couple of weeks later, and he said, 'You left some books.' He brought them by. I ended up sleeping on a couch with friends the rest of the semester."

Yemen is a conservative Muslim country, but Awlaki did not bring this prudish intolerance from Sanaa to Fort Collins. It smacks of the callow certainty of the recent convert. And there was another factor, as Ghassan Khan pointed out. In both Yemen and Saudi Arabia, Khan said, social contacts can be quite stratified by class and religious views. As a teenager in Sanaa, Awlaki would have been unlikely to spend much time with religious hard-liners. In America, a very diverse Muslim minority was thrown together by circumstances. "I grew up in Saudi Arabia, and I never met people like the Tablighi," Khan said. "If Anwar had stayed in Yemen, I don't think he would have changed." Nasser al-Awlaki shared that view. He told a visitor years later of his son's embrace of piety, "What happened, happened in America."

Nasser al-Awlaki was conventionally religious, family members say; to grow up as a Muslim in Yemen is a bit like growing up as a Baptist in the rural American South—the fundamentals of belief, scriptural knowledge, spiritual vocabulary, and worship come with the territory. But along with his first cousin, Saleh bin Fareed al-Awlaki, Nasser had attended the British-run Aden College, a private high school on the Arabian Sea that was no hotbed of Islamism. And unlike Qutb, he was overjoyed with what he found in America after arriving on a Fulbright scholarship in 1966. He was the classic aspiring Third World technocrat, coming to America in search of education and taking his new skills and broadened worldview home to try to help his struggling country. In that mission he succeeded spectacularly, serving as minister of agriculture and in high-level university posts, and eventually dispatching two of his three sons, first Anwar and then Ammar, to America with the expectation that they would follow a similar path. Religion was very much a sideshow in the family's life, and Nasser was concerned that it might derail his sons, family members say. When the middle son, Omar, began to visit the mosque in Sanaa too often for his father's liking, Nasser actually prohibited him from going there. "He said, 'If you want to pray, pray at home and don't congregate with others,'" said the youngest brother, Ammar. "He was afraid he'd be politically inclined toward the Muslim Brotherhood," which had a branch in Yemen, Ammar recalled.

Anwar's American citizenship was an accident of his father's education. He was born on April 22, 1971, in Las Cruces, New Mexico, where his father was a graduate student in agricultural science at New Mexico State University. Four months later, the family moved to Lincoln, Nebraska, where Nasser worked on his PhD at the University of Nebraska. Finally the family relocated to St. Paul, Minnesota, moving into a house near Nasser's teaching job at the

College of Agriculture of the University of Minnesota. Anwar went to Chelsea Heights Elementary School near Como Park in St. Paul, and his father described him as "a cute little boy who enjoyed himself very much in school and outside." His parents had parties with other graduate students from around the world and went on vacation to northern Minnesota's lake country in the summers, swimming, fishing, and hiking. "Anwar had a beautiful childhood in America," his father said. Nasser and Saleha's second child, a girl, was also born in the United States.

But work in Yemen called, and the family arrived back in Sanaa on the last day of 1977. Anwar was enrolled in Sanaa's only private school, Azal Modern School, where he quickly caught up, though his English was better than his Arabic. He stayed in the school, favored by Yemen's elite, until graduation in 1989, a kid who carried piles of books on vacation and took a particular interest in history. Islam was part of the curriculum at Azal, as at every school in Yemen, and Anwar prayed and fasted during Ramadan like everyone else, his father said. He showed no special interest in religion and in his high school days never spoke of becoming an imam. In fact, his brother Ammar remembers their mother repeatedly putting a prayer rug in Anwar's suitcase before he left for Colorado State and Anwar repeatedly taking it out; his attitude seemed to be, Ammar said, "I'm going to America and I won't need this."

But Anwar, like his schoolmates, was excited by the jihad of the mujahedeen, the holy warriors fighting for Islam—with the help of the United States—against the Soviet Army in Afghanistan. The concept of jihad, malleable and disputed within modern Islam, would become central to Anwar al-Awlaki's evolution, and here it makes its first notable appearance. For boys of their generation, said Walid al-Saqaf, a neighbor of the Awlaki family in Sanaa in the 1980s, the guerrilla war to oust the godless Soviets was an inspiring, heroic cause. "There was constant talk of the heroes who were leaving Yemen to join the fight and become martyrs and go to paradise," recalled Saqaf, now an Internet activist in Yemen. In the Awlakis' neighborhood, families would regularly gather to watch the latest videotapes brought by young men returning from the war. "I recall Anwar as a skinny teenager with brains," Saqaf said.

Students who did especially well in school were permitted to opt out of military service and instead spend a year teaching. For Anwar, who was no athlete, this escape from the drudgery and physical toll of army service held great appeal. So for a year after high school he taught in an elementary school in Dhela'a, an hour's drive from Sanaa. A decade later, applying to start a doctoral program in education, he recalled the stint with pleasure: "That was my first exposure to the field of teaching, and I loved it."

By all accounts Nasser was a loving and supportive father, but he did not hesitate to direct his son's education. He thought Anwar should get an engineering education and specialize in hydrology and water resources, a topic Nasser had himself written about and a critical need in Yemen, where groundwater sources have been dwindling for decades. Nasser spoke with friends at the US Agency for International Development in Sanaa, who advised him to consider Colorado State, which had a strong hydrology program. According to Nasser, his USAID friends also advised him to have Anwar apply for an American government scholarship reserved for foreigners and say he was Yemeni, which was not untrue—he grew up with dual citizenship. (Much later, Anwar wrote: "My father at the time was a Minister of Agriculture and the Americans were happy to make some exceptions for him.") The day after he landed in Chicago on June 5, 1990, however, Anwar applied for a Social Security card and listed his place of birth as Sanaa, presumably a deliberate misstatement to protect his scholarship offer. Some twelve years later, after the country had been unimaginably altered and Awlaki had taken an unexpected path, government officials would discover and pursue the old teenage falsehood.

At some point after the blowup with Ghassan Khan, Awlaki seems to have settled into a less obstreperous, more reasonable style. But his new devotion to Islam lasted. He became an active member of Colorado State's Muslim Student Association, serving for two years as association president and chairman of *dawah*, or outreach, at the little mosque at the edge of campus, said Yusuf Siddiqui, a friend and fellow MSA activist. Siddiqui said that in the wide range of Muslim students Awlaki would have been considered a moderate, somewhere between the most rigid conservatives and the libertines who shrugged off bans on drinking and sex. He was elected MSA president in a race against a Saudi student who was far stricter. "I remember Anwar saying, 'He would want your mom to cover her face. I'm not like that,'" Siddiqui said.

But in the pre-9/11 era, few university officials paid much attention to the internal politics of the Muslim minority on campus, and the most conservative contingent expressed quite extreme social and political views. "I felt like the MSA was a bunch of radicals and fundamentalists," said a Muslim woman, born and raised in Kuwait, who studied at Colorado State when Awlaki was there but didn't know him. She recalled an aggressive male student with a big beard declaring in a panel discussion that Muslims who lived like most American students on campus "were going to hell." The woman ended up settling in the United States but said she was no longer a practicing Muslim.

Siddiqui said that Awlaki's flawless American English sometimes made fellow students forget that his adolescence, and the shaping of his personality, had taken place in the very foreign setting of Yemen. "If you made some pop culture reference, he might not recognize it," said Siddiqui, who had grown up in Colorado. Once, on a picnic jaunt to Big Thompson Canyon about a half hour's drive from campus, Anwar astonished his American and Americanized friends by climbing a nearby mountain barefoot. "He just said, 'That's how we do it in Yemen,'" Siddiqui recalled. Sometimes it was hard to know whether Awlaki's behavior reflected his upbringing in Yemen or his newfound religiosity. Once, when a female American student stopped by the MSA to ask for help with math homework, "He said to me in a low tone of voice, 'Why don't you do it?'" Siddiqui said. The budding ladies' man that Khan had observed in the early months of freshman year now, after his embrace of Islamic piety, felt uncomfortable being alone with a female student.

As an MSA activist, Awlaki was becoming more overtly political, and naturally his attention fell on the Afghan jihad that had been so powerful a part of his milieu as a teenager in Sanaa, where he had spent many hours watching videotapes of the jihad and hearing the tales told by Yemeni men returning from battle. In the winter break of his sophomore year, in late 1991, he took off for Afghanistan, by then legendary among Muslims around the world as the place where a band of devout warriors of Allah had defeated a superpower. After the Gulf War, he wrote later, in a possibly embellished account published in *Inspire* magazine, "I started taking my religion more seriously and I took the step of traveling to Afghanistan to fight." The notion of a skinny, pampered American college student taking up arms in a brutal guerrilla war may seem like a stretch, and it is quite possible that Awlaki was glorifying a bit of jihad tourism. The Soviet Army had pulled out nearly two years earlier. But it was not implausible that he aspired to join the fight: as he prepared to leave, the Soviet-backed regime in Kabul still held power, and various rival factions of mujahedeen were still battling government forces, though the combat was scattered and nothing like it was at the height of the war.

Not surprisingly, the experience appears to have been a letdown. Anwar's younger brother, Ammar, later asked him about his Afghanistan trip. Anwar said he had not fought because there was so much snow and it was so cold. According to Ammar, Anwar had responded disgustedly, "We did nothing." Ammar added, "When Anwar says we did nothing, it means that Anwar, who used every minute of his day, was frustrated." Undoubtedly anticipating resistance, Anwar did not tell his father about the Afghan trip until after it had occurred, Nasser al-Awlaki said. "I actually only knew about that trip after he returned to the US, and I was glad he had returned to continue his studies," Nasser said. "I think he stayed only a few weeks and it was after the war ended there, when Americans were traveling there freely."

In the version published later in *Inspire*, Anwar himself suggested that he had found the experience so moving that he was prepared to drop out of Colorado State and join the mujahedeen in Afghanistan, but his plans were overtaken by events. "I spent a winter there," he wrote, returning to Colorado "with the intention of finishing up in the US and leaving to Afghanistan for good. My plan was to travel back in the summer." But in the spring of 1992, the last Soviet-backed leader, Najibullah, resigned: "Kabul was opened by the mujahedeen and I saw that the war was over and ended up staying in the US." But if Afghanistan had been a frigid disappointment, he didn't let on. He wore a distinctive Afghan hat all over campus, a please-ask-me-about-it affectation that spoke of a young man trying on an identity. He started quoting Abdullah Azzam, a prominent Palestinian scholar who provided theological justification for the Afghan jihad and was a mentor to Osama bin Laden.

Given Awlaki's later career, his belated visit to the most famous and celebrated modern jihad takes on special meaning, even if he never got near combat. It is also an opportunity to set aside the indelible coloring of 9/11 and recall that the stirring saga of the Afghan mujahedeen, with which Awlaki had grown up and which inspired his college travel, was an American-funded, American-backed, American-celebrated affair. Each year of his presidency, Ronald Reagan had lavished praise on the grizzled, bearded Islamists he called "freedom fighters," and he had backed their David-and-Goliath battle with billions in covert aid via the CIA. "To watch the courageous Afghan freedom fighters battle modern arsenals with simple handheld weapons is an inspiration to those who love freedom," he wrote in one of his annual Afghanistan Day proclamations. "Their courage teaches us a great lesson—that there are things in this world worth defending." Like the CIA strategists and American politicians whose vision would be hailed in the book and movie *Charlie Wilson's War*, Awlaki was inspired by the victory of the mujahedeen. But while the Americans credited the outcome to the Stinger missile and an open congressional checkbook, Awlaki attributed the triumph to Allah.

Awlaki's extended absence in the wilds of Afghanistan had left him way behind in his studies. Ghassan Khan remembers him turning up in a fluid dynamics class late in the spring semester and pleading with his former roommate to share his notes from the class. "He said, 'I really need to get an A on the final, because I got a zero on everything else,'" Khan said. Not long after that, Awlaki learned that he had lost his US government scholarship, a move he later suggested might have been punishment for his growing Islamic activism. But by his own admission, and the recollection of some classmates, he had missed many classes because of both his travels and his extracurricular interests, so his suggestion of political martyrdom is not especially convincing. "Shortly after my scholarship was terminated, I enquired for the reason behind such a drastic step," he wrote. "The answer I got was that my grades were dipping too low. It is true that my focus had now shifted away from school and my grades suffered because of my travel to Afghanistan and my role as head of the Muslim Student Association on campus." His Colorado State transcript confirms the deteriorating grades: despite borrowing Khan's notes, he got an F in that fluid dynamics course, and his grade point average for the whole 1991–92 school year was a meager 1.0, a D average. His father said he thought the scholarship had ended because of USAID budget cuts, which is possible, though it is easy to imagine his embarrassed son offering his father that explanation rather than owning up to his woeful performance. Nasser confirmed that he had paid his son's tuition and expenses for his last two years at Colorado State.

But if the door to academic stardom was closing, another door was opening. The Islamic Center of Fort Collins met in a modest, one-story brick house in a residential neighborhood adjoining the Colorado State campus; it had been a church until Muslim students and professors, who had met in borrowed rooms since the 1960s, bought it for $149,000 in 1980 and finally had a permanent home for worship, study, and charitable activities. By the early 1990s, said Moin Siddiqui, a retired professor of statistics and mosque leader, Friday midday prayers, or *jummah*, was drawing 150 men and 30 women from diverse backgrounds. "You'd have a bunch of Pakistanis, a bunch of Malaysians, a bunch of Saudis, a bunch of Libyans. They studied hydrology, veterinary medicine, civil engineering, statistics," he said. Without the budget to pay a full-time imam, students and professors took turns preaching the Friday sermon. It was a comfortable, low-pressure setting for an ambitious young man to try his hand at preaching, and Awlaki took advantage of it. He soon found that he had a knack for it.

If he could boast of no deep religious training, he knew much of the Koran and the hadith, the sayings of the Prophet Muhammad. He spoke fluent English, and he had a light touch. "He was very knowledgeable," said Mumtaz Hussain, a Pakistani immigrant active in the mosque for two decades. "He was an excellent person—very nice, dedicated to religion." Awlaki expressed no anti-American sentiments, said Hussain, whose son served in the National Guard. "This is our motherland now. People would not tolerate sermons of that kind," he said.

His choice of courses seems to reflect a growing excitement about preaching. In the summer term in 1992, he broke out of his strict engineering curriculum and took a course on public speaking, as well as introductory classes in literature and philosophy. In the spring of 1993 he signed up for "The Literature of Social Protest," and in his final term in the summer of 1994 he took "Studies in Persuasion," earning an A in both of those courses. As the months passed and his reputation at the mosque flourished, Anwar began to imagine an alternative to the path his father had set out for him, the lockstep sequence from an American engineering degree to a post in Yemen working on water supplies.

Many years later, on his blog, Awlaki would say that Thomas Gradgrind, Charles Dickens's notoriously utilitarian headmaster in *Hard Times*, reminded him of "some Muslim parents who are programmed to think that only medicine or engineering are worthy professions for their children." It sounded like a personal gripe. Anwar managed to pull up his grades considerably, earning all A's and B's his senior year. By taking courses all four summers, he managed to graduate in 1994 with a bachelor's of science in civil engineering and an overall GPA of 2.41, a low B-minus. His father naturally wanted him to use the degree, and he took an entry-level job at an engineering consulting company in Denver. "That would be the topic at the lunch table here in Sanaa when Mom and Dad would talk about it," Anwar's young brother Ammar remembered. "They were happy about it, thrilled about it, when he was a trainee." But he quit after a matter of weeks, to his father's dismay. "I discussed the issue with him, and I tried to encourage him to continue his career as a professional engineer, because that kind of career will benefit the people of Yemen after he decides to return to Yemen," Nasser said. But by then Anwar had managed to get a part-time job as an imam at the Denver Islamic Society, and it was obvious that his heart was in preaching, not hydrology.

Days after receiving his degree in August 1994, Anwar flew to Abu Dhabi for a wedding—his own. The Awlaki family was modern and westernized in many respects, but in this case they opted for tradition. The match was an arranged affair in which Anwar and his bride, Gihan Mohsen Baker, the daughter of his father's second cousin, appear to have had limited say. Like many well-off people from southern Yemen, the bride's family had left the country after a Marxist regime seized power in the south in the late 1960s, seeking their fortune in fast-developing cities like Abu Dhabi in the Arab states of the Persian Gulf. Saleh bin Fareed al-Awlaki, Anwar's wealthy uncle and a respected sheikh who had earned a fortune while living in the Gulf, helped play matchmaker. (Bin Fareed was Nasser's first cousin and thus technically Anwar's first cousin once removed, but Anwar called him uncle.) Anwar's parents "asked me if I would speak to my cousin and to his daughter and her mother," Bin Fareed recalled. "They asked, 'Is he the right man?' We said, 'Yes, he's the perfect man. Plus, he's our blood.'" Anwar was twenty-three, a beanpole with an unruly beard at six-foot-one and 135 pounds; Gihan was nineteen. They settled in Denver, and their first child, a boy they named Abdulrahman Anwar al-Awlaki, was born there on an August afternoon a year later.

By most accounts, Awlaki's preaching in the early years was unobjectionable even to those American Muslims who were especially wary of hints of radicalism, which could attract unwanted attention from the authorities or alienate non-Muslims. There were mentions of the plight of the Palestinians and criticism of sanctions on Iraq for depriving ordinary Iraqis of medicine and food, an issue to which Awlaki would often return in later years. The tenor of Awlaki's message was unambiguously conservative in terms of social values. Like many an evangelical Christian pastor, Awlaki preached against vice and sin, lauded marriage and family values, and parsed the scripture, winning fans across a range of generations. As an American citizen in his mid-twenties, equally at home in Arabic and American-accented English, Awlaki was a rarity. Most imams at American mosques were older immigrants who spoke English with a heavy accent or not at all and had little understanding of American youth culture. Awlaki could meet young Muslims on their own turf and sympathize with their awkward position between two cultures, one at home, the other at school. But he impressed Arab immigrant parents and grandparents, too, as a bright young man who could discuss spiritual matters or practical problems in Arabic. "He had a beautiful tongue," said one of the pillars of the Denver mosque, a Palestinian American in his sixties. "He had a nice voice. He had earned the knowledge he needed."

But the same elder recalled a painful dispute at the end of Awlaki's time at the mosque, known as Al Noor, or "the light." A Saudi student at the University of Denver told the older man that he had decided, with Awlaki's encouragement, to travel to Chechnya to join the jihad against the Russians. The elder thought the Saudi's plan was ill-advised and confronted Awlaki after Friday prayers. He told Awlaki that the young man should not go on jihad without the permission of his parents, citing the hadith, the sayings of the Prophet. Their argument grew louder, with a small group of worshippers pausing to watch. "My way was *dawah*," or inviting people to accept Islam and its teachings, he said. "His way was *jihadi*." As their dispute escalated, the elder said, "I told him, 'Don't talk to my people about jihad.' He left two weeks later."

Years later, said the elder, who was reluctant to be quoted by name about controversial topics, he felt vindicated when the 9/11 attacks showed what loose talk of jihad could lead to. "This jihad situation started long ago. It wasn't dealt with then, and it's grown and grown," he said. "Some of these leaders are brainwashing the young people." He said he counseled young Muslims studying in the United States to stay out of politics: "I tell them, 'You're here to get your education and go back and serve your people. That's your jihad.'"

Indeed, the concept of jihad, literally "struggle" in Arabic, is as flexible and disputed as "freedom" in American political discourse. Jihad can be the struggle within oneself to do the right thing, the struggle to raise your children as honest and caring people, or the nonviolent struggle against injustice in the world. But its most common meaning in everyday parlance is, of course, that of an armed struggle for Islam. In official American government pronouncements, as well as American public sympathies, the Chechen jihad against the often-brutal Russian military sometimes got implicit or open sympathy. In the months before Awlaki's dispute with the Al Noor elder, in 1996, the State Department regularly condemned Russian military atrocities in Chechnya and the relentless bombing of Grozny, capital of the autonomous republic in Russia's mountainous south. Given Awlaki's own adventure visiting Afghanistan, it is easy to imagine him offering religious sanction to a Saudi student a few years younger to follow his dream. The Saudi student at the Denver mosque did follow Awlaki's advice, went to join the fight—and died in Chechnya in 1999, the elder said.

Awlaki's reputation for preaching in Denver got him an invitation to become the head imam at another mosque, Al Rribat al-Islami, in San Diego, a city whose sunny climate and seaside setting must have been hard to resist. Al Rribat means "retreat" or "fortress," and the mosque had been founded by Saudi and other Gulf students who felt that the city's main mosque, the Islamic Center of San Diego, known as Abu Bakr, was too liberal. Al Rribat occupied a handsome stucco building with blue-green tile under a towering palm tree, and Anwar and Gihan and their growing family—Abdulrahman now had a younger sister, Mariam—moved into a modest house next door. Now, at the early age of twenty-five, he was in charge of his own mosque. Again, his reviews were excellent, and he seemed to take to the idyllic Southern California lifestyle.

"He lit up when he was with the youth," said Jamal Ali, forty, an airport driver. He played soccer with younger children and took teenagers paintballing—a common outing for church youth groups, too, without the association with training for jihad that it later took on from a terrorism prosecution in Virginia. The young imam found himself counseling people far older than he was, and he was still finding his way, Ali said. "I saw him evolving in trying to understand where he fit into Islam," he said. Awlaki read lots of books on leadership; he later let his younger brother, Ammar, help himself, and Ammar found a well-thumbed copy of Stephen R. Covey's 1989 mega-bestseller, *The Seven Habits of Highly Effective People*, in his collection.

Lincoln W. Higgie III, an art dealer in his late fifties who lived across quiet Saranac Street, found Awlaki to be an engaging and thoughtful neighbor who apologized about the parking problems that came with the flood of Friday worshippers. On Thursdays, Higgie remembered, Awlaki liked to go fishing for albacore, and sometimes he would bring over a sample of the catch, deliciously prepared by his wife. The Awlakis' toddler son and daughter would play on Higgie's floor, chasing his pet macaw, while the men compared notes on their travels. "I remember he was very partial to the Blue Mosque in Istanbul," Higgie said. He detected no hint of hostility toward or discomfort with non-Muslims like himself.

Awlaki's family also stayed in close touch. His father spent six months in San Diego in 1997, enjoying time with his grandchildren.

And when a scheme to invest in gold and minerals caught his son's eye—not the first or last time Anwar would be attracted by a supposedly lucrative investment—Nasser loaned him some $20,000. (He "lost everything," Nasser later recalled with a rueful laugh.)

Anwar invited his brother, Ammar, now seventeen, to spend the summer of 1998 with him in California, and the teenager had a memorable time. On the sidewalk outside the mosque after Friday prayers, he sold jars of famed Yemeni honey for a total of $700, a neat profit of $600 over what he had paid at home. Alongside the honey, he sold cassettes of his brother's lectures on the lives of the prophets of Islam. The bigger San Diego mosque, Abu Bakr, had offered Anwar a job, which he turned down, Ammar said. But the discussions led to a regular series of lectures by Anwar at Abu Bakr, and those talks became the basis of the lectures that a few years later, recorded professionally, would make Anwar famous among English-speaking Muslims.

"He was very popular, charismatic," Ammar recalled, "hanging out with the younger guys more than older guys. That was the start of the Internet—e-mail, AOL, all that stuff. He had a computer in his office at the mosque, and that's where he spent most of the time. The rest of the time we'd go mountain climbing, camping. We had some fun camping—the two of us and guys from the mosque." Ammar said he grew sick of eating fish ("It was fish all the time—salad with fish, rice with fish"), but he had fond memories of accompanying his brother on early-morning trips on a big fishing boat with about fifty people aboard, catching yellowfin tuna and barracuda. They would clean their catch in the kitchen, and Anwar's wife would complain about the mess, Ammar said.

Anwar, clearly buoyed by his own success, encouraged his younger brother to resist family pressure in his choice of a career. "He would tell me, you know, 'Be a lawyer, be an artist, be an author—don't be an engineer or a doctor, because you can find an engineer or doctor to do that for you.' He always insisted that, 'Ammar, don't choose what Dad and Mom choose for you. Choose what you think you can find yourself in.'"

To most everyone he knew, Awlaki's life seemed to be going remarkably well. But there were darker currents in both Anwar's personal life and his professional life during his San Diego years. Twice, in 1996 and 1997, the young husband and father was arrested for soliciting undercover police officers posing as prostitutes on a notorious strip not far from the mosque, and once he was charged for loitering near a school. In 1999, alarmed by his contacts with suspected militants, the FBI opened an investigation, closing the inquiry with no charges the following year. Those episodes would remain unknown even to some close acquaintances at the time. Years later, after 9/11, those earlier arrests and suspicious contacts would get new scrutiny, as investigators tried to understand whether Awlaki might have had a secret life far beyond his dalliances with streetwalkers.

For now, however, his growing renown drew speaking invitations from mosques around the country. In February 2000, with a few associates, Awlaki incorporated a company in Nevada to sell his sermons and lectures on CD, calling the company Al Fahm Inc., for the Arabic word for "intellect" or "insight." His father, who had visited him in San Diego and seen his success at the mosque and beyond, had given up on trying to steer him back to engineering. But Nasser al-Awlaki still worried about Anwar's career choice—and especially about what it would mean if he chose to return to Yemen. "I told him, If you come back to Yemen, you'll be just another imam, and there are thousands of imams in Yemen," Dr. Awlaki recalled. "The best thing for you, my son, is really to have another career." Nasser al-Awlaki used his connections with Sanaa University to get Anwar a scholarship to do a master's degree in educational leadership at San Diego State. Then he persuaded him to go on to complete a PhD and helped arrange for the government to support that, too. By his father's account, Anwar decided to leave his job at the San Diego mosque to begin a doctoral program elsewhere. He was accepted by the University of California at Santa Barbara, but he heard that the program at George Washington University in the nation's capital was better. The fees were far beyond what his government scholarship would pay, so George Washington agreed to waive all fees if he would take on a part-time role as the university's Muslim chaplain, giving occasional religious classes and counseling students. Even with his tuition covered, however, his $800-a-month scholarship from the Yemeni government was not enough to support his family, so he would have to find a job.

Then he got a recruiting call from a far bigger mosque that served the thriving, diverse Muslim community right outside the nation's capital. Dar Al-Hijrah—the name means "land of migration," aptly capturing the jumble of nationalities and languages represented at Friday prayers—was a powerhouse.

L ater the mosque would have to fend off hyperventilating accusations of guilt by association with terrorists, notably Awlaki himself, and would be given a scurrilous label in the right-wing media, "the 9/11 mosque." Given that subsequent history, the motive of Dar Al-Hijrah leaders when they offered Awlaki a job as imam at the end of 2000 was more than a little ironic: they hired him specifically because they were worried about the dangers of radicalization. They feared that Dar Al-Hijrah, in suburban Falls Church, Virginia, was losing young people to a nearby, more overtly militant storefront mosque, one whose underground feel was underscored by its name: Dar al Arqam, for the owner of the safe house in Mecca where the Prophet Muhammad and his earliest followers met in secret. "The mosque's objective in hiring Anwar was, they had had a series of imams who did not speak English and were not engaged with the youth," said Johari Abdul Malik, a longtime Muslim chaplain at Howard University who became director of outreach for Dar Al-Hijrah in 2002. At Dar al Arqam, a charismatic bioscientist named Ali al-Timimi was drawing young people with a hard line: that voting was *haram*—forbidden by Islamic law—because it elevated man's law over God's law, and that serving in the American military was outlawed because US forces might fight against Muslims. Dar Al-Hijrah, though its leaders might express strong anti-Israel views and oppose social equality for women, took a far more accommodating stance toward American life. For some young people with an assertive approach to their faith, the mosque's leaders were far too accommodating.

"They weren't offering the edginess that young cats need," said Abdul Malik, an African American convert to Islam who spent years counseling college students. "Young cats wanted someone to say, 'I'm not joining the military—they're killing Muslims. What do they say at Dar Al-Hijrah about that? If you go to Dar al Arqam they're laying it out, brother!'"

Awlaki had been happy in San Diego, but success was feeding

his ambitions. He had forged his own preaching career, in the face of his father's skepticism, in Fort Collins and Denver. He had proven in San Diego that he could successfully run his own mosque. He was launching an audio publishing venture to reach a larger audience. And though he was not yet thirty, Dar Al-Hijrah was one of the nation's biggest mosques, and its location in the Virginia suburbs of Washington would give Awlaki a chance to perform on a more prominent stage. The 2000 presidential campaign was well under way, and Anwar told his father that he supported George W. Bush, the Republican nominee, whose conservative social views matched his own. He even mused excitedly about the possibility that his new job as imam might win him an invitation to the White House. He agreed to start at Dar Al-Hijrah in January 2001 and left the San Diego job in June for an extended visit to Yemen.

4

AN EXQUISITE WEAPON

Estimating a man's height on the basis of video footage shot from fifteen thousand feet was not so easy. And the lanky, bearded Saudi's appearance was not yet, in early September of 2000, nearly so iconic as it would become a year later. But this guy in the grainy images beamed back from the Predator flying over Afghanistan to Langley, Virginia, was clearly very tall. And the dance of deference—he moved like a shark with a bodyguard of pilot fish, aides approaching to consult him and then scurrying away—marked him as the leader. It was Osama bin Laden, the CIA analysts were sure.

This was videotape shot two weeks earlier and now being reviewed and shared with bosses, part of a rushed project called Afghan Eyes. The goal was to test the notion that the cameras on the Predator, a UAV, or unmanned aerial vehicle, reminiscent of a gangly intelligent insect, might be good enough to allow operators to identify the terrorist. But say the Predator had found Bin Laden—what then? Sure, the video analysts could alert the Pentagon of a Bin Laden sighting, and a volley of cruise missiles could be loosed from a ship or submarine toward Tarnak Farms, Al Qaeda's training camp near Kandahar. But it would take four to six hours for the missiles to reach their target. Where would Osama bin Laden be in six hours? They had no idea. An attack would kill whatever luckless souls had wandered into the target area; if things went really wrong, the missiles would miss Bin Laden and his deputies and kill a bunch of women and children.

So what are we going to do, the analysts muttered, just watch him? This was the guy who in 1996 had declared war on America and whose acolytes in 1998 had blown up the embassies in Nairobi and Dar es Salaam, operations of staggering crudity that killed far more Africans than Americans. He had vowed to reach "the far enemy," America, and his rhetoric was drawing a motley mix of followers from all over the world.

In September 2000, as the CIA wrestled with what to do about Bin Laden, Anwar al-Awlaki was visiting his family in Yemen, was applying for a doctoral program, and would soon be preparing for his new job at the Virginia mosque a short drive from CIA headquarters. Barack Obama was an Illinois state senator who, soundly beaten in his race for Congress the previous year, was wondering whether his political career had reached its ignominious end. Terrorism barely ranked on the issues that concerned Americans; in April, 75 percent of those polled told Gallup they were "not too worried" or "not worried at all" about becoming a victim of terror. Just 4 percent were "very worried," the lowest proportion on record.

But at the CIA, the Pentagon, and the National Security Council, a few officials had become preoccupied with Bin Laden and his grandiose threats. Sometimes to the perplexity of their colleagues, they spent every day worrying about what might be coming. Just days after the Gallup survey, on April 25, 2000, Richard Clarke, the White House counterterrorism adviser, had sent a memo to the Counterterrorism Security Group, an interagency committee that advised President Clinton, then in his final year in office. Clarke proposed that the CIA fly Predators over Afghanistan to look for Bin Laden. The committee gave its consent. The advent of the drone as a counterterrorism tool was under way.

Now, five months later, at the CIA's Counterterrorism Center, the Afghan Eyes analysts were polishing their ability to scan hours of video and spot what mattered. They saw the man they believed to be Bin Laden a second time in late September. They kept watching, burning with frustration, and their imaginations inevitably ran to a technological revenge fantasy: What if the Predator toted a missile along with its camera? What if the instant they got confirmation of the tall guy's identity they could fire at the push of a button? What if, some morning between a boring early staff meeting and a desultory lunch, they could kill Bin Laden, spend the afternoon writing it up, and still get home for dinner with the kids?

The drone revolution in counterterrorism began in moments like those. That fall and winter, in secret tests at China Lake in California and Nellis Air Force Base in Nevada, Air Force teams showed that it was possible to load a one-hundred-pound Hellfire missile under each of the Predator's twenty-five-foot wings and fire them without burning up the aircraft or sending it into a tailspin. At a meeting in a sixth-floor conference room at CIA headquarters in the spring of 2001, senior agency and military officials debated whether it was time to launch some armed Predators over Afghanistan and try to take a shot at Bin Laden. The strongest advocate was Charlie Allen, a blunt-spoken CIA veteran, then the agency's assistant director for intelligence collection, who had pushed the Predator program hard along with a few other officials, including Vice Admiral Scott Fry, director for operations at the Joint Chiefs of Staff, and especially Richard Clarke, who had stayed on in the Bush White House as counterterrorism adviser.

"We need to begin now to use the lethal capabilities of this system," Allen recalled telling the group. Colleagues say he stood and pounded the table in fury as the counterarguments came back at him: The armed Predator was too new, too experimental, to use in so important an operation. Sure, the tall man on the video resembled Bin Laden, but how could they be sure whom they were shooting at? Some CIA leaders worried about the cost that the agency, without the Pentagon's endless bankroll, might have to bear. Some Air Force generals found it hard to be enthusiastic about airplanes without pilots.

Allen persisted. "We're going to regret this if we don't strike as soon as we can," he recalled telling the group. "My view was: Decapitate the leadership. If you don't get Bin Laden, and you get his lieutenants, you're starting to lessen his capabilities." The skeptics offered more reasons for caution: In some tests, the Hellfire missiles had punched through buildings and buried themselves in the ground, detonating too late. The control system to link operators stateside with the Predators over Afghanistan was an unproven, jury-rigged design involving signals bounced off a communications satellite over Southeast Asia. The meeting ended without a decision to strike. Nor did a countermanding order come from the White House, since Clarke was having trouble persuading the new George W. Bush team to take up the Predator issue—or even to talk seriously about the terrorist threat. He had called for an urgent meeting to discuss the Al Qaeda threat in the first days of the Bush presidency, on January 25, 2001. He finally got his meeting on September 4, 2001.

"I lost that fight," Charlie Allen said in an interview years later. He didn't like pondering "hypotheticals," he said, but he couldn't help himself. "Bin Laden in September 2000 had his entire leadership there," Allen said, "and his guards were totally unaware that the UAV was watching." What if the consensus in early 2001 had gone the other way, and the novice drone operators had gotten lucky and hit Bin Laden or wiped out his deputies? "History would have been very different, sir," Allen told me. "It would have been tremendously different. The intellectual candlepower, and the fire, and those fanatically obsessed with striking the United States would have been killed."

After September 11, 2001, the objections to the armed Predators quickly dissolved. The first real-world Predator strike hit the camp of Mullah Omar, the Taliban leader, on October 7, 2001, killing two of his bodyguards. A new era in warfare had begun, with unpredictable consequences.

The Predator would be the first drone to become famous—and infamous—generating newspaper editorials, protest marches, secret legal opinions, and outlandish artworks. What few Americans knew was that it was the descendant of generations of unmanned American aircraft, dating almost to the origins of aviation. Flying, after all, was inherently dangerous for human beings, who were poorly designed to sail through the air. Failure was lethal. If the idea was human transportation, there was no avoiding the danger. But if a flying robot might somehow be controlled from the ground and dispatched on a mission to pose as an enemy plane for target practice, or to take aerial photographs, or eavesdrop, or blow up a strategic target, why not try it?

By 1918, the US Army was experimenting with the Kettering Bug, a pilotless biplane with gyroscope guidance that could carry 180 pounds of explosives for about forty miles before dive-bombing into a target. The Bug was never used in combat, but by World War II, in Operation Aphrodite, daring pilots were assigned to steer bomb-laden "robot" aircraft toward Nazi Germany before bailing out short of the target and turning control over to radio operators on the ground. A young lieutenant named Joseph P. Kennedy Jr., elder brother of the future president, was one of two pilots killed on the first Aphrodite mission when the aircraft's ten tons of munitions exploded prematurely over Suffolk, England. This line of development, in which the unmanned craft itself became the weapon, would eventually lead to the cruise missile.

Meanwhile, Radioplane, a company founded by Reginald Denny, a British boxing champion, opera singer, actor, and aviation enthusiast, pioneered a different kind of drone, one capable of surviving for reuse. During World War II, the army bought thousands of Radioplane aircraft, eight-foot-long, radio-controlled wooden models, mainly for use in aerial target practice or to draw enemy fire and expose antiaircraft installations. Among Radioplane's assembly-line employees was eighteen-year-old Norma Jeane Dougherty, who posed smiling and holding a wooden propeller for a US Army public relations program run by a young army captain. Dougherty would soon become better known under her assumed name, Marilyn Monroe; the captain, Ronald Reagan, would also pursue a Hollywood career before turning to other work.

The value of surveillance UAVs was underscored in 1960, when the piloted Lockheed U-2 was shot down first over the Soviet Union, with the arrest and interrogation of the surviving pilot, Francis Gary Powers. Two years later another U-2 was downed over Cuba during the Cuban missile crisis, killing the pilot, Rudolf Anderson. Partly as a result, unmanned spy planes really came into their own with the war in Vietnam, where the United States sent unmanned surveillance aircraft on more than three thousand missions. Among the most prominent craft were the Ryan Aeronautical Company's models, which were given distinctly nonthreatening nicknames: the Lightning Bug and the Firefly. Usually launched at a high altitude from a piloted aircraft, they carried cameras and sometimes electronic intercept equipment and could be retrieved in midair using a helicopter.

But military planners long pondered the possibility of a reusable drone that could drop bombs or fire missiles. In a project code-named Have Lemon, the Air Force Flight Test Center at Edwards Air Force Base in Southern California attached a Maverick missile to a Ryan model called BGM-34A and conducted the first live test on December 14, 1971. A weight to balance the missile was hung on the drone's opposite wing and dropped at the moment the missile was released, to keep the aircraft stable.

By 1981, the Association for Unmanned Vehicle Systems was a decade old and had the money and clout to draw as keynote speaker the famous Hungarian-born physicist known as the father of the hydrogen bomb, Edward Teller. At a press conference, the seventy-three-year-old Teller declared that "the unmanned vehicle today is a technology akin to the importance of radars and computers in 1935." That sounded like hyperbole at the time—perhaps Teller was being gracious to his hosts—but his detailed remarks look prescient in retrospect. (Less prescient was his claim, a decade before the Soviet collapse, that "the Soviet Union is ahead in practically every military field" and that "we need to catch up.") Teller said that in addition to being small, cheap, and expendable, "unmanned vehicles become really useful when they are intelligent"; they could carry "every extra sensory organ that you can dream of"; they could "be used for reconnaissance, for attack or for defense—for anything you please." He insightfully predicted their value in agriculture, fire fighting, and crime fighting. Even Teller's diagnosis of the major cause of the Air Force's dilatory and reluctant approach to drones both before and after 1981 was right on target. "The Air Force is built around fliers—and unmanned vehicles put fliers out of business. And that is a serious problem," he said.

Twenty years later, the irresistible force of 9/11 changed all that. Soon, former Top Gun fighter pilots were retraining for what they wryly called the Chair Force, mastering robotic aircraft by remote control. In Afghanistan and Iraq, both the Predator and its bigger, newer cousin, the Reaper, would become an indispensable part of the American combat arsenal. The CIA, recognizing a growth area, began to bulk up what would eventually become, in the tribal area of Pakistan, the biggest paramilitary program in its history. Within a decade, the Air Force would be training more drone pilots than fighter pilots and bomber pilots combined.

A cranky debate about what to call this new class of armed aircraft would go on for years. The Air Force had long called them UAVs, but some objected that this latest generation of aircraft were by no means "unmanned." In fact, each Predator had a team of more than one hundred people behind it: not just a pair of hands-on operators but intelligence officers to guide its movements, video analysts to assess what it saw, ground mechanics to maintain its engine and other gear, another team to load its weapons and launch it, and a string of satellite communications technicians to make sure the complex controls and video download worked right. Most of these jobs were worked in shifts around the clock, pushing the total manpower much higher. If they were not "unmanned," could they be drones? Many official military documents had called them "drones" for decades, but historically that name had been technically reserved for only those vehicles used to fill in for enemy aircraft in target practice.

So the Air Force came to prefer the term RPA, for "remotely piloted aircraft," or RPV, for "remotely piloted vehicle," and government officials at all levels tried to steel themselves to stick to that technically correct language. But as the media and the broad public became aware of these strange flying machines, and especially as their possibilities beyond surveillance and killing drew attention, a simple, one-word moniker was vastly more attractive than a military abbreviation or a tongue-tangling phrase. For most people, a drone would be a drone, no matter what anybody in authority said.

Though the first Predator strikes in Afghanistan in late 2001 had been controlled from a parking lot outside CIA headquarters in Langley, Virginia, the Air Force pilots flying the growing fleet of armed drones were soon relocated to a desolate area of Nevada. Creech Air Force Base, as many military veterans noted, oddly resembled some of the landscapes in Afghanistan, Pakistan, Iraq, and Yemen that the drones surveyed. "If you could have cut out a hunk of Iraq's terrain around Baghdad and matched it to anywhere in the United States, that would have been in Nevada," one Predator pilot, Lieutenant Colonel Matt Martin, wrote about his move there. "Various shades of desert brown crumpled by the fist of a giant stretched to the horizon, broken only by green waterways. Creech was in the middle of nowhere." An hour's drive from Las Vegas, near the tiny hamlet of Indian Springs, the base had been built in a hurry after Pearl Harbor but for decades had been a backwater called Indian Springs Air Force Auxiliary Field. But it came back to life in the mid-1990s when the Air Force decided to operate the new surveillance Predators from a hodgepodge of trailers and low-rise buildings there. In 2005, in recognition of its growing importance in the post-9/11 wars, it was given the name of an eminent retired general, Wilbur Creech, and that vaguely menacing motto: Home of the Hunters.

The Predator, made by the San Diego–based General Atomics, had a wingspan of fifty-five feet, nearly twice its length. It weighed, literally, half a ton, not counting the six hundred pounds of fuel. Its bulbous front, which gave it a feeling of barely containable brain-power, housed a satellite antenna. The underside of the nose held the cameras, whose multiple streams could be fused into a single video image beamed back to Creech or the CIA or the military's Joint Special Operations Command. The propeller, in back, pushed it along at a cruising speed of just eighty miles an hour, pokey by airplane standards. Its strangest feature was the tail, which angled sharply downward on both sides, as if some vandal had climbed up and stood on the flanges until they bent. The drones cost up to $4 million apiece—not big money at the Pentagon, but the total fleet cost, with ground control stations and satellite networks, would eventually run into the billions. With a standard cruising altitude of fifteen thousand feet, three miles up, they were often out of sight and inaudible, but when they were in range and the wind was right the Predators made a jangling buzz that many compared to a lawnmower engine. The sound, and the occasional silver glint of sunlight off the fuselage, heralded a strange, new threat for those living below, whether they were Al Qaeda commanders or children herding goats.

At Creech, each Predator in the country's growing fleet had a core team of two: the pilot, who used his joystick to fly the plane, and the sensor operator, or SO, who ran the increasingly complex array of gear it carried. There was an optical video camera to view the landscape; an infrared camera that could penetrate light cloud cover and distinguish warm objects such as vehicle engines and human beings; synthetic aperture radar, able to provide high-resolution images of large landscapes, effective even in bad weather; a laser designator that could "sparkle" a vehicle or building, as the operators called it, allowing a missile to follow the laser trail to the target; and, sometimes, sophisticated eavesdropping equipment to pick up cellular calls, walkie-talkie traffic, and other electronic signals. They worked night shifts, when it was daylight in Al Qaeda territory. They sat in the dark before a bewildering array of screens, with distant landscapes

unrolling before them. They learned to zoom in on a suspicious compound, circling and circling the aircraft while trying to make sense
of the people and vehicles coming and going. It was called "pattern
of life," and it was what you studied for hours, sometimes, before you
decided you were watching a legitimate target, got clearance for a
kill, took aim, and fired the missiles, hoping for the best.

One intelligence veteran who had spent years high up in the chain
of command offered to re-create for me the kind of exchanges he had
with drone operators in advance of approving a strike.

How long have you had capture of the target?
    Two hours.
*Give me the history of the compound: When have you seen anyone
other than a military-age male in that compound?*
    I'll get back to you.
How's the weather?
    Weather's fine.
How much fuel?
    We got three more hours, but we got the next Predator on
    orbit.
Okay. Call me back in two hours.

So, two hours later:

See any women and children? Where are they?
    They're in the family quarters.
Can you see cooking fires over there?
    We see no cooking fires.
*Okay, give me a bug splat. [Which is a kill radius. It's a blob that
appears on the operator's screen, giving the computer's estimate of
the strike zone in three colors—green being safe, red being dead,
and yellow in between. It depends on the munition and the angle.]
Which way do you want the Hellfires to come in?*
    It's going to be easiest to do it from the northwest.
*Okay, show me a bug splat from the northwest. Oh, shit, I don't
like that—you've got the energy coming in from the northwest,
you're hitting the guest quarters here and the energy's still going
to the family quarters over there. I don't like that at all. Now*

show it from the southeast. You gotta come in this way, it hits the guest quarters here, all of the energy goes away from the family compound. What's the PK, probability of kill, there? Oh, it's pretty good. Okay, let's do it from the southeast.

The patient prestrike analysis that drones permitted made believers out of many of the government officials who wanted a weapon that matched the terrorist enemy, whose numbers were small but who often found refuge in lawless territory or hid among civilians. Michael Hayden, who as CIA director had proposed the drastic increase in drone strikes in Pakistan to President Bush in 2008, told me that the armed drone was "an exquisite weapon when you want to be both effective and moral. It gives you a sense of proportionality. It gives you a sense of distinction—legitimate and not-legitimate targets. So for this kind of war, when the target is an individual or a small group of individuals, I just can't think of any other way of doing it."

Hayden's view was representative of the upbeat accounts from high-level American officials of the drone's capabilities. There was no question that the drone held huge promise of precision by comparison with the alternatives available to kill suspected terrorists: a bomber dropping heavy ordnance, a fighter jet firing missiles as it raced overhead, certainly an invading ground force. But tellingly, as a few drone pilots dared to break the silence and speak up about their own experiences, their accounts were less sanguine. Lieutenant Colonel Matt Martin, for instance, whose book *Predator* makes clear his support for the program in which he worked as a drone pilot, nonetheless candidly acknowledged the daunting responsibility of firing missiles and the significant chance that a drone operator could hit the wrong people. "If his hand twitched at the last instant, if he breathed wrong, the missile might go astray and take out the house full of people next door or the group of old men smoking and joking down the block," he wrote. Martin recounted harrowing cases in which he saw innocent civilians killed.

Once, an old man appeared just after Martin had fired a missile, "tottering along" toward the target in Baghdad's Sadr City; it was unclear whether he was killed or only injured by the blast. Another time, two boys on one bicycle—one ten or eleven years old, the other smaller and balanced on the handlebars—suddenly came into view as the missile shot toward the ground, riding toward a truck with in-surgents milling around it. Martin described how in that instant he recalled having pedaled his little sister on his own bike in similar style as a boy in Indiana; he thought, too, of the old man whom he had hit inadvertently, an episode he said "had plagued me ever since." Senior security officials often emphasized the technical advantages of drone strikes, including an ability to divert a missile *after* it had been fired in exactly such a situation. But in this case, diverting the missile from the boys on the bike would have endangered other nearby civilians, Mar-tin wrote. "Mesmerized by approaching calamity, we could only stare in abject horror as the silent missile bore down on them out of the sky. It could not be diverted without the risk of even greater carnage." The boys died, their "bent and broken" bodies visible in the rubble after the smoke cleared, Martin wrote in his admirably honest account.

The debate about war, and how it should be conducted, now ex-panded to the question of killing by remote control. Opponents of the drone program pictured Americans watching distant, alien people on a screen and using a joystick to fire a weapon at them—and inevita-bly thought of video games. "Because operators are based thousands of miles away from the battlefield, and undertake operations entirely through computer screens and remote audio-feed, there is a risk of developing a 'PlayStation' mentality to killing," Philip Alston, the United Nations' special rapporteur on extrajudicial execution, wrote later in a phrase that became a rallying cry for drone critics. The analogy was irresistible; the Air Force was actually looking for the skills of avid video gamers.

But those who had spent time at Creech knew that the psycho-logical toll on drone pilots and sensor operators was, paradoxically, far greater than on those who flew traditional fighters and bombers. Matthew Atkins, an Air Force lieutenant colonel who after long ex-perience believed in the value of drone strikes, wrote an essay in 2014 to refute those who considered killing from thousands of miles away "cold, clinical and impersonal." In fact, he said, "Nothing could be farther from the truth." Modern warfare had largely gotten away from the hand-to-hand combat of earlier epochs, and killing at a distance was the norm, whether from conventional air strikes, or artillery fire, or cruise missiles. In such circumstances, Atkins said, you rarely saw the enemy. But the team of drone operators not only saw the target, they lingered over it. "In order to deliver maximum pressure on an enemy network and minimize collateral damage, intelligence personnel spend hundreds, if not thousands, of hours watching and studying potential targets," Atkins wrote. "This method of killing takes a toll on our nation's watchers and finders." If the target had a family, the operators might watch him with his wife and children, eating dinner in a courtyard or hugging a daughter goodbye. "And when you recommend that target folder for approval, you do so with the explicit knowledge that you are recommending the death of not just an enemy of our nation, but a person. This creates an intense moral and psychological burden that intelligence personnel carry with them every day."

The same point was made by drone pilots who, unlike Atkins, were deeply disenchanted with the campaign. Brandon Bryant, who had operated drones over Afghanistan, told the radio and television program *Democracy Now* that he had "watched this guy bleed out . . . and his right leg above the knee was severed in the strike. And he bled out through his femoral artery." The image, he said, was "pixelated, but, I mean, you could see that it was a human being, and you could see that—what he was doing, and you could see the crater from the drone—from the missile, and you could see probably the body pieces that were around this guy." His point in talking publicly about his experience, he said, was to show that drone operators "aren't killer robots. They're not like unfeeling people behind this whole thing." He believed the government, with its obsessive secrecy about drone warfare, had done a poor job of "humanizing the people that do it. And everyone else thinks that the whole program or the people behind it are a joke, that we are video-game warriors, that we're Nintendo warriors. And that's really not the case." Security officials often hailed the fact that drones took on terrorism without putting Americans in harm's way. That proved to be a gross oversimplification. The casualties were emotional and psychological, but they were casualties all the same.

The very first experiment in the armed UAVs' new capability for pinpoint killing outside a conventional war zone came in Yemen. That CIA Predator strike in the Arabian desert in November 2002 would capture in microcosm many of the issues that would become prominent over the next decade as the notion of killer drones gradually caught the public imagination.

The target was the head of Al Qaeda in Yemen, Qaed Salim Sinan al-Harithi, also known as Abu Ali. In his mid-forties—an old man by jihadi standards—he had the kind of Al Qaeda résumé that merited the deepest respect from youthful recruits: he had received formal military training in the army of the United Arab Emirates as a young man; he had fought with Bin Laden against the Soviets in Afghanistan; and he had been directed by Bin Laden to organize a training camp in Yemen. In 2002, with the CIA and other agencies consumed with the global hunt for Al Qaeda operatives, Harithi was high on their list. The National Security Agency had multiple phone numbers he had used in the past, and on November 3, 2002, a computer at the NSA's headquarters at Fort Meade, Maryland, sounded the alert. The satellite phone signal was located in the wasteland of Marib province in Yemen's tribal territory. An analyst actually recognized Harithi's voice, and an armed CIA Predator took off from Camp Lemonnier in the little nation of Djibouti in the Horn of Africa, crossed the Gulf of Aden, and headed inland. (Much later, Djibouti would ban armed drones for several years.)

In an odd coincidence, the American ambassador to Yemen, Edmund Hull, was on his way to Marib that very day for a visit to a regional hospital and discussions on development projects there. An Al Qaeda cell in Sanaa, alerted to the ambassador's travel plans, took a shot at a helicopter as it took off, evidently believing it might be the ambassador's. In fact, it belonged to Hunt Oil Company, and one Hunt worker was slightly injured by the gunfire. But as Hull and his entourage met tribal leaders in Marib and toured the hospital, the ambassador got word from the embassy: the Predator had spotted Harithi's SUV as it sped along a desert road. One Hellfire missile had missed, but the second had destroyed the car, instantly killing Harithi and five other men. The Yemeni government, which had approved the American strike on the grounds that the US role not be disclosed, dispatched a helicopter to check the scene and confirm the deaths. Yemeni officials gave reporters a false cover story: Al Qaeda members had been killed, the officials said, when a bomb they were transporting accidentally detonated.

At CIA headquarters and at the White House, the operation

looked like a stunning success, proving the reach of a formidable new technology to use against isolated terrorists. A veteran Al Qaeda leader and his posse had been eliminated; US and Yemeni counterterrorism officials had closely cooperated; the strike, on a desert road, had spared civilians. The promise of the Predator—clean, uncomplicated victories against a shadowy, scattered enemy—seemed fulfilled.

Then the complications began. First, there was the discovery that when things blow up and people are killed on the ground, secrecy is not plausible and cover stories quickly fall apart. The day after the strike, the Associated Press and other news outlets reported accurately, citing anonymous sources, that the strike was no lucky accident but a missile strike from a CIA Predator. Secretary of Defense Donald Rumsfeld hinted gleefully at a Pentagon news briefing that it might just be an American operation, saying of Harithi that "it would be a very good thing if he were out of business." The next day the deputy defense secretary, Paul Wolfowitz, made it official, telling CNN that "it was a very successful tactical operation." The secrecy that the Americans had promised had barely lasted forty-eight hours.

The Yemenis were furious. President Saleh made it clear that he would approve no more strikes, leading to a gap in American operations in Yemen that would last for seven years, during which Al Qaeda would build its strength in the country, especially after a major prison break in 2006. Though there was little popular outcry over the killing of Harithi, Yemeni officials had demanded secrecy because they correctly saw the possibility of a backlash. In a traditional, tribal Muslim society, American military action would inevitably breed resentment, they knew. The Yemeni reaction to that first strike underscored the impossibility of covering up American strikes and the fragility of the diplomacy necessary to sustain them.

Next, there was the legal and policy controversy, subdued at that point but unavoidable. That the American government was killing people outside a war zone raised obvious questions that many reporters tried to answer. A couple of days after the strike, I called Loch Johnson, who had served as a staffer on the Senate's Church Committee when it investigated CIA assassination plots in the 1970s and was an intelligence historian at the University of Georgia. He used the "a" word that government officials were trying to avoid. "It's a highly lethal machine the CIA is using to carry out assassinations,"

Johnson told me. "If you're going to accuse someone of being a terrorist, should you present some evidence? Should you arrest them and give them a trial? Is America going to send drones into any country we choose to kill people we think are terrorists?" His remarks anticipated the main issues in a much-needed debate, one that would be delayed for a decade by excessive secrecy. At the least, Johnson said, there should be congressional oversight and public discussion. "I think these questions merit much closer attention than they've received," Johnson told me. Another expert, Larry Taulbee, a political scientist at Emory, called the strike legitimate, noting that "there's a self-defense case to be made here" and saying that having to worry about lethal drone strikes could hinder Al Qaeda's plotting. But Taulbee also warned of the possibility of a backlash, provoking retaliatory attacks or recruiting new, young militants for Al Qaeda.

The first drone strike outside a war zone had stirred up a hornet's nest of legal, practical, and political issues. The United States was entering into a new kind of warfare, and the need for Congress to take up the matter in public hearings was already obvious. But the congressional debate on targeted killing would be delayed for more than a decade because Congress would be intimidated by classification rules imposed by intelligence officials and enforced by President Bush and, for a time, by President Obama. Those of us watching drone developments noticed an odd paradox: at national security conferences, when think-tank experts or journalists discussed the use of unmanned aircraft to kill terrorists, government officials and members of Congress would clam up. In other words, the people with real, inside knowledge of the pros and cons of drone strikes were the only ones not permitted to speak about them. The first substantive public hearings on drone strikes would take place only in 2013.

One final lesson from the Harithi strike was that despite the remarkable capabilities of the Predator to observe and record activities on the ground, the operators' view was far from complete. The BDA, the Bomb Damage Assessment, was inevitably subject to inaccuracies and omissions. Contrary to the initial impressions of American drone operators, it would turn out that one Al Qaeda operative in Harithi's car, Rauf Nassib, had survived and escaped. He would bedevil counterterrorism authorities for years to come. And American intelligence officials learned only after the strike that among those killed was an

American citizen, Kamal Darwish. Darwish had joined Al Qaeda, and no one at the CIA shed tears over his demise. But the belated discovery added just a whiff of doubt to the celebration: Was it worrisome that the United States government had killed an American without knowing it or intending it?

The Harithi strike, a serious blow to Al Qaeda in Yemen and a demonstration of military and intelligence prowess, also showed more subtly the real limitations of the technology. In the years to come, the CIA and the Pentagon's Joint Special Operations Command would be killing people whose identities were uncertain, overlooking civilian deaths in poststrike assessments, stirring passions over sovereignty among foreign leaders, and fueling fury at the United States with uncertain consequences for long-term American security.

Still, there was no mistaking the visceral appeal to counterterrorism officers of the destruction that the armed drone could hurl, literally, from the heavens. When the military first began buying the Hellfire missile in the 1970s, the name was lamely explained as shorthand for "Helicopter-Launched Fire and Forget Missile." That was obviously only part of the story. Warriors liked the biblical resonance, which would be echoed in a later missile, the Brimstone, and in the larger armed drone called the Reaper. The shower of superheated metal fragments from the five-foot-long Hellfire when it detonated in a car or house left nothing alive. In a battle against religious fanatics who believed those who did not share their version of Islam were doomed to burn forever in hell, America was responding with her own version of hell on earth.

5

WE ARE THE BRIDGE

In the disorienting days after the 9/11 attacks, Ammar al-Awlaki, now a college student in New Mexico, e-mailed his older brother, Anwar, in Virginia, to hear the young imam's thoughts on the momentous events and find out whether he might be appearing on American television to comment. An answer came back late on the night of Friday, September 14. Earlier that day Congress had passed a joint resolution "to authorize the use of United States Armed Forces against those responsible for the recent attacks launched against the United States," a measure that would become the legal basis not just for more than a decade of war but for targeted killing with drones as well. Late that afternoon, President George W. Bush had stopped by the smoldering ruins of the World Trade Center and grabbed a bullhorn. When a worker yelled, "We can't hear you," Bush replied, "I can hear you. The rest of the world hears you. And the people who knocked these buildings down will hear all of us soon." It was a time of boiling emotions, bewilderment vying with anger, tough talk masking deep fear.

Now, at midnight, Anwar al-Awlaki began his brief message to his brother with the abbreviation for *As-salamu alaykum*, or "Peace be upon you," the standard Muslim greeting.

> AA Ammar
> I personally think it was horrible. I am very upset about
> it. Anyway, maybe tomorrow they will have me on for
> an hour. I will let you know if it will go ahead. The media

**are all over us. At Jummah today we had ABC, NBC,
CBS, and the Washington Post. I hope we can use this
for the good of all of us.**

The quick reply captured in capsule form the chaos that had engulfed Anwar al-Awlaki's world as the imam at Dar Al-Hijrah, one
of the country's largest mosques in one of the globe's most saturated
media markets. It was an unfiltered glimpse, in a private message to
a family member, of Awlaki's condemnation of the 9/11 attacks as
"horrible," a notable clue for tracing his evolution. But it also showed
how the tragedy had catapulted a young preacher into a spotlight of
blinding brightness, with television cameras jostling for space at *jummah*, or Friday prayers. And perhaps it contained a hint of Awlaki's
ambition, which might have sounded crass in a public message, to
take advantage of the tragedy for some collective moral purpose—to
"use this for the good of all of us."

The next morning the national trauma would become intensely
personal for Awlaki. The FBI's frantic quest to identify the hijackers
and track their activities in America quickly found that two of them,
Nawaf al-Hazmi, twenty-five, and Khalid al-Mihdhar, twenty-six,
childhood friends from Saudi Arabia, had worshipped at Awlaki's
mosque in San Diego for months while he was the imam. Hazmi and
a third Saudi hijacker, Hani Hanjour, twenty-nine, had later turned
up across the country at Dar Al-Hijrah. It was an alarming pattern
that brought two FBI agents to the door of Awlaki's modest brick
rancher on Kaywood Drive in Falls Church just hours after he had
sent the e-mail to his brother. It was the first of at least three interviews over the next few days.

From the FBI's written account of the interviews, notes recorded
on a standard form called a 302, Awlaki appears to have been alter-
nately cooperative and combative. The agents walked him through his
biography and his extensive travels of the previous months, but when
they asked about the hypersensitive topic of jihad, Awlaki balked.
"When questioned as to whether or not AWLAKI lectured on the
Jihad, AWLAKI stated, 'I would like not to comment on that,'" the
agents wrote. "However, he further stated that he 'absolutely strongly
condemns the attacks.'" Under the circumstances, Awlaki may have
been wary of addressing the complexities of the concept of jihad in

Islam for fear of fueling the agents' suspicions, preferring to stick to a straightforward condemnation of the plot. Likewise, when the agents asked to see Awlaki's passport, he declined: Awlaki "advised that he did not feel like showing it to the SAs at this time because it was upstairs," they wrote, using the abbreviation for "special agents." Awlaki's motive here is hard to discern, but he may have been concerned that the agents would use the stamps in the passport to try to trip him up on details of his travels—or confiscate the passport to prevent him from leaving the United States.

Three more times, agents visited. In the second interview, two days after the first, Awlaki had to correct the misspelling of his first name—the agents, showing their unfamiliarity with common Arabic names, had written it as "Answar." The agents thought they might have caught the imam in a lie. He had said in the first meeting that he had been absent from the mosque when FBI investigators showed around an array of photos of the suspected hijackers. This time Awlaki said he had recognized a face from the photo array: it was one of the hijackers from the San Diego mosque, Hazmi. Awlaki told the agents that on one occasion, when he had just returned from a visit to Saudi Arabia, Hazmi had stopped him in the mosque and complained that the imam had not contacted him during the trip, since Hazmi had been home in Saudi Arabia on a visit at the time. Awlaki said he had never pegged Hazmi as especially devout because he didn't wear a beard or pray five times a day. He described Hazmi as soft-spoken and shy.

The cleric said he did not recognize al-Mihdhar, Hazmi's roommate and constant companion, though he recalled Hazmi often being with another man, who he had assumed was his brother. The agents met Awlaki for a third interview on September 19—three interviews in five days—but this time, recognizing that the intensity of the FBI scrutiny called for legal representation, he told them to come to the Springfield, Virginia, office of his lawyer. He expressed skepticism about the notion that Hazmi could have been a hijacker, saying he was "so slight of build that he might have trouble slaughtering a chicken."

What they learned during the repeated questioning, along with simultaneous interviews with Awlaki's West Coast contacts and a review of travel and credit card records, did not persuade the agents to arrest Awlaki. That was notable, since in those anxious days it did not take much to prompt the FBI to take a Muslim suspect into custody. But agents remained suspicious. At least one worshipper at the San Diego mosque described long, closed-door meetings between Awlaki and Hazmi, and an FBI document later described Awlaki as Hazmi's "spiritual adviser." Awlaki's cagey manner and intermittent hostility prompted the agents to open a formal investigation of him. His phones would be monitored and a surveillance team would watch his movements day and night, though for months he would remain unaware of the cars trailing him through DC traffic. The FBI decision would have far-reaching and unintended consequences.

Reporters run in packs, and never more so than when a big news story is driving news competition. In the history of the modern United States, there had never been a news story bigger than 9/11, nor one more difficult for Americans to grasp. Why, went the instantly clichéd question voiced by cable anchors and news magazine covers, do they hate us? Newspapers needed quotes, authoritative voices to frame and begin to answer difficult questions. Television needed talking heads and pictures—images beyond the relentlessly looping video of the jetliners hitting the towers.

So it was that the phones began to ring incessantly at Dar Al-Hijrah. Falls Church was an inner suburb—even in the capital's unpredictable traffic, a TV crew could hop across the Potomac from downtown Washington and get to the big mosque in less than half an hour. Word spread fast: here was an imam with near-perfect American English and a knack for the sound bite. Just as important, he seemed to be a *moderate*, a vague label but one that meant a news organization could be pretty safe in treating him as legit. He was unlikely, in other words, to say anything crazy on the air. The interview requests poured in—the networks, PBS, NPR, *The New York Times*, the *Washington Post*—everyone wanted a little time with Anwar al-Awlaki. And no, the television producers would say, we don't have any agenda. And yes, I'm afraid next Tuesday is not soon enough. And what's the lighting like inside the mosque? "He was enjoying the limelight," said Johari Abdul Malik, who joined the staff at Dar Al-Hijrah at about this time. "And he wore it well."

After issuing a press release condemning the attacks, Awlaki and the mosque's leadership had decided to close the building for a few days, concerned that Dar Al-Hijrah might become a target for public rage. "Most of the questions are, 'How should we react?'" Awlaki told a reporter, describing the concerns of worried Muslims. "Our answers are, especially for our sisters who are more visible because of the dress: Stay home until things calm down." There were threats, and Awlaki told a reporter that one Muslim woman had stumbled into the mosque after being attacked by a man with a baseball bat.

But mosque leaders were also surprised and heartened by the outpouring of support from non-Muslim neighbors. Some nearby churches offered volunteers to escort Muslim women worried about venturing out. One neighbor, Patricia Morris, noticed the big iron gates at Dar Al-Hijrah closed for the first time and consulted a Palestinian friend, who said Muslims in Falls Church were "very scared." So Morris organized a candlelight vigil around the reopened mosque at 7 p.m. on the Friday after the attacks, drawing about thirty people. Muslims leaving evening prayers gave white roses to those at the vigil as a gesture of thanks for their solidarity. Awlaki posed for the *Washington Post*, smiling alongside Morris inside the mosque's school and expressed relief at the "very positive" responses from other neighbors as well, including eighty people in a nearby apartment building, who sent a statement saying, "We want your congregation to know that we welcome you in this community."

At that first Friday *jummah* after the attacks, with reporters awkwardly perched around the sanctuary, Awlaki was quite aware of the expectation that he would denounce the bloodshed in New York, Washington, and Pennsylvania. He had every reason to believe that the FBI would be monitoring the service. He began by reading a condemnation of the attacks from a prominent Egyptian-born Islamist scholar, Yusuf al-Qaradawi, citing a voice with particular authority for Dar Al-Hijrah's immigrant-heavy congregation: "Our hearts bleed for the attacks that targeted the World Trade Center as well as other institutions in the United States," Qaradawi wrote, before adding a quick caveat to make clear that he was not fully embracing America's record—"despite our strong opposition to the American biased policy toward Israel."

Then Awlaki offered his own, distinctly American spin. "We

came here to build, not to destroy," he declared. "We are the bridge between America and 1 billion Muslims worldwide."

It was a fascinating, tantalizing notion, put forward at an especially charged moment. In the conflict that had suddenly roared to life between America and Muslims, American Muslims were, whether they liked it or not, the bridge. Perhaps now, Awlaki suggested, they could become the mediators, the peacemakers, the explainers. And this bespectacled imam, with his Arabic garb and his American speech, epitomized the possibilities. That was what the journalists had seen and why they rushed to question him. An article in *The New York Times* took note of Awlaki's sudden prominence, identifying him as a rising star who "at 30 is held up as a new generation of Muslim leader capable of merging East and West: born in New Mexico to parents from Yemen, who studied Islam in Yemen and civil engineering at Colorado State University." On NPR, a reporter said that Awlaki "sees himself as a Muslim leader who could help build bridges between Islam and the West."

Awlaki was himself just beginning to grasp his potential, the possible scale of his influence and future renown. Some have greatness thrust upon them, Shakespeare wrote—with comic intent, in *Twelfth Night*, it was true, but then there was something comically absurd about the television trucks maneuvering in the mosque parking lot, the reporters' sincere but woefully ignorant questions, the ego boost of catching one's own name in the country's most important newspapers, one's own bearded face on the evening news. Some have greatness thrust upon them, and Awlaki—an Internet addict who had rushed to Best Buy after the attacks to buy a television to watch the coverage—sensed it was happening to him. *I hope we can use this,* he had written to his brother, *for the good of all of us.*

In October, he sat down for questions from Ray Suarez of *NewsHour* on PBS, who stopped by after visiting the Old Town Islamic Bookstore in nearby Alexandria, where four bricks and a note threatening Muslims had come through the window the night after the attacks. At Awlaki's little house, a few minutes' drive from the mosque, Suarez later recalled, the reporter and the preacher "drank tea and snacked on nuts and dried fruit while seated on the carpet in his comfortable, book-lined basement." The lanky Awlaki "had to fold his long bony legs like a grasshopper to join me on the floor." They "talked about world history, US relations with Muslim countries, and speculated on how the coming era would be shaped by the terror attacks," Suarez said.

In the resulting *NewsHour* segment, Awlaki described the pressure on all Muslims in the wake of Al Qaeda's assault: "I think that every one of us now feels that if we go on a plane, we would be looked at with some suspicion. And for a whole community to feel like that, I mean, it makes the community feel that they are under siege, they're under scrutiny. It's a very uncomfortable feeling."

In a sermon excerpted on the show, Awlaki denounced the carnage of 9/11—and in the same breath condemned what he considered to be American crimes, in particular the deaths attributed to years of American-led sanctions against Iraq. But in addition he played up the unique perspective of Americans who also happened to be Muslims:

> You would find that the perception of the Muslims in the Muslim world about America is quite different than the perception of the American Muslims about America. Why? Because the American Muslims, they know what America is about. Yes, we disagree with a lot of issues when it comes to the foreign policy of the United States. We are very conservative when it comes to family values. We are against the moral decay that we see in the society. But we also cherish a lot of the values that are in America. Freedom is one of them; the opportunity is another. And that's why there is more appreciation among the American Muslims compared to the Muslims in other parts of the world.

It was a comment, echoing Bush's paeans to American freedom, that might be cheered even by American conservatives who at that moment were reflexively hostile to Islam. The United States had just invaded Afghanistan, an aggressive patriotism was being expressed with ubiquitous flags and country-music anthems—and here was a Muslim imam endorsing American exceptionalism in language any patriot could appreciate.

In the traumatic weeks after the attacks, Awlaki participated with seeming sincerity in interfaith services and discussions, sharing stages and microphones with rabbis and priests. "My recollection of him at that point was as a voice for moderation," said Father Gerry Creedon, then priest at a Catholic parish in Arlington, Virginia, who repeatedly encountered Awlaki on the circuit and spoke with him privately as well. "He struck me in his personality as a gentle man, very well read and intelligent." Simon Amiel, an organizer with the campus Jewish organization Hillel, recalled working with Awlaki on an event to bring together Jewish and Muslim students at George Washington University. Awlaki spoke about the parallel traditions of Islam and Judaism and was "cordial and friendly," Amiel recalled.

In November, for the video unit of the *Washington Post*, Awlaki agreed to star in a sort of Islam-101 film explaining Ramadan, the month of fasting in the Islamic calendar. It was an intimate view, with Awlaki at home and in the mosque, in Western clothing and traditional robes and cap. He was shown eating dates and praying quietly at home before dawn, then leading a subdued crowd in the morning prayer at the mosque. "Ramadan is a chance for us to get away from the worldly indulgences, everything that is material," he said. Awlaki addressed some of the issues that he knew bothered or puzzled non-Muslims, such as the separation of the sexes during worship. "There's a section for the sisters and a section for the brothers," he explained, speaking without defensiveness or condescension. "The reason for the separation during all the worship services is because in the time of worship there should be no distraction."

Awlaki offered some mild political comments in the *Post* video, but without rancor. "I think that in general Islam is presented in a negative way," he said. "I mean there's always this association between Islam and terrorism, when that is not true at all. I mean, Islam is a religion of peace." With close-ups of the imam's wire-rims as he checks his e-mail, a shot of his six-year-old son, Abdulrahman, sitting on his lap, and a pan of his family breaking the day's fast with dinner in a friend's modest suburban apartment, the video was warm and appealing. (It won a first prize that year for the videographer, Travis Fox, from the White House News Photographers Association.) Years later, it would still be easy to find on YouTube. It would hint at a path not taken: Awlaki as a respected American spokesman for Islam, helping Muslims negotiate between their religion and their country, speaking out critically on American foreign and domestic policy while gently reassuring non-Muslims that they had nothing to fear from their neighbors.

It was also, unquestionably, not the whole story of Awlaki's evolving views of terrorism and of America. In the tangled, complex world of American Islam, there were many competing influences and divisions, and sorting them out was difficult even for well-informed believers. As an imam serving a diverse congregation and speaking publicly, Awlaki had to be tactful and inclusive. He readily joined the interfaith gatherings that were suddenly so popular after 9/11 and played down the schisms within his own faith. Non-Muslims probably would not have noticed it, but he was clearly on the conservative side of the spectrum of Islam in America. Most scholars would have characterized him in 2002 as clearly part of the Salafi movement—the conservative school of Islam that called for a return to the original ways of the early Muslims, the *salaf*s or ancestors. His lectures and sermons invariably began with stories from one of three sources considered legitimate in the Salafi assessment: the Koran; the hadith, or sayings and traditions of the Prophet Muhammad; and the lives of the companions of Muhammad and the other prophets of Islam. His style resembled that of a fundamentalist Christian preacher who begins with what he sees as the literal truth of the Bible, finds the right passages, and then applies them to contemporary life. By default, Awlaki, like many Muslim clerics, thought of humanity as divided into two camps: Muslims and non-Muslims. Implicit in his sermons was the assumption that for Muslims loyalty to the *ummah*, the global community of believers, took precedence over loyalty to any particular nation. Muslim Americans, in Awlaki's view, were first of all Muslims and only secondarily Americans.

Muslims attuned to the nuances of language and emphasis had a view of Awlaki that might have surprised the journalists who described him as representing a "new generation" of clerics. "I would not have called Awlaki a moderate," said Ahmed Younis, a Muslim lawyer and activist who heard him preach several times in the years before 9/11 and pegged him as a conservative, if not rigid, Salafi. "Moderation is not just about violence. It's about everything. He was not an extremist—just a little politicized, tapping into history. But not especially progressive."

In retrospect, it is easy to see Awlaki's views evolving from the initial, emotional reaction that he had shared privately in the e-mail to his brother—that the attacks were "horrible" and that he was "very upset." As the weeks passed, like many others, he was put off by the notion, commonly voiced at the time, that Americans had suffered a "loss of innocence" and were somehow unique as a target of large-scale killing. He seemed determined not to take sides either with Muslims overseas who cheered the plotters or with an aroused and self-righteous America. When he condemned the attacks on New York and Washington, he simultaneously condemned American actions that, in his view, had resulted in the deaths of innocents—Muslim innocents. He pushed a moral equivalence that few Americans were in a mood to hear. In his segment on Awlaki, Suarez of PBS included a snippet of a sermon in which Awlaki attempted this balancing act, using the early reports that the attacks had left six thousand dead:

> The fact that the US has administered the death and homicide of over one million civilians in Iraq, the fact that the US is supporting the deaths and killing of thousands of Palestinians does not justify the killing of one US civilian in New York City or Washington, DC, and the deaths of 6,000 civilians in New York and Washington, DC, does not justify the death of one civilian in Afghanistan. And that is the difference between right and wrong, evil and good, that everybody's claiming to talk about.

Looking back years later, Suarez gave a shrewd assessment of Awlaki, who clearly had impressed him deeply. "While talking of his feelings of grievance, he chose his words carefully," Suarez said. "One could walk away from the Friday sermon, or from the interview, struck by how in his rhetoric he could dance right up to the edge of condoning violence, taking the side of anti-American forces in the Muslim world, and then, just as carefully, reel it back in, pulling the punch, softening the context, covering the sharp-edged scalpel of his words in a reassuring sheath." Despite the reassurances, Suarez said, Awlaki was "uncompromising in his view that the United States had much to answer for in the Islamic world," saying that "the US needed to change its approach just as much as Muslims did."

That attempt at balance animated Awlaki's public statements. Osama bin Laden, Awlaki told the *Washington Times* in October, "has been able to take advantage of the sentiment that is out there regarding U.S. foreign policy." Again, he proffered an equipoise of wrongs. "We're totally against what the terrorists had done. We want to bring those who had done this to justice," he said. "But we're also against the killing of civilians in Afghanistan." In an online chat with the *Washington Post*, he repeated the mantra, while throwing in, as a sweetener, some praise for American liberties: "Keep in mind that I have no sympathy for whoever committed the crimes of Sept. 11th. But that doesn't mean that I would approve the killing of my Muslim brothers and sisters in Afghanistan. Even though this is a dissenting view nowadays—but as an American I do have the right to have a contrary opinion."

To a dispassionate observer, Awlaki's balancing act looked logical: 9/11 was a horror, after all, because utterly innocent people had died, and equally innocent people had died of malnutrition and disease in Iraq as a result of American-led sanctions and were now dying in the bombardment of Afghanistan. The same two-part, pacifist message ruffled few feathers when it was expressed by Catholic priests or Lutheran ministers, as it often was in that period. But for Muslims, there was no dispassionate standard. The moment demanded that they prove their loyalty to the United States without qualification.

For many Muslims, the resounding phrase of President Bush after 9/11—"Either you are with us, or you are with the terrorists"— seemed to announce a new set of rules, unforgiving and accusatory, to be specially applied to them. Criticize American foreign policy too severely, it implied, and you have effectively decided to join the terrorists. To underscore the point, Bush implied that Al Qaeda's attacks had nothing to do with American foreign policy—with its stationing of troops in Saudi Arabia, for instance, or its support for Israel. "Americans are asking: Why do they hate us?" Bush said. "They hate our freedoms," he answered, "our freedom of religion, our freedom of speech, our freedom to vote and assemble and disagree with each other." But for American Muslims like Awlaki, those words began to ring ironically in the fraught months after 9/11: for them to exercise freedom of speech by criticizing America's foreign policy record was to invite suspicion and bitter rejection.

The Bush speech to Congress, interrupted with applause twenty-nine times in forty-one minutes, was widely quoted and framed the mainstream American reaction to the attacks. It was also a frontal assault on Awlaki's attempt to define himself as the man in the middle. In effect, the president of the United States was saying that in this crisis Muslim Americans had to embrace their country, right or wrong. Any attempt to express a nuanced view, linking Al Qaeda's atrocities to American foreign policy, was out of line; it meant you were "with the terrorists." So much for Awlaki's notion that he and fellow Muslim Americans could serve as a bridge, or for his hope to "use this for the good of all of us."

There was a double filtering process going on, as the fall of 2001 progressed and Awlaki tried out this role of bridge builder that he had assigned himself. First, there was the sorting that was natural for journalists, who tended to set aside any dissonant notes in the narrative as they portrayed Awlaki as a peace-loving family man, as appalled as anyone by the September atrocities. In the outtakes of the *Washington Post* video, for instance, Awlaki strongly condemned the US war in Afghanistan, said he didn't trust the American media, and said he relied on Arabic and European news sources to tell the truth about the war. He had been upset by the Gulf War as a college student, and now, he suggested, history was repeating itself: "We have the memories of Iraq fresh in our minds—we were told in 1990 this was going to be a war against Saddam Hussein. Well, after ten years he's still in power and the ones who are suffering are the Iraqi people—one million in Iraq died." Now, with the new war in Afghanistan, he said, "we're hearing that, well, the reason is to get the terrorists—but then, here we go, I mean—casualties for the civilians." He described a bomb flattening a mud house in Afghanistan, killing a father and his seven children—an episode he claimed was omitted from US press coverage. "This leaves a strong imprint on us," he said, arguing that such mistakes were bloody disasters "that our fellow citizens in America don't see." None of those comments made it into the final Ramadan video, and not because of any sinister intent. It just didn't fit the story.

Second, there was the imam's own careful calibration of how to reach out through the national media to Americans who, after years of never giving Islam a thought, were suddenly obsessed with it and frightened by it. Asked by NPR to discuss the competitive voices of Osama bin Laden and Muslim moderates—implicitly including him—Awlaki said, "It is the radical voices that are taking over" and "All of the moderate voices are silenced in the Muslim world." When the religion reporter for *The New York Times* called him for a story about how prominent Muslims had toned down the pre-9/11 rhetoric that had been fiercely critical of the United States, Awlaki was happy to oblige. As often in this period, he displayed a subtle skill in gauging what the reporter was looking for and then delivering it. "In the past we were oblivious," he said. "We didn't really care much because we never expected things to happen. Now I think things are different. What we might have tolerated in the past, we won't tolerate any more." He acknowledged that previously "there were some statements that were inflammatory, and were considered just talk, but now we realize that talk can be taken seriously and acted upon in a violent radical way."

Actually, though the *Times* and NPR made no mention of it, Awlaki himself made a few inflammatory statements in the days after 9/11. Like any politician who offers a restrained performance on *Meet the Press* on Sunday morning and takes a different tone while speaking to a fired-up partisan crowd on Sunday night, Awlaki adjusted his message to his audience. On September 17, answering questions on the Egyptian theologian Qaradawi's IslamOnline.net, a popular gathering spot for Muslims on the web, Awlaki was indeed "moderate" in most of his answers. He framed the 9/11 attacks as a "heinous crime," praised Bush and other top American officials for warning against discrimination against Muslims, and said that "many Muslims" were among the fallen police officers and firefighters "who are the heroes of this tragedy." He acknowledged "extremism" among Muslims and declared: "We should come out strong in our disapproval and condemnation. This is a chance for us to show the real face of Islam." But when he fielded a question about the hidden hand of Israel in the September 11 plot, a ridiculous conspiracy theory beginning to circulate online, Awlaki not only accepted the premise—he went on to fan the flames:

Q: *What do you think about the possibility of involvement by Israeli Mossad?*

A: Add to that the fact that there has been an uprising in Palestine that was becoming very popular while the popularity of the Israeli response was plummeting. Israel was going through a serious PR crisis. Israel has even hired U.S. public relations firms to try to clean up its reputation and Ariel Sharon's damaged image.

Also there were lawsuits filed against the war criminal Ariel Sharon in Belgium. That was a serious blow to Israel to have its highest official in such a position.

Now doesn't the timing of the attacks raise a question mark???

Later in the same exchange, Awlaki called the evidence emerging in the first few days "perplexing" and floated a cockamamie theory of his own to steer the blame for the attacks away from Muslims, noting the sinful lifestyles of the accused hijackers: "You have a right to be confused. It appears that these people were victims rather than hijackers. It seems that the FBI went into the roster of the airplanes and whoever has a Muslim or Arab name became the hijacker by default."

It was hard, Awlaki wrote, to imagine "someone who was drunk the previous night, or in a strip bar, things that are agreed upon among Muslims as major sins in Islam, to give up their lives the next day for the sake of a religious claim. It doesn't make sense at all. There is something peculiar happening???"

Awlaki's willingness to engage in such errant speculation was revealing. But he didn't repeat the outlandish claims, at least publicly, after evidence clearly implicating Al Qaeda was reported. Like many Muslims in the first days after the attacks, he was trying to make sense of a befuddling set of facts and engaging in wishful thinking that his own beleaguered religious minority might yet avoid blame for the tragedy.

In sorting out what Awlaki really felt or believed as he coped with the aftershocks of 9/11, it is worth taking note of just how young and unformed he was as he started the job outside Washington in January 2001. He had not yet turned thirty. He was just seven years out of college. He had not made a final decision on what career to pursue—or whether to settle permanently in the United States or

Yemen. His father, after losing the battle to keep him on an engineering track, had switched tactics and now hoped his eldest child
would still follow in his footsteps by earning an American doctorate
that could prepare him for high-level posts in Yemen, which desperately needed talent like Anwar's. His application to the doctoral
program at George Washington University was quite revealing. It
required a two-page "Statement of Purpose," written in the summer
or fall of 2000, in which he came across as strikingly uncertain, even
immature, hardly the smooth-talking imam mastering media interviews just a year later. The statement was a mix of boasts about academic achievements, half-baked apologies for academic lapses, and
a not-quite-convincing claim that all his life has been a preparation
for an EdD degree at George Washington. It was a combination any
veteran admissions officer would recognize, but it did not suggest a
fully formed worldview or a settled career plan.

In the national high school examinations given in his graduation year, Awlaki asserted, he had scored in the top twenty out of
fifty-two thousand students who took the exams. "My inclination
was towards human and social sciences," he wrote. "But the tradition was that students with high grades should go into medicine or
engineering," he added, tactfully leaving his father out of it. Hence
his choice of civil engineering as his major at Colorado State. He
blamed his abysmal grades his sophomore year on his unsuitability
for the engineering field (not mentioning his Afghan adventure): "I
wasn't enjoying my major at all. At the same time I was enjoying and
doing well in the elective courses, which I handpicked to satisfy my
true desires." After he graduated from college in 1994, he said, he
had learned of a World Bank program starting up in Yemen to build
four community colleges and to train the faculty and staff to serve in
them. "That provided me with an opportunity to enter into the field
I loved most: Teaching," he wrote. He had talked with the Yemeni
officials in charge of the community college project, and "They are
granting me a full scholarship to pursue a doctorate degree." He had
delayed starting the degree, he said, only to "thoroughly investigate
my options. I spent lengthy days and nights surfing the net, visiting
one university website after another." And then, the requisite flattery:
"The *only* curriculum that perfectly satisfied my aspirations was the

HRD program at GWU," he wrote, adding italics to emphasize his attraction to the human resource development program.

A strong recommendation from his adviser at San Diego State predicted that after he finished his doctorate "he will become an education leader in the higher education system of Yemen," running one of the new community colleges or helping to train faculty for other institutions. In case that seemed like mere speculation, it was backed up by another recommendation from a top official of Yemen's Ministry of Education, who wrote that he had been advising Awlaki for three years on his training. "We are preparing Mr. al-Awlaki to lead a Technical Education Department at the University of Sanaa, Faculty of Education," the official wrote. "A new department in the making." Awlaki ended his "Statement of Purpose" with a banal description of his "research interests," whose vagueness betrays indecision at best: "My research interests," he wrote, "would be in the integration of the different skills and knowledge learned in the program." If anything might have sunk his application, surely it would have been this hapless declaration of . . . nothing at all. But he was a student with a decent record, an evident eagerness to learn, and sponsors back in Yemen. George Washington had dispatched a letter admitting him to the doctoral program, with a major field of education administration and policy studies, on December 12, 2000, just a few weeks before Awlaki was to report for duty at Dar Al-Hijrah.

What was most astonishing about all the paperwork Awlaki submitted for the degree was what he left out. He did not say a single word about his work as an imam at two mosques over the previous seven years. In his statement of purpose, he wrote at length about his one year of teaching elementary school in Yemen when he was eighteen and did not mention the teaching experience he had undoubtedly accumulated as a cleric and counselor in Denver and San Diego from age twenty-three to twenty-nine. That this was no oversight is proven by the résumé he prepared for the George Washington application. Under "Experience" it lists the stint in the Yemeni elementary school more than a decade earlier, and an even older part-time job as a "data analyst" on a World Bank project when he was in high school. But it omits the successively more impressive jobs he had held as an imam. It made for a strangely skimpy résumé for a twenty-nine-year-old, to say the least.

What could possibly have motivated Awlaki to censor the vast majority of his work experience—experience quite relevant to the field of education—as he applied to the doctoral program? George Washington officials clearly learned about his clerical experience, since they offered him the Muslim chaplain post. But the written application remains a puzzle. Conceivably Awlaki, or someone who advised him, thought George Washington University might look askance at his mosque career and doubt his claimed devotion to the field of education. Perhaps, even in the pre-9/11 period, he was worried about anti-Muslim or antireligious sentiments among American university administrators. What seems beyond dispute is that when Awlaki started at Dar Al-Hijrah at the beginning of 2001, with the encouragement of his father, he was seriously considering taking up a post in academic administration in Yemen. His father confirms it. "I convinced him that he should have a career in education," Nasser al-Awlaki said. "And I said, 'If you want to record things about Islam, that's no problem.'" In other words, his father suggested that he pursue a conventional academic path and relegate his preaching to a part-time affair, sort of a hobby. That would be another road not taken.

If he began his work in Falls Church with doubts about how it would go, they must soon have been put to rest. He connected with the more sophisticated Muslim community of northern Virginia just as he had in Denver and San Diego. Umar Lee, a young American convert who was active at Dar Al-Hijrah, recalled a dynamic, friendly preacher with a winning personal touch. By comparison with older immigrant clerics, "Anwar was just a much cooler guy," Lee said. "He was walking through the lobby one day, and he said, 'Hey, Umar, how you doing?' I don't think we'd even been introduced," but Awlaki had figured out who Lee was and remembered his name. "He'd see us playing basketball and walk over and play with the ball. He wouldn't join the game, but he'd talk to us," Lee said.

In February 2001, Awlaki led a group of American Muslims on hajj—the pilgrimage to Mecca that is considered one of the five pillars of Islam. Hale Smith, a San Francisco attorney and Muslim convert who was on the trip, recalled Awlaki as "very Americanized," "low-key, quiet and reasonable." Smith found Awlaki "extremely conversant with the fine points of Islamic law" but also open-minded, willing to acknowledge that some sayings attributed to the Prophet Muhammad were "fake or very weakly authenticated." Smith was put off by the male chauvinism and "medieval thinking" of some Saudi clerics they met and found the common sense Awlaki brought to religious texts to be a welcome contrast.

To all appearances, Awlaki was a modern American imam on the ascent, and official Washington was taking notice. In July he was invited to preach at the regular Friday Muslim prayers in the US Capitol. He extolled the Prophet Muhammad to a standing-room-only audience of Muslim congressional staffers, lobbyists, and bureaucrats as a sort of model statesman who was "extremely successful as a head of state" but who "never had to compromise his integrity." His remarks were caught by a film crew shooting a documentary about Muhammad. Then a local Islamic institute that helped train Muslim chaplains for the US military asked Awlaki to lecture the trainees, who would soon be counseling Muslim American soldiers.

Speaking invitations poured in from much farther afield as well. In August, less than a month before 9/11, he spoke at a conference named "Allah's Final Revelation to Mankind" at the University of Leicester in the United Kingdom. On September 1, he delivered a speech entitled "Tolerance: A Hallmark of Muslim Character" at the Islamic Society of North America conference in Chicago, asserting that "Muslims had the best track record of tolerance in the world" when they held power. A week later, he flew to California to address a fund-raiser for Jamil al-Amin, the former H. Rap Brown, a Muslim convert and imam whose forthcoming murder trial had become a cause célèbre for activists. He flew home on the morning of September 11, 2001, and learned of the attacks in New York as he rode in a taxi from Washington's National Airport to the mosque, smoke rising from the Pentagon a few miles away. He had no idea, or so investigators would conclude, that three of the nineteen men who had just died carrying out the atrocity had heard him preach in San Diego and Falls Church.

In October, despite the whirlwind of his life and work in the aftermath of the attacks, the entrepreneurial Awlaki found time to apply for and receive a copyright on his lecture series, "Lives of the

Prophets." The lectures had been recorded and published earlier in 2001 by an Islamic publisher in a Denver suburb, Al-Basheer Company for Publications and Translations, first on eighteen cassettes and shortly thereafter on twenty-three compact disks. This was the enterprise whose humble beginning had been on the sidewalk outside the San Diego mosque, with little brother Ammar selling homemade cassettes, along with the Yemeni honey.

The lectures, and the growing collection of Awlaki CDs, would play even more of a role than his media appearances in spreading his fame across the world of English-speaking Muslims. In San Diego, he had created a company, Al Fahm Inc., with a businessman who worshipped at the mosque, Sam Eulmi. But they couldn't come to terms, Eulmi said, and Awlaki then connected with Al Basheer, run by a Saudi, Homaidan al-Turki, who would later go to prison in Colorado for abusing his Indonesian housekeeper. Despite that controversy, Al Basheer was a successful enterprise for some years, and Awlaki was its unrivaled star.

In news reports, Awlaki's early lectures and sermons on CD are often mixed up with his later, militant speeches and declarations. That is a mistake. They are utterly traditional—a rendering into engaging English of classic stories from the earliest days of Islam. If there are hints of militancy or endorsements of violence—and suspicious listeners have found a few—they are buried in allegory and history. Only in hindsight's distorting rear-view mirror can his accounts of episodes from the Koran and the hadith, the Prophet's sayings, be taken as a sign of dangerous radicalism. It would be akin to declaring that a rabbi's recounting of David's use of a slingshot to do in Goliath was evidence that the rabbi endorsed terrorism. In fact, in "Lives of the Prophets," his first major set of recordings, Awlaki was translating and retelling Al Bidayah wa'an-Nihayah (The beginning and the end), a sort of encyclopedia of Islam written by the fourteenth-century scholar Ibn Kathir, who lived near Damascus. Ibn Kathir was a revered *muhaddith*, or transmitter of stories about the Prophet from the hadith, and *mufassir*, or interpreter of the Koran. Awlaki's skillful retelling and interpretation were part of a long and respected Islamic tradition, and Muslims in the United States, Canada, and the United Kingdom ordered the CDs by the thousands. They were grateful for a contemporary narration of the foundational stories of their religion—in clear English that their children could understand.

Awlaki spoke with warmth and simplicity, achieving the kind of intimacy that distinguishes the finest natural storytellers. "These are the best of stories, because they are dealing with the best of creation," Awlaki said at the opening of the first lecture, covering the story of Adam, after a revved-up introduction using reverb to create an echo effect. Allah commanded the Prophet to "narrate these stories unto the *ummah*," the community of believers, Awlaki said, "so it becomes a duty upon us to relate these stories." Like any Christian preacher introducing Bible stories, Awlaki admonishes his listeners to ponder the meaning of the stories he will recount. "These stories are not to entertain us," he said, "these stories are for us to derive lessons and reflect." The importance of the stories, he explains, is that the early figures of Islam—the Prophet Muhammad; the other prophets, including Moses and Jesus; and the Sahaba, or companions of the Prophet—"are the best, and we need to have role models." His emphasis on showing young people the right path was especially notable. "If we are not going to provide our children, our youth, with role models" from among the heroes of Islam, Awlaki said in that first lecture, "they're going to find role models somewhere else, because human beings cannot live without role models. Every human being," he said, "has role models—if they are not good, they're going to be bad." It was a point that would be made often in the coming years by those who were fearful of what Awlaki himself had become.

In late January 2002, as the popularity of Awlaki's growing collection of CDs was taking off, he got an unusual invitation. The Defense Department's Office of General Counsel had a series of luncheon speakers, and a bureaucrat working there had heard Awlaki give a talk to residents of a luxury apartment complex in nearby Alexandria. She had been impressed both by "the extent of his knowledge" and by how he "handled a hostile element in the audience." He had condemned Al Qaeda and 9/11—presumably a minimal requirement for an invitation to one of the institutions targeted in the attacks—and Pentagon staffers knew that the defense secretary, Donald Rumsfeld, "was eager to have a presentation from a moderate

Muslim." On February 5, the luncheon took place, Awlaki spoke, and no one appears to have been scandalized.

A wlaki was steering a cautious course across a polarized political landscape. He denounced Muslim extremism while trying not to offend the sensibilities of his conservative Muslim congregation, which included many immigrants raised on angry denunciations of Israel and other presumed enemies. His task wasn't getting easier. As the weeks passed after 9/11, Muslims in America felt increasingly under scrutiny and pressure. The time of sympathetic candlelight vigils had passed; now Awlaki's congregants traded stories about insults to women who covered their hair and about Muslims who received the cold shoulder from once-friendly workmates. Now, too, worshippers at Dar Al-Hijrah began to feel the heat from government agencies that were seared by their failure to prevent the attacks and terrified that new plots might be in the works.

Many Muslims in the United States resented being implicitly blamed for the mass murders on 9/11, in which they had played no part and which their leaders had immediately and repeatedly condemned. Tales of FBI investigators or immigration agents knocking unannounced at the homes of Muslims in northern Virginia, many of them doctors, engineers, and accountants, stirred anxiety. Some worshippers at Dar Al-Hijrah spotted strangers wielding video cameras in the parking lot after Friday prayers. As the FBI and other agencies stepped up a frantic hunt for Al Qaeda sleeper cells in America—cells that would turn out essentially not to exist—people in Awlaki's congregation traded stories of rude and ill-informed investigators turning up at their workplaces and homes, asking, for instance, their view of Osama bin Laden. (That seemed a naive question; presumably a real Al Qaeda operative would be shrewd enough to not to share his real views of his boss with the FBI.) Immigrants who had fled repressive governments in the Middle East with their all-powerful *mukhabarat*, or intelligence service, began to sense a similar heavy government hand in America. The initial wave of fear began to give way to anger. Then came Operation Green Quest and two days of federal raids on more than a dozen Islamic institutions, businesses, and homes in northern Virginia.

When Awlaki stepped to the microphone at Dar Al-Hijrah to address the crowd at *jummah* prayers on Friday, March 22, 2002, his voice shook. His fury was palpable. He spoke not of Islamic history or the requirements of life as a good Muslim, his usual themes, but of the heavy-handed raids, which had hit the community like a tornado. He called the federal sweep a "campaign . . . against the Muslim community" and said it was "an indication of the dangerous route this war on terrorism is taking." He read a long list of the Islamic institutions targeted in the raids, names well known to many of the hundreds of people gathered for prayers. He called it "strange and amazing" that among the targets was the Fiqh Council of North America. Fiqh is Islamic jurisprudence, and Awlaki noted that the Fiqh Council, a committee of revered religious scholars, had actually issued a fatwa, or ruling, approving the American invasion of Afghanistan. Many Muslims considered that council's rulings "very mild or watered-down"—yet the council, too, was raided. "What is next," Awlaki asked, "and who will be safe?"

The raids were the culmination of Operation Green Quest, a hunt for sources of money for Al Qaeda, and involved some 150 agents of the US Customs Service, the Internal Revenue Service, the Immigration and Naturalization Service, and the Bureau of Alcohol, Tobacco and Firearms, among other agencies. In the end, it produced much smoke but little fire; though at least two targets of the raid were convicted of crimes unrelated to Al Qaeda, the national 9/11 Commission would ultimately conclude that "the United States is not, and has not been, a substantial source of al Qaeda funding." Operation Green Quest, which some FBI officials saw as a ham-handed effort of other agencies to get in on the post-9/11 action, became the subject of turf battles and was finally shut down in 2003.

The complaints voiced by Awlaki, who was speaking for many in his mosque, were aimed not at the notion of hunting for terrorist financing but at the operation's unselective sweep and cowboy clumsiness. The agents had not limited themselves to raiding offices but had burst simultaneously into the homes of many Muslim leaders, carting away truckloads of computers, documents, and books. Awlaki harped in particular on one episode that would resonate for years in the community: agents had handcuffed the wife and daughter of one

Muslim leader at gunpoint and held them for four hours, not allowing them to get their head scarves—grossly disrespectful treatment
in a conservative Muslim home. His voice uncharacteristically rushed
and strained, Awlaki pronounced a grave conclusion: "So this is not
now a war on terrorism—we need to all be clear about this. This is a
war against Muslims. It is a war against Muslims and Islam. Not only
is it happening worldwide, but it is happening right here in America,
that is claiming to be fighting this war for the sake of freedom while
it's infringing on the freedom of its own citizens—just because they're
Muslim, for no other reason."

It was a long way from Awlaki's comments a few months earlier
about Muslims' appreciation for American freedom. If he had previously been working to calm non-Muslims' fears about Islam, and
Muslims' fears about the American government—well, the authorities were now making that impossible. "The government knows very
well that there's a lot of anxiety among the American public when it
comes to Islam, because the people don't know what Islam is about
and they don't know what we stand for. Therefore conducting such
a search at this particular time is very sensitive—it's sending a very
wrong message to the American public. . . . Why tie in these American Muslim institutions to what has happened on September 11 when
there's no connection?"

Just six months earlier, he had stood in the same spot, before a
crowd of worshippers at Dar Al-Hijrah, and declared: "We are the
bridge between America and 1 billion Muslims worldwide." Now,
his efforts to build that bridge, to be the interpreter and go-between,
seemed to have run aground. It would come as a disappointment but
not really a surprise to his many admirers when they learned that just
days after delivering this fiery sermon Awlaki decided to leave the
United States for good. It made sense, after all. The Green Quest
raids had been the last straw. The wave of hostility to Islam, instead
of subsiding, had gained new force. The very government that was
supposed to enforce the rights of all Americans seemed to have decided, on the basis of dubious or nonexistent evidence, that American
Muslims and their institutions must be "with the terrorists."

In fact, however, that was not the whole story. Awlaki's decision
to leave the United States was far more complicated than it appeared.
Even after the raids that had so infuriated and depressed him and his

congregation, he had been planning to stay. What Awlaki learned just a few days after his fiery sermon would terrify him and put his career in extreme jeopardy. The discovery that prompted his sudden departure involved matters that he could never discuss in a Friday sermon.

6

TOTALLY PLANNING TO STAY

On December 13, 2001, a mild but blustery day, Anwar al-Awlaki drove his white Dodge Caravan across the Potomac into Washington and parked west of Dupont Circle. He'd purchased the used minivan when he'd moved to Virginia to accommodate his growing family—after seven years of marriage, he and his wife, Gihan, had three children. Such solo drives had become routine for him, though the settings varied; sometimes it was a motel in a seedier part of the city, or tonier lodging in the sprawling Virginia suburbs. This time it was the Marriott Residence Inn on P Street toward the end of the holy month of Ramadan. In his *Washington Post* online chat a few weeks earlier, he had explained that Muslims abstained from sexual activity during Ramadan between sunrise and sunset. It was 2:30 p.m. when he made his way to Room 1010, where a young woman from Texas awaited their appointment.

He was a computer engineer, born in India and now living in California, Awlaki told her. He was polite and apologized for sneezing so much, explaining that he was suffering from hay fever. He handed over $220 and she performed oral sex on him. He "finished very quickly" and asked her for another round, the woman would later recount. But she was trying to raise the money to go to college in Florida and said he'd have to pay another $220. He said he'd pay again only for full sexual intercourse. She declined and he went on his way. He was a busy man, after all.

After their testy, inconclusive interviews with him in September, FBI counterterrorism agents were worried that Awlaki's contacts with the 9/11 hijackers might not have occurred by chance, as he had claimed. So starting two weeks after 9/11, they had assigned the bureau's Special Surveillance Group to keep tabs on him. SSG operatives are not agents and don't carry guns; they tend to have less education and training than agents and have the straightforward job of following their quarry by car and on foot and taking notes and sometimes pictures. In Awlaki's case, the agents soon learned from the SSG watchers that the imam indeed had a rich secret life. But it had nothing to do with terrorism.

In the months after 9/11, the watchers from the SSG followed Awlaki to assignations with prostitutes at the Wyndham City Center, the Melrose, the Monarch, Avenue Suites, the Swissotel, and more. Agents would follow up with the women later the same day or the next day, asking about Awlaki's words and actions. He liked the lights on, the agents learned. He found the escort services online and booked their services under his real name. Sometimes he asked for intercourse, sometimes oral sex, and sometimes he just watched the woman stimulate herself while he masturbated. The women had no complaints (though one, checking him out through the peephole in the hotel room door when he knocked, thought he resembled Osama bin Laden). He was "clean," "sweet," and "very nice," they said. If he harbored anti-American feelings or was concocting secret terrorist schemes, he showed no sign of it.

The pages and pages of scribbled notes from the surveillance teams and the typed interviews with escorts contained few surprises. Awlaki had been picked up twice in San Diego soliciting prostitutes, but he had not been deterred. Despite his more demanding schedule and the higher stakes now that a spotlight was trained on him in Washington, it had become a habit he could not, or did not want to, break. His FBI tails even followed him as he took the subway to the Pentagon to appear as a luncheon speaker.

The imam who had preached at the Capitol, whose CDs were in the homes of the devout, who was regularly quoted as a spiritual authority, skulked secretly around the city, violating the moral rules he taught. In one surveillance photo, he made his solitary way down a city sidewalk to his next assignation, hands in the pockets of his trench coat, seemingly lost in thought. It is a glum picture, and the FBI files make for dispiriting reading—the cringe-worthy wanderings of this married father of three and the depressing snippets of the biographies of the women. ("She comes from a poor family in New Hampshire," the agents reported of the woman at the Melrose, "and is doing this kind of work strictly for the purpose of making money.") As a humiliating coda, the FBI tails also dutifully followed his wife on her shopping trips and the entire family on outings to the Smithsonian's National Museum of Natural History and dinner at a Phillips Seafood restaurant.

His sexual escapades were unremarkable, of course; the existence of the sex industry that served him was proof enough of that. But for a man in his position they were also stunningly reckless. As many a Christian minister had discovered the hard way, a public sex scandal could blow to bits a promising religious career. Awlaki was violating fundamental tenets of the conservative Islam he preached: repeatedly committing adultery; lying about his background, even as he revealed to a series of prostitutes his real name; squandering his family's limited budget at a rate of $300 or $400 an hour. In one of his sermons, he had denounced *zina*, or fornication, blasting American television for spreading *zina* all over the world and declaring that Allah had sent AIDS as punishment. "The movies and the nudity and the destruction of this culture is now global," he declared, in an echo of his decade-old college argument with his roommate over TV. To be exposed now before his congregation and his growing national and international audience as a hypocrite and flagrant sinner would be a devastating blow, almost certainly career-ending.

And though Awlaki didn't know it, as the salacious reports made their way up the chain of command at both the FBI and the Justice Department, senior officials began to consider doing exactly that. In June of 2002, the FBI's top counterterrorism official, Pasquale D'Amuro, sent a twenty-page memorandum to James A. Baker, counsel at the Justice Department's Office of Intelligence Policy and Review, laying out the tawdry details and seeking approval to use intelligence reports for a federal prosecution under a statute known as the Travel Act, formally titled "Interstate and Foreign Travel or Transportation in Aid of Racketeering Enterprises." One passage in the memo: "How Anwar Awlaki's Behavior Meets the Criminal Elements Defined Above." The feds were not especially interested in Awlaki's peccadilloes as such. But they continued to document his life in excruciating detail. Even if they found no evidence of terrorist ties, they might be able to use the file on his visits to prostitutes to pressure him to become an informant or, if they decided he was a dangerous influence, to discredit him with a federal criminal case.

The underlying problem was that even after months of intensive scrutiny of his past and present, the investigators were still sufficiently worried about his possible connections to terrorism that they did not feel they could clear him. The hints of militancy, dubious connections, and suspicious coincidences in his record would disturb American authorities for years. They would be studied with concern by both the Congressional Joint Inquiry into 9/11, which completed its work in December 2002, and the 9/11 Commission, which published its report in July 2004. Despite all of the investigations, officials would continue to struggle to answer a basic question: Before 9/11, had Awlaki been a secret militant with a connection to the plotters of the worst terrorist attack in American history? Or was he more or less what he claimed to be in 2002—a conservative Muslim cleric who was critical of American actions abroad but condemned mass violence?

To weigh the evidence, it might be useful to make the strongest case for Awlaki's secret militancy and then examine its weaknesses. Even if no definitive answer is possible, barring the discovery of some unknown diaries or secret communications, the exercise helps place the story of Anwar al-Awlaki up to his thirty-first birthday in April 2002 in the broader context of Islam in America.

The case for the prosecution might start on January 15, 2001, with the arrival at Los Angeles International Airport of the two future hijackers, Nawaf al-Hazmi and Khalid al-Mihdhar. Hazmi spoke a little English, Mihdhar spoke none, and neither had lived in the West, so they were notably ill-equipped to navigate American life. The principal organizer of the 9/11 plot, Khalid Sheikh Mohammed, recognized the problem. Though he would urge the other hijackers to keep to themselves during their time in America, he authorized Hazmi and Mihdhar to seek help from mosques and from the local Muslim community, he later told investigators.

Within two weeks, the two Saudi citizens met a fellow Saudi, a business student with Saudi government ties named Omar al-Bayoumi, who offered to help them get settled if they moved to San

Diego, where he lived. On February 4, Bayoumi helped them move into a San Diego apartment complex, cosigning the lease and paying the first month's rent and deposit. Between that day and February 18, four calls were recorded between Bayoumi's phone and Awlaki's phone. Some FBI investigators believed that Bayoumi had loaned his phone to Hazmi and Mihdhar and that the calls were actually between Awlaki and the future hijackers. In the months that followed, some worshippers at Al Rribat al-Islami, Awlaki's San Diego mosque, thought they recalled Hazmi, or both of the Saudis, in lengthy closed-door discussions with the imam in his office. The notion of a close relationship was also supported by the fact that Hazmi later turned up at Dar Al-Hijrah in Virginia after Awlaki began working there in 2001, as did a third hijacker, Hani Hanjour.

Two men who had roomed together in New Jersey, a Jordanian named Eyad al-Rababah and a Syrian, Daoud Chehazeh, came under FBI investigation for their contacts with the hijackers at Dar Al-Hijrah. Chehazeh did not cooperate but was given political asylum anyway, a decision some members of Congress criticized as foolish. Rababah admitted helping Hazmi and Hanjour find apartments and move; some FBI agents, and the 9/11 Commission, believed he might have been given that assignment by Awlaki, though they had no proof. Rababah was later deported to Jordan, and the web of connections has never been fully understood, according to former FBI agents who worked on the case.

Awlaki's contacts with the hijackers seemed all the more significant because they came against a background of years of FBI suspicion of terrorist ties, including a short-lived previous criminal investigation. Alone, none of the facts about Awlaki before 9/11 came anywhere near making a criminal case. But together, they made a perplexing skein of connections.

During his years in Colorado, for instance, Awlaki had at least some contact with a Palestinian-Kuwaiti named Ziyad Khaleel, who was vice president of the Denver Islamic Society in the early 1990s, when Awlaki was at Colorado State. Khaleel, it would later turn out, was an active Al Qaeda supporter who would later earn a modest footnote in history by purchasing a battery for Osama bin Laden's satellite phone in 1996.

In 1998, when he was in San Diego, Awlaki had signed on as vice president of a nonprofit organization, the Charitable Society for Social Welfare, whose ostensible purpose was to raise money for "orphans, refugees and the needy" in Yemen and to support youth clubs in American cities. The society had been sponsored by a prominent Yemeni cleric, Abdul Majeed al-Zindani, whom the United States would later place on the list of designated terrorists, and an FBI agent later testified that it was "a front organization to funnel money to terrorists."

Did Awlaki have any inkling that Khaleel had ties to Bin Laden, or that some of the money he helped raise in the United States might end up with extremists? It's impossible to say. But the connections disturbed FBI counterterrorism investigators, who opened a terrorism investigation on Awlaki in San Diego in June 1999. The bureau closed the investigation in March of 2000 after finding no evidence of a crime, even though they noted that Awlaki had recently been visited by an associate of Omar Abdel Rahman, the so-called Blind Sheikh, who was serving a sentence of life in prison for plotting to blow up New York City landmarks.

Then there were a few discoveries that had been made after September 11, 2001. A police search of the apartment in Hamburg, Germany, of Ramzi bin al-Shibh, a Yemeni member of Al Qaeda who helped plan the 9/11 attacks, turned up a piece of paper with the phone number of Dar Al-Hijrah, Awlaki's Virginia mosque. And investigators would discover that a sort of communications hub for the scattered conspirators of 9/11 was a satellite phone in Yemen that belonged to the father-in-law of Khalid al-Mihdhar, one of the hijackers who had prayed in Awlaki's San Diego mosque.

In mid-2000, Mihdhar angered his bosses in Al Qaeda by leaving San Diego when he learned his first child had just been born in Yemen. That meant Mihdhar was visiting his wife, baby daughter, and father-in-law in Sanaa roughly at the same time that Awlaki was visiting his family in the same city, between his jobs in San Diego and Falls Church. Hence, when an Al Qaeda team attacked the guided missile destroyer USS *Cole* on October 12, 2000, in the Yemeni port of Aden—a plot investigators believed Mihdhar probably knew about in advance—both the imam and the soon-to-be hijacker were in Yemen.

The mind boggles at this pile of maybes. But a final, provocative detail might be added to the indictment: Lincoln Higgie, the neighbor of Awlaki in San Diego to whom the cleric would sometimes bring fish he had caught, recalled an odd encounter. About a month before 9/11, he said, Awlaki, who had moved to Virginia eight months earlier, stopped by Higgie's house after retrieving the last of the belongings he had left at his former house next to the mosque. The men had a friendly chat, Higgie recalled, and Higgie urged his former neighbor to stop by whenever he was in the area. According to Higgie, Awlaki offered a puzzling reply. "He said, 'I don't think you'll be seeing me. I won't be coming back to San Diego again. Later on, you'll find out why,'" Higgie said. "I thought it was a little strange."

Stitching all these novelistic details into a unified theory of Awlaki's secret radicalization takes a bit of imagination. First, recall that Awlaki had embraced a starkly intolerant brand of Islam, at least for a time, in his freshman year at Colorado State. Imagine that Ziyad Khaleel, who went battery shopping for Bin Laden, met Awlaki when both were in Colorado and quietly brought him into the Al Qaeda fold. Say that the future hijackers Mihdhar and Hazmi found Awlaki and his mosque not by chance but because Mihdhar's father-in-law back in Yemen, running the satellite telephone hub for Bin Laden's plotters, directed his son-in-law to the cleric. That would explain the closed-door meetings that some fellow worshippers remembered the men having at the mosque. Consider the possibility that Awlaki knew perfectly well that the Yemeni charity for which he was serving as American vice president was in fact raising money for terrorism. And say that Awlaki's odd conversation with his former neighbor, Lincoln Higgie, was a bit of operational sloppiness revealing that the cleric knew in advance that the 9/11 attacks were coming.

It is a case that has won at least a few believers in the suspicious community of hard-bitten American terrorism-watchers. It deeply worried the top investigators for both the Congressional Joint Inquiry into 9/11 and the 9/11 Commission. Philip Zelikow, the commission's executive director, said he considers the Awlaki question "one of the three largest loose ends in our investigation of the plot." The commission's report noted the lingering doubts of some (though by no means all) FBI agents about Awlaki's possible ties to the hijackers and declared, "We share that suspicion," which Zelikow described to me as "a grave statement." It is certainly conceivable that Awlaki was somehow in on the plot, and it is impossible to disprove. But let's step back and examine the theory for flaws and weaknesses.

Perhaps the biggest cautionary note is that FBI investigators considered and eventually rejected the notion that Awlaki was a covert member of Al Qaeda who knew in advance about the plot. Asked
for its bottom line on this question, the bureau gave me an unequivocal statement: "Extensive investigation by the FBI has not developed
any evidence that Awlaki had advance knowledge of or involvement in
the 9/11 attacks, nor has the FBI developed evidence that he knowingly provided support to any hijacker in furtherance of that plot."
This judgment is based in part on still-secret intelligence the bureau
collected. Heavily redacted FBI documents indicate that both the
first investigation in 1999–2000 and the second one, opened immediately after 9/11, involved "ELSUR," or electronic surveillance. So
apparently nothing in intercepted telephone conversations or e-mails
suggested a link to the 9/11 plot. The FBI may have conducted an in-
competent investigation, of course, and the bureau certainly has reason
to play down the possibility that it was bamboozled by a sleeper agent
for Al Qaeda. But FBI investigators with the power to eavesdrop, conduct surveillance, read classified intelligence reports on Al Qaeda, and
consult with American and foreign intelligence and counterterrorism
agencies—and with every incentive to make a terrorism case against
Awlaki in 2002—could not do it. That counts for something.

Some FBI investigators also raise logical objections to the notion
that Awlaki was in on the plot. They argue that Osama bin Laden
and Khalid Sheikh Mohammed would not have been likely to trust
the fate of their entire plot to an American cleric who had lived in
the United States for more than a decade, no matter who vouched
for him. They point out that Awlaki's behavior after the attacks—
not trying to flee, but sitting for repeated interviews with the FBI—
suggests that he had no concern about being exposed as an Al Qaeda
agent. And they observe that years later, when Awlaki had openly
embraced Al Qaeda's philosophy and goals, he had every reason to
enhance his own militant résumé by claiming a role in the terrorist
network's biggest success. He never did so, and—to the contrary—
implied that he opposed terrorism at the time.

Then there is the testimony of family members like his brother
Ammar, who got that e-mail at midnight on September 14—a private

exchange, not a statement before the Washington press corps—in which his brother condemned the attacks as "horrible." The brothers talked and met in the months afterward, and Ammar never doubted that Anwar disapproved of the mass killing.

But what of the web of circumstantial evidence that seems to document Awlaki's links to the militant world? It might merely reflect the small world of American Islam. Awlaki was an active, religious young man at Colorado State when Ziyad Khaleel, with the Bin Laden connection, was an imam an hour away in Denver; it would hardly require a conspiracy for them to be acquainted. Devout young men like Mihdhar and Hazmi, disoriented when they landed in America, might naturally have sought support and advice from a savvy local imam—without confessing to him their monstrous plans. The label that later came to be paired with Awlaki's name—"spiritual adviser" to one or both future hijackers—appears in early FBI documents but seems to be based on nothing more specific than the vague recollections of worshippers who thought they had seen the men, or at least Hazmi, in the imam's office.

For what it's worth, Awlaki himself, who had acknowledged knowing Hazmi in San Diego, said later that he had no idea that Hazmi had moved to the Washington area and prayed at Dar Al-Hijrah. He correctly pointed out that suggestions of his complicity in the 9/11 Commission report were mere speculation: "If you follow the paragraphs on me you'll find the word 'MAY' repeated more than three times: 'MAY have met them when they first arrived in San Diego, MAY have introduced them in Washington to such and such to help them out, this MAY be more than just a coincidence.'" Likewise, Mihdhar and Awlaki could easily have been in Sanaa at the same time in 2000 without meeting; both had family matters to deal with. And recall that as late as mid-2000, when he applied for the George Washington University doctoral program, Awlaki seemed to be considering abandoning his religious career altogether to become an educational bureaucrat—hardly a likely option for a dedicated Islamic extremist.

Even Lincoln Higgie's seemingly damning encounter in August 2001—an irresistible Hollywood moment—is by no means definitive. His memory of the exchange has varied over time. In 2003, he told a 9/11 Commission investigator that Awlaki had told him "something very big was going to happen, and that he had to be out of the country when it happened." When I first spoke with Higgie in 2010, he did not recount Awlaki talking about "something big"— just that Awlaki had said that he might be going abroad, that he would not return to San Diego, and that the reason would be clear later. Asked about the discrepancy in 2014, Higgie said he thought that perhaps Awlaki had referred to "something" happening, but not "something big." In our conversations in both 2010 and 2014, Higgie told a parallel story about something else that had happened shortly before 9/11: an American art dealer friend, he said, had been warned by Pakistani business contacts that they had to ship artworks to the dealer quickly. Why? he asked his friend. "Something's going to happen," the friend replied. Of course, the linchpin of Awlaki's supposed remarks—which would have been a staggering failure of discretion if he really knew about the plot—was that he had to leave the country. But he did not leave the country for many months after 9/11.

There is no doubt that Higgie recalls a puzzling remark from Awlaki; his housemate confirmed that Higgie spoke about it at the time. But in the agitated hindsight that follows a momentous event, much looks portentous and suspicious. When Higgie read that his friendly former neighbor had contacts with the hijackers, he undoubtedly combed his memory for exchanges with Awlaki, searching for clues to what was coming, and perhaps reading too much into ambiguous words.

When all the evidence is considered, the notion of Awlaki having a well-hidden secret life in Al Qaeda is unpersuasive. It's possible that Awlaki had a sense that Hazmi, and perhaps Mihdhar and Hanjour as well, were involved in some kind of operation and that he was sufficiently ambivalent not to probe deeply or alert the authorities. When the attacks occurred, and he saw the mass murder of innocents, he may have been sincerely shocked and disturbed, as his public and private statements implied. "I think Awlaki had to know that something was going on," said Bob Bukowski, an FBI agent, now retired, who investigated the ties of Rababah and Chehazeh to Awlaki and to the hijackers. "I don't think he necessarily knew the details of the plot." One more anecdote from the months after 9/11 lends more support for such a conclusion.

———

As his renown spread, Awlaki fended off preaching invitations from mosques all over the country. But one he accepted in early 2002 came from Las Cruces, New Mexico, where he had family ties: he had been born there, while his father studied at New Mexico State University, and now his younger brother Ammar was a student there. Anwar flew down for a couple of days, gave a sermon at the local mosque, and spent time with his brother. One night, Ammar recalled, the two of them had a dinner invitation from a local Yemeni immigrant family. Anwar proposed walking—to his brother's surprise, since the house was about five miles away. The long walk gave them a chance to speak at length about 9/11, Al Qaeda, and the battle for Muslim hearts and minds. As they walked, Ammar recalled, Anwar spoke in strikingly harsh tones about Al Qaeda. Ammar, nineteen at the time and barely versed in the different political forces within the Muslim world, had noticed that some Saudi students at the mosque were "a little sympathetic" toward the 9/11 terrorists, suggesting that the United States had deserved a comeuppance. "I expected that Anwar would say, 'Okay, they had good intentions. . . . They chose the wrong means.' But Anwar was totally against it." What was especially memorable, he said, was that Anwar seemed furious at Al Qaeda, which he seemed to see as a dangerous rival for the loyalty of Muslims and which he said had "set us back twenty years in our efforts." He even seemed to relish the prospect of strong American action against Al Qaeda. "And he said, 'Look, now let's see who wins. Who's going to spread Islam?'"

"I remember he opened my eyes," Ammar recalled. Listening to his brother, he said, he came to understand divergent approaches to religion: "Okay, there's jihadists who believe they can bomb and spread Islam, but oh, there are guys who live in the States like Anwar who are trying to spread Islam in peaceful ways, who think you don't spread Islam by attacking. I remember he was not impressed at all by Osama bin Laden."

Ammar returned the visit toward the end of March 2002, flying to Washington, where Anwar picked him up in his minivan. The younger brother's real motive, in fact, was to borrow the van and drive to New York to visit a girl he'd taken an interest in. Before he left Washington, however, he spent a few days with Anwar, hanging around the mosque and sampling some of the ethnic restaurants that

Anwar liked. Neither Anwar nor Ammar knew it, but an FBI surveillance team followed them on their rounds: driving by the White House and Pentagon, shopping at Borders, dining at a kebab place and at Legal Seafood. At first, in the FBI reports, Ammar was just "UMEM," or unknown Middle Eastern male; then the FBI watchers figured out that he was the cleric's younger brother.

As Ammar, the admiring younger brother, remembered it, he was eager to see Anwar return to Yemen and follow in his father's footsteps in helping out a country that needed him. So not long after he arrived in Washington, Ammar asked Anwar lightheartedly just how long he intended to stay in the United States. "And he goes, like, 'Forever,'" said Ammar, whose American English is even more colloquial than his brother's was. "I asked him how long he might stay, because I thought Anwar was a charismatic guy, one of a kind. If he came to Yemen, he'd do something, he'd be something special in Yemen. At the time that's what I thought. I looked up to Dad and what he'd done in Yemen. I wanted Anwar to be the same. But he said, 'No, I'm going to spend the rest of my life in America.'" With his preaching success, his CDs, and his emergence as a national voice since 9/11, he apparently had set aside the plan to take an education post at Sanaa University. Between his thriving career at the mosque and beyond, his location near the center of American political power, and his pleasant lifestyle, he had no intention of leaving, Ammar said. "He had started on his PhD. We'd go out and have amazing seafood in Washington restaurants. We'd go to Chinese restaurants. He was showing me around. He was totally planning to stay."

It was a notable exchange. According to the FBI surveillance logs, Ammar arrived in Virginia on March 23—the day *after* Awlaki's fierce March 22 "war against Muslims" sermon in response to the federal raids on Islamic institutions. It has been a common assumption that after that outburst of anger and frustration Awlaki was fed up and ready to leave the country, disillusioned by the wave of hostility to Muslims. But Ammar's account suggests otherwise—that even after the sermon, Anwar fully intended to stay in the United States.

The language of the sermon itself actually supports that conclusion. Awlaki framed the struggle of Muslim Americans to insist on their rights in the face of discrimination and police abuse as parallel to the earlier struggle of African Americans, with which he had become familiar. He had visited prisoners while living in San Diego, had read Malcolm X, and had spoken just days before 9/11 at the fund-raiser for Jamil al-Amin, the former H. Rap Brown, a prominent leader in the black liberation movement of the 1960s. And in the angry March 22 sermon he held up African Americans as a model for American Muslim empowerment and actually mentioned the case of al-Amin, whom he portrayed as an innocent man facing unfair murder charges. He called for unity—"This was an attack on every one of us"—and support for Muslim political organizations "by your money, by your manpower and also by your advice and ideas." At the emotional peak of the sermon, Awlaki made the comparison with the civil rights movement explicit:

> As Muslims, if we allow this to continue, if we do not stop it, it ain't gonna stop! It's not gonna stop! If you don't stand up in the struggle and make your voices heard and unite and make it clear to the authorities that you're not going to allow your necks to be stepped over and your rights to be infringed upon, then only Allah knows where it's gonna stop. . . . Because there are no rights unless there is a struggle for those rights. And the history of America in that sense is very clear. African Americans in this country had to go through a struggle. Their rights were not handed to them.

The sense of the sermon was that yes, times are tough—but that Muslims must unite and fight, not cower or flee. It fit Anwar's explanation to his brother a few days later that he planned to stay indefinitely in the United States. But then, suddenly and dramatically, something changed.

Just a few days after their conversation about Anwar's future, Ammar showed up at the mosque at the time of the evening prayer, known as *isha*, the last of the five daily prayers. He was surprised to discover that his brother was not leading the prayer. "He was in the mosque—his car's there," Ammar said. "If he's there, he's the leader of the prayer—but he wasn't leading the prayer." Ammar sought out his brother and found him looking pale and more upset than he had ever seen him. "He was in such a mental state, so devastated that he couldn't even lead the prayer. . . . He was angry, upset, sad, maybe confused." Ammar asked him what had happened. "And he said,

'We'll talk about it.'" Ammar was appalled and intensely curious about what could have caused such distress.

The next day, he accompanied his brother to a library or some other public place—Ammar can picture the setting but doesn't remember exactly where they were. Anwar found a meeting room where they could be alone and astonished him with his next request: "He told me to take the battery out of my phone, and he did the same." Then his brother explained to Ammar what had so distressed him: a conversation that he had had the previous night, just before the evening prayer was to begin.

"He said, 'Something happened last night that made me reconsider my stay here in the States. I was told that the FBI has a file on me, and this file could destroy my life. I'm now rethinking my options, and one of them might be as drastic as leaving the States.'" Anwar said he was leaving in a few days for a long-planned visit to the United Kingdom, where he was scheduled to speak at a Quran Expo in Birmingham. He just might not come back, he said.

Anwar did not tell his brother who had revealed the existence of the FBI file on him or what it contained. Given Anwar's evident anguish and secretive manner, Ammar did not press him for details. He knew vaguely that some Dar Al-Hijrah members had connections to Hamas, the Palestinian group that had been designated by the United States since 1997 as a terrorist organization, and he wondered whether allegations of support for Hamas might be involved. But he found the episode as bewildering as it was upsetting. A day or two after the conversation, Ammar drove to New York to visit his friend. Anwar flew to England and spoke at the Quran Expo but canceled his return trip. He would return to the United States only one more time, seven months later.

A long-secret document reveals just how Awlaki learned on that night in March 2002 of his FBI file and what it contained. The bureau had not confronted him, nor had any of Awlaki's friends or colleagues learned of the file's existence and tipped him off about it. Instead, the tip came from inside Awlaki's secret life in the hotels and motels around the nation's capital: he had received a warning call from a manager of one of the escort services he regularly patronized, who told him that "an agent named 'Wade' had been there asking questions about him." The agent, Wade Ammerman, later told four interviewers from the 9/11 Commission that he believed the escort manager's call—monitored by the bureau under a court order approving eavesdropping—made Awlaki "nervous" and prompted him to change his plans.

This explanation fits all the facts. Awlaki had been questioned by counterterrorism agents first in San Diego in the 1999–2000 investigation and then repeatedly after 9/11. But months had passed, and he had no reason to believe that the bureau would be able to build a terrorism case against him; in fact, investigators did not believe they had a case. Hence Awlaki's assurance in telling Ammar only days earlier that he expected to stick with his thriving clerical career in the United States for many years to come. Now, however, with the alarming call from the escort service, Awlaki would have realized for the first time that his many visits to prostitutes had been monitored by the FBI. The nature of the questions that agents had asked the escort service manager likely would have made clear that they knew a great deal about his extraclerical activities.

He was right: however thin the evidence tying him to militancy, the bureau's Awlaki file was overflowing with lurid details of his paid sexual encounters. Though Awlaki didn't know it, bureau officials were indeed studying the possibility of charging him, as the June 2002 racketeering memo would show. He was being quite realistic when he told his brother that the prostitution file could "destroy my life." It could plausibly be used to put him in jail. It could be leaked to the media, shattering his career, his reputation, and his family life. Or perhaps even worse, from the point of view of psychological pressure, it could be used by the FBI to blackmail him into becoming an informant, an agonizing possibility for a strong-minded cleric who was urging Muslims to stand up to a bullying government. It was an intolerable threat that Awlaki did not dare confront and could not mitigate. He could only flee.

In a tale full of twists that might have gone a different way, this was an especially provocative turn. The FBI's blanket surveillance was intended to find his ties to terror, and what it found did not add up to anything close to a criminal terrorism case. But because the bureau stumbled onto his visits to prostitutes, and because Awlaki found out about it, he abandoned his life in the United States, with dire ultimate consequences both for American security and for Awlaki himself. In other words, his main reason for leaving the United States was not Americans' anti-Islamic prejudice, as many have assumed, but his own anti-Islamic behavior. His aspiration to serve as a bridge between America and Islam, already challenged by the Operation Green Quest raids and the growing tension between the authorities and many Muslims, was over. He could no longer function as an American imam, living every day under the shadow of his own hypocrisy and the FBI's knowledge of it. He would have to find something else to do with his life.

As he flew to London at the end of March 2002, Awlaki was heading into an environment far more tolerant of militant Islamic rhetoric than the post-9/11 United States. Both in the diverse British Muslim community and on the political left in Britain, there was substantial support for the notion that 9/11, however regrettable for its victims, represented a kind of rough justice for an arrogant America. When he left American soil, Awlaki left behind more than the constant fear of exposure for his involvement with prostitutes or prosecution for his past associations with militants and the hijackers. In the United Kingdom, he no longer faced the stark with-us-or-with-the-terrorists choice that Bush had pronounced.

He spoke at the Quran Expo in Birmingham, as planned, but he canceled his return trip. Instead, he went to stay with his wealthy uncle, Saleh bin Fareed al-Awlaki, who happened to be at his estate in Bournemouth, the resort town on England's south coast. Bin Fareed asked him about the fallout from 9/11, and Anwar told him he had been questioned by the FBI but never detained or charged, with no restrictions on his travel. "I asked him, 'What are you doing here in London?'" Bin Fareed recalled. "And he said, 'I want to spend a few weeks here to preach in mosques and universities.' So he went to London and he went to the north of London and came back to see me two or three times. He was moving freely and he was not afraid of anything to be done against him."

At Dar Al-Hijrah, officials were shocked by Awlaki's sudden decision to leave, but they took the move in stride, hopeful that they could persuade him to return. The mosque prepared a letter on April 20, about three weeks after his departure, to use to answer inquiries about where the imam had gone. By dressing up his sudden and highly inconvenient disappearance as a sort of planned sabbatical, mosque officials left open the possibility of Awlaki's return. "Mr. Al-Awlaki's Islamic knowledge and experience is phenomenal," the letter said, "and the center wishes to continue employing him. It is in that regard that we have decided to transfer Imam Al-Awlaki to Yemen in order to take extensive Islamic law classes with scholars that are qualified to teach it."

By the time the letter was written, Awlaki had arranged for his family to leave Virginia and fly to Yemen, where they moved into his parents' spacious house in Sanaa. He began to divide his time between Yemen, where his family always welcomed him, and London, where he was developing a reputation as a charismatic speaker, building upon his successful CDs. Nussaibah Younis described memorably in the *Guardian* the weekends she spent as a British Muslim teenager taking the bus to Islamic conferences. "Once you've been on the circuit for a while, you get a ratings system going: when old, first-generation Pakistani men get up to speak you skip out into the corridor for a cup of coffee and a gossip." But the Americans tended to be compelling, and Awlaki was among the best, she recalled. "When I hit 17, I attended a 10-day Islamic studies course and was thrilled to discover that Awlaki was the centerpiece of the schedule," wrote Younis, now with the Project on Middle East Democracy. "He taught us about the life of the prophet Muhammad for three hours a day and it was mesmerizing. He taught by telling stories. He spoke about the Prophet Muhammad, his wives, his companions and their lives with such passion, intimacy and humor—it was as though he knew them first hand. His stories were so good because he wasn't afraid to see the humanity in the characters he described. He spoke about their weaknesses as well as their strengths, about jealousy, anger, love and lust." Younis and the other students could have no idea that when he spoke of such "weaknesses" as lust he was speaking from deep personal experience.

In October 2002, Awlaki did something unexpected. At the urging of his father, he interrupted his budding career as a lecturer in Britain to make one last trip to the United States. Nasser al-Awlaki, who knew nothing of the prostitution file, was clinging to his dreams for his talented son. Anwar was still officially in the doctoral program at George Washington University. Perhaps he could finish his studies and still get a worthy position at Sanaa University or in the Yemeni government. Alternatively, maybe it was not too late to capitalize on his considerable fame in the United States and make a good life there after all. Awlaki, his wife, and the youngest of their three children flew via Riyadh to JFK International Airport, arriving early on the morning of October 10. They were taken aside for secondary screening, held for three hours, and finally told they were free to fly on to Washington. Eight years later, in *Inspire* magazine, Awlaki recalled that customs officials seemed "quite baffled" by the situation. "I got an apology from one of them with a weird face on him. Actually I myself was shocked and asked them: Is that it? They said, yes sir, that's it. You are free to board!" In what would be his final public encounter with his government on American soil, the future terrorist was given a comment card—just in case he wanted to complain about his treatment at the hands of immigration agents.

Despite his lightly sarcastic tone in recalling the episode, it seems likely that Awlaki was feeling less smug at the time. He had fled the country in a hurry seven months earlier, after all, after the escort service had tipped him off about his FBI file. He knew that the FBI had plenty of evidence to embarrass or arrest him, and during the long wait at JFK he may well have wondered whether his father's pressure to give life in America one more chance might now end in disaster.

In fact, his return was even riskier than he could have known. In the months before his plane landed, the law enforcement bureaucracy had prepared two possible prosecutions. Both of them, however, turned out to be so convoluted that they did not ultimately pass muster with senior Justice Department prosecutors. First, there was that twenty-page FBI memo four months earlier that had proposed a racketeering case based on his crossing from Virginia into the District of Columbia to buy the services of prostitutes. Prosecutors declined to go along with the idea. Second, there was the discovery of a long-ago Awlaki lie by a determined Diplomatic Security Service officer, Ray Fournier, who was assigned to the Joint Terrorism Task Force in San Diego. Fournier discovered that on Awlaki's application for a Social Security card back in 1990 he had falsely given his birthplace as Aden, Yemen, presumably in order to safeguard his US Agency for International Development scholarship for foreign students. The statute of limitations on a fraud charge related to the scholarship or the Social Security application had long since passed. But Fournier argued that since Awlaki had used his Social Security number to renew his American passport in 1993, a charge of passport fraud—with an unusually long ten-year statute of limitations—was still possible. On the basis of his theory, a warrant was issued for Awlaki's arrest in June 2002.

When Fournier heard a few months later that Awlaki was actually on his way to the United States, his efforts seemed to be coming to fruition. "We were all pleased that a target of this importance was going to be picked up," Fournier said. "He would have gotten a year at most, but we could have talked to him. We could have seen who visited him, who called him." It was a blatant proposal for a fishing trip, but Fournier's quest for more answers from Awlaki would later be echoed by the two major investigations of 9/11: leaders of both the Congressional Joint Inquiry and the 9/11 Commission believed that Awlaki's connections had warranted deeper investigation.

But the federal prosecutor who was in charge of terror investigations in Colorado at the time, David Gaouette, ordered the arrest warrant withdrawn. He discovered that Awlaki had used his correct New Mexico birthplace when seeking a replacement Social Security card in 1996. As a result, Social Security officials said they would testify at any future trial that Awlaki was entitled to the Social Security number, that it was valid, and that Awlaki had himself corrected his erroneous application. It did not look like a viable fraud case to four veteran prosecutors who looked it over. Gaouette, who later served as US attorney, said that he and his colleagues knew little about the terrorism suspicions surrounding Awlaki but that they could not approve Awlaki's arrest on the basis of Fournier's insistence that the cleric was "a bad guy." "We can only arrest people for a legitimate charge," Gaouette said. "We follow the laws. We follow the Constitution."

It is far from clear, in any case, that the FBI agents most knowledgeable about Awlaki, in Washington and San Diego, actually wanted him arrested. A still-classified memo regarding Awlaki was sent by the FBI director, Robert Mueller, to the attorney general, John Ashcroft, on October 3, 2002—a week before Awlaki's arrival, probably about the time US intelligence learned of his travel plans. So the question of what to do about Awlaki appears to have been considered at the highest levels of government. In addition, documents show that Special Agent Wade Ammerman, of the bureau's Washington Field Office, an Awlaki specialist by that point, was contacted in the flurry of calls on the morning of October 10. He appears to have done nothing to support Fournier's efforts to have the cleric detained. It is possible that Ammerman and his colleagues, having already questioned Awlaki at least three times, believed it would be more fruitful to let the cleric roam the United States while keeping him under close surveillance.

And that leads to a mysterious nighttime encounter, later in October 2002, between Awlaki and Ali al-Timimi, the rival, radical Virginia cleric whose popularity with young Muslims had prompted Dar Al-Hijrah to hire Awlaki in the first place. In a highly controversial case, Timimi, an American-born biologist, was later sentenced to life in prison for encouraging some of his youthful followers to go to Afghanistan and fight American troops. In challenging his conviction, his lawyers said that Awlaki showed up at Timimi's house one night and pressed him for help in recruiting fighters for jihad. Timimi found Awlaki's conduct odd, his lawyers said, and began to suspect that he was wearing a wire and working for the FBI.

On its face, the notion that Awlaki might have been pressured into helping the FBI has a lot to recommend it. Perhaps the bureau did not protest the withdrawal of the Awlaki arrest warrant because it had other plans for him. Agents could easily have approached Awlaki quietly, perhaps even at JFK, threatened him with exposure or prosecution, and enlisted his help in the ongoing investigation of Islamic militants in Virginia. One heavily redacted FBI document related to the Awlaki investigation, dated October 22, 2002, has the synopsis "Asset reporting," suggesting either that Awlaki might have became an "asset," or source, or that someone else was reporting to the FBI about him.

But the bureau flatly denies that Awlaki was cooperating. FBI agent Ammerman, in his long-secret interview with the 9/11 Commission, describes Awlaki's nighttime meeting with Timimi—both men were probably under surveillance—but gives no indication that Awlaki was working with the FBI. Asked whether the FBI played any role in directing Awlaki to visit Timimi, recording their meeting, or questioning Awlaki about the meeting after it happened, a bureau spokeswoman sent a one-word written answer: No.

7

STEALTHY, AGILE, AND LETHAL

When Senator Barack Obama stood at the podium at Washington's Woodrow Wilson Center on August 1, 2007, to deliver his first major address on national security, he had a lot to prove. Just three years earlier he had been an obscure Illinois legislator. Now as a very junior US senator, he was proposing to take the helm of the country in the midst of two wars, with Al Qaeda still threatening attacks. Even to many who were captivated by Obama's personal story, the notion of this former community organizer as commander in chief seemed a stretch. This was his chance to persuade the doubters, who were legion, that he was capable of leading the country at a fraught time for national security and military affairs.

Obama, reading from a teleprompter and looking considerably younger than his forty-five years, devoted much of the speech to a reprise of his famous opposition to the invasion of Iraq. His prescience about the war, he suggested, set him apart from all his rivals for the Democratic presidential nomination—notably Senator Hillary Rodham Clinton, who had voted to authorize the invasion. Congress had "rubber-stamped the rush to war," becoming its "co-author," he said. "Because of a war in Iraq that should never have been authorized and should never have been waged," he declared, "we are now less safe than we were before 9/11."

Five years earlier, at an antiwar rally in Chicago's Federal Plaza, Obama had warned that a US invasion would "only fan the flames of the Middle East, and encourage the worst, rather than best, impulses of the Arab world, and strengthen the recruitment arm of Al Qaeda." By 2007, it had all come true, and Obama's warning had become a central plank in his appeal to American voters. If he wanted to bask in his 2002 stance against the invasion, it was hard to blame him. The Bush administration's rationale for the war, Saddam Hussein's weapons of mass destruction, had long ago been exposed as a cruel hoax. Panglossian predictions that American troops would be "greeted as liberators" (from Vice President Dick Cheney, a supposed hard-eyed realist) and that the invasion would be a "cakewalk" were quoted only as the object of bitter ridicule. The war was burning through some $10 billion a month, and 3,647 American troops had been killed and more than 27,000 wounded. The headlines on the day of Obama's speech were grimly familiar: "Three U.S. Soldiers Killed," "Car Bomb Kills 17 in Central Baghdad," "Sunni Arab Bloc Quits Iraqi Government."

But the sound bites from 2002 of the young state senator speaking out against "a dumb war . . . a rash war" failed to capture the caution and care with which he had framed his argument at the time. The refrain of Obama's 2002 remarks was not the motto of a peacenik: "I don't oppose all wars," he said—three times. He evoked the history of combat that he believed to be righteous: the Civil War, which drove "the scourge of slavery from our soil"; World War II, in which his grandfather and other troops liberated Hitler's death camps and "triumphed over evil"; and the military response to 9/11, asserting, in a not entirely convincing show of personal bravado from this skinny lawyer, that "I would willingly take up arms myself to prevent such tragedy from happening again."

Now, three months into his campaign for president, as he laid out his approach to national security, Obama knew that reminding voters that he would have kept America out of Bush's Iraq quagmire was not enough. That was what he would *not* do. But what *would* he do?

If the speech had an affirmative core, it was Obama's tough talk on terrorism—specifically the threat posed by militant sanctuaries in Pakistan to both the US homeland and to American troops in Afghanistan. Pakistan's president, Pervez Musharraf, was distracted by his own problems, Obama said, and was not doing enough. A few weeks before Obama's speech, my *New York Times* colleague Mark Mazzetti had reported that the Bush administration had prepared to grab Al Qaeda's No. 2, Ayman al-Zawahri, at a 2005 meeting in Pakistan, only to cancel the raid as too risky. A week after Mazzetti's story, I had written about a new National Intelligence Estimate that said Al Qaeda had regrouped in Pakistan and gave a dark assessment of a revived terrorist threat. Obama and his team had seized upon both stories as they drafted the speech.

"There are terrorists holed up in those mountains who murdered 3,000 Americans," Obama said. "They are plotting to strike again. It was a terrible mistake to fail to act when we had a chance to take out an Al Qaeda leadership meeting in 2005. If we have actionable intelligence about high-value terrorist targets and President Musharraf will not act, we will."

If he wanted to make a splash with that vow, he succeeded. But it was not quite what he had intended. His opponents spotted what they saw as an obvious greenhorn mistake and pounced. Obama was vowing, they claimed, to invade the sovereign territory of an allied country. Hillary Clinton, who had repeatedly labeled Obama "naïve," took him to task for "telegraphing" US moves; a few months later, in a presidential debate, she spoke scornfully of his remarks: "He basically threatened to bomb Pakistan, which I don't think was a particularly wise position to take." Christopher Dodd called Obama's comment "irresponsible." Joe Biden called Obama "uninformed." Most memorable was the strafing he got from Mitt Romney on the Republican side: "In one week he went from saying he's going to sit down, you know, for tea, with our enemies, but then he's going to bomb our allies. I mean, he's gone from Jane Fonda to Dr. Strangelove in one week."

Obama, returning fire, reemphasized the fact that his opponents had voted to authorize the Iraq War: "I find it amusing that those who helped to authorize and engineer the biggest foreign policy disaster in our generation are now criticizing me for making sure that we are on the right battlefield and not the wrong battlefield in the war against terrorism." Maneuvering against far more experienced foreign policy hands, he would play his Iraq trump card again and again.

But it was not an invasion of Pakistan that Obama had in mind. Nor was it bombing in the traditional sense. There was a new weapon that had already captured his imagination, though the exaggerated secrecy that plagued American security debates made it too sensitive for a member of Congress to speak about it publicly except in the most oblique language. "I will not hesitate to use military force to take out terrorists who pose a direct threat to America," Obama said at the Wilson Center. "I will ensure that our military becomes more stealthy, agile, and lethal in its ability to capture or kill terrorists."

No one in the broader public quite got it at the time. But Obama was talking about the drone.

In the weeks before his Wilson Center address, Obama had huddled with the foreign policy team he had assembled for the campaign to probe the policies he had in mind and to test the treacherous politics of terrorism for a candidate with his thin résumé. By late 2006, Obama had begun to reach out to a few experienced government hands to ask them not to commit to any presidential candidate because he might get in the race. Among them were Richard Clarke, the iconoclastic terrorism expert who had worked for both Clinton and Bush and had subsequently blasted the Bush administration's failure to heed his warnings about a coming attack; Susan Rice, who had worked on Clinton's National Security Council staff and was a protégée of Madeleine Albright, the first female secretary of state; Jeh Johnson, a former federal prosecutor and Air Force general counsel; and a few gray eminences, notably Lee Hamilton, a congressman from Indiana for thirty-four years before becoming a favorite appointee to troubleshooting boards, notably as vice-chairman of the 9/11 Commission. Acting as staff for the brainstorming sessions was Denis McDonough, not yet forty, an aide to Tom Daschle, the former Senate majority leader, who had joined the Obama team earlier in 2007 after his friend Mark Lippert, a navy reservist, was deployed to Iraq. Ben Rhodes, just shy of thirty, an aspiring novelist who had spent five years as a speechwriter for Hamilton, was the wordsmith working with the senator on national security and foreign policy. They gathered in folding chairs in a distinctly unpresidential two-bedroom apartment above a Subway outlet on Massachusetts Avenue in the capital to hash out what Obama should say.

Those who did not already know Obama well soon discovered that he was neither a pacifist nor an ideologue, though both opponents on the right and admirers on the left consistently misunderstood this. At heart, for better or worse, Obama proposed to be a ruthless pragmatist, especially when it came to counterterrorism. If the staggering expenditure of young lives and national treasure in the two big wars was meant to make America safe from terrorism, he thought, it was a perverse way to go about it. Occupying Muslim countries for years with a small city's worth of heavily armed and sometimes trigger-happy Americans was proving ineffective or counterproductive. On top of it all, the Bush war on terror—the very phrase rankled Obama, who saw it as intellectually ridiculous; the war was on Al Qaeda, he thought, not its tactics—had repeatedly violated the fundamental principles that Americans had for decades held dear. Secret detention and torture had squandered international support, ceded the moral high ground in a battle of ideas, and handed the enemy a potent source of propaganda.

But inaction was not an option, given the dire news from Pakistan. What if you could kill the terrorists without killing anyone else? What if you could do it without putting American lives at risk? The armed drone seemed to provide exactly the necessary third choice between doing nothing, on the one hand, and invading countries, on the other. For a presidential candidate whose main ambitions lay in the domestic arena, the drone seemed a godsend. It could lower the American profile in the Muslim world, depriving Al Qaeda of the foil that had allowed it to recruit an Iraqi branch of the terror network and reinvigorate anti-American passions. It offered the opportunity to take decisive action without the agony of American casualties.

In the discussions above the Subway shop, Obama had begun to articulate a simple principle that would become a mantra early in his presidency: Let's kill the people who are trying to kill us. The number of Al Qaeda plotters whose aim was to attack Americans was in the hundreds. Yet several hundred thousand Iraqis and Afghans, and some four thousand American troops, had died in the two big wars since 2001. That tragic mismatch, in Obama's view, had deepened America's predicament. The drone, it seemed, if used judiciously, offered a way to scale the solution to the problem, picking off America's real enemies one by one. At the time of Obama's 2007 speech, there had been just a dozen drone strikes in Pakistan and only one in Yemen; the large-scale drone campaign in the tribal area of Pakistan would not be started for another year, in the last six months of George W. Bush's second term. But to Obama and his advisers, the promise of killing with pinpoint accuracy from thousands of miles away—if CIA and Joint Special Operations Command claims were to be trusted—held indisputable appeal.

"The drones were coming into sight as the best available tool— maybe the only tool—to reach the safe havens," recalled Lee Hamilton, who as president of the Wilson Center in 2007 introduced Obama to the audience at his national security speech and was impressed by the brash young candidate. Hamilton, who had spent all the years since completing the 9/11 Commission report focused on the terrorist threat, was deeply frustrated that Al Qaeda could still operate with impunity from sanctuaries in Pakistan. "My point of view was rather simplistic—I thought something had to be done," he said. "The drone was the only thing we had to get at 'em." There was little consideration in those early discussions, Hamilton said, of collateral damage, political backlash, or the dangers of proliferation. "It was full speed ahead," he said.

Obama's aggressive, if murky, vow to take tough action, so easily misconstrued, was seen by his rivals as a clumsy political ploy, the blunder of an amateur trying to look tough. It did, of course, result from a political calculation: if he was critiquing the Bush record he had to offer a persuasive alternative. But there was more to it than that. Obama was attracted to technological solutions, especially if they seemed to offer a moral advantage. For a candidate who was revolutionizing the use of the Internet for fund-raising, recruitment, and messaging, technology seemed to offer solutions. For a guy in his forties who was never without his BlackBerry, there was nothing intimidating about the digital age. In health care, he promised that electronic records and shrewd management could cut costs and eliminate dangerous errors. In energy, he was smitten by solar, wind, and biofuels, fuel efficiency and "clean coal." And in combating terrorism, he saw invading countries as decidedly old school, something left over from the era of the telegraph. The drone, using some of the same technology that was now creating the smart phone boom, might be the new, more humane way to protect the country.

If any American was prepared by his own background to understand the contradictions of Anwar al-Awlaki's struggle for identity, it might have been the young Barack Hussein Obama, who wrote a whole book about his own diverse influences and difficult quest. The parallel was arresting: two men born in the United States to foreign fathers of Muslim ancestry and taken in childhood to live overseas in a Muslim country before returning stateside. Still, except in the overheated speculation of conspiracy-mongers on the far right, or just far out, Obama's exposure to Islam was quite superficial and largely confined to childhood. The deeper analogy might be with the temptations of radicalism for a young man who finds himself alienated from the society around him, as Obama did off and on throughout his adolescence and young adulthood. Obama, a decade older than Awlaki, spent years puzzling over his relationship to the American mainstream and its values. As he negotiated the conundrum of race—even in the relatively soft atmosphere of an elite private school amid Hawaii's ethnic mélange—he experienced the casual humiliations and frustrations of a racial minority. And at times, in reaction, he assumed an angry, radicalized stance.

In *Dreams from My Father*, Obama describes his "fitful interior struggle" as he grappled with how to interpret his own mixed ancestry. "I was trying to raise myself to be a black man in America, and beyond the given of my appearance, no one around me seemed to know exactly what that meant." As he tried on the trappings of racial identity—learning to "curse like Richard Pryor," trying out the dance moves from *Soul Train*, spending hours on the basketball court—Obama acknowledges that he "was living out a caricature of black male adolescence, itself a caricature of swaggering American manhood." His small circle of black friends, "teenagers whose confusion and anger would help shape my own," endlessly mulled over the mysteries of discrimination in the minutiae of their lives. He simmered over the "trap" that American life seemed to have set for him: "Following this maddening logic, the only thing you could choose as your own was withdrawal into a smaller and smaller coil of rage, until being black meant only the knowledge of your own powerlessness, of your own defeat. And the final irony: Should you refuse this defeat and lash out at your captors, they would have a name for that, too, a name that could cage you just as good. Paranoid. Militant. Violent. Nigger." It is a striking description. Reading about the frustration of powerlessness, and the decision to lash out, it is hard not to think of Awlaki's post-9/11 transformation, and of those he would inspire.

In the end, that was the road Obama did not take. He spent time as a teen with an older black man, Frank Marshall Davis, who had been a leftist firebrand but had mellowed by the time young Obama paid his visits. He delved through the riches of African American literature and memoir, taking particular interest in Malcolm X and his turn away from racial hatred at the end of his life. Of course, Awlaki was also a fan of Malcolm X, and in a brief window after 9/11 he overtly embraced the African American struggle for civil rights as a model for Muslim Americans. But Awlaki left that model behind when he abandoned the United States and embarked on a steadily more militant career. Obama's talent and enterprise, and the encouragement of many powerful and admiring mentors, swept him forward on a path to success, prestige, and power.

Sorting through Obama's early career for anything that might shed light on the counterterrorism policies he would adopt as president is a futile mission. In the work of a community organizer, a Chicago lawyer, and an Illinois state senator, there is little that touches on the subjects that would later engross Obama at the Tuesday terrorism meetings in the Situation Room.

But in Obama's part-time work teaching constitutional law at the University of Chicago law school there is territory worth exploring. As president, in the Awlaki case, he would be forced to make a decision on grave constitutional questions, and some civil libertarians would accuse him of violating the Fourth and Fifth Amendments. He would draw on the government's top lawyers to consider the legality and constitutionality of killing Awlaki, and he would accept and act on their advice. And critics of the decision would use his status as, in the sarcastic phrase of journalist Jeremy Scahill, "the constitutional-law-professor-president," to suggest that he must know better and that his actions therefore carried a whiff of hypocrisy.

Between graduating from Harvard Law School and running for the US Senate in 2004, Obama spent about a dozen years teaching part-time at Chicago as "lecturer" and then "senior lecturer." He taught courses on constitutional law and voting rights and a seminar called "Current Issues in Racism and the Law." Former students recall an engaged, informal, and Socratic professor who was less interested in pushing his own views than in challenging students to express their own. "You rarely got his opinion or his view," said Salil Mehra, who took Obama's seminar and is now a law professor at Temple University. "If we got a direct statement, it was biographical or observational—part *Dreams from My Father*, part *Seinfeld*."

That was true, he and other former students said, when the class discussed an intriguing essay Obama assigned for the racism seminar in 1994: "Is It Right and Wise to Kill a Kidnapper?" by Frederick Douglass. It was Douglass's commentary on a riveting drama that was playing out in 1854 in the abolitionist hotbed of Boston. An anti-slavery mob tried to free an escaped slave, nineteen-year-old Anthony Burns, who was to be returned to bondage in Virginia under the Fugitive Slave Act of 1850. In the ensuing riot, a "truckman" or driver for the US marshal named James Batchelder was stabbed to death. A few days later, Douglass published his audacious commentary in his newspaper, posing a fundamental moral question: Might it be justified to kill a man whose vicious crime undermined the security and well-being of an entire society?

Society has the right, Douglass argued, to protect itself against those who would endanger it: "This right of society is essential to its preservations; without it a single individual would have it in his power to destroy the peace and the happiness of ten thousand otherwise right minded people. Precisely on the same ground, we hold that a man may, properly, wisely and even mercifully be deprived of life. Of course life being the most precious is the most sacred of all rights, and cannot be taken away, but under the direst necessity; and not until all reasonable modes had been adopted to prevent this necessity, and to spare the aggressor."

A century and a half later, Obama would wrestle with the targeted killing of suspected terrorists. Douglass's argument was a striking precursor to those he would embrace. The right of a society to "peace and happiness" in the face of a threat from a supremely dangerous individual; the condition that the malefactor be killed only under "direst necessity"; the requirement that "all reasonable modes" be tried short of killing—all would be recognizable as the Obama administration faced the Awlaki threat in 2010.

Anyone returning a free man to bondage, Douglass had written, "labeled himself the common enemy of mankind," and killing such a person was a positive moral good. "We hold that he had forfeited his right to live," Douglass wrote of the driver in the essay the young law professor had assigned. Nearly two decades later, Obama would echo Douglass's reasoning in justifying killing by drone.

I f slavery and abolition were the animating moral issues of American life in the mid-nineteenth century, then terrorism and the response to it were surely the equivalent in the early twenty-first century. In the years after 9/11, those of us covering the American campaign against Al Qaeda repeatedly found ourselves confronting moral and legal issues of gravity and consequence: secret detention; interrogation and torture; leaks to the press and the unprecedented crackdown on them; the targeted killing of suspected terrorists. Terrorism and the fear it generated pressed on elected and unelected officials weighty questions of right and wrong, sometimes in excruciating tangles. Again and again, the United States would drop principles that had defined it on the world stage, embracing practices it had long condemned.

In his Chicago years, Obama's natural interests mostly lay elsewhere. As he taught his law school courses and made the endless trips between Chicago and Springfield to serve in the Illinois Senate, his steadily growing political ambitions focused mainly on the deep troubles of America at home. But when the World Trade Center towers fell, he surely knew that the tragedy would cast a shadow for many years over the future of American politics. He had just turned forty, and he had been a state legislator for nearly five years, with his eye always on national office. He was asked by the *Hyde Park Herald*, his neighborhood newspaper in Chicago, to offer a written comment on the attacks by Al Qaeda. His sweeping and authoritative tone— almost comically overweening from a lowly state senator—revealed his poorly disguised ambition. He wrote as if he had already been rehearsing in his mind just what he might have said were he already in the White House: "Certain immediate lessons are clear, and we must act upon those lessons decisively." Along with the obvious calls for tougher airport security and better intelligence, he made a tough statement about Al Qaeda's plotters: "We must be resolute in identifying the perpetrators of these heinous acts and dismantling their organizations of destruction."

But though it was barely a week after the attacks, Obama added some less conventional, more far-sighted notes. He talked about the need to understand what motivated the attackers—"the sources of such madness"—which he speculated was "a fundamental absence of empathy" that was not "innate" in any religion or culture but could be "channeled by particular demagogues or fanatics." He wrote of American "rage" but cautioned that US military action in response must consider "the lives of innocent civilians abroad" and that Americans must avoid "bigotry" in their response. In the long run, he wrote, the country must "devote far more attention to the monumental task of raising the hopes and prospects of embittered children" around the globe who might be tempted by such apocalyptic violence.

In the years between 9/11 and his presidential campaign, Obama was rarely asked about terrorism, even after his election to the US Senate in 2004. But shortly after crushing Republican Alan Keyes in the Senate race, hoping to keep riding the publicity wave to sell his memoir, Obama embarked on a promotional blitz for the reissued *Dreams from My Father*. In the unlikely setting of a Barnes & Noble in New York City, he gave a long, thoughtful answer to a question about the nature and causes of the terrorist threat. The video is still viewable on YouTube, and again Obama tried to broaden the perspective on terrorism beyond the use of force. He spoke of how children in Pakistan without real prospects and trained in a fundamentalist madrasa might turn to extremism "not only for advancement but just some sense of meaning in their lives." The American response, said the senator-elect, had to address root causes:

> Our foreign policy and our perspective with respect to how to deal with terrorism has to reflect not only the interest in stopping the immediate threat of terrorism but also in creating a foreign policy that promotes justice, that promotes economic development, that promotes the rights of women. Those are all central aspects to dealing with terrorism. Ultimately terrorism is a tactic—we're not fighting terrorists, we're fighting people who engage in terrorism but have a whole host of rationales and excuses for why they do this, and to the extent that we can change the sense of opportunity in many of these countries and we can change the manner in which we function in these countries in more positive, proactive ways, then we're not going to eliminate terrorism entirely, but

we're at least going to be able to make more of a dent then if all
we're resorting to is military firepower.

His answer drew enthusiastic applause from the huge crowd. This
was no ordinary book tour. *Dreams* had sold a modest nine thousand copies initially, but Obama's Democratic National Convention
speech and Senate race had made him famous, and the new edition
leapt onto bestseller lists. He hired Robert Barnett, the Washington agent and lawyer favored by presidents, to shop around a new
book project and got a $1.9 million advance for three books, a con-
tract that would vault him for the first time into the ranks of the
truly wealthy. The first book to result, *The Audacity of Hope* in 2006,
was a far more cautious, far less original work than *Dreams*, and one
patently designed to fill out his portrait for a national audience. It
reflected his most heartfelt interests—the index had three times as
many references to "health care" as to "terrorism"—but it also gave
him a chance to sketch his views on the Al Qaeda problem more
thoroughly. He took an easy shot at the Bush administration's legal
calisthenics over detention and torture, saying he believed that "we
have played fast and loose with constitutional principles in the fight
against terrorism." He declared that "the battle against international
terrorism is at once an armed struggle and a contest of ideas, that our
long-term security depends both on a judicious projection of military
power and increased cooperation with other nations." In reminiscing
about Indonesia, where he had lived as a child, he expressed regret
at "the growth of militant, fundamentalist Islam" there. Most significant, perhaps, was Obama's discussion of when the United States
could and should unilaterally use force against terrorists. He called
the post-9/11 attack on Al Qaeda and the Taliban "entirely justified"
and elaborated in a lawyerly statement of doctrine worth quoting at
length:

I would argue that we have the right to take unilateral military
action to eliminate an *imminent* threat to our security—so long
as an imminent threat is understood to be a nation, group, or individual that is actively preparing to strike U.S. targets (or allies
with which the United States has mutual defense agreements), and
has or will have the means to do so in the immediate future. Al

Qaeda qualifies under this standard, and we can and should carry out preemptive strikes against them wherever we can. Iraq under Saddam Hussein did not meet this standard, which is why our invasion was such a strategic blunder. If we are going to act unilaterally, then we had better have the goods on our targets.

It was a striking shift of emphasis. Though he would base his presidential run in part on criticism of the Bush security record, Obama endorsed the Bush notion of "preemptive" strikes, even when they were unilateral. It presaged Obama's splashy vow the following year in his big national security speech that he would "not hesitate to use military force to take out terrorists who pose a direct threat to America."

Many Americans, and many foreigners, would later be surprised by Obama's decision to escalate drone strikes. But his intentions were hidden in plain sight. His emphasis on the imminence of a threat, as well as his insistence that we "have the goods" on strike targets to avoid blunders, raised issues that would become flash points in his presidency.

In the Muslim world, any attention to candidate Obama's vow to go after terrorists was overwhelmed by the spectacular possibility that a black man whose middle name was Hussein and who was sharply critical of many Muslims' nemesis, George W. Bush, might become the American president. Mohammed al-Asaadi, the Yemeni newspaper editor and activist, happened to be in Maryland in 2007 at an American Federation of Teachers gathering when AFT officials introduced him to the stumping Obama. The two men chatted for a few minutes, and Asaadi was struck by the candidate's knowledge of Yemen, then not at the top of the news. Obama asked him about the conflict with the Houthis, the Shiite rebels involved in a slow-burning insurgency near the Saudi border. "He asked, literally, 'How are those rebels doing up there in the north?' I told him I was shocked he would ask such a specific question. The guy knows Yemen already, which is really good. He asked, 'How is the situation overall?' I said, 'The rebels are in the north and Al Qaeda is in the south and people are sandwiched in between.' He laughed at that." Like many Yemenis, Asaadi said, "I had high hopes."

On election night, at the barricaded American embassy in Sanaa, the affable ambassador, Stephen Seche, hosted a reception for Yemenis. Some of the local guests were in tears, so moved were they by the promise of an Obama presidency.

A few weeks before that presidency officially began, on December 9, 2008, Obama visited a secure room in the Kluczynski Federal Building in Chicago for his fullest briefing so far on the CIA and its covert action programs, notably the drone program. A SCIF, or sensitive compartmented information facility, has to be eavesdropping-proof, and this one was a cramped, windowless room in the Mies van der Rohe skyscraper. There was a media frenzy in the city that day: the pugnacious Illinois governor, Rod Blagojevich, had just been arrested on corruption charges. But Obama's focus was far from the Chicago political scene where he had gotten his start.

On one side of the table were Obama, vice president-elect Joe Biden, retired general Jim Jones, who would be Obama's national security adviser, and two security aides to Obama and Biden, Mark Lippert and Tony Blinken. On the other side were Mike McConnell, the director of national intelligence, and Michael Hayden, the CIA director, and aides to both men. Starting when he became the Democratic nominee, Obama had received limited intelligence briefings. But as president-elect he was now being let in on the most sensitive secrets of all, the CIA's covert action programs. Hayden led Obama through some of the CIA programs that he had repeatedly blasted on the campaign trail: secret detention and brutal interrogation for Al Qaeda suspects. Waterboarding and the harshest of the rest of the methods that had so stained the United States' reputation had been dropped, but the CIA program still officially existed. Hayden laid out its purpose and limits, trying once again to defend it: fewer than one hundred prisoners had passed through the secret black sites, he said; just one-third had been subjected to any kind of "enhanced" interrogation methods; and just three had been waterboarded. (Evidence would later surface that more than one hundred prisoners had been held at the black sites and that waterboarding had in fact been used on more than three prisoners.) Obama asked about the six "enhanced interrogation techniques" that were still authorized, and Hayden demonstrated them on David Shedd, a deputy to McConnell who played the captive terrorist: facial slap, belly slap, facial hold, attention grasp, dietary manipulation, and sleep deprivation. Obama's stony stare and lack of questions suggested what would soon become clear: he was already determined to shut the program down. But Biden, more loquacious, engaged in some dueling with Hayden, asserting that the CIA's rendition program had deliberately sent prisoners to other countries "to be roughed up," a charge Hayden denied.

The atmosphere was tense, as might have been expected given Obama's unsparing language on the campaign trail about the CIA program and how it had violated American values. And there was another, more personal complication. Obama had let supporters know that he intended to nominate John Brennan, a CIA veteran who had been listed as a campaign adviser but had first met the president only after the election, to replace Hayden as CIA director. Hayden was distressed; he had wanted to keep the job, in part as a signal that the intelligence agencies were not part of the partisan political spoils system. But Brennan had come under attack from liberal bloggers and human rights advocates who believed that, as a senior CIA official in the early years of the Bush administration, he bore responsibility for torture. Brennan insisted that the interrogation program had not been part of his job and that he had opposed the brutal methods. But in late November he would withdraw from consideration for the CIA job. At the time of the briefing, Obama's intentions for the job were uncertain.

When Hayden's briefing moved on to the drone program in Pakistan, Obama's demeanor changed. He leaned forward, listened intently, and began to ask more questions. Hayden recounted how, a few months before, Bush had approved the CIA's proposal to radically step up the pace of strikes, when it became obvious that Pakistani authorities were tipping off some of the targets. Obama's questions were practical: he wanted to understand how this program identified its targets, sought to minimize civilian deaths, and measured the effects of the strikes. They were not hostile questions. It was a bit of a surprise to the intelligence officials: here, at least, was a CIA program that the new president did not hold in contempt.

To anyone who had pondered the entirety of Obama's 2002 "dumb war" speech, or read closely his endorsement of preemptive strikes against Al Qaeda in *The Audacity of Hope*, or understood Obama's Pakistan comments in the 2007 speech—to anyone who had correctly pegged Obama as a pragmatist, not an ideologue—his interest in the drone program might not have been a surprise. To the former law professor, there was a distinction that meant a great deal: torture was always illegal, under both domestic and international law, and even the Bush Justice Department had ultimately withdrawn the legal opinions approving waterboarding. By contrast, targeted killing by a government, under specified conditions, could be legal. But for the intelligence officials, as for most Americans, such nuances were drowned in an ocean of political rhetoric—from Obama's supporters, from his critics, and sometimes from Obama himself—that had created the impression that he was a liberal who would junk the whole Bush counterterrorism agenda.

When Hayden had finished explaining the "RDI" program—rendition, detention, and interrogation—Obama had told him curtly that Greg Craig, the incoming White House counsel, would be in touch. (A month later, Craig indeed would give Hayden advance notice of the first-day executive order ending the detention and interrogation program.) But when Hayden finished his briefing on the drone program, the CIA director said that it would continue to operate as described unless and until Obama directed otherwise.

The president-elect simply nodded.

PART THREE   2002–2009

8

THAT WAS THE TRANSFORMATION

Awlaki was in lecture mode, as he so often was in 2003. His wife and children were in Sanaa, and he had plenty of time to write and speak. He was offering a formal series of lectures in the basement of the East London Mosque and various other locations, occasionally on forays to other British cities. His renown in Britain's Muslim community was growing, and his flirtation with violence was becoming more obvious. His topic was, as usual, Islamic history: a fourteenth-century work by Ibn Nuhaas, who died fighting in Egypt, popularly known as the Book of Jihad. To speak publicly about jihad, even in Britain, where radical rhetoric was far more common than in the United States, was to play with dynamite, Awlaki knew. So he began with a disclaimer: "Now, I want to state in the beginning and make it very clear, that our study of this book is not an exhortation or an invitation to violence or promotion of violence against an individual, or a society or a state—this is purely an academic study. We are studying a book that is 600 years old. . . . It is purely an academic study of an old, traditional book."

And then he was off into twelve lectures totaling sixteen hours, exploring the nuances of jihad, which he called a "very important part" of *fiqh*, or Islamic jurisprudence. His young, male listeners stuck with him: these were stories of ancient Muslim heroes like Salamah Ibn al-Akwa, who could run faster than horses and whose exploits defending Islam were legendary. When confronted by four enemies of the Prophet Muhammad who had been sent to kill him, Ibn al-Akwa coolly told them, "I can kill any of you I like but none of you will be able to kill me," to which one of the frightened would-be attackers replied: "I think he is right!" (At this line, Awlaki's audience broke up in laughter.)

For young British Muslims, many of whom felt marginalized or alienated, Awlaki brought to life an exotic world of camels ridden into battle, of victory feasts around desert campfires, of miraculous powers for the soldiers of Allah, and of *jannah*, the paradise that would be the reward of those who died defending the faith. It was a world of black-and-white moral judgments in which the Prophet and his companions, like superheroes in a Hollywood movie, ultimately vanquished those who plotted against them. Many of Britain's most famous, or infamous, Muslim activists were screamers, drawing attention with their thundering denunciations of Western lifestyles, foreign interventions, and politicians. Awlaki's style was completely different. He spoke in a low-key, scholarly manner, but with warmth, humor, and color.

On their face, his stories were not so different from the David-versus-Goliath tales of the Old Testament, in which the heroic Israelites, with God on their side, routinely smote their enemies. But of course, two years after 9/11, in a world turned upside down by Al Qaeda's self-proclaimed jihad, Awlaki spoke in a charged political field. His very choice to spend sixteen hours talking about jihad's place in the turbulent early years of Islam, analyzing the motives for violence and the rewards for martyrdom, was a clear-eyed political statement. Sayyid Qutb, the Egyptian ideologue who had been so disturbed in the late 1940s by American women, was credited with rescuing the Book of Jihad from obscurity. Abdullah Azzam, the charismatic Palestinian leader of the anti-Soviet jihad in Afghanistan, whom Awlaki often quoted after his college visit there, was widely cited praising the book as a worthy guide.

Awlaki was using history as a kind of code, in which the heroic jihad of the past was used to teach and encourage the heroic jihad of the present, but in a way that would not get him in trouble with British authorities. Awlaki's disclaimer that his words were not an exhortation to violence, like so many disclaimers in the commercial world, was pro forma: a technical, legal requirement not meant to be taken especially seriously. In context, according to those who heard him speak at the time, his disclaimer seemed to be delivered with a wink:

You know I have to say this, but of course I don't mean it, because my lectures are absolutely an exhortation to violence against the enemies of Islam.

Certainly that was what many of those who listened to Awlaki's talks in Britain, following him from city to city, came to believe. Among the audience at one of Awlaki's lectures on the Book of Jihad in December 2003, it later turned out, were three of the four men who would later bomb three subway trains and a double-decker bus in London on July 7, 2005. The presence of the three future suicide bombers at the lecture in the town of Dudley, near Birmingham, would come to light because a counterterrorism informant working with British authorities was also in attendance. If Awlaki suspected he was being watched, he was right. Awlaki "was pretty clever in passing on his message," said Shahidur Rahman, a British-born Muslim activist and self-described militant of Bangladeshi ancestry, who became a devotee of the cleric in 2003 at the age of twenty. Years later, Rahman spoke about his first meeting with Awlaki with undiminished awe and affection. "It was during the time of the evening prayer. I was standing next to him and I was quite happy that Awlaki was standing next to me and he was smiling. I was very proud. . . . He was normal—he was so softly spoken and would sit with people." Rahman and several friends decided to attend Awlaki's December 2003 lecture series on Umar ibn al-Khattab, a beloved companion of the Prophet, about whom Muhammad said: "If there were to be another Prophet after me, it would have been Umar." Awlaki delivered the lectures in the white-walled basement of the East London Mosque, dressed in a white *thobe*, a long-sleeved traditional robe, and a modest but elegant turban.

With admiration, Rahman recalled what he perceived as Awlaki's double game: "He would talk about the life of Umar al-Khattab and at the same time talk about the surrounding issues. So it would hit the audience automatically in their hearts and minds." For example, Rahman said, "he would talk about the kuffar"—the pejorative term for non-Muslim, *kafir* singular, *kuffar* plural. "How could a kafir be your friend," Rahman remembered Awlaki asking, "if Allah says in the Koran that Allah doesn't like the unbelievers?" Indeed, Awlaki's comments about the *kuffar* in the Umar al-Khattab lectures have had a long life on the Internet, usually with the title "Never Ever Trust the Kuffar." After recounting a seventh-century story of betrayal and deception at the hands of a non-Muslim, Awlaki offered an extended twenty-first-century punch line for his young audience: "The important lesson to learn here is: Never, ever trust a *kuffar*. Do not trust them. Now, you might argue and say, 'But my neighbor is such a nice person. My classmates are very nice. My co-workers—they're just fabulous people, they're so decent and honest. And you know the only problem is that we Muslims are giving Islam a bad name. If these terrorists would just stop what they're doing. . . .'"

Not so, Awlaki explained. You can't judge the unbelievers on the basis of your non-Muslim friends and colleagues—"Joe Six Pack or Sally Soccer Mom," he called them, showing off his colloquial American English. They might well be "decent and nice people," he acknowledged, perhaps thinking of favorite American professors, or of non-Muslim neighbors like Lincoln Higgie, who lived across from the mosque in San Diego. But they, he said, are "not the ones pulling the strings." The Koran warns that the leaders of the *kuffar* are those with power, and they are not to be trusted, he explained.

Rahman said he and his friends learned from Awlaki that they could have only two possible relationships with a non-Muslim. "We can give him dawah"—that is, proselytize him to try to convert him to Islam—"or we fight jihad against them," Rahman said. "This is something that made sense to me at that time." It still made sense to him in 2010, when my colleague Souad Mekhennet managed a rare feat by getting Rahman and two of his friends to speak candidly, on the record, about their still-radical views.

Awlaki was instructing his young, British followers, who lived in a country that was more than 95 percent non-Muslim and a city (London) that was about 88 percent non-Muslim, that the vast majority of their compatriots could not share their values and could never truly be their friends or allies. Unless the unbelievers could be taught to accept Islam, the only religiously sanctioned option was to fight them. A more pernicious message in a modern, multicultural society could hardly be imagined, but Awlaki embedded it in quiet, engaging, humorous tales from the seventh century.

Rahman remembered with contempt the "so-called scholars" who would not give straight answers at that time when young men asked about the legitimacy of suicide bombings, or what he called "sacrifice operations," that they were seeing on news broadcasts from Iraq and elsewhere. "They would say, 'You know what? This is disputed, and we cannot talk about this.'" Sheikh Anwar, by contrast, "was not afraid," Rahman said. Using tales from the Koran to illustrate his points, Awlaki "said suicide is not allowed in Islam—but a self-sacrifice operation is different," his follower recalled. Awlaki was careful never to mention Osama bin Laden by name, Rahman said, but his intent was clear. "He would never mention Sheikh Osama, but we would know that he would speak about the mujahedeen and he would tell us, 'You know who the ulema are,'" referring to scholars with an authoritative interpretation of Islam.

Rahman marveled at Awlaki's ability to convey an incendiary ideology without getting into trouble with British authorities. "I was wondering at that time, how was it possible that the Sheikh could pass on such a message?" Rahman said. "How could he be in a moderate masjid," or mosque, "and say what he is saying, but at the same time do it in a way that he doesn't get caught?" In fact, in a Britain increasingly polarized over the threat of extremism, Awlaki did not draw anything like the opprobrium heaped on other, openly militant preachers who shouted from stages and outdoor platforms in London or Birmingham. But his influence may have been just as subversive as theirs, undercutting mainstream clerics' claims that Al Qaeda represented a distortion of Islam.

Just two years earlier, speaking in the *Washington Post*'s Ramadan video, Awlaki had protested the dark accusations being lodged against his faith: "I mean, Islam is a religion of peace." He had told his brother privately that the 9/11 attacks were "horrible." In San Diego, he had been a warm and generous neighbor to non-Muslims like Lincoln Higgie. In Virginia, after 9/11, he had joined priests and rabbis at interfaith gatherings, calling for peace and brotherhood. Now he was blithely lecturing on jihad and explaining to impressionable young men the fine distinctions between suicide and self-sacrifice. He was casually denigrating all non-Muslims as *kuffar*, worthy of only conversion or attack. What had happened?

Part of what had changed was Awlaki's setting. In America, said Ahmed Younis, the American Muslim activist who had heard him preach in the United States, "he had to appeal to Americanism." In the States Awlaki had often praised American freedoms and tolerance for minority religions like Islam. Surrounded by "Joe Six Pack and Sally Soccer Mom," he had criticized some American policies but found it difficult to vilify the United States without reservation, while speaking via the media to a broad American audience.

But on the Muslim lecture circuit in London, Birmingham, Essex, Leicester, Glasgow, and other cities where he appeared in 2002 and 2003, hostility to America was unrestrained. The difference, in part, was explained by demographics. Muslim immigrants to America had been cherry-picked by immigration authorities over the decades, and most were well educated and reasonably well integrated into the larger community. Muslim Americans approximately matched the American average in income and education. In the United Kingdom and the rest of Europe, the picture was quite different. Muslim immigrant families in Britain, most of whom had resettled under liberal rules from Pakistan, India, and other parts of the old British Empire, were a larger proportion of the population, and they often lived in more isolated ethnic communities. On average, they significantly lagged behind their non-Muslim neighbors in education and income. "The first time I went to London," said Younis, a well-educated native of California, "I thought I was in Karachi."

Awlaki's ambitious nature, in this new setting, found a new channel. In the United States, his ambition had found its most successful expression as the middleman between America and Islam, a position that had drawn huge and friendly media attention and led to his preaching at the US Capitol and speaking at the Pentagon. Now, in Britain, Awlaki discovered that his exclusively Muslim audiences were often looking not for bridge building but for a justification of their sense of grievance. If they felt the sting of discrimination and disdain from the British majority, Awlaki provided a scholarly explanation: the world was divided into Muslim believers and the *kuffar*, the unbelievers who were misguided at best, sinister at worst.

Awlaki rarely drew on his own experience in his talks, preferring the more detached pose of the scholar. But he had been at the hub of a Muslim community outside Washington under intense and hostile scrutiny after 9/11, and he knew the FBI had followed him on his secret sexual escapades. He had abandoned a promising PhD program and a flourishing career in the United States. There was a deeply personal side to his polarizing talk.

But another element in Awlaki's shift, unquestionably, was the United States' developing track record in response to 9/11. Awlaki's disillusionment can be traced through a series of articles he wrote in 2002 for the *Yemen Observer*, an English-language newspaper in Sanaa, at the invitation of its editor, Mohammed al-Asaadi. Addressing the international expatriates and educated Yemenis who were the *Observer*'s small audience, Awlaki tried his hand at more explicit criticism of American policies. His first article, in May 2002, criticized American support for Israel, including what he called "the Israeli-controlled US media," which he blamed for pressing Palestinian officials to condemn suicide bombings while giving Israel a pass. In July 2002, Awlaki wrote scathingly of the American war on terror, saying it had eroded civil liberties in the United States and given cover to the governments of India, Russia, and Israel for human rights abuses against Muslims. "The US has set an extremely dangerous precedent with its actions," he wrote. He questioned whether the American campaign had accomplished anything, noting that Bin Laden and other Al Qaeda leaders were still at large. "Americans are less secure than ever before," Awlaki wrote. He asserted that "thousands of innocent civilians have lost their lives" in Afghanistan and elsewhere, concluding with sarcasm: "The terrorizing of innocents everywhere has been the great success of America's War on Terror." The next month, in August 2002, he took on the escalating campaign of the Bush administration against Saddam Hussein's Iraq, declaring: "The US should not invade Iraq. . . . Simply, the US should leave the whole Middle East alone." Seven months later, American troops were in Baghdad, and Awlaki's lectures were becoming less restrained in their contempt for those he saw as the enemies of Islam.

Terrorist movements had often benefited from an overreaching response by the governments they targeted. Again and again through history, extremist violence had provoked an aroused government to go too far, engaging in brutal and sweeping actions, and thus inadvertently assisting the terrorists' recruiting efforts. By the spring of 2003, the United States seemed to be unthinkingly following that historical pattern. The extraordinary wave of sympathy for America as a victim of mass murder, which had extended even into much of the Muslim world, was gone. Shocking photographs of Muslim prisoners at Guantanamo Bay, Cuba, shackled in orange jumpsuits, had become one count in a growing indictment of American conduct shared by both Muslims and many non-Muslims in Europe and beyond. If the American invasion of Afghanistan had been predictable, perhaps even understandable, the invasion of Iraq in early 2003 was not.

Al Qaeda had based its declarations of war on America in 1996 and 1998 on a claim that the United States wanted to conquer Muslim lands. That claim, initially based on the small contingent of American troops in Saudi Arabia, had seemed implausible, even lunatic, when it was first proclaimed by Osama bin Laden. But now, with American troops patrolling the streets of Kabul and Baghdad, it began to make sense. The predictions of the extremists were coming true. By the fall of 2003, when it was clear that the Bush administration's assertions about Saddam Hussein's nuclear and biological weapons programs had been false, the notion that the United States' real motive must be control of the oil and lands of the Muslim Middle East gained credence. A young British Muslim might easily conclude that the United States, backed by the British and other allies, really was pursuing a global crusade against Islam.

Untying the tangle of factors—ideological and psychological, personal and political—that produce radicalization is never easy, but in Awlaki's case some of the threads can be made out in retrospect. His own sexual behavior, along with the scrutiny of the FBI, had helped send him fleeing from the United States, cutting short a promising public career as an American imam. He had found an encouraging audience for his most radical tendencies in Britain, and he enthusiastically played to his new audience. As an American imam, he routinely had to deal with the larger society, counseling Muslims with personal or financial troubles, speaking to non-Muslim audiences, encountering ministers and rabbis. But in the United Kingdom, his duties and circle of contacts dramatically narrowed. With no responsibility for a mosque, he was immersed in his lectures, puzzling out with other fundamentalist Salafis the lessons that early Islam could teach. To anyone who objected to his portrayal of believers and nonbelievers in constant conflict, Awlaki needed only to point to current events. Under George W. Bush, American had used bogus claims about weapons of mass destruction to send an army to the very heart of the Arab world; opened secret prisons where Al Qaeda suspects were tortured; and locked up a hodgepodge of Muslims at Guantanamo Bay, Cuba, for years without trial.

For Awlaki, the tales of the embattled early Muslims, and the least tolerant passages in the Koran and the hadith, now seemed to be not just historical artifacts but prescient guides to the present and future. The six-century-old Book of Jihad suddenly took on new relevance, and Awlaki was there to explain it.

Yet Awlaki's British acolytes, who saw a confident and charismatic leader, might have been surprised to learn that to his family and friends in Yemen he still seemed a bit at sea. In 2002 and 2003, he was commuting between London and Sanaa, and in Sanaa he was staying in his father's big house on upscale Rabat Street. His father and mother, along with Anwar's sisters, lived on the second floor. Anwar, with his family, and his brother Omar had separate apartments on the third floor. His youngest brother, Ammar, had an apartment on the fourth floor, only half of which was finished.

His father took some pride in Anwar's growing reputation among English-speaking Muslims as a preacher and lecturer, but he continued to believe his son needed a doctorate and a more conventional career. "I encouraged him to complete his PhD in Britain but he couldn't do that because of the high fees charged at British universities," Nasser recalled. With no doctorate, the plan from 2000 for Anwar to start a new department of technical education at the University of Sanaa was off. Recognizing that the lecture circuit in Britain would not offer an adequate living in the long run, Anwar experimented with ways he might make a living in Sanaa. Using his father's money, he invested in real estate, but he found the work didn't suit him, and, in a repeat of his experience with a gold and mineral scheme in San Diego, he lost the money. He discussed with friends and colleagues the possibility of getting his own religious television show in the Gulf, but no offers were forthcoming. He seriously considered opening a language school; Sanaa was a magnet for Westerners who wanted to learn Arabic, and there was no shortage of ambitious young Yemenis who wanted to improve their English. But Anwar never started the business.

The fact was that, despite his increasingly outspoken criticism of the West and vocal hostility to non-Muslims, he was dispirited by the corruption and inefficiency in Yemen and really would have preferred to settle in America or the United Kingdom, family members said. He had greatly enjoyed his time in the West, his father said, "working within the Muslim community with educated people from other Muslim countries, and with young people. I think he would have preferred to go back to Britain or the United States once the situation for Muslims after September 11 became less difficult."

There is a surprising piece of evidence to support this conclusion: Awlaki had gotten in touch with the FBI to explore the possibility of a return to the United States. In the autumn of 2003, Awlaki called one of the FBI counterterrorism agents who had interviewed him after 9/11, Icey Jenkins, a veteran who had served in Saudi Arabia and headed the bureau's investigation of the 1996 Khobar Towers bombing, which killed nineteen US servicemen. He left a telephone message on her voicemail, saying, "This is Anwar, you interviewed me after 9/11," leaving his e-mail address, and asking to talk to her. She was astonished to hear from him and was working on other matters, so she passed the message to Wade Ammerman, the Awlaki specialist in the FBI's Washington office, who followed up by e-mail and phone. Ammerman told 9/11 Commission investigators on October 16, 2003, that he believed Awlaki "may want to return to the US." In an e-mail Awlaki sent to the FBI on October 27, 2003, he complained about reports in the media and the 9/11 Commission that he had been a "spiritual adviser" to two hijackers, which he considered a gross distortion of his passing contacts with men who had worshipped in his mosque. "I am amazed at how absurd the media could be and I hope that the US authorities know better and realize that what was mentioned about me was nothing but lies," he wrote. But Awlaki had also read that the FBI was reportedly looking for him, and while he said he had nothing new to add to his previous interviews, he did say he was "around and available" and could meet with agents in England or Yemen. After a slow round of calls and e-mails, Awlaki and Ammerman made a plan to meet in London in March 2004. But Awlaki evidently got cold feet about a meeting or simply got busy with other things. When Ammerman tried to finalize arrangements in late 2003, Awlaki did not reply, and by January 2004 his Yahoo e-mail address was no longer working.

The truncated exchange pointed to yet another alternate path for the Awlaki story. Had the FBI seized the initiative quickly to clarify his legal position—told him he faced no charges but should tone down his rhetoric—he might conceivably have returned to the United States. He could have resumed his old job at Dar Al-Hijrah, picked up where he had left off in his PhD program at George Washington University, and restarted his career as middleman between America and Islam. But the FBI was evidently quite satisfied to keep a suspicious but not prosecutable character at a distance, and the bureau seems to have made no effort to get back in touch after the e-mails began to bounce. Nor did the 9/11 Commission, which in late 2003 and early 2004 repeatedly sought help from the FBI in trying to set up a meeting with Awlaki, ever succeed in talking to him.

Of course, even if the FBI had assured him that it did not plan to charge him, the prostitution file would have hung over his head like a sword of Damocles. Apart from that, he may have worried that circumstantial evidence—his contacts with the 9/11 hijackers and other known militants—might be used against him to build a case on the vague charge of "material support" for terrorism. It was not an idle fear. By mid-2003, after all, his sometime rival in Falls Church, Ali al-Timimi, whose appeal to young people had prompted Dar Al-Hijrah to hire Awlaki and who had since made several joint appearances with Awlaki in Britain, was expecting indictment. Timimi ultimately would be charged, convicted, and sentenced to life in prison for encouraging his young followers to fight US troops in Afghanistan, a sentence that shocked many civil libertarians.

In fact, in Britain, too, despite its greater tolerance for public militancy, Awlaki began to feel the government was watching him. At some point in 2004 he was banned from returning to the country, according to British news reports. "I think the UK police, Scotland Yard, were looking for him and he had to leave the UK," said Mohammed al-Asaadi, the *Yemen Observer* editor who had published his critiques of US foreign policy. "He was afraid they would take him easily and give him to the Americans—that's why he left."

When Awlaki settled permanently in Yemen, some of his friends and relatives believed the government should give him a good job. He had an excellent education, spoke fluent English, was personable, and came from a powerful tribe, they argued. Why not put him to work? Both his father and his uncle tried to help, but to no avail.

Why, exactly, he had trouble getting a job is uncertain. It may be that the appeal of preaching meant that his heart was not in the search. He may have been picky, given his views of government corruption. Potential bosses may have been intimidated by Anwar's American education or wary of his religious inclinations.

Whatever the reasons, Awlaki was quite conscious of being left behind as his friends and former classmates from the elite Azal Modern School—among them Ahmed Ali Saleh, the son of Yemen's president—moved up the ladder in ministries, the Yemeni military, and private companies. "I mean, to see his classmates as high-ranking officers, and he was more highly educated than others, and he's in the streets," said his uncle, Saleh bin Fareed al-Awlaki, whose view captured the sense of entitlement of the aristocracy in a poor country. "I am sure that if he got a chance—if he had been given a post like his colleagues, I'm sure he would have been happy." Awlaki seems to have confided his frustrations and disappointed hopes to his uncle. "He was always talking that he spent his time to be educated, and he was sad about his future." When he decided to move permanently to Sanaa, Bin Fareed said, Anwar had imagined, "'I will come, I will get a chance to work or do my duty for my country. But I have never been given a chance.' He was so sad that his education was ignored." Remarkably, Anwar sometimes spoke of a return to the United States as a sort of backup plan; his relatives didn't know the FBI backstory that probably would have dissuaded him from such a move. "He would always say, 'Thank God I'm an American citizen and I have a second home to go back to, if things go wrong in Yemen,'" his uncle said.

In retrospect, the law of unintended consequences may have been at work. American and British suspicions toward Awlaki, of which Yemeni authorities were quite aware, may have helped thwart any plan on the government's part to steer this son of a former minister and university official into a prominent post. With other options foreclosed, Awlaki pursued his religious vocation with new energy. Since he had been essentially self-taught, with no formal Islamic education, there was plenty of room to improve his credentials.

At Sanaa's Iman University, whose conservative Salafi curriculum drew devout young men from many countries, he gave a series of lectures on Islam in medieval Spain, a fascination of his since age thirteen, when his family had toured Spain on the way to the Stanford computer course. The university's founder, the prominent Yemeni cleric Abdul Majeed al-Zindani, invited him to take any courses that he wished, and he made regular visits to the hilly, rough-hewn campus in the northern part of Sanaa. He visited Saudi Arabia and spent time with a controversial cleric and erstwhile critic of the Saudi monarchy, Salman al-Awda, who had been imprisoned for five years in the 1990s. He moved to the town of Hodeidah on Yemen's west coast, where the university had a college of shariah, or Islamic law, for three months of study. And he closeted himself for hours, preparing and recording new lecture series on CDs—a successful business, but one his father said brought him less than $20,000 a year.

Ammar al-Awlaki, who was living at home for most of 2003 and 2004 as his older brother traveled back and forth to London, recalls that Anwar was engrossed in his religious work. He worked in a book-filled office in the family home and was "always busy," which Ammar, as the admiring younger brother, found a little frustrating. "He was full throttle at the time—doing his sermons, translating books," preparing English versions of classic Islamic texts so that he could record them. If Anwar accepted an invitation to the home of friends or relatives, "he would stay like fifteen or twenty minutes and he wants to leave. We'd have lunch with family members, relatives, we'd have a big feast and he'd be the first one to leave, to go back to his office or have an appointment."

Looking back at that period in his brother's life, Ammar saw it as critical: "That was the transformation period, I think. I sensed it. I didn't see it, but I started to sense it." Anwar was preoccupied with a political-theological debate that was boiling across the Muslim world about the Iraq War and that could be expressed in shorthand as jihad versus *fitna*. Was the fight against the Americans and their allies in Iraq jihad, a legitimate battle for Islam, obligatory for believers? Or was it *fitna*, pointless discord in which no side was in the right?

More broadly, this was a debate about the place of the United States in the cosmology of Islamic belief. Anwar, who a few years before had praised American freedoms and spoken of bridging the gap between the United States and a billion Muslims, spoke explicitly of how his views were changing. "I remember him saying, 'You know, in 2001 I had a clear stance. But now I'm debating it,'" Ammar said. In mid-2003, he recalled, the brothers sat in Anwar's home office and mused about the changing world. Ammar reminded his older brother of the days when he had preached about the distinctive role of Muslim Americans, who had a foot in both worlds. But with the rise of the insurgency in Iraq in 2003, "Anwar was looking at it from an Islamic point of view—is it legal? Is it Islamic? Is it jihad, or is it *fitna*?" Anwar's teacher in Saudi Arabia, Salman al-Awda, had declared the insurgency *fitna*, but Anwar wasn't convinced. He knew that Awda had been imprisoned by the Saudi rulers and wondered whether the scholar was hedging his position to avoid more trouble.

The unavoidable discussion of America and Iraq strained Anwar's relationship with his father—or rather, Anwar censored himself to reduce the strain. When the report of the Congressional Joint Inquiry into 9/11 was released in July 2003, Awlaki's name was redacted, but there was little doubt as to the identity of the San Diego imam who "reportedly" had served as "spiritual adviser" to two hijackers. The congressional report noted the FBI's pushback against this description of Awlaki, saying the bureau asserted that "the imam was a 'spiritual leader' to many in the community." The *Washington Post* featured Awlaki in its advance story on the congressional report. The following year, in June of 2004, a story in *U.S. News & World Report* described Awlaki as a major mystery in the 9/11 story and publicly reported his prostitution arrests in San Diego for the first time. The magazine described (with some exaggeration) his "fiery anti-American rhetoric" while at US mosques and called him a "skirt-chasing mullah."

For Nasser al-Awlaki, with his deep fondness for America, the news reports that now linked his son to the atrocity of 9/11, however peripherally or unjustly, were excruciating. Anwar knew that his father had always seen mixing politics with religion as playing with fire. He steered clear of theological talk when his father was present.

Nasser, the practical man of science and progress, was critical of the American war in Iraq, but he couched his criticism in strictly political terms. "Everyone discussed it politically," Ammar said. For Anwar, however, the Iraq War was primarily a religious issue. He was intrigued by how the war should be judged according to shariah, or Islamic law, and which clerics had issued which fatwas, or religious rulings, regarding the fighting, Ammar said. While Anwar would happily discuss such matters with Ammar, he clammed up when his father was around, acutely aware that his religious analysis would only reopen the wound inflicted by his son's association in press reports with the attacks on America.

In September 2004, Ammar left for further study in Canada, convinced that however tactful Anwar might be around his parents, he was deeply alienated by the Iraq War and was fundamentally shifting his views. Ammar did not see his brother at that point as "fully transformed, as the Anwar that the rest of the world knew afterwards," he said. But, he added, "I believe, yes, 2004 is the turning point."

If there is a piece of work by Awlaki that marks that turning point, it is the five-hour set of lectures that he released in 2005, "Constants on the Path of Jihad." None of his works would prove as influential. J. M. Berger, one of the most insightful chroniclers of Awlaki, described "Constants" as "maybe the single most influential work of jihadist incitement in the English language," one that again and again would surface as a critical influence in terrorism plots. It occupies a place midway between the earnest Islamic history of Awlaki's early CDs and his open embrace of terrorism in later Internet messages for Al Qaeda in the Arabian Peninsula (AQAP).

Stylistically, "Constants" is indistinguishable from Awlaki's most innocuous CDs, and that may be the key to its impact. No histrionics signaled the shift. By 2005, many Muslims of various ages and ideological stripes knew his voice from his traditional sermons and his lectures on Islamic history; his boxed CD sets were in their glove compartments, and his calm storytelling made their commutes to work more tolerable. In other words, he was already in the door when his message grew more radical. His was a trusted voice with an evolving message, and the change resonated with many Muslims for whom the Iraq invasion and the excesses of the American campaign against terrorism had already planted seeds of doubt.

Like most of Awlaki's lecture series, "Constants" is not original work. It is Awlaki's loose English translation of a post-9/11 treatise by Yusef al-Ayeri, a Saudi associate of Bin Laden who had fought the Soviets in Afghanistan and went by the nom de guerre "Swift Sword." He helped found the Saudi branch of Al Qaeda, which would later become AQAP, argued in his writings that the Iraq invasion was a boon for jihad, and ran jihadi websites until May 2003, when he was killed by Saudi security forces. In his retelling, Awlaki trimmed some of the most obviously provocative details, including Ayeri's references to Osama bin Laden and Al Qaeda. Whether the omissions represented residual doubts about endorsing Al Qaeda's strategy or simply a wariness of provoking the authorities is uncertain. But his embrace of violent jihad was unequivocal. He ridiculed contemporary Muslims who condemned such attacks by saying, "There's nothing in Islam that allows using violence"—though he had himself expressed that view after 9/11. To say such a thing simply to get along with the *kuffar*, or unbelievers, he said, was "compromising your religion."

To Ayeri's dry text Awlaki brought his flair for storytelling. But he also sprinkled contemporary references through this mainly historical work, quoting Donald Rumsfeld, the American defense secretary, and *U.S. News & World Report*. He criticized the cowardice of Muslims who had enthusiastically supported the anti-Soviet jihad in Afghanistan but who did not show the same fervor for fighting the Americans there. In religious terms, both were legitimate jihad, he said; the "hypocrites" were simply terrified of the United States. Westerners tried to use language to strip violence of its Islamic meaning, he said. "Whenever you see the word *terrorist*, replace it with the word *mujahid*," Awlaki said. "Whenever you see the word *terrorism*, replace it with *jihad*. The only reason they're not using the words *mujahid* and *jihad* is those are words in the Koran—so you can't replace those." He lauded Sayyid Qutb, the Egyptian father of modern jihad who had been hanged in 1966 for plotting to assassinate Egypt's president, as a martyr who, he said, "wrote with ink and blood." He singled out for praise "martyrdom" attacks by Muslims who came from prosperous backgrounds, because "it completely destroys the theories of the *kuffar*" about such violence being motivated by suicidal despair, poverty, and oppression and "forces them to look at the true reason"—the defense of Islam.

The central message of Ayeri's work and Awlaki's lectures was that Islam, like any religion, had both constants and variables. The first and most important constant was that "jihad will continue until the Day of Judgment" and thus (as the other constants elaborated) did not depend on any specific leader or place. This was Ayeri's polemic against Muslim scholars who tried to set limits to jihad, suggesting that it might be suspended or dropped depending on the circumstances. The lectures also presaged Awlaki's later call for homegrown, individual attacks,

notably in *Inspire* magazine: by suggesting that jihad could not be limited by leaders or lands, he paved the way for the argument that devout
Muslims in the West should not wait for orders before carrying out
acts of jihad. Awlaki, channeling Ayeri, described jihad as the unceas-
ing duty of every Muslim. "Giving up on the banner of jihad is defeat.
What does the enemy want from us?" The enemy does not care about
prayer or reading the Koran, Awlaki said. "What they're asking from
us today is one thing specifically: Stop jihad. No more jihad. If we give
them what they want, then we have lost," he said. "Any Muslim today
who is not fighting *jihad fe sabilillah*," Arabic for "jihad for the sake of
Allah," "is supporting the enemy by giving him this victory for free."
Any Muslim today, Awlaki said. His message, by 2005, was getting
pretty hard to misunderstand.

Saeed Ali Obaid lived not far from the Awlaki family's Rabat Street
home. One night, unable to sleep, he rose at around 3 a.m. and
walked to the neighborhood mosque to pray. The mosque was closed,
but he called to the guard, who let him in. Inside, in the darkened
prayer hall, Anwar al-Awlaki was leading about one hundred young
men in prayer. Surprised, Obaid stepped into a corner and listened.
He heard nothing radical, he said, but the scene was striking to him
nonetheless. It suggested how large and organized Awlaki's following
had become and how careful he was to avoid too high a profile. "To
me it was a training camp," Obaid said. What Obaid saw as Awlaki's
American traits—his organization, punctuality, friendliness, skill at
conflict resolution—all added to his appeal, he said.

Early in 2006, a young Danish convert living in Sanaa was invited to the Awlaki home for a banquet. Morten Storm was a former
biker-gang enforcer who had grown tired of his violent friends and
discovered Islam in a public library, taken the name Murad Storm,
and embraced the militant Salafism of Awlaki. "I warmed to him
immediately," Storm wrote in his memoir, an invaluable eyewitness
account of Awlaki in his later years in Yemen. "He was urbane and
well-informed, with a scholarly air and an undeniable presence. He
exuded self-assurance without coming across as arrogant." At one
point in a pleasant evening, Awlaki's ten-year-old son, Abdulrahman, born in Denver, came to consult his father about his homework.
Storm remarked on the close bond between father and son and was

impressed that Abdulrahman helped amuse Storm's much younger son, despite the difference in their ages.

Awlaki seemed to be trying to "tap into a wider pool of radicals in the Yemeni capital and beyond," Storm wrote. Storm offered his own home in Sanaa for a weekly Islamic study circle at which Awlaki would teach a small, multinational group of devotees. "He loved being our mentor, seeing his every word absorbed," Storm recalled. "Sitting cross-legged on the floor with notes in front of him, poised and eloquent, he liked to show off his intellect and learning, peering occasionally over his glasses at us." But there were darker notes as well. Awlaki accused the FBI of leaking fabricated reports of his two arrests for soliciting prostitutes; in truth, the reports were not fabricated but documented in San Diego police records, and the FBI had kept secret his many visits to prostitutes in Washington, DC. "They did everything they could to humiliate me, to make me a laughing-stock among Muslims," Awlaki told Storm, by the Dane's account. One night Awlaki lingered after the rest of the study group had left Storm's house. "He fixed me with those dark eyes and said simply: '9/11 was justified,'" Storm recounted. If his account was accurate, Awlaki had traveled a long way since his bitter condemnation of 9/11 during the walk with his brother in New Mexico some four years earlier.

Being "blocked" in his pursuit of a more conventional career, his uncle said, Awlaki channeled all his ambition into the role of a teacher and leader of devout young people, which he had tried out in the United States and mastered in Britain. "Because he did not have a job, he had more time to move and preach here and there, and he was very, very popular, very influential," Bin Fareed said. If there had been fewer constraints on his message in Britain than in the United States, then in Yemen, a religiously conservative country with a long history of Islamic militancy, there was even greater acceptance of a worldview that portrayed Muslims as the victims of Western oppression and searched for contemporary answers in ancient religious doctrine. Mohammed al-Asaadi, the *Observer* editor, thought the interaction with young devotees may have pushed him toward extremism. "He found listening ears and open hearts for his speeches, sermons, and also his guidance," said Asaadi, who remembered seeing Awlaki driving around town in his SUV. "And wherever you find someone listening to you who would like to sacrifice his life for what you say, the natural human reaction would take it one step further."

While living in Sanaa in 2006, Awlaki stirred up family trouble by announcing that he was taking a second wife, a teenager whose brothers were among the cleric's dedicated fans, Nabil and Tareq al-Dahab, the militant sons of a prominent tribe in northwest Yemen. By one account, they offered their sister to Awlaki as a kind of tribute to their idol; in any case, his decision was not taken well by either his first wife or his own westernized family, for whom polygamy was a vestige of older times. Awlaki set up his new wife in a separate apartment in Sanaa. Later, in 2008, he would take a third wife, a devout Muslim woman who had arrived from New Zealand, though she evidently became disenchanted and left Anwar and Yemen after just four months of marriage. His behavior recalled the compulsive sexual appetite that had driven Awlaki to risky assignations with prostitutes. And taking additional wives was unquestionably a step away from his American upbringing, an embrace of old Islamic custom.

Yemeni authorities, under the eye of President Saleh, did pay close attention to what they were hearing about Awlaki from the American and British governments. Starting in 2003, as the Congressional Joint Inquiry and the 9/11 Commission examined the lingering mysteries involving the San Diego hijackers, the FBI came under criticism, privately and sometimes publicly, for failing to get to the bottom of Awlaki's role. As early as September 2003, the London-based Arabic daily *Al-Sharq al-Awsat* reported that the FBI office at the America embassy in Yemen was looking for Awlaki; of course, it would not have been hard to find him, either at his family's home or at well-publicized public appearances in Britain.

Yemeni authorities called Awlaki in for questioning on several occasions, and he suspected American pressure was responsible, according to Asaadi, the editor. "He was telling me, 'I'm not a person who would justify killing or who is in favor of killing—I am a Muslim. But the way they are harassing me, the way they are chasing me, the way they are liaising with the Yemeni authorities to detain me is something annoying, something disturbing,'" Asaadi said. "The more pressure he got from the authorities, the more radical he became." By 2005, eyewitnesses recall seeing surveillance cars regularly parked outside the Awlaki family home on Rabat Street. Once again Awlaki was being watched, and this time there was little effort at discretion. "I saw someone outside the house chewing qat in his taxi at 3 a.m.," said a former neighbor, speaking of the ubiquitous leaves chewed for their mild stimulant effect by most Yemenis. "I said, 'What the hell are you doing?' 'Chewing qat,' he said."

The FBI had staked out a position during the 9/11 investigations that Awlaki was neither a conspirator in the plot nor a significant threat—a position that, of course, helped them defend their failure both before and after 9/11 to fully probe his connections. The bureau formally closed its Awlaki investigation in May 2003 "for lack of evidence of a pattern of activity suggesting international terrorism." In July 2004, when the bureau got a tip of some kind on Awlaki (the exact nature of the tip is redacted from public documents), officials decided not to pursue it. "ANWAR AWLAKI is no longer in San Diego Division and is believed to be out of the country. No interview will be conducted."

But in January 2006, an FBI source reported that Awlaki had just crossed the border from Canada into Vermont, and the bureau's Washington Field Office opened a new investigation. It was a bogus tip, as agents soon discovered—Anwar was leading a busy life in Sanaa. Nonetheless, with his recording of "Constants on the Path of Jihad" making the Internet rounds and turning up in terrorism investigations, counterterrorism agents decided to keep the file open. The next month, concerns about the threat from Yemen were rekindled when at least twenty-three Al Qaeda operatives escaped from the Political Security Organization's maximum-security prison in Sanaa in a jailbreak widely suspected of having inside help. So in April 2006, the new case was transferred to the FBI's San Diego office, which had first looked into Awlaki in 1999–2000, and files covering both eavesdropping and surveillance on Awlaki were transferred there from Washington. Clearly, the bureau was worried about a cleric who was openly endorsing violent jihad and carrying a US passport.

Perhaps it was a coincidence. But eight months after the FBI reopened its investigation, Yemeni authorities made the unusual decision to act against this son of a prominent family. Awlaki was arrested in Sanaa, along with two other Yemenis, and imprisoned about three miles away from his family's house at the Political Security Organization's prison, where the 2006 jailbreak had occurred.

The prison was a sprawling complex just below the parched brown hills that seemed to merge without a clear boundary into the stone buildings of the capital. It occupied several city blocks, surrounded by barbed wire and guard towers, protected from suicide bombers with police roadblocks and tire shredders. Anwar's parents were horrified, and his father and uncle immediately began to lobby their government contacts, up to President Saleh, to get him released.

Nominally, at least, his arrest on August 31, 2006, resulted from his intervention in a tribal dispute over a kidnapping. Though the kidnapping case might appear to have been just a pretext for the authorities to get him off the streets, Awlaki's father confirmed that it was the real reason for his arrest, and Awlaki himself later told AQAP's media wing that he was taken into custody because of "a local accusation." News reports later linked Awlaki, under the pseudonym Abu Atiq, to a thwarted September 2006 Al Qaeda plot to attack oil installations in Marib and Hadramout provinces. Separately, Yemeni press reports linked the man called Abu Atiq to a group of eight foreigners who were arrested in October 2006 and accused of running guns to militants in Somalia. In his eighteen months of imprisonment, however, Awlaki was never charged with a crime, and it remains uncertain whether those accusations had any merit.

Whatever the real reason for his arrest, Yemeni authorities, with their usual wary eye on American counterterrorism dollars, soon consulted John D. Negroponte, the director of national intelligence. In effect, the Yemenis told Negroponte: We are holding an American citizen who has been linked to the 9/11 hijackers and whose name keeps surfacing in America. What do you want us to do with him? Negroponte told the Yemeni officials that the United States did not object to his detention, according to American and Yemeni officials.

Word soon got around among Muslim activists in the West. The British group Cageprisoners, founded by a British citizen formerly imprisoned at Guantanamo Bay, Moazzam Begg, sent out a notice that got wide circulation: "A respected scholar, Imam Anwar Al-Awlaki, has been arrested in Yemen. This deeply saddens many of us, especially those who have widely benefited from his lectures and courses on tapes and CDs, and during his visits to the UK." The appeal, urging a letter-writing campaign, said that Awlaki "may be subject to injustices and torture."

A legend would later arise that Awlaki was moderate in his views until he was arrested and physically tortured in the Sanaa prison. While torture in custody was not unusual in Yemen, Awlaki never publicly mentioned ill treatment. His father, who visited him in prison and heard his account afterward, said he was never beaten or physically tortured, quite possibly because of the prominence of his family. By Awlaki's own account, for more than sixteen months of his eighteen-month incarceration, he was kept in solitary confinement—a form of isolation that, while used in many American prisons, is considered by many human rights activists to be a form of psychological torture. During the second half of his imprisonment, authorities permitted weekly visits from his family. In any case, Awlaki's evolution to more and more radical views and his endorsement of violence clearly had begun long before his 2006 arrest.

Prison appears to have had a profound effect on him, in part because it allowed ample time for study and contemplation. In Awlaki's later account, in interviews and on the blog he started after his release, his incarceration became almost a blessing. This may have been self-dramatizing on his part, or a reluctance to give his captors the satisfaction of knowing they had made him suffer, but it has the ring of truth. Prison held the promise of transforming a thirty-five-year-old man who had, in fact, been a bit lost—the prostitutes, the failed business schemes, the pressure from family to be something other than an imam—into an authentic Islamic hero, a martyr suffering for his faith like many of the most famous figures in the history of the religion. The Prophet himself had been celebrated for his asceticism. Awlaki now seemed to relish his own physical deprivation.

If the move from Washington to London had narrowed his world mainly to like-thinking religious fundamentalists, now his world narrowed still further, quite literally. His first nine months in prison, he said later, were spent alone in a bare, eight-by-four-foot basement cell illuminated by a bare bulb hanging from the ceiling that was on twenty-four hours a day. He slept on a two- to three-inch-thick mattress on the floor and had a plate, a water bottle, and another bottle for urination, he said. He was allowed no visitors and no contact with other inmates, and he could speak to the guards "in whispers and only for urgent needs." But he was also given a Koran. "In this environment," he wrote on his blog after his release, "there is nothing to do and nothing to read but the Quran, and that is when the Quran reveals its secrets," when it "literally overwhelms the heart." He would "recite it with eagerness for hours" and "never lose my concentration." His recitation, he wrote, "would carry me outside of this world and I would completely forget about my situation until a warden would slam the door open for restroom time or to take me for interrogation."

The Koran alone did not occupy him entirely over the long days and nights. He requested Islamic books, but "a particularly mean Prison Head" turned him down. So he asked his family for English books. They were selected by his mother, Saleha, who had come from a humble tribal background (her husband once called her "a Bedouin from Shabwah," the Awlakis' territory in southern Yemen), had earned a high school equivalency certificate in the United States, and had ultimately received a degree in English literature from Sanaa University, to the lasting pride of Nasser al-Awlaki and the entire family. She chose novels by Charles Dickens and Thomas Hardy, which held considerable appeal for Anwar, and plays by Shakespeare, which decidedly did not ("Shakespeare was the worst thing I read during my entire stay in prison"). At Anwar's request, Nasser included the copy of *Moby-Dick* that an American colleague had given him in the United States when Anwar was six, saying that he should read it when he was older. He was not especially impressed with Herman Melville's epic but remarked, "In jail, anything is good," even the Yemeni government newspapers he usually scorned.

In recounting his reading, Awlaki provided a disclaimer in keeping with his conservative Salafi principles: "Now, I want to stress that I do not encourage any serious Muslim brother or sister to waste time with novels." He suggested, not especially convincingly, that his real reason for reading the English literature was to refresh his language skills. And he made exceptions for Orwell's *Animal Farm* and *1984*, which he thought offered insight into "how the West is treating Muslims today," and for David Attenborough's *Life on Air*, a memoir by the British naturalist and broadcaster. In an aside that is a reminder of the kinship between fundamentalist Muslims and fundamentalist Christians, Awlaki added: "I was disappointed to find out that such a person, one who has firsthand knowledge and experience with some of the most amazing signs of Allah, is a person who believes in evolution and shows no signs of believing in a creator."

Awlaki eventually got access to Islamic books, despite the initial ban, and immersed himself in them. He pored over the works of Ibn Taymiyyah, a deeply conservative Islamic scholar who even in the fourteenth century had called for Islam to return to its authentic roots. He had been imprisoned for his views and died in prison, perhaps lending his story greater resonance for the imprisoned Awlaki. But apart from the Koran, the books that won his most outspoken praise were those of Sayyid Qutb, the Egyptian leader of the Muslim Brotherhood whose imprisonment in 1966, followed by his execution, again gave Awlaki a tacit connection. Qutb, whose ruminations on the fleshly temptations of American life were so memorable, wrote massive books that included his detailed thirty-volume commentary on the Koran and his blistering critiques of modern Muslim states, whose leaders he believed should be overthrown to make way for genuinely Islamic rule. "Because of the flowing style of Sayyid I would read between 100–150 pages a day," Awlaki wrote. "In fact I would read until my eyes got tired," eventually covering his weaker left eye and continuing with his right eye until it "just shut down." Awlaki was swept away by Qutb, widely considered the father of modern radical Islamism. "I would be so immersed with the author I would feel that Sayyid was with me in my cell speaking to me directly," he wrote. "So even though I was in solitary confinement I was never alone." The young American imam, once known for his friendly and outgoing approach to his diverse congregations and to his neighbors, now was closeted with a single intellectual companion, one who had preached a bitter and exclusive faith.

By the testimony of a somewhat worshipful Al Qaeda member who knew Awlaki and was imprisoned at the same time, he projected calm and dignity, as if to show that the machinations of his enemies could not disturb his sense of spiritual contentment. The fellow prisoner, Harith al-Nadari, described his friend as even "more steadfast" than before his arrest, showing no "distress or boredom." "He was the same man I knew from before. A man with a kind smile," Nadari recounted, a "tranquil self that is confident in Allah and His decree." Other prisoners backed down from their radical views in order to earn better treatment, Nadari wrote later. "He refused to soften his position when others did through taking the excuse of being under coercion," and thus the prison authorities left him in solitary confinement.

Even allowing for exaggeration by the admiring Nadari, the portrait of Awlaki's self-conscious cultivation of the image of a principled religious leader with unshakable convictions is quite convincing. He had long lectured on the Salaf, the ancestors, and now, it seemed, he was emulating the great figures from the days of the Prophet. "In the seclusion room, he divided his time between worship and reading," Nadari recalled. "That allowed him to sail in a sea of folders of *Tafseer* and jurisprudence, fatwa and history"—in other words, commentary on the Koran; writings on Islamic law; Islamic rulings; and the early history of Islam that he had taught for so long.

As Awlaki reveled in his uninterrupted reading time, his father and uncle lobbied feverishly for his release from prison. They made an extraordinary team: the former agriculture minister, who had been appointed by President Saleh, and the wealthy businessman and tribal leader. Both had been distressed by what they saw as Anwar's drift into radicalism and his failure to find success in a secular career, but they knew of nothing he had done to justify his arrest. They met multiple times with President Saleh and his intelligence director, General Ghaleb al-Qamish, who assured them—with whatever degree of sincerity—that Anwar was imprisoned without charges only because of unbearable pressure from the Americans. Their repeated access to the president and his powerful security chief, who had been in office together for nearly three decades, attested to the clout and reputation of the family. At different times, they spoke also with the Saudi Prince Bandar bin Sultan, who had served as ambassador to the United States until 2005, and Abdulwahab al-Hajjri, Yemen's ambassador to Washington for many years. But for months Yemeni officials were polite but unmoved.

"At the beginning they said, 'Oh, we want to keep him for a while and then we will tell you,'" Bin Fareed said. "They never gave us any reason at the beginning, but they said, 'You can be sure he's in a safe place, a nice place.'" When Bin Fareed went to see Qamish, the general assured him "we have nothing against him at all" and flattered the uncle by praising the nephew, whom he portrayed as a brilliant thinker and teacher. "We sit with him, we talked and we thought we would change his thinking, what he believes," Bin Fareed recalled Qamish telling him. "And we do not find anything wrong with this young man except he's a religious leader. And instead of us educating him, he was educating us. And we became very influenced by him." Still, Qamish directed him to President Saleh for an explanation of why he could not be released. The president told Bin Fareed, "'Be cool, don't worry, don't be angry. He's our son, the same as he's your son, and he's well looked after.'" Eventually, after months of this run-around, Qamish acknowledged that he had a thick file of correspondence with American officials about Awlaki and that they insisted he stay in prison. Qamish said Yemeni officials had repeatedly asked the United States for solid evidence against Awlaki supporting his involvement in terrorism or other crimes "so we can take him to the court. And they kept telling us tomorrow, after tomorrow—but till today they have not given us anything, not even a single paper."

The US-Yemeni correspondence remains classified, and it is hard to be certain how serious the demand from Washington was to keep Awlaki locked up after Negroponte's initial green light. Yemeni authorities had, of course, kept Awlaki under surveillance long before his arrest, and American pressure was a handy excuse for the Saleh administration in many instances. But the American track record for brushing aside concerns about rights and erring on the side of security was well established by 2006. Believing that the United States was the problem, Nasser al-Awlaki persuaded his son to talk to two FBI agents, who visited for two days in mid-2007, about a year after his arrest. They asked him mainly about the 9/11 hijackers, according to his father, evidently trying to complete the investigation that the 9/11 Commission had felt was superficial and inconclusive. Certainly at this point there is no evidence that US officials had any basis to charge Awlaki with a crime. He was talking about jihad, but that was not illegal. It was unlikely that they had more evidence than the Yemenis on his involvement in the alleged oil attacks or Somali arms shipments—if he was, in fact, involved. And Yemeni authorities had not charged him.

By Awlaki's account, his exchanges with the visiting FBI agents were testy but largely respectful. He later boasted to Harith al-Nadari, his fellow prisoner, that he had taken charge of the interview, acting the role of the sheikh. "He entered the office . . . like a boss," Nadari recounted later. "He chose to sit on the most appropriate seat, ate from the fruits prepared by the Yemenis to host the Americans and poured

Snapshot of Anwar al-Awlaki, thirteen (right), with his father, Nasser, at Yosemite National Park during the family's summer trip to the United States, 1984. COURTESY OF THE AWLAKI FAMILY

Nasser al-Awlaki, Anwar's father, who studied and taught in the United States and served as Yemen's agriculture minister and university chancellor, at home in Sanaa, 2015. HAMED SANABANI

Imam Anwar al-Awlaki with one of his children, Abdullah, at a dinner during Ramadan, 2001, in Washington. A *Washington Post* video featured Awlaki explaining the holy month. VIDEO BY TRAVIS FOX

Anwar al-Awlaki at Dar al-Hijrah outside Washington with neighbor Patricia Morris, who organized a candlelight vigil to support worshippers at his mosque after 9/11.

TRACY A. WOODWARD/*WASHINGTON POST*

After the 9/11 attacks, Awlaki, shown here preaching in a PBS news report, drew national media attention as an eloquent imam who condemned 9/11 and could explain Islam.

An FBI surveillance photo of Awlaki on his way to a prostitute in Washington, February 2002. When he learned what the FBI knew about his regular visits, he fled the United States, saying it could "destroy" him.

FBI agent's notes on an interview with a prostitute about Awlaki's visit, January 2002. She called him "sweet."

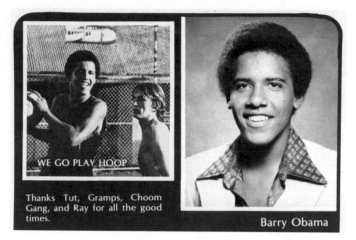

WE GO PLAY HOOP

Thanks Tut, Gramps, Choom Gang, and Ray for all the good times.

Barry Obama

Obama in his high school yearbook at Punahou School, Hawaii, 1979. He wrote later of the temptation of radicalism, the possibility that he might withdraw "into a smaller and smaller coil of rage. . . . Should you refuse this defeat and lash out at your captors, they would have a name for that too, a name that could cage you pretty good. Paranoid. Militant. Violent. Nigger." PUNAHOU SCHOOL

Obama campaigning in Seattle, 2007. His vow that year to attack terrorists inside Pakistan if necessary drew scorn from rivals. Few realized that he was thinking of drones. ALLISON HARGER/FLICKR

The MQ-1 Predator: the Bush and Obama administrations came to rely on the armed drone to kill suspected terrorists in Pakistan and Yemen. Proponents said it was the most precise way to eliminate terrorists, but poor intelligence repeatedly led to civilian deaths. US AIR FORCE

Morten Storm, a Danish biker-gang member who embraced radical Islam, traveled to Yemen and in 2006 became part of a study circle under Anwar al-Awlaki. He later grew disillusioned and became an agent inside Al Qaeda in Yemen for the CIA and Danish and British intelligence. COURTESY OF MORTEN STORM

Yemen's stunning capital, Sanaa, where Anwar lived at his father's house and then was imprisoned for eighteen months in 2006–2007. He left the capital in 2008 and soon joined Al Qaeda. FRANCO PECCHIO/FLICKR

A video released by Al Qaeda in the Arabian Peninsula (AQAP) in 2014 showed (l to r) Awlaki, Umar Farouk Abdulmutallab, and Nasir al-Wuhayshi, the head of the group, together before Abdulmutallab's attempted airliner bombing.

Take not the Jews and the Christians for your allies and protectors.

After the Christmas 2009 airliner attack over Detroit, AQAP released a video that included this excerpt from the martyrdom message recorded in advance by the would-be bomber, Umar Farouk Abdulmutallab, twenty-three. He told the FBI that Awlaki had helped direct the plot, prompting Obama to add Awlaki to the kill list.

I would like to forward my message to the American people, also to the Muslims in the west in general and particularly in America

By March 2010, when he recorded this video, Awlaki was openly calling for killing Americans, including civilians. He dressed in military garb, with the Al Qaeda flag and the ceremonial dagger of Yemeni tribesmen in his belt.

Among others influenced by Awlaki's calls for violent jihad from 2009 to 2015 were (top row, left to right) Nidal Hasan, who killed thirteen people at Fort Hood; Zachary Chesser, a blogger who wanted to fight in Somalia; Roshonara Choudhry, who stabbed a member of the British Parliament; Tamerlan and Dzhokhar Tsarnaev, the Boston Marathon bombers; and (bottom row) Said and Cherif Kouachi, who killed twelve people in Paris at *Charlie Hebdo*.

Starting in 2010, Awlaki and his American protégé, Samir Khan (right), often posed with weapons in Al Qaeda propaganda.

Awlaki and Khan put out *Inspire*, a quirky magazine that both urged attacks and offered instructions on how to carry them out.

Obama relied on his counterterrorism adviser, John Brennan, who became a close and trusted aide, to manage drone strikes. PETE SOUZA/WHITE HOUSE

Obama announced Awlaki's killing, without explicitly saying he had ordered it, on September 30, 2011, at a retirement ceremony for the chairman of the Joint Chiefs of Staff, Adm. Mike Mullen, at Fort Myer, Virginia.

Obama discussed his decision to target Awlaki in a May 2013 speech. But he never mentioned the drone strike two weeks later that killed Denver-born Abdulrahman al-Awlaki, sixteen, who had left his grandfather's house in Sanaa to find his father. He was killed along with a teenage cousin; the strike was aimed at an Al Qaeda operative who was not there. COURTESY OF AWLAKI FAMILY

In the years since he and his son were killed, Awlaki's influence has only grown, as his sermons on Islamic history and calls for attacks have proliferated on YouTube and other Internet forums. Admirers have posted many tributes to him, including this Al Qaeda video, which calls him "the martyr of *dawaah,*" or Islamic teaching.

a cup of tea for himself." Awlaki told Nadari that the FBI agents were determined "to find any tiny violation that would permit them to prosecute him back in an American court. It was an interrogation, he said. Nevertheless, they didn't find what they were searching after and they returned frustrated." In an account he gave to a British supporter shortly after his release, Awlaki spoke somewhat mysteriously of the prison interview with the FBI. "There was some pressure, which I refused to accept, and that led to a conflict that occurred between me and them, because I felt that it was improper behavior from their behalf," Awlaki recounted. "That was solved, however, later on, and they apologized." It is conceivable that the agents pressured Awlaki to inform on Americans or Yemenis suspected of militancy and that he rejected the request. But whatever was said, it did not lead to Awlaki's release or to criminal charges. The limbo continued.

Inside the Bush administration there was an intermittent debate about Awlaki's fate, and some officials, including the FBI director, Robert Mueller, expressed uneasiness that an American citizen was being incarcerated indefinitely without charges and with American connivance. Some American officials believe a green light eventually came from Washington for Awlaki's release. But by the account of Awlaki's father and uncle, the release occurred shortly after they met again with President Saleh at the president's Aden residence. Bin Fareed told Saleh, "If you have any evidence against him, you take him to the court and we will never ever object." In fact, he said, "If anything proves that he's got anything to do with anything, with terrorism, we don't mind if you execute him the next day. Or, as he's a US citizen, if the United States has anything to prove against him, we don't mind if you deport him and send him to the States to court." According to Bin Fareed, President Saleh laughed and said again that he had repeatedly pressed the Americans for any evidence against Awlaki. After promising and then failing to deliver such evidence, the president said, the Americans gave him a more candid account of their concern. Saleh said the American officials' real worry was that Awlaki was "a very well known personality and very influential religious man in the United States" and that "when he gives a speech, thousands and thousands of people will listen to him." In view of that potent influence, Saleh said, the Americans told him that "we think that it will be good for him and good for us and

Yemen to keep him in jail—in prison—for a few years until people forget about him."

Again, it is impossible to say for sure whether any American official actually made such a statement or whether it was a product of President Saleh's fertile imagination. But Bin Fareed said that he and Nasser al-Awlaki did believe that Anwar was a pawn in a game Saleh was playing with American authorities, whom the Yemeni president ceaselessly courted for counterterrorism aid. So they pressed Saleh, suggesting that he should not knuckle under to the American pressure, and eventually Saleh suggested that Anwar might be released if someone would guarantee that he would stay out of trouble. At first Saleh proposed that Bin Fareed give the guarantee himself. But then he realized that he would have a hard time pressuring a tribal leader if things went wrong and asked that they arrange for such a guarantee from a Yemeni businessman instead. Before they could recruit a businessman, however, the mercurial president changed his mind again. "He said, 'Don't worry, I will allow him out without anyone signing for him, because I take your word and I have nothing against Anwar.'" He was indeed released after a week or so in mid-December.

Word reached Washington on December 19, 2007, that an American citizen, whose government had connived in his imprisonment without charges, was free: "AmCit Terror Suspect Released from Yemeni Custody," the cable from the American embassy in Sanaa announced. By then, American officials, evidently worried that Awlaki might try to return to the United States, were already at work on a criminal case against him. Heavily redacted e-mail exchanges released by the FBI do not make clear the nature of the charges under consideration; the statute of limitations on any prostitution charge would probably have expired, and charging Awlaki for his generic and historical praise for jihad seemed like a stretch. But a criminal complaint of some sort was drafted, apparently with a double purpose: deterring Awlaki's return to the United States and, if he did return, giving authorities at least a chance to arrest and question him. "It would buy us a couple of weeks and HQ wants to pursue it as an option," wrote one counterterrorism agent. The agent said Yemeni authorities had been asked to inform Awlaki that if he returned to the United States he "faces potential criminal exposure." In the end, however, the plan was dropped. On December 31, an FBI official wrote to colleagues: "I think that collectively we have decided not to go forward with a criminal case. First this is an extremely weak criminal case. Second, we are not inclined to bring charges against someone with the whole plan that we would dismiss the case if and when he was arrested." It was at least the third time federal law enforcement officials had considered charging Awlaki with a crime, following the floating of prostitution and then passport fraud cases in 2002. Each time they had decided not to proceed.

Well read and well rested, and with no plans to travel to the United States, Awlaki resumed his habitual frenzy of activity. Morten Storm, his Danish acolyte, saw him a week after his release and found him pale and thin, hardened in his views and paranoid about spies. Less than two weeks after his release, on December 31, 2007, the day the FBI was giving up on the idea of charging him, Awlaki gave a long-distance interview to an enthralled Moazzam Begg, the founder of Cageprisoners, which had lobbied for his release. A British Muslim activist who had been held for three years by the United States in Afghanistan and at Guantanamo Bay, Begg sought in his questions to draw a parallel between his imprisonment and Awlaki's, and they agreed on the comfort of the Koran while behind bars.

By February of 2008, Awlaki had registered a website, www.anwar-alawlaki.com. On May 31, 2008, he thanked the unnamed "brothers who are behind the idea of this website" and who set it up for him. He reveled in the new reach it gave him, exceeding even the tens of thousands of CDs he had sold. "In the old times it used to take a few days to travel, for example, from Makkah," or Mecca, "to Medina which are only 450km apart. Now we can communicate all over the globe within seconds; text, audio and video, all within seconds. So I would like to tell all of the brothers out there whom I personally know and whom I spent memorable time with: Assalamu alaykum and insha Allah I will never forget you. And to those whom I grew to know through these modern means of communication but the circumstances have separated me from meeting them, nevertheless, I still feel a bond with them and I love them for the sake of Allah because they have chosen to follow Islam."

A few days later an American fan wrote: "Imam Anwar, Do you

plan on coming back to VA to visit your old community? Or to attend conventions in the US?" Awlaki answered: "I do not intend at the moment on visiting the US. So please convey my salaams to my brothers and sisters in VA." He began to post some of the lectures that had made his reputation, comment on current events on his blog, and hear from admirers via his "Contact the Sheikh" page. In June he wrote the first of many posts telling the story of his imprisonment and his reading while incarcerated.

Theo Padnos, the American writer who spent months among the questing young Muslims who had come to Yemen from all over the world, described the powerful effect of prison on Awlaki's appeal. "This prison spell was a gift from Allah, and bound Awlaki much more tightly to his fans," Padnos explained. "The battle he now fought purified his soul, and opened up to him the mysteries of the sacred writings. His ordeal, as several of his fans pointed out on the website, never threatened his faith in God; it brought him inner strength. This is the experience of which these young Muslims in the West dream. To have had it is the truest Islamic credential in today's world."

But even as Awlaki was reaching out to his fans with new authority, Yemeni security officials would not leave him alone. "After he was allowed out, from the first minute he was out, he told me several times, 'I do not feel safe and I am not free,'" said Bin Fareed, who had done so much to get him out of prison. Anwar told him, "They count my breathing, and wherever I go, two people will always follow me. If I go to the mosque, they are right and left of me. If I jump in a taxi, they will be following me in another car. If I go to eat in a restaurant or if I have a cup of tea in a coffee shop, they will be around me. If I go and see a friend they will be following me." Fed up with the scrutiny—and possibly with other motives as well—Awlaki decided to leave the capital and move south to his family's tribal territory of Shabwah province. First he moved to the provincial capital, Al Ataq. Then he moved to his grandfather's empty house in the family's village, Al Saeed, a mud-brick hamlet of about one hundred people. By the account of his uncle, who had a big house in the village and saw him regularly, Anwar split his time between his new home and the village mosque, where he preached, led prayers, and became a sort of problem-solving authority. "He'd sit most of his time in the mosque. People would ask him questions—people would have family problems, children problems, and they would ask him, and he would advise them what to do," Bin Fareed said. Somehow, from this backwater, he managed to get Internet access, and he kept posting on his blog every week or two, often taking a militant stance.

But his new, wild setting did not please the authorities. General Qamish, the intelligence chief, once again summoned Bin Fareed to tell him that "the Americans" wanted Anwar back in Sanaa, or, failing that, in another city—Aden or Mukalla on Yemen's south coast. The motive was not entirely clear, but it seemed American officials were loath to see Awlaki go too far off the grid. If he was not in a city, he might be impossible to keep under physical surveillance, and he would be likely to send fewer e-mails and make fewer calls, conceivably escaping even the long electronic reach of the NSA, especially in Shabwah, where Al Qaeda had a foothold. Bin Fareed demurred, telling Qamish that if Awlaki was a dangerous influence it was better to keep him in Al Saeed, a tiny village where he was surrounded by relatives. "So I think it's the right place for you, for him, for the Americans, and for us," Bin Fareed said he told Qamish. "It's far away from everything." But Qamish insisted, and Bin Fareed dutifully made the five-hour drive from Aden to the village and told Anwar about the request.

Anwar was polite and repeated his thanks for his uncle's help in getting him out of prison. But he refused to leave. "No way will I accept to move my place, and I will live here," Anwar said, according to his uncle. Bin Fareed sweetened the request with an offer to let Anwar live with him in his seaside villa in Aden—a far cry from his primitive village life. It did no good. "No, I don't like it," Anwar told his uncle. "Please allow me to live here."

Even as he became the most prominent radical imam on the web, showing his mastery of the new tools of blogging, Facebook, and YouTube, Awlaki had retreated into the protection and isolation of one of the oldest forms of social organization: the tribe. The twenty-first-century American-born preacher, multilingual, multinational, and technically savvy, was now in the village where his great-great-grandfather had built a fortress, where his forebears had struggled for generations, and where tribal traditions held more sway than government or law.

9

WWW JIHAD

One day in December 2005, a group of young Canadians stood in a snowy Ontario field around a laptop, transfixed by Awlaki's calm voice reciting "Constants on the Path of Jihad." Six months later, the Toronto 18 were arrested and accused of plotting a sensational, if implausible, series of attacks, including storming Canada's parliament and beheading the prime minister.

In March 2007, Albanian immigrant brothers in New Jersey were caught on tape exclaiming about Awlaki's brilliance in explaining the obligation to defend Islam. "You gotta hear this lecture," said an excited Shain Duka, as an informant's hidden microphone recorded the conversation.

"They kicked him out of the US, and now they locked him up in Yemen," said his brother, Dritan Duka. "He was talking about jihad—the truth, no holds barred, straight how it is." Two months later, the brothers were charged with plotting to attack Fort Dix.

If in the years after he retreated from Washington and London to Yemen Awlaki seemed to some of his family to be frustrated and adrift, a ballooning number of fans formed a different impression. Here was a Muslim cleric who had the Arabic knowledge and the American confidence to pronounce uncomfortable, even dangerous truths. Here was a smart, young English speaker unafraid to follow the Koran and the hadith wherever they led. Awlaki's PhD plans may have been thwarted and his schemes involving real estate deals and language schools may have failed. But his online fans didn't know or care about that. His Islamic teaching was kindling volatile emotions across the English-speaking world. It is worth stepping back to consider what powered his popularity. Why was Awlaki, in the cacophony of voices competing for the attention of young Muslims, so successful in winning their loyalty and, in some cases, moving them to action?

The web matured to provide the tools Awlaki needed just in time to help him reach English-speaking Muslims with his exciting and enraging call: Your faith is under attack, and it is your duty to fight back. In 1998, Awlaki's brother was selling cassettes of his early, unobjectionable sermons on the sidewalk in San Diego, a decidedly analog effort. Later, after leaving the United States, Awlaki spoke of trying to get his own television show on one of the big Gulf broadcasters. That didn't happen. But as the Internet matured he was quick to exploit its possibilities. He mastered the voice and video messaging service Paltalk to lecture to big virtual audiences, with his lectures announced in advance on Islamic websites. His lectures began to spread effortlessly across the web and around the world, fans passing them to their friends and posting them on site after site. In 2005, the year he recorded one of his greatest hits, "Constants on the Path of Jihad," three young PayPal employees were developing YouTube, which would soon become the platform that would give Awlaki's message its greatest reach. "He appreciated the power of the Internet, and more than other jihadi scholars, opened up himself for online dialogue with young Muslims—men and women—as he encouraged them to submit questions and to contact him through email," said Rita Katz, founder of the SITE Intelligence Group in Washington, which monitors militant web activity.

The Internet seemed especially suited to the propagation of contentious messages that, in an earlier era, would never have made it into a newspaper or onto radio or television. In the privacy of their homes, young Muslims in the United States, Canada, and Britain were increasingly taking to their computers to satisfy their curiosity about the radical strains of Islam that seemed to terrify their governments. "Extremists are more and more making extensive use of the internet," Britain's Home Office said in a report delivered to Parliament on the July 7, 2005, bombings of London's subway and buses. "Websites are difficult to monitor and trace; they can be established anywhere and have global reach; they are anonymous, cheap and instantaneous; and it requires no special expertise to set up a website."

Historians of terrorism have often found that personal contact is critical in pushing a young man (and it is still, almost always, a man) across the boundary from simply fantasizing about an attack to plotting one. Often enough, in the terrorism cases the FBI brought in the years after 9/11, the personal contact came in the form of a well-paid bureau informant who hung around a mosque enthusiastically advocating violence, a pattern that drew legitimate criticism of the bureau's counterterrorism tactics. But long before they met the provocative informant, the would-be jihadis had usually spent many hours alone on the web, marinating in the endless debates about the obligations of Islam, the Western assault on the faithful, and the heroic deeds of young men daring to fight back, documented in stirring videos. In the menacing world of the online call to jihad, the figure that loomed steadily larger in the view of both the radicalized young men and their enemies in police and intelligence agencies was Anwar al-Awlaki.

As Awlaki became notorious, there was recurring confusion about the nature and timing of his influence. By 2003, boxed CD sets of Awlaki's lectures on the life of the Prophet Muhammad and the lives of the other prophets of Islam, his stirring tales of the early heroes of the religion, were in tens of thousands of homes and cars of Muslims in the United States, the United Kingdom, and Canada. Those recordings suggested an allegiance to the conservative Salafi school of Islam, whose devotion to the early followers of Muhammad implied a critical view of modern and secular life. But the early Awlaki did not yet fall into the small minority of Salafi believers who advocated violent jihad to return the world to the supposed ideal state of the seventh century, the Salafi-jihadis as they were sometimes called. By no stretch of the imagination could those CD collections alone have motivated anyone to commit an act of violence. To believe that listening to Awlaki's early CDs caused terrorism would be as egregious as concluding that listening to gospel records caused people to attack abortion clinics because most clinic bombers owned gospel records.

This distinction between the early and later Awlaki was sometimes overlooked. In later years, when investigators found Awlaki's material amid the CDs and notebooks and thumb drives and laptops scooped up in a counterterrorism search, his name came to be a kind of explanation: *So that's why they came up with this crazy plot—they had been listening to Awlaki.* That was an oversimplification. "If you were a second generation Muslim living in Britain from the late-90s onward and were interested in your religion, Awlaki would be among your favorite scholars," said Alexander Melagrou-Hitchens, an expert on Islamic militancy in Britain and author of several insightful papers on Awlaki. "Pretty much every Muslim I know here listened to Awlaki back in the day—so having his stuff and listening to it was by no means a remarkable or strange thing to be doing and certainly didn't mean that one was a jihadist."

As a careful tracking of his work shows, Awlaki evolved steadily from 2002 on toward an open scorn for non-Muslims and an endorsement of violent jihad. In some of his lectures in Britain in 2003 and 2004, and certainly by 2005, with "Constants," Awlaki's message had become overtly approving of violence, openly hostile to those he called *kuffar*, and dismissive of less martial interpretations of Islam. The significance of his early CDs is not that they encouraged terrorism; they did not. But the early recordings established his mainstream popularity, creating a more receptive audience for his later, militant message. Having established his reputation as a sober and scholarly preacher, he was more likely to get a hearing from his fans when he turned up the heat in his lectures and sermons. For that reason, Awlaki's former fellow imam at Dar Al-Hijrah in Virginia, Johari Abdul Malik, began to warn young people away even from Awlaki's most innocuous early recordings, calling the CDs "gateway drugs." By the time the Toronto 18 and the Fort Dix plotters were extolling Awlaki's call to jihad, it seems fair to draw a line from his words to their deeds.

There was still uncertainty about what was cause and what was effect: Did a disaffected young man discover Awlaki's incendiary material because he had already embraced militant Islam and was eagerly Googling "jihad" on the web? Or were Awlaki's lectures denouncing the *kuffar* and lionizing the mujahideen—and the connections he made between gripping tales of early Islam and the plight of Muslims today—actually radicalizing people? By 2007, that question was being debated in the cubicles and conference rooms of the CIA, the National Counterterrorism Center, and the State Department. And at the FBI, which was casting a broad net in hopes of picking up anyone in the United States who was even considering the virtues of violent jihad, the ubiquity of Awlaki and his prolific, steadily more radical lectures became impossible to miss.

By 2008, said Philip Mudd, then a top FBI counterterrorism official, Awlaki "was cropping up as a radicalizer not in just a few investigations, but in what seemed to be every investigation." Mudd had worked in the CIA for years before being recruited by the rival FBI in 2005, just as Awlaki's name began to be mentioned in government's inner circles. Mudd said that Awlaki had become a formidable opponent, calling him a "magnetic character" and a "powerful orator in a revolutionary movement." An April 2008 FBI memo referred to Awlaki as "a known Al Qaeda facilitator and operative," though any intelligence supporting that label is redacted from the public version. In October 2008, Charlie Allen, the CIA veteran who had pushed for early drone strikes, then serving as the intelligence chief at the Department of Homeland Security, denounced Awlaki in a public speech: "Another example of Al Qaeda reach into the homeland is US citizen, Al Qaeda supporter, and former spiritual leader to three of the September 11th hijackers, Anwar al-Awlaki, who targets US Muslims with radical online lectures encouraging terrorist attacks from his new home in Yemen." Allen's comment marked the first time a government official had gone public with the growing worry about Awlaki's influence.

In late 2001, Awlaki had aspired to be, along with other Muslim Americans, a bridge between the West and Islam. Now he was becoming a bridge of a different kind, carrying his admirers along on the same journey he himself was making, from a conservative, but essentially accommodationist, mainstream Islam to its radical, intolerant, and violent offshoot. Instead of explaining Islam to the West and the West to a billion Muslims worldwide, as he had once spoken of doing, he was instructing Muslims that the West was an irreconcilable enemy of the faith and that violence might well be the only legitimate response.

In a much-debated 2007 report, the New York City Police Department's intelligence division had tried to break down the radicalization process for Western Muslims to a series of four predictable stages. Some civil libertarians objected to the whole emphasis on rad-icalization, which they thought shifted dangerously away from vio-lent acts to extreme ideas. The vast majority of people who embraced radical ideas never did anything illegal, they pointed out. Viewing religiosity as a step toward terrorism was just to invite the pointless profiling of Muslims.

But with the opposite goal, Al Qaeda itself showed this same de-sire to break down the inchoate evolution of militants into easy-to-understand steps. In early 2009, the group posted on the web its own guide to radicalization, called "A Course in the Art of Recruitment," describing five stages that bore a rough resemblance to the NYPD's. The police department and the terror network were both driven to try to find the hidden secrets that turned someone into a terrorist.

Without being so systematic about it, Awlaki had devised a par-ticularly potent formula for captivating and motivating young people. Part of his effectiveness was his mastery of both the Arabic sacred texts and of the English in which his main audience lived their lives. Part was his warm and disarmingly informal style of speaking. Part was his skill in negotiating, with the help of more technically expert advisers, the shifting communications technology between 2001 and 2008, moving from audio cassette, to CD, to Paltalk, to his own in-teractive website and blog, and finally to Facebook and YouTube.

But those were just the medium. Underlying his success were two fundamental human drives: first, the motivating power of religion; and second, the universal quest of the young, young men especially, for identity, companionship, and adventure in pursuit of a cause. Like Osama bin Laden in the Arab world and charismatic radicals in other Muslim subcultures—or European Christians who went to fight in the Crusades—Awlaki in his English-speaking sphere tapped those two deep wellsprings of human action and combined them into a single, intoxicating message.

In a courageous comment on the 9/11 attacks, a Roman Catho-lic priest who had witnessed the assault on the World Trade Center paid grim tribute to the staggering force of religious faith. Monsignor Lorenzo Albacete, a theologian and physicist, was asked by the PBS show *Frontline* a few months after the attacks for his initial reaction on that day and gave an arresting answer:

From the first moment I looked into that horror on Sept. 11, into that fireball, into that explosion of horror, I knew it. I knew it before anything was said about those who did it or why. I recognized an old companion. I recognized religion. Look, I am a priest for over 30 years. Religion is my life, it's my vocation, it's my existence. I'd give my life for it; I hope to have the courage. Therefore, I know it.

And I know, and recognized that day, that the same force, energy, sense, instinct, whatever, passion—because religion can be a passion—the same passion that motivates religious people to do great things is the same one that that day brought all that destruction. When they said that the people who did it did it in the name of God, I wasn't the slightest bit surprised. It only confirmed what I knew.

Albacete's candor about what he called "this thirst, this demand for the absolute," has stayed with me for more than a decade. He elevated the bitter and bewildered initial debate about the atrocities of 9/11 to a higher, more abstract plane, where the universal force of any religion to sanctify extreme violence was clear. The instinct in the West to identify Islam as the source of terrorism is understandable but provincial; it mistakes this moment in history, with its temporary array of economic and political forces, as permanent. The larger point is that religion gives life meaning for the faithful. Measured against the imperatives of faith, the killing of one or one hundred or ten thousand people is a trifle—a minor sacrifice compared to the awesome goal for which the killers imagine they are committing such slaughter.

The sociologist Mark Juergensmeyer published *Terror in the Mind of God: The Global Rise of Religious Violence* in 2000—and revised it after 9/11, which came along the following year as if to prove his point. "Within the histories of religious traditions—from biblical wars to crusading ventures and great acts of martyrdom," Juergensmeyer argued, "violence has lurked as a shadowy presence. It has colored religion's darker, more mysterious symbols. Images of death have never been far from the heart of religion's power to stir the imagination." His analysis seems particularly apt for explaining Awlaki's routine use of the glorious violence of the Islamic past to justify violence in the Islamic present. Juergensmeyer may fail fully to explain the slaughter motivated by modern, nominally secular ideologies such as those constructed by Hitler and Stalin—but in their utopian promises and absolutist claims, Nazism and Soviet communism clearly functioned as state religions. The point is that there must be a cause of great majesty, offering a vision of future paradise, to persuade people to commit terrible acts of violence. For someone trying to fathom Al Qaeda's gruesome crimes, it is instructive to step back and consider the mass murders committed through the ages in the name of Christianity, Hinduism, Buddhism, and innumerable smaller sects. To recall the beheadings, the burnings at the stake, the sectarian bombings, and the pogroms of fanatics of other faiths and other eras is not to rationalize grievous violence committed in the name of Islam but to try to understand its source.

But if Awlaki, like other contemporary advocates of violent jihad, exploited the unbridled passion of religion, he also aimed his appeal at the young men who were most exploitable. The same search for identity by affiliation with a group and a cause that helps recruit young men to Al Qaeda also sends them, depending on the country and the era, to urban gangs, tribal militias, and military service. The drive to become part of a larger movement, with rules, goals, and charismatic leaders, motivates some to join the Marines, others to join the Crips or the Latin Kings, and still others to join Hamas. Sometimes, though not always, the group is united by a collective focus on a single, dehumanized enemy.

Over the years, as a journalist covering terrorism, I have struggled to comprehend what seemed incomprehensible: the worldview that not only justified but celebrated the slaughter of innocent human beings with no connection to religious or ideological conflict. I have found it instructive to consider the role of the military in the culture and values of the United States. With pride as well as trepidation, American parents send their sons and daughters off to war to fight in far-off countries. Americans speak of the military's mission as sacred, even when it entails mass killing. American soldiers fight for their nation, and when they die for their nation they are reflexively celebrated as heroes, even if the purpose and legitimacy of the war (as in Vietnam or Iraq) are the subject of furious debate at home. To question their sacrifice is considered unpatriotic—indeed, blasphemous.

Substitute *ummah,* the community of believers in Islam, for *nation,* and the worldview of an Awlaki becomes much clearer. For Muslims who have taken a critical step and concluded that their loyalty to fellow Muslims must come before their loyalty to fellow citizens, the notion of fighting to protect the *ummah* takes the place of fighting to protect the nation. As a marine considers defending the United States of America to be his duty, so a young Muslim jihadi sees defending Islam and the community of believers as his duty. And if the jihadi believes the United States is at war with Islam, then killing the Americans who are fighting that war, and even the American civilians who are funding the war, suddenly becomes not monstrous but legitimate, even noble.

This is not to suggest a moral equivalence between state warfare and stateless terrorism. In the distorting mirror of Awlaki's definition of jihad, for instance, American civilians automatically became enemies whose murder was justified and indeed celebrated. During the Iraq War, while American soldiers killed thousands upon thousands of civilians, their deliberate slaughter was officially prohibited and in some cases was prosecuted as a crime. That is a distinction of huge value and significance. The point is that within the framework of any ideology or religion brutal violence can take on the presumption not only of justice but of heroism. It can be a potent lure to a young man looking for camaraderie and a cause.

A wlaki's lectures offered escape from the aimlessness, pettiness, and frustration of many young lives and admission to a world of seeming moral clarity, a noble cause under assault from powerful enemies. He aroused his listeners by admitting them to a club of sorts: the comforting brotherhood of brave young men who were running grave risks for their faith and looking out for one another, and who saw themselves as the righteous heirs of courageous ancestors who had stood up for Islam over many centuries. The power of his achievement is captured by the comments on Awlaki's blog, which for its eighteen months of active operation, from May 2008 to November 2009, became an Internet clubhouse for earnest, aspiring defenders of Islam. Especially striking is the worshipful attitude that Awlaki seemed to inspire in those who wrote in, including a reader named Ibraheim: "May Allah keep Anwar and all of us on the straight path and know brother Anwar that I love you for the sake of Allah and it would be a dream of mine to meet you in person one day and learn from you!"

Will McCants, a Princeton-trained scholar who was closely tracking the online jihadi world in 2008, was struck by the central position that Awlaki occupied. "The sun in that solar system was Awlaki," McCants said. "All the others linked to him."

In January 2009, when Awlaki posted a piece very much in the spirit of the web—what would later be dubbed a "listicle"—called "44 Ways of Supporting Jihad," it drew 737 comments in ten days. Most of them expressed gratitude for the imam's advice. Awlaki placed violence at the center of jihad but offered an expansive set of options for the eager but inexperienced to get involved: supporting the mujahideen, the fighters, with money; helping the family of a *shaheed*, or martyr, or the family of a prisoner; "Fighting the lies of the Western Media"; or engaging in "physical fitness" and "arms training," presumably as a step toward joining the actual fight. At No. 29 on the long list was "WWW Jihad," an area in which Awlaki himself now was setting the example. "The internet has become a great medium for spreading the call of Jihad and following the news of the mujahideen," he wrote.

It is not hard to picture the Muslim teens and twenty-somethings reading this latest missive from Awlaki in basements or bedrooms in Muslim neighborhoods in Dearborn, Michigan, or Toronto's Thorncliffe Park, or East London, where the challenges of Muslim communities might connect with his vision of embattled Islam. Here, on the web, away from the sharp eyes of their parents or wary local imams, they could engage in fantasies about their own roles or ask questions about their doubts and concerns. In the erratically spelled comments on Awlaki's "44 Ways," among the usual juvenile high jinks ("lol maybe you should open your own blog just learn english first") and earnest requests ("Ya sheikh can you please download the video lecture you gave at the East London Mesjid here on the website . . . all of us our dieing to hear it inshallah"), there are darker posts. A British reader calling himself Abu Maryam begins with hero worship:

Shaykh, That was an awesome document tackling questions about Jihad from almost every angle. Already your name sprawls all over google, muslim sites around the globe wait eagerly for you to publish your articles so that they can convey the truth to the masses. Here in the UK you've got a massive following of youth that are questioning the islam that they have been brought up upon against the Islam they see before them conveyed through teachings from yourself and other pious scholars on the right path.

Abu Maryam apologizes to "the brothers and sisters here for taking up space more than necessary" as he reaches out for counsel to Awlaki and to others reading the blog. He has immersed himself, he explains, in reading the likes of Ibn Taymmiyah, the fourteenth-century scholar whose work enthralled Awlaki in prison. As a "next step" Abu Maryam is wondering how to reach certain Saudi sheikhs he believes have the right ideas "so as to strictly stay away from the innovations practiced by friends and family." ("Innovations" in Salafi terminology are a negative: heretical departures from the ways and teachings of the Prophet Muhammad and his early followers.) He is "frustrated" by the "flurry of articles" he's seen on the Internet from Saudi scholars who claim that "there is no justification of Jihad in places like Iraq or Gaza in current times." If radicalization is a path, Abu Maryam is clearly on it: "I am struggling to understand how if Jihad is valid in its physical form, how can it be carried out without inflicting physical casualties on surrounding innocents against the saudi fatawas [rulings by religious authorities] that say that suicide bombings and martyrdom operations killing innocents are *haram* [forbidden]. Please can you clarify for me, I don't have a great deal of understanding."

For every young Western Muslim who crossed the line and began plotting violence or traveled to Yemen or Pakistan to join Al Qaeda, there were hundreds or thousands more like Abu Maryam, intrigued by the battle with the supposed enemies of Islam but too fearful or ambivalent to act. By sweeping huge numbers of people into that recruiting pool, Awlaki added new recruits to the small minority who would take the next step and join the battle. Again and again, his devotees turned up in criminal cases.

Among the avid readers of Awlaki's blog was a Virginian named Zachary Chesser, who signed his comments on the blog "Zakariya" and styled himself Abu Talhal al-Amreeki in his other prolific online posts. Never was there a clearer case of a young man in a frantic search for an identity. As a teenager, Chesser got deeply into heavy metal music, notably the shock-rock act Marilyn Manson, reveling in satanic lyrics. His senior year at suburban Oakton High School, twenty minutes from Awlaki's former mosque and only a little farther from CIA headquarters, he was written up in the yearbook as "the only Caucasian member of the school's break-dancing club" (the others were mostly Korean Americans). "I loved it so much that my parents would threaten to make me quit the club if I didn't get good enough grades," he was quoted as saying. Plus, he said, it was a good way to meet girls.

But by the time the yearbook was out, break dancing was passé: Chesser had met a Muslim girl, had converted to Islam, and was scaring fellow members of the school's Muslim Student Association with warnings that they were headed for hell if they didn't dress more modestly. The girl broke up with him, but he quickly met and married another young Muslim woman, briefly attended George Mason University, and turned his huge capacity for enthusiasm to what Awlaki had dubbed "WWW Jihad." He created a YouTube channel under the name LearnTeachFightDie, which he alarmingly described as the proper stages of a true believer's life. His online rants drew the first visit from a concerned FBI agent in June 2009, just a year after his high school graduation.

Predictably, by then, Chesser had become a fervent fan of Awlaki, including recorded talks on CD called "Dreams and Dream Interpretations." Chesser began e-mailing the imam, in part to ask his help in interpreting a dream in which he had turned up in Somalia to fight with al-Shabab, the Islamist insurgency there. Awlaki wrote back twice, to the delight of Chesser, who also posted an account of his dream as a comment on Awlaki's blog. By December 2009, he had started his own forum, themujahidblog.com, posting one article called "Open Source Jihad"—a term that Awlaki would later borrow for how-to articles in his own *Inspire* magazine. Soon Chesser was helping run a better-known radical site, RevolutionMuslim.com.

He even pursued an online argument with Jarret Brachman, a well-known American terrorism analyst whose criticism of Awlaki had offended Chesser. Brachman wrote later that the two became "what you might call hostile friends, sparring over a wide array of topics."

Reading back over Chesser's early antics, one is tempted to smile at his callow superenthusiasm for whatever happened to catch his fancy. It is easy to imagine such a kid straightening out by sopho-more or junior year in college and channeling the same frenetic en-ergy into business or biochemistry. In Chesser's case, that would not happen. In April 2010, Chesser posted at RevolutionMuslim.com an ominous warning to the makers of *South Park*, the irreverent ani-mated show that had once been his favorite, because an episode had included a caricature of the Prophet Muhammad dressed in a bear suit. Chesser wrote that the show's creators, Trey Parker and Matt Stone, "will probably end up" like Theo van Gogh, the Dutch film-maker murdered by a Muslim extremist in 2004 after making a film critical of Islam. Along with the statement, Chesser posted a photo of Van Gogh's corpse and audio clips from Awlaki's lecture "The Dust Will Never Settle Down," in which Awlaki argued that "our enemies have successfully desensitized us" and that the reaction to cartoons portraying the Prophet and other insults to Islam had not drawn an adequate response. "Horrendous things happened! Blasphemy to the greatest extent! But what is the reaction? Very little!" said Awlaki, who contrasted this passivity with the early Muslims' resort to the sword to avenge offenses against the Prophet. Chesser's menacing statement made the news and led to a final rift with his parents.

Finally, on July 10, 2010, Chesser was stopped at JFK Interna-tional Airport in New York, where he was trying to board a plane on his way to Somalia to fight with al-Shabab. He was informed that he was on the no-fly list and, questioned about his online posts about Awlaki, told a Secret Service agent at the airport that he "did not necessarily disagree with Awlaki." He was arrested eleven days later and was eventually sentenced to twenty-five years in prison for "ma-terial support" to al-Shabab, threatening Parker and Stone, and other crimes. Chesser was twenty-one. Just over two years had passed be-tween his introduction to Islam and his terrorism arrest. In court, he expressed remorse and suggested that he was puzzled by his own swift passage. In a written statement, he said he was "ashamed and

bewildered. . . . I know that I will spend many years trying to understand why I followed the path that has led me here."

I f counterterrorism officials viewed Awlaki as a critical contributor
to Chesser's transformation, it was not just because of the smitten
young man's own online testimony to his hero. It was because, as the
FBI's Philip Mudd said, they were seeing the phenomenon again and
again. By the time Chesser pleaded guilty in October 2010, the collection of characters charged with plotting or carrying out violent attacks
and claiming the influence of Awlaki was extraordinarily diverse.

There was Najibullah Zazi, the Afghan immigrant who was arrested in September 2009 at age twenty-four for plotting to blow up
the New York subway, and who explained later that he had had little
interest in Islam until he and his two codefendants listened to more
than one hundred hours of lectures by Awlaki and a militant British cleric. A former fry cook and Muslim convert in his late twenties, Michael C. Finton, tried to blow up the Federal Building in
Springfield, Illinois, later that month; his MySpace page featured a
quotation from Awlaki about his imprisonment in Yemen. There was
Roshonara Choudhry, a British university dropout—and a rare case
of a woman committing this sort of crime—convicted of stabbing
a member of Parliament, Stephen Timms, in East London in May
2010. She said she had listened obsessively to more than one hundred hours of Awlaki's sermons before deciding that Timms should
be punished for voting in favor of the Iraq War.

There was Paul G. Rockwood Jr., thirty-five, a Muslim convert
who became an Awlaki devotee and began to make lists of Americans he believed should be murdered as enemies of Islam; he got
eight years for making false statements to the FBI. There were Mohamed Mahmood Alessa and Carlos Eduardo Almonte, New Jersey
men arrested at JFK in June 2010 on their way to join al-Shabab.
They had played Awlaki tapes for an undercover informant. A Texas
man, Barry Bujol, twenty-nine, was arrested the same month as he
tried to leave the country and join Al Qaeda in the Arabian Peninsula
(AQAP) in Yemen; he had exchanged e-mails with Awlaki, who sent
him a copy of "44 Ways of Supporting Jihad."

Were Awlaki's lectures critical in turning all these fans into
would-be killers? Or had they sought out Awlaki's material because

they were already committed to violent jihad? In all of the cases, it was a dance of radicalization in which Awlaki was a central figure but by no means the only influence. Such nuances went largely unexamined at the time; media reports and Justice Department press releases duly took note each time Awlaki turned up in an investigation. But whether he was cause or effect or both, Awlaki by 2010 was a celebrity unequaled in the counterterrorism universe by anyone other than Bin Laden.

And in the view of some Americans who tracked terrorism, the threat he posed had eclipsed even Bin Laden, whose Al Qaeda associates in Pakistan were being steadily knocked off by Obama's drone strikes. As the core of the terror network shrank, AQAP—the only Al Qaeda affiliate that was operationally focused on attacking the United States—was clearly on the rise. At a Washington conference in April 2010, Representative Jane Harman, a Democrat with years of experience overseeing the intelligence and counterterrorism agencies, declared that "terrorist number one in terms of a threat against us is an imam named al-Awlaki." At a New York Police Department briefing, an intelligence analyst called him simply "the most dangerous man in the world."

The two men who had done the most to elevate Awlaki to that exalted, if hyperbolic, status were Nidal Hasan, who had shot up Fort Hood in November 2009, and Umar Farouk Abdulmutallab, who had flubbed the airliner attack over Detroit the following month. Despite their differences in age (Hasan was thirty-nine, Abdulmutallab just twenty-three), geography, and ethnicity, their psychological kinship was striking. Both were lost and lonely souls who, despite what on paper looked like considerable accomplishments, were desperately searching for meaning in their lives. Both were preoccupied with finding a worthy mate and struggled to balance sexual attraction with the strictures of their conservative brand of Islam. Both had heard Awlaki in person and had followed his work online as true believers. For both men, Awlaki was not a passing influence but a guide who became, over the course of several years, the center of their ideological universe, with grave consequences. He was indeed their bridge to extremism, and it is quite plausible, if unprovable, that without him they would not have made the journey.

And there was one more parallel: the American counterterrorism juggernaut got worrisome information on both men before their attacks, lost track of it, dug it out when it was too late, and made it the centerpiece of later recriminations and investigations into what had gone wrong.

Major Hasan, the army psychiatrist, had attended Friday prayers at Dar Al-Hijrah when Awlaki was preaching there; his mother's funeral was held at the mosque in May 2001. Frustrated by his failure to find a wife, distressed by the deaths of his parents, he had become steadily more religious. Sitting alone at night in his apartment, he had discovered Awlaki's new online life as his more radical works began to circulate on the web in 2005. He kept tracking the cleric in 2006–7, as his authenticity was reinforced by his imprisonment, which was diligently chronicled by his online supporters. Hasan was still watching in 2008, when Awlaki launched his own website and blog, offering a virtual mosque where his followers could gather, hear from him, and debate among themselves. For Hasan, Awlaki's unforgiving new message was an implicit reprimand—What was a good Muslim like him doing in the American army? But it also offered a way out. Perhaps Sheikh Anwar would tell him that it was not too late to switch sides and join in the defense of the *ummah*.

Starting on December 17, 2008, Hasan began sending Awlaki messages via the "Contact the Sheikh" link on Awlaki's website, asking his opinion on the proper Islamic view of certain kinds of violence. His first query asked about US army sergeant Hasan Karim Akbar, who in 2003 in Kuwait had thrown four grenades into the tents of his fellow soldiers and then fired his rifle at them in the ensuing chaos, killing two and injuring another fourteen troops. "Would you consider someone like Hasan Akbar or other soldiers that have committed such acts with the goal of helping Muslims/Islam (Lets just assume this for now) fighting Jihad and if they did die would you consider them shaheeds," or martyrs? Nidal Hasan asked. Like so many others who consulted Awlaki or listened to his lectures, Hasan was trying to distinguish between violence that was *halal*, religiously sanctioned, and violence that was *haram*, forbidden. The messages capture him in the transition from loyalty to the United States, which he had vowed to defend when he joined the army after high school in 1988, to loyalty to the Muslim *ummah*. Akbar's horrifying attack on his own comrades in the 101st Airborne, Hasan suggested, might *seem* to be an act of betrayal. But in a larger, religious framework, he wondered, would killing fellow soldiers who are themselves preparing to fight against Muslims qualify as a legitimate act of jihad?

Awlaki ignored that query and most of the rest, but he engaged briefly after Hasan told him that he was organizing a contest to award $5,000 to the author of the best essay on "Why is Anwar Al Awlaki a great activist and leader" submitted to a local online publication in the Washington area, the *Muslim Link*, and that he wanted Awlaki to award the prize himself. Hasan added a personal PS: "We met briefly a very long time ago when you were the Imam at Dar al Hijra. I doubt if you remember me. In any case I have since graduated medical school and finished residency training." This remarkable piece of sycophancy stirred Awlaki to respond for the first time, but Hasan had overshot the mark: "I don't travel so I won't be able to physically award the prize and I am too 'embarrassed' for a lack of the better word to award it anyway," Awlaki wrote back. Hasan followed up with a note explaining that plans for the contest had been thwarted by the cowardice of others. He added an offer to send money if Awlaki needed it and, in a postscript, asked for his help with his so-far-dismal search for a compatible woman: "PS: I'm looking for a wife that is willing to strive with me to please Allah," he wrote. "I will strongly consider a recommendation coming from you."

Awlaki replied with a friendly note, asking Hasan to tell more about himself and offering to keep an eye out for a prospective wife. Hasan sent a fulsome biography and several more notes, but Awlaki did not reply again.

In other words, contrary to many later news reports, Awlaki offered no encouragement in his personal e-mail messages to Hasan for the idea of killing fellow American soldiers. But that was not the whole story. On his blog, Awlaki went on to address the very questions that were so troubling Hasan in the months before his shooting spree at Fort Hood. In July 2009, the month Major Hasan was transferred to Fort Hood, Awlaki posted a blistering attack on his website denouncing Muslim soldiers who would fight against other Muslims. His focus was on the armies of Muslim countries allied with the United States, which he called "the number one enemy of the ummah." But his scathing denunciation would certainly have applied to a Muslim fighting in the US Army, a concern that preoccupied Hasan, who knew he might face deployment to Afghanistan. "The blame," Awlaki wrote, "should be placed on the soldier who is willing to follow orders whether the order is to kill Muslims as in Swat," a valley in Pakistan where security forces were fighting militants, "bomb Masjids as with the Red Masjid," a mosque in Islamabad that was the site of a 2007 siege, "or kill women and children as they do in Somalia, just for the sake of a miser[ly] salary. This soldier is a heartless beast, bent on evil, who sells his religion for a few dollars." Hasan had not heard back from Awlaki in the previous seven months, but he followed his writings assiduously, and this must have come as both a searing insult and a call to arms. Hasan's idol was, in effect, calling him a "heartless beast" who was selling out Islam—and was connecting with Hasan's own shifting feelings. Just a month earlier, when another admirer of Awlaki, Abdulhakim Mujahid Muhammad, born Carlos Bledsoe, had shot two soldiers outside the military recruiting station in Little Rock, one fatally, Hasan reportedly shocked his army colleagues by seeming to praise the attack, saying that "this is what Muslims should do, they should stand up to the aggressor."

So by October, when Hasan was officially given the news he had dreaded—that he was being sent to Afghanistan—he had internalized the catechism of militant Islam that Awlaki had helped popularize: that the world's population was divided into two irreconcilable groups, believers and unbelievers; that the unbelievers, led by the American military, were waging a ruthless war on Muslims; that any Muslim participating in that war on Muslims was a traitor and a sellout; and that the only appropriate response was to take the battle to the enemy. He had bought a handgun and, in a twist Awlaki might have understood, had begun to visit the strip club next to the gun shop, paying for lap dances in a private room. On November 4, he began to give away his food, clothing, and furniture to his neighbors, giving one neighbor two sport coats and a business suit still in a dry cleaning bag. "You should sell these," he suggested. The rest, he said, should be given to the Salvation Army. On the morning of the shootings, November 5, he stopped by the home of another neighbor, Lenna Brown, who was having coffee with a friend. He gave both women brand-new copies of the Koran and suggested that they read the verses on Maryam, the Islamic rendering of the Virgin Mary story. Brown asked where he was going, and he answered Afghanistan. She asked Major Hasan how he felt about deployment, and he paused. "I am going to do God's work," he said.

For months he had tried to entice Awlaki into a real exchange on substantive matters, notably the obligations of a Muslim who finds himself in the American military. The imam, wary or just busy, had ignored most of his sixteen messages. But four days after Hasan had yelled "Allahu akbar!" and shot dead twelve soldiers and a Defense Department civilian, Awlaki finally weighed in with his endorsement, 420 words that began: "Nidal Hassan is a hero. He is a man of conscience who could not bear living the contradiction of being a Muslim and serving in an army that is fighting against his own people. This is a contradiction that many Muslims brush aside and just pretend that it doesn't exist. Any decent Muslim cannot live, understanding properly his duties towards his Creator and his fellow Muslims, and yet serve as a US soldier."

Awlaki presented the case as crystal clear: "The only way a Muslim could Islamically justify serving as a soldier in the US army is if his intention is to follow the footsteps of men like Nidal." And, Awlaki added, every American Muslim faced the same quandary, if not in the stark terms of the military: "The heroic act of brother Nidal also shows the dilemma of the Muslim American community. Increasingly they are being cornered into taking stances that would either make them betray Islam or betray their nation. . . . The American Muslims who condemned his actions have committed treason against the Muslim Ummah." It was a revealing turn of phrase: the *ummah* took precedence over the nation, and Muslim Americans who did *not* betray their country were guilty of treason.

Of the 180 comments that appeared before the web-hosting company took down Awlaki's site, the vast majority approved of Hasan's shooting rampage and praised Awlaki for having the courage to endorse it. One writer, calling himself Abu Mubarak, connected the assault on Fort Hood with the drone attacks Obama was escalating, suggesting that the real terrorists wore American uniforms. "When a drone is sent into afghanistan, or iraq, or palestine," Abu Mubarak wrote, "and kills 13 'suspected terrorists' and injures another 30, as they were walking down the street, or drinking coffee in a cafe, where is the outcry of the Muslims and condemnations from the Americans? So if Nidal was a drone, would that have made it any more acceptable?"

In the weeks before Hasan's November 5 attack, as the army psychiatrist made his preparations, Umar Farouk Abdulmutallab was making his own lethal plans. He had completed an engineering degree at University College London in 2008, residing at the expense of his father, a wealthy Nigerian banker, in a building where apartments sold for millions of pounds. But very much like Awlaki years earlier, Abdulmutallab had decided that his father's plans and an engineering career were not the future he wanted; the all-consuming fervor with which he had embraced Islam pretty much ruled that out. After finishing his degree, he had applied for and received a two-year visa to visit the United States, trying it out with a two-week Islamic studies course in Houston. Then, after what must have been tense negotiations with his parents, he agreed to enroll in a business course in bustling Dubai, where his father hoped he might be insulated from extremist influences.

But in the world of WWW Jihad, geography was no obstacle. Abdulmutallab abandoned his business course, left Dubai, and flew to Sanaa on August 1, 2009—admitted to Yemen, where his mother's family came from, in part because he held a valid American visa, a sort of gold stamp of approval for other countries worried about terrorism. His goal was clear: to find his way to Awlaki and volunteer for jihad. Within a few weeks he had connected in Sanaa with a member of Awlaki's underground network, explained his goal, and given the man the number of his Yemeni cell phone. Soon he got a text from Awlaki asking him to call. In a brief conversation Awlaki—undoubtedly wary of a trap—asked the young Nigerian to write a full explanation of his desire to join the jihad. Abdulmutallab, always the diligent student, took several days over his treatise, essentially an application to join AQAP. When he sent it to Awlaki, the imam replied that he would find a way for Abdulmutallab to join the fight.

For Abdulmutallab, it must have been a thrilling moment: he had passed the test set by his hero, the new father figure who had eclipsed his own father, whom Umar Farouk now condemned for un-Islamic behavior. The young man had first seen Awlaki four years earlier on his first visit to Yemen, where he spent the 2004–5 academic year at the Sanaa Institute for the Arabic Language, one of many language schools in the Yemeni capital. The details of their encounters that summer are uncertain, but Abdulmutallab appears to have heard Awlaki lecture at Iman University on its ramshackle campus north of town, which drew Salafi students from many countries. It is also quite possible that the Nigerian joined the throngs of young men flocking to hear Awlaki preach or talk in several mosques around the city.

Abdulmutallab's prolific blog posts from before, during, and after that Yemen summer give a sense of a thoughtful, diligent, diffident, somewhat naive eighteen-year-old, wistfully searching for romantic and religious fulfillment and beginning to pull away from his family's control and expectations. After a three-year immersion in London's Islamic scene, he had embraced a rigid faith, nothing like his family's liberal approach to religion. In May of 2005, on an Islamic online forum, he fretted that even though he had tried to sign up for a version free of advertisements he could still see ads featuring the distraction of *haram*, or forbidden, photographs of women. "I didn't mind it b4 but now i see haram pictures of women with uncovered hair," Abdulmutallab wrote. In many cultures, including many Muslim subcultures, the idea of a teenager somberly complaining that he could not avoid glimpses of women's hair on the web might have sounded comical. But he was deadly serious.

In January, when he joined the Islamic forum at gawaher.com (the name was Arabic for "jewels"), his first post was titled "I Think I Feel Lonely." Reaching out to the devout for comfort he could not get from his University College classmates, he explained that he felt obliged to avoid the partying that was the core of student social life. "Hence i am in a situation where i do not have a friend," he wrote. "i have no one to speak too, no one to consult, no one to support me and i feel depressed and lonely. i do not know what to do." Predictably, he was especially torn over his lack of a love life and the sinful thoughts and actions that seemed to rule him. "As i get lonely, the natural sexual drive awakens and i struggle to control it, sometimes leading to minor sinful activities like not lowering the gaze," he wrote. This problem, he added, "makes me want to get married to avoid getting aroused." But few parents wanted to see their daughters married to an eighteen-year-old, he wrote. The Prophet "advised young men to fast if they can't get married but it has not been helping me much," Abdulmutallab added. The humor was unintentional.

He found heartfelt support from both men and women on the web forum, and after settling in at the language school in Sanaa he took on the job of advising others on the forum who were considering studying in Yemen. "Alhamdulillah," praise God, he wrote, "i finally got my wish. After a hard battle deciding where to go and what to do, i finally ended up in Yemen. I'm doing a 3 month arabic course and so far it is just great." Soon he was describing the weather, giving phone numbers, advising on women's housing arrangements, and enjoying the position of authority. To study the language of the Prophet in the land of the Prophet; to meet people as devout as he was; to attend the lectures of scholars like Awlaki—all of it seemed to capture the imagination of the earnest Muslim from West Africa. It also planted the seed for his return in 2009.

On November 19, 2009, exactly two weeks after Hasan committed his massacre, Abdulmutallab's worried father, Alhaji Umaru Abdulmutallab, who had just turned seventy, showed up at the US embassy in Abuja, Nigeria. He was one of Nigeria's wealthiest men, and he was accompanied by Nigerian security officials. His son was in Yemen and had cut off communications, he told the Americans, and he feared he might have joined Al Qaeda. It was a terrorism warning of rare clarity and authority, not unlike the complaints from some of Nidal Hasan's military colleagues about his increasingly open embrace of extremist views. The senior Abdulmutallab's dire message was accepted by the State Department, the CIA, and the National Counterterrorism Center, duly placed in the computer files, and then essentially ignored. Alhaji Abdulmutallab would learn his son's fate five weeks later, at the same time as the powerful American intelligence agencies and the rest of the world, with the news of an airliner landing in Detroit.

10

I FACE THE WORLD AS IT IS

It was Obama's inauguration week in January 2009, a time of historic pronouncements and lofty predictions. On Tuesday, a frigid day, the new president touched on the terrorist threat that had shaped the previous American decade, but he framed his new approach as one rooted in ideals. "For those who seek to advance their aims by inducing terror and slaughtering innocents, we say to you now that, 'Our spirit is stronger and cannot be broken. You cannot outlast us, and we will defeat you,'" Obama told the spirited crowd massed on the National Mall, where people climbed into the trees to try to catch a glimpse of the stage. In Yemen, as it happened, Yemeni and Saudi militants had chosen that day to announce a new alliance called Al Qaeda in the Arabian Peninsula (AQAP), but that was an obscure news brief probably unnoticed by anyone in the exuberant crowd. Obama invoked earlier generations who had "faced down fascism and communism" not just with military force but with "sturdy alliances and enduring convictions." "Our security," he said, "emanates from the justness of our cause, the force of our example, the tempering qualities of humility and restraint." On Wednesday, with a phalanx of retired generals and admirals standing behind him and photographers snapping away, Obama signed executive orders banning torture, shuttering the CIA's black sites, and promising to close Guantanamo within a year. "We intend to win this fight," he declared. "We are going to win it on our own terms."

Now, on Friday, just the fourth day of his presidency, in a detailed intelligence briefing in the Oval Office, the president was facing the grimmer facts of the terrorism fight. Vague euphemisms like "We intend to win this fight" were replaced by gruesome details of actual missile strikes. Michael Hayden, the outgoing CIA chief, went over plans for the latest drone operations in Pakistan, showing photos of recent strikes, explaining the guidance systems of drone-fired missiles, the blast radius of a Hellfire—all the technical details of targeted killing. Obama's new team was there to learn: General Jim Jones, the new national security adviser; Admiral Dennis Blair, the director of national intelligence; John Brennan, the counterterrorism adviser; and Rahm Emanuel, the White House chief of staff. Hayden's reputation as a "great briefer" had powered his rise from lowly intel officer in Guam to director of the National Security Agency (NSA) and then of the CIA. Now he was on the way out—Obama had decided to nominate Leon Panetta as CIA chief—but Hayden wanted to impress the new crowd.

Obama was attentive and asked numerous questions. The drone, after all, offered him the middle ground he wanted between the wasteful big wars and doing nothing. It offered the extraordinary chance to take out terrorists without risking American lives. Hayden, who had proposed and run the escalated drone campaign in Pakistan for some six months, and who would describe the drone to me as "an exquisite weapon," was the right man to sell this program. The CIA director left the White House convinced that he had done an excellent job. He was shocked the next day to get a call from Emanuel telling him that he had overdone the briefing: you will not brief this president like that again, Emanuel said. The chief of staff wanted to spare Obama the details of this grisly business. As president, Obama had endless responsibilities, and he needed to ration his time. Emanuel was concerned that the new president might get entangled in security issues to the detriment of domestic priorities.

As it would turn out, Emanuel was wrong. Obama would insist on deep personal involvement in the drone program. He knew that what Bush had started, and what he was now expanding, had no real precedent in American history: the killing of suspected enemies in twos and threes and tens, based on secret intelligence, in countries where the United States was not at war. He did not trust the agencies carrying out the strikes to grade their own work. He felt it was his responsibility to invest the time—hours each week—to keep abreast of the operations and often to exercise his own judgment about what was justified and what was too risky. Obama, after all, had insisted throughout the campaign that he, unlike Bush, would show that American security could be assured without violating American values.

Just how difficult this could be was illustrated by the first two CIA drone strikes of his presidency, carried out in Pakistan on the very day that Hayden gave his briefing. Obama would learn in the next day or two that civilians had been killed in both strikes, including several children, though the details remained in dispute, as was so often the case. The toll prompted Obama to ask the agency for even more information on its efforts to avoid killing civilians and its criteria for judging success and failure. The shock of those first strikes helped shape Obama's decision to get involved and stay involved.

"He is determined that he will make these decisions about how far and wide these operations will go," Tom Donilon, then Obama's deputy national security adviser and eventually Jones's replacement, told me in a later interview. "He's determined to keep the tether pretty short."

Obama's short tether for the CIA and the Joint Special Operations Command (JSOC) was a break with Washington tradition. There was an old White House term—"plausible deniability"—to describe how a president's aides sought to distance their boss from fraught decisions. The notion was that American power would make something happen in a faraway place, but the hand of the United States—and certainly the hand of the American president—would not be seen. Historically, those decisions often involved trying to kill perceived foes of the United States. In 1960, for instance, President Dwight Eisenhower had suggested at a meeting with security aides that it would be a good thing if Patrice Lumumba, the Congolese firebrand whose leftist views the United States feared, were somehow to be removed from the picture. He issued no written order, and his musing would become public only in the recollection of a notetaker four decades later. But aides took it as an instruction, and the CIA began to organize an assassination plot. (The CIA station chief would hurl the poisoned toothpaste he had been given for the job into the Congo River. Lumumba would soon be killed, but not by CIA assassins.)

When the Senate's Church Committee, so named for its chairman,

Senator Frank Church of Idaho, investigated intelligence misdeeds in the mid-1970s, the committee reported: "Non-attribution to the United States for covert operations was the original and principal purpose of the so-called doctrine of 'plausible denial.' Evidence before the Committee clearly demonstrates that this concept, designed to protect the United States and its operatives from the consequences of disclosures, has been expanded to mask decisions of the president and his senior staff members." And one of the most curious documents to surface from the archives of American intelligence, a CIA assassination manual that appears to date from the early 1950s but was declassified only in 1997, explained in detail that when the United States killed an enemy, it would not be as the result of a written order from the president:

> Assassination is an extreme measure not normally used in clandestine operations. It should be assumed that it will never be ordered or authorized by any U.S. Headquarters, though the latter may in rare instances agree to its execution by members of an associated foreign service. This reticence is partly due to the necessity for committing communications to paper. No assassination instructions should ever be written or recorded. Consequently, the decision to employ this technique must nearly always be reached in the field, at the area where the act will take place. Decision and instructions should be confined to an absolute minimum of persons. Ideally, only one person will be involved. No report may be made, but usually the act will be properly covered by normal news services, whose output is available to all concerned.

It was a creepy, disturbing document, hinting that the official version of American history might just omit unsolved murders carried out by government operatives on their own initiative and perhaps disguised as accidents—a tactic the manual also recommended. It reflected the pre–Church Committee era when the CIA operated virtually without oversight, an era that Obama abhorred.

For there was more to Obama's "short tether" on drone strikes than the practical question of keeping a close eye on lethal operations. In a way, Obama was engaged in a struggle over history. Never shy about comparing himself to Lincoln and Franklin Delano Roosevelt, the new president had a sweeping sense of his potential importance. As he had said often on the campaign trail, he believed his job was not just to keep America safe but to restore its principles to the fight against terrorism after the grave lapses under Bush.

Obama knew the policies he abhorred had been championed by Vice President Dick Cheney, who had brought his own sense of history to bear on the response to 9/11. Cheney had been White House chief of staff to President Gerald Ford from 1975 to 1977, when the Church Committee carried out its unprecedented inquisition into the CIA, the FBI, and the NSA. Cheney believed that the inquiry had gone too far and that the remedies that resulted from the committee's exposure of assassination plots and spying on Americans unconstitutionally infringed on the president's power. After 9/11, Cheney had famously spoken about the need to work "sort of the dark side" against Al Qaeda. His was the loudest voice for ignoring or overturning restrictions on the executive branch and returning to the pre-Church days of unfettered eavesdropping and covert operations.

When he arrived at the White House, Obama was determined, in effect, to restore the Church Committee's legacy—to prove, as he said repeatedly, that America did not need to make a "false choice" between its security and its ideals. When he gave the major national security speech of his early presidency, at the National Archives on May 21, 2009, he declared: "I believe with every fiber of my being that in the long run we also cannot keep this country safe unless we enlist the power of our most fundamental values." Reprising themes from the campaign and inauguration, Obama said that those values had been on display during World War II, when the United States had "shut down torture chambers and replaced tyranny with the rule of law." During the Cold War, he said, standing for the right values had permitted the United States to "overpower the iron fist of fascism and outlast the iron curtain of communism." But after the shock of 9/11, he said, "unfortunately, faced with an uncertain threat, our government made a series of hasty decisions. . . . We went off course." Now, Obama suggested, the "season of fear" when the country had abandoned its principles had passed. "And where terrorists offer only the injustice of disorder and destruction, America must demonstrate that our values and our institutions are more resilient than a hateful ideology."

Speeches were easy. Figuring out what to do about threats was hard, and from the early days of Obama's presidency the looming signs of trouble from Al Qaeda in the Arabian Peninsula were evident. "There was complete shock when the new team came in and saw what shape Yemen was in," said one counterterrorism official. He said the Yemeni-Saudi coalition of Guantanamo graduates and hardcore extremists who had formed AQAP seemed ambitious and competent. Drone strikes in Pakistan, stepped up in Bush's last months and escalated further by Obama, seemed to be dismantling the core of Al Qaeda there, albeit at the cost of some civilian casualties and a growing political backlash. But in Yemen, where US intelligence was far sketchier, militants had mounted a complex assault on the American embassy in September 2008, using rocket-propelled grenades, automatic weapons, and at least two car bombs. The attack had killed twelve people, eleven Yemenis and one Yemeni American, in addition to six of the attackers. The embassy was situated on a hill in Sanaa's northwest, not far from a poor neighborhood seen as a hotbed of Al Qaeda sympathy, and it had become a virtual fortress.

Obama's top security aides began making regular stops in Sanaa, pressuring Yemen's cagey president, Ali Abdullah Saleh, to take on AQAP. Saleh had long been viewed in Washington as an unreliable ally mainly interested in extorting cash from American coffers. But Saleh offered more and more expansive promises as he received in succession in 2009 a number of senior Americans, including Steven Kappes, the deputy director of CIA, and General David Petraeus, the head of Central Command, who oversaw all military forces in the Middle East. By the time John Brennan, Obama's counterterrorism adviser, arrived in September, he had dropped all limits on American counterterrorism operations, according to the diplomatic cables later made public by WikiLeaks, the antisecrecy group. "President Saleh insisted that Yemen's national territory is available for unilateral CT operations by the U.S.," a cable said, using shorthand for *counterterrorism*, "while at the same time placing responsibility for any future AQAP attacks on the shoulders of the USG," or US government, "now that it enjoys unfettered access to Yemeni airspace, coastal waters and land." Saleh played up the chances of another attack on the

American embassy or other Western targets but declared: "I have given you an open door on terrorism, so I am not responsible."

It was a remarkable situation: the leader of a nation giving another country a blank check for military action in his land, asking in return only that he escape all blame for what happened. For this extraordinary surrender of his country's sovereignty, Saleh got his reward: an invitation to meet Obama at the White House. But for the United States, the broad permission would open the door to grave missteps whose consequences would linger for years.

The CIA station and the military attaché's office at the US embassy in Sanaa were getting steadily more crowded in the second half of 2009, as analysts and undercover officers arrived from the United States to beef up scrutiny on AQAP. A joint operations center in the capital where Yemeni and American counterterrorism officers worked together also was bustling. But in a classic catch-22, the same security threats that had drawn more American spies and special operations teams to Yemen made it risky for them to travel the country, develop sources, or sometimes even get permission to leave embassy premises. The Americans had to rely far more than they liked on reports from counterparts in Yemeni security agencies, who were viewed as a mixed bag both in competence and in sympathies.

With HUMINT severely constrained, SIGINT became all the more important. In plain English, that meant that because human spies could not easily mingle with Yemenis to recruit and meet with agents, eavesdropping, or signals intelligence, had to bear a double burden. The eavesdropping station inside the embassy run by the Special Collection Service, which did local eavesdropping on Yemeni government offices and suspected Al Qaeda sympathizers in Sanaa, was critical. The SCS, whose impressive headquarters was hidden away on a corner of the Agriculture Department's research farm in Beltsville, Maryland, had been created in the late 1970s to settle a turf war between the CIA and the NSA; it was jointly run by officers from both agencies, usually operating under cover from embassies and consulates. Now the office juggled a growing stream of requests, directing high-tech antennas toward the cellular calls and military and police radios within its range. Both manned and unmanned surveillance aircraft cruised over Al Qaeda's turf in the tribal provinces,

monitoring cell traffic and the walkie-talkie radios the militants favored for short-range communications.

Back at the NSA's big station in San Antonio, Texas, a team was
assembled to study Yemen's communications system and how the
NSA might better tap into it. From April until August 2009, technicians pored over charts of underwater cables, spreadsheets of communications satellite links, and statistics on Yemen's nascent Internet
and cellular networks. The analysts discovered that there were only
about 320,000 Internet users and six million mobile phone subscrib-
ers in a population of about twenty-six million, though both numbers
were rising fast. There were barely a million landline phones, nearly
all in the cities. The analysts identified a few key telecommunica-
tions officials and computer system administrators who might be useful eavesdropping targets or, if hacked or bribed, sources of technical
information. The SSAD team, as the Texas analysts were called, for
Special Source Analysis and Discovery, also got more creative, studying whether a militant in Yemen posting a YouTube video might inadvertently reveal his location. The team compiled elaborate charts
of telephone call routing, looking for spots vulnerable to intercept.
They dug up cell phone numbers for important Yemeni officials and
suspected terrorists. And they paid particular attention to international calls from Yemen to Pakistan's tribal areas, where Al Qaeda's
leadership was hiding.

By early December 2009, the intelligence net was picking up dire
signs of impending attacks. The targets were uncertain, but
American officials believed that Western embassies and hotels favored
by foreigners were likely to be on the list. For months, some American military analysts had argued for strikes against AQAP. Now the
CIA reported that bombers in Abyan province in Yemen's south were
preparing to don suicide vests and to head for Sanaa, almost certainly
intending to attack the US embassy. General Petraeus pushed hard for
what he said was a rare opportunity to take out a large number of militants. The situation seemed to meet Obama's criterion for action: a direct threat to American lives. But General James Jones, then Obama's
national security adviser, said officials knew intelligence on targets in
Yemen was still a work in progress, especially compared with Pakistan. "It was case by case and trying to get some assurances that in

fact that target was where we thought he was, who we thought he was, would be there when we thought he was," Jones said in an interview. "It was more difficult because it was kind of an embryonic theater that we weren't really familiar with." The president nonetheless approved a strike, proposed by the Pentagon, on a suspected AQAP training camp near the village of Al Majala in Abyan.

For Obama, it was a momentous step. He had come into office with the hope of remaking relations with the Muslim world, in part by reducing the American military presence there. Now, with the military and intelligence agencies declaring an emergency, he felt he had no choice but to go in the opposite direction, expanding the American war on Al Qaeda into a new and volatile Arab country. On the night of December 17, 2009, Petraeus oversaw the strike from his Tampa headquarters, with Obama's senior security aides in touch by video link from the Situation Room. Djibouti, twenty miles from Yemen across the slender Bab el Mandeb Strait, still would allow only surveillance Predators to be flown from its territory. Under pressure to move fast, military commanders used the only weapon available—volleys of cruise missiles from a US Navy vessel in the Arabian Sea.

Yemeni ground forces struck in several locations in coordination with the American missile assault. In the cubicle warrens of American intelligence agencies, at the CIA, the Defense Intelligence Agency (DIA), the NSA, and beyond, there was excitement. "We'd been wanting to do strikes forever at that point," recalled one counterterrorism analyst who had spent 2009 watching AQAP organize, recruit, and plot attacks.

Yemen's embassy in Washington put out a statement claiming that the dawn attack on what it called "Al Qaeda's hideout" had been carried out by "Yemeni counterterrorism units backed by the air force." Within hours of the strikes, Yemen announced that Obama had called to congratulate Saleh on Yemen's "successful terror raids." The clumsy misdirection did not hold up for long. Within a day, American officials, speaking anonymously, began to hint to reporters in Washington that the air strike at Al Majala had not been a strictly Yemeni affair. *The New York Times* wrote that "American firepower" had been involved. ABC News broke the news that US cruise missiles had been used.

Two weeks later, on January 2, 2010, after the underwear bomb episode on Christmas, Petraeus returned to Sanaa, "congratulated President Saleh on recent successful operations against AQAP," and informed him that American security aid would be increased sharply to $150 million in 2010. In one of the more cynical moments in recent diplomatic history, Saleh cheerfully assured Petraeus in a ninety-minute discussion that he would keep up the charade. "'We'll continue saying the bombs are ours, not yours,' Saleh said, prompting Deputy Prime Minister Alimi to joke that he had just 'lied' by telling Parliament that the bombs in Arhab, Abyan, and Shebwa were American-made but deployed by the ROYG," the Republic of Yemen Government, the cable said.

On closer examination, the upbeat cable actually revealed astonishing ignorance of what the United States had done. When Saleh told Petraeus that "mistakes were made" in the December 17 strike, resulting in excessive civilian casualties in Abyan, the American general denied it. "The General responded that the only civilians killed were the wife and two children of an AQAP operative at the site, prompting Saleh to plunge into a lengthy and confusing aside with Deputy Prime Minister Alimi and Minister of Defense Ali regarding the number of terrorists versus civilians killed in the strike." The cable said that "Saleh's conversation on the civilian casualties suggests he has not been well briefed by his advisors on the strike in Abyan." The self-satisfied tone of the cable was misplaced. In fact, according to multiple Yemeni and international investigations, Saleh was right and Petraeus was shockingly misinformed. He, not the Yemeni president, was the one who had "not been well briefed by his advisors."

The most careful and thorough study of the Al Majala attack, by Human Rights Watch, would conclude that the strike had killed the main target, an Al Qaeda operative named Saleh Muhammad Ali al-Anbouri, better known as Muhammad al-Kazami, and possibly as many as thirteen other militants, though evidence for the precise number is sketchy. With the idiosyncratic logic of military planners, the Pentagon's JSOC called the names on its secret kill list "objectives," and it had decided to name targets in Yemen after towns in Ohio. So Kazami was dubbed "Objective Akron" in targeting documents. But the strike that killed Objective Akron also hit the tents of two extended Bedouin families, killing at least forty-one civilians, including nine women, five of them pregnant, and twenty-one children.

One of the first outsiders to reach the grisly scene, hours after the strike on December 17, was Anwar al-Awlaki's uncle, Saleh bin Fareed al-Awlaki. Bin Fareed was a leader of the Awaliq tribe (also transliterated Awlak and several other ways) from which the family got its surname. When a catastrophe befell his people, they naturally summoned him. He made the three-hour drive from his seaside villa in Aden and found a horrifying landscape of missile craters and burned tents, with blood and body parts everywhere. The local Bedouin families had been paid to provide food, laundry, and other services to the Al Qaeda camp, but there was no evidence and no likelihood that they shared the militants' ideology or posed any direct threat to Americans. The families' herds, some 1,500 goats, sheep, cows, and donkeys, had been slaughtered along with the families.

"Old women," Bin Fareed said in an interview, growing emotional as he remembered the massacre. "Children. I mean, we collect the remains—we don't know if it belongs to dogs, goats, or human beings. So we buried it all together." Yemeni officials had ordered Yemeni Air Force MIG fighters to fly over the site shortly after the missiles hit to try to cover American involvement, but Bin Fareed said the deception was obvious even the day of the strike. Officials later claimed that the Al Qaeda camp was an inaccessible mountain hideout, comparing it to Tora Bora in Afghanistan, but Bin Fareed reached it with no difficulty in his SUV. "It was about ten minutes from the main road in a small car," he said.

Nor did the killing stop with the strike. One or more of the American Tomahawk missiles that hit the site were armed with cluster munitions—a warhead stuffed with 166 yellow cylinders the size of soda cans, designed to shatter into some three hundred metal fragments. The international Convention on Cluster Munitions, banning their use, was proposed at an international conference in Dublin in 2008, came into force in 2010, and has been signed by 113 countries. But the signatories do not include Russia, China, or the United States. One motivation for the ban was the danger from unexploded bomblets, and indeed in Al Majala at least four curious children and adults who picked up the yellow cans in the days after December 17 were killed and another dozen or more injured.

Bin Fareed was outraged, and after helping bury corpses and body parts he drove to his house in Shabwah province and spread word that tribesmen should mount a protest at the site. He also took steps to launch an inquiry by Yemen's parliament, in which he served, to document the results of the strike. Tens of thousands of angry local people rallied two days later on the hills surrounding the craters. But television cameras focused most of their attention on a handful of Al Qaeda members atop a hill, lifting their Kalashnikovs in the air and denouncing the United States and the Yemeni government. Bin Fareed said he grabbed his rifle and wanted to confront the Al Qaeda gunmen for trying to hijack the protest but was restrained by his friends. For him, the presence of a handful of Al Qaeda militants and the media coverage of a brief speech by one of them were a disaster, threatening to distort the sincere outrage of the tribes into an expression of support for Al Qaeda.

One White House aide recalled that it took weeks before an after-action report on the Al Majala strike confirmed the damage. "The president wasn't happy with it, and so we went through a very long process led by Brennan to tighten up how we take lethal action in Yemen," the aide said. "We were aware of the blowback on the ground and how off things had gotten."

The full impact of the December 17, 2009, strike would not be evident for months. But the debut of American military action in Yemen would turn out to be a resonant catastrophe for the United States. Anyone who studied the asymmetric battle against terrorism recognized the crucial role played by perceptions of fairness and injustice, good intentions and bad, competent allies and blunderers. But the campaign had begun with clumsy cover-ups of American involvement, cruise missiles and cluster bombs utterly unsuited for precise strikes, and collateral damage so extreme that it would permanently poison public opinion. With a single strike, the United States had yielded the moral high ground in Yemen.

By the time of the Al Majala strike, Obama was presiding over a jury-rigged bureaucracy constructed to handle targeted killing. Its work in Pakistan had become all but routine, and the White House signed off on strikes there in advance only if they posed unusual risks. About twice a week, CIA drones flying over Pakistan's tribal area fired a volley of missiles at suspects on the ground, killing scores of people each month. Obama had approved one strike in Somalia in September 2009 and the first Yemen strike in December, and he had decided to personally approve all strikes in those countries in advance. The message of the expansion seemed clear: What the United States was doing in Pakistan was not just an emergency measure or an adjunct to the conventional war next door in Afghanistan. Wherever the United States discovered someone it considered to be a dangerous enemy, it would strike.

Each Tuesday, Obama would descend from the Oval Office to the Situation Room, the basement command center whose sleek mahogany-and-electronics look resulted from a major update during Bush's second term, for the weekly terrorism meeting. With John Brennan at his side, the president would run through the agenda: the rogues' gallery of Al Qaeda suspects, reports on plots afoot and plots foiled, questions about how best to meet the threat. Sometimes there would be a show-and-tell from the agencies—the CIA for Pakistan, JSOC for Yemen and Somalia, including before-and-after shots of a strike. Or the agencies would present a brief biography of a suspected terrorist who had been named to the kill list. When Yemen was the main topic, as it often was in the months after the Christmas Day bombing attempt, the ambassador to Yemen, Stephen Seche, or the CIA station chief in Sanaa would join the discussion by video link.

Sometimes Obama would draw out his security cabinet on how the contest was going, or grow contemplative and remind everyone in the room of the fateful nature of their task. When a debate about civilian casualties in drone attacks began to heat up in 2010, Obama would sometimes point out, somewhat defensively, that there might well be civilian casualties from a decision *not* to proceed with a proposed strike: like the three thousand civilians who had died on 9/11, they would be the victims of an Al Qaeda plot that a drone strike might have disrupted. Whether a strike was approved or rejected, the president often remarked, civilian lives were at stake.

At one Tuesday meeting a few weeks after the underwear bomb episode, the president took a moment to peruse a chart from the intelligence agencies: fifteen Al Qaeda suspects in Yemen with Western ties, some with connections to Awlaki. The country faced adversaries without uniforms, often indistinguishable from the civilians around them. The mug shots and brief biographies resembled a layout from a high school yearbook. Several were Americans. Two were teenagers, including a girl who looked even younger than her seventeen years. "How old are these people?" asked Obama, the father of two daughters, according to two officials present. "If they are starting to use children," he said of Al Qaeda, "we are moving into a whole different phase."

The suspects on the chart were not yet being proposed as drone targets, but Obama knew that some of them soon could be. He was the ultimate arbiter of a "nominations" process to designate terrorists for kill or capture, and there were virtually no captures by American agencies, though allied governments sometimes imprisoned militants on the basis of US intelligence. Before names were added to the "kill list," a term the media used but the White House didn't like, Obama and his aides often pored over terrorist suspects' biographies on what some officials wryly called "baseball cards." When the CIA sent word that there was a rare opportunity for a drone strike on a top terrorist—but that his family was with him—it was the president who had reserved to himself the final moral calculation.

Since his time in the Senate, Obama had seen the drone as a possible answer to both the technical and moral challenges of counterterrorism. The terrorists were few, and the Bush years had proven that a big conventional fighting force was no way to take them on. The most highly praised counterterrorism strike in Iraq, in 2006, used five-hundred-pound bombs to kill Abu Musab al-Zarqawi, the ruthless Jordanian-born militant who declared himself "emir" of the Islamic State of Iraq. But it was a paradoxical victory: Zarqawi headed a jihadi insurgency that had not existed before the American invasion (and one that would survive his death, spread to Syria, and become a much bigger menace in the years to come). Bush's war, in other words, had created the militants that commanders were then congratulated for killing.

By that measure, a program consisting solely of targeted strikes with no ground troops seemed eminently sensible. Obama, said Ben Rhodes, his deputy national security adviser, considered targeted strikes "a way of minimizing the chance of getting drawn into a bigger conflict by successful terrorist attacks that create a groundswell of opinion for more aggressive action." A little killing, in other words, might prevent a lot of killing. The drone, CIA and JSOC operators claimed, offered unequaled precision because it allowed the analysts and the drone pilots to loiter for hours or days and study what they called the "pattern of life" on the ground. When the strike came, a Hellfire missile could take out a car or part of a house, leaving neighboring buildings unscathed. At Obama's urging, after a 2010 strike killed several women and children in Pakistan, the CIA actually reduced the size of the explosive munition on the Hellfire missile. Let's kill the people who are trying to kill us, was the president's regular refrain.

It all seemed logical and reasonable, and drones seemed to be one of the few government programs that both Republicans and Democrats liked. The political consensus in Washington was such, in fact, that it was easy to miss the profound shift that targeted killing represented. The single-minded pursuit of enemies had changed America and its leaders. Like Bush and his advisers—indeed, like the American people—Obama and his aides had themselves been *radicalized* by the threat posed by Islamic radicals. Before 9/11, anyone proposing to use missiles in a country where we were not at war to kill suspected terrorists week after week would have been met with strong opposition. The Bush administration, in fact, had repeatedly and explicitly condemned Israel's practice of killing Hamas leaders and other militants with missiles and other weapons. On July 5, 2001, Secretary of State Colin Powell reiterated the American stance: "We continue to express our distress and opposition to these kinds of targeted killings." The following month, just two weeks before the Al Qaeda attacks, the State Department spokesman, Richard Boucher, declared that "Israel needs to understand that targeted killings of Palestinians don't end the violence, but are only inflaming an already volatile situation and making it much harder to restore calm." At that time, an American official who recommended that an American citizen overseas suspected of terrorism should be killed with a missile would surely have been met with incredulity and scorn. But 9/11 had changed the definition of what was preposterous, what was merely prudent, what was un-American, and what was unthinkable.

Even the Norwegian Nobel Committee, it seemed, was not bothered by Obama's approval of drone strikes, since it had stunned the White House and the country in October 2009 by awarding him the peace prize. The choice seemed a strained effort by Europeans to underscore their disgust with George W. Bush, and it only fed conservatives' belief that the American president was some kind of Euro-socialist interloper driven by an alien ideology. For Obama, the prize was an untimely embarrassment—an *Onion* story come to life. The president later said that he and his political adviser David Axelrod had expected many political challenges, but "the one thing we didn't anticipate was having to apologize for having won the Nobel Peace Prize."

Preparing for his December 2009 acceptance speech in Oslo, Obama asked his speechwriters to dig up readings from Thomas Aquinas and others—not on peace but on the concept of just war. When he spoke, he did not flinch from the paradoxical position he was in, as commander in chief overseeing two grinding wars and a covert drone campaign. He cited such previous laureates as Gandhi and Martin Luther King, but only to distinguish his own position from theirs. As the head of a state at war, Obama said, "I cannot be guided by their examples alone. I face the world as it is, and cannot stand idle in the face of threats to the American people. For make no mistake: Evil does exist in the world. A non-violent movement could not have halted Hitler's armies. Negotiations cannot convince Al Qaeda's leaders to lay down their arms. To say that force may sometimes be necessary is not a call to cynicism—it is a recognition of history, the imperfections of man and the limits of reason."

This moralistic strain in Obama's public statements found an echo in the voice of John Owen Brennan, whose Jesuit education at Fordham University gave him an affinity for such talk that was unexpected from a grizzled twenty-five-year veteran of the CIA. The deep suspicions of human rights activists about Brennan's role in the agency during the Bush years had prompted them to speak out against and scuttle Obama's plan to make him CIA chief. But Obama believed Brennan's claim that he had no role in torture; after all, Brennan was the highest-ranking former CIA officer to endorse Obama's presidential run in its early stages. Quite aware of his own inexperience in the national security realm, Obama appreciated what he saw as Brennan's respectful, low-ego, factual style of briefing. He knew it would be invaluable to have a guy like Brennan as a filter for the information coming from the CIA and other agencies: Brennan would know when agency officials were manipulating the facts, omitting policy options they did not like, feuding over turf, or bluffing about threats. So Obama asked Brennan to become his counterterrorism adviser, a job in which he would see the president daily, sometimes awaken him in the middle of the night with news of threats or decisions about strikes, and win Obama's deep gratitude. As the threat from Al Qaeda's Yemen branch began to eclipse the terror network's Pakistan core in 2009, Brennan's former experience as CIA station chief next door in Saudi Arabia made his counsel even more valuable. He forged ties with Yemeni officials, including Ali Abdullah Saleh, the erratic president, and made regular trips to both Sanaa and Riyadh on behalf of the president.

More surprisingly, Brennan won over many of his critics in the human rights world in Obama's first year in office. They heard from allies in the administration that Brennan was the most consistent voice for closing Guantanamo and that he acted as a check on the drone strikes. People like Harold Koh, the State Department's legal adviser, who had been an outspoken liberal critic of the Bush counterterrorism programs, found that Brennan was an unexpected ally in interagency debates. One colleague likened Brennan to a dogged police detective, tracking terrorists from his cavelike office in the White House basement; another called him the priest whose blessing had become indispensable to Obama.

Such descriptions would grate on outsiders, including cynical former CIA colleagues of Brennan, who saw him as a deft politician and a facilitator for the stepped-up drone program. Civil libertarians who had come to a positive view of Brennan would wonder if they had been duped some five years later when, as CIA chief, he would work to refute and delay the Senate Intelligence Committee's massive exposé of the agency's interrogation program. Another notable dissenter was Dennis Blair, the retired admiral who lasted a year as director of national intelligence before being fired after several bureaucratic scuffles with Leon Panetta, the CIA director. Blair told colleagues that Obama was only the latest of many presidents to be "captured" by the CIA. Rather than helping Obama objectively assess CIA claims and demands, Brennan was actually the CIA's very effective agent in the White House, Blair believed. He thought the

White House was far too narrowly focused on names on the kill list. "The steady refrain in the White House was 'This is the only game in town'—reminded me of body counts in Vietnam," said Blair, who had begun his navy service during that war.

But if the CIA was winning over the president, it was partly because of those body counts. By many accounts, the agency's drone program in Pakistan seemed to be getting results. There was little public controversy over civilian casualties; that would come later, sparked in part by the excellent work of the Bureau of Investigative Journalism in London and other groups. In the second year of his presidency, Obama's morning reading included the unnerving stream of terrorism threats highlighted in the President's Daily Brief, a striking number of which were traceable to Awlaki, his Al Qaeda branch, and his web-driven acolytes in the West. Now, in a satisfying evening-up of the score, there was also a swelling tally of foreign militants who had been, as the portentous euphemism put it, "removed from the battlefield." Especially in Pakistan, it seemed, anyone Al Qaeda promoted into a management position could count on an early martyrdom.

There were challenges in assessing who was and was not a militant dedicated to violent jihad in Yemen, but Anwar al-Awlaki posed no such problem. Both in words and in deeds he left no ambiguity about his loyalties and intentions. In the series of statements he released via the Internet from his hideouts in Shabwah province, Awlaki declared that it was every Muslim's duty to kill Americans, including ordinary citizens. Awlaki gave an interview to a sympathetic Yemeni journalist, Abdulelah Haider Shaye, who had aggressively covered the civilian deaths in the strike on Al Majala. Shaye would later be imprisoned in Yemen for three years with the encouragement of the Obama administration, which claimed he was working closely with AQAP. In the interview, Awlaki offered a backhanded endorsement of American democracy to answer the most difficult question for Al Qaeda: How could it justify killing random civilians?

"The American people live in a democratic system and they are responsible for its policy," Awlaki told Shaye. "It is the American people who elected the criminal Bush to two presidential terms and elected Obama, who is no different than Bush." Civilians "are the ones who spend on the army and they are the ones who send their children to be recruited. So they are responsible," Awlaki said.

Some civil libertarians argued that however reprehensible Awlaki's views were, all of it was mere talk—free speech, protected by the First Amendment. But even in his speech, Awlaki was arguably pushing against the limits of constitutional protection. The Supreme Court's ruling in *Brandenburg v. Ohio*, a landmark 1969 First Amendment case, involved one of the most dangerous homegrown terrorist groups in American history. The court overturned the conviction of an Ohio Ku Klux Klan leader who had talked at a rally about the possibility of what he called "revengeance" if the government continued "to suppress the white, Caucasian race." The ruling declared that advocacy of violence could be punished as a crime only if it was "directed to inciting or producing imminent lawless action and is likely to incite or produce such action." Certainly the great majority of Awlaki's sermons and lecture series before 2010 would merit First Amendment protection under this standard; hailing the example set by those who fought for Islam centuries ago or advising Muslims to "never trust the kuffar," the unbelievers, would be well within the limits of free speech.

But by late 2009, Awlaki's advocacy of violence had become open and unconditional. He was explicitly seeking to incite attacks, and the growing number of arrests of his followers for plotting violence suggested, too, that his online speeches were "likely" to "produce such action," in the words of the *Brandenburg* decision. The trickiest word in the Supreme Court's ruling was "imminent," and the concept of the imminence of a threat would become the subject of many legal debates about targeted killing. Were Awlaki's calls for violent action "directed to inciting or producing *imminent* lawless action"? Or would that require that the cleric accompany Abdulmutallab to the Amsterdam airport and order him to board the plane? At the least, the notion that Awlaki's online calls for violence fell within the realm of protected speech appeared debatable.

In any case, as the scores of American intelligence analysts now working on Awlaki and AQAP had learned, Awlaki was no longer limiting himself to talk. In FBI interviews in late January and February 2010, Abdulmutallab had described to FBI agents in detail how Awlaki had helped plan and direct his airliner attack, connecting him with Al Qaeda, sending him to the bomb maker Asiri, arranging his martyrdom video, and reminding him to detonate the bomb only after reaching American territory. The government, with its self-defeating penchant for excessive secrecy, kept the details under wraps, allowing some opponents of targeted killing to argue that Awlaki was only a propagandist.

Then, in the weeks after the failed Christmas attack, Awlaki began exchanging encrypted e-mails with a Bangladeshi man, Rajib Karim, who worked in information technology for British Airways in Newcastle, England. After being put in touch by Karim's brother, Tehzeeb, who had traveled to Yemen to meet the cleric, Awlaki wrote Karim to explore how he might assist with a new airliner attack. "Our highest priority is the US," Awlaki wrote in early February 2010, though Scotland Yard would not decipher the messages for months. "Anything there, even on a smaller scale compared to what we may do in the UK would be our choice. So the question is with the people you have is it possible to get a package or a person with a package on board a flight heading to the US?" There could be no doubt that "we" meant AQAP. Karim replied that he would do his best: "Like you say I also agree that US is a better target than UK, but I do not know much about US. I can work with the bros to find out the possibilities of shipping a package to a US-bound plane." Karim also expressed some doubts about the legitimacy of civilian targets such as the London subway or passenger aircraft, asking Awlaki for a "refutation" of religious authorities who condemned such attacks.

Awlaki had no such qualms. He pressed Karim for information that could guide AQAP's bomb maker, Ibrahim al-Asiri, in further design changes to get explosives through airport security. "BTW," Awlaki wrote, using casual shorthand for "by the way," "did any of the brs [brothers] you mentioned get training on x-ray machines or understand their limitations"?

Such detailed brainstorming about mounting terrorist attacks, former American intelligence officers said, turned up regularly in intercepts of Awlaki's private messages starting in early 2009. Some caught Awlaki discussing the possibility of a cyanide or ricin attack in the United States. The talk about how to evade detection at airports especially terrified American aviation officials. They considered Asiri an evil genius and feared he was finding ways, with Awlaki's help, to circumvent the billions of dollars' worth of improved airport security measures since 9/11.

There was no uncertainty inside the Obama administration about Awlaki's actions and intentions. But did that mean that Obama had the constitutional and legal authority to order him killed? In the weeks after the Christmas bombing attempt, David Barron and Marty Lederman, the two former Bush critics now in the Justice Department's Office of Legal Counsel (OLC), were under intense pressure to complete a legal opinion on the legal and constitutional status of a presidential authorization to kill Awlaki.

They worked under huge disadvantages. Both were considered brilliant legal scholars, but neither had any experience in intelligence, counterterrorism, or the accumulating record of targeted killing in Pakistan and Yemen. While the subject cried out for consultation with experts in multiple fields, they could not share their assignment with outsiders. The importance of the opinion counseled an unrushed consideration of the novel issues a kill order would raise, but the White House, the CIA, and the Defense Department all wanted an answer. If Barron and Lederman took their time and the drones over Yemen missed a clear chance to kill Awlaki, it was conceivable that a terrorist plot could come to bloody fruition as a result. If they rushed their approval for the deliberate hunting and killing of an American citizen for the first time outside either a conventional war or capital punishment, they would be setting a precedent that history might come to view as reckless and dangerous. Not least, both men were acutely aware that their liberal admirers would be quick to accuse them of hypocrisy—of granting a Democratic president leeway they would have denied to his Republican predecessor—if their legal reasoning was not rock-solid.

From the OLC offices on the fifth floor of the Justice Department, they reached out to the CIA and Defense Department for the entire intelligence record on Awlaki. The top-secret reports, transcripts of intercepted phone calls, and decrypted e-mails that came back could be reviewed only in a Justice Department SCIF, or sensitive compartmented information facility—a room specially shielded against spies' electronic probes. When they wanted to solicit the views of other lawyers elsewhere in the government, their draft opinion had to be hand-carried by a courier—the classification level was too high to permit the use of e-mail. Each hard copy was watermarked with the name of the department receiving it, to make it easy to trace any illicit photocopy.

Even at high levels in the government, officials who saw the unexpurgated case against Awlaki were surprised. Harold Koh, the State Department's legal adviser and another former Bush critic, had followed the Awlaki saga and thought of him as a propagandist who could probably not be legally targeted. But he asked his staff to round up a stack of intelligence reports on the renegade cleric, canceled his appointments, and holed up for hours in a tiny State Department SCIF. What he learned took him by surprise. The documents showed that Awlaki was not just a hotheaded preacher or an above-the-fray religious authority issuing general fatwas, but the active, aggressive detail man revealed in the e-mails to Karim and the exchanges with Abdulmutallab. "When I saw that he had clearly given an order to blow up an airliner over US soil—which is essentially a criminal order to kill hundreds of innocent civilians—I didn't think of him as a mere propagandist," said Koh in an interview after Awlaki's role in the plot had been declassified for Abdulmutallab's sentencing. "I was actually shocked that that particular fact hadn't been highlighted earlier."

After a month of long days, Barron and Lederman completed their initial legal analysis. In early February, days after Abdulmutallab had begun telling a more complete story about Awlaki's role in the plot to FBI investigators, the Justice Department informed the White House orally of their conclusion: killing Awlaki would violate neither the Constitution nor the executive order banning assassination. With the legal advice in hand, Obama did not wait. On the morning of Friday, February 5, the president and his security cabinet met at the White House and approved, with no dissent, the addition of Awlaki to the kill list. "If this had happened a year earlier in the administration, I think there might have been greater resistance—from State, potentially from Justice," said Michael Leiter, who participated in the discussions as director of the National Counterterrorism Center. "But a year and a half in, whether it was Christmas Day or other events, you had a lot of people in the administration who were watching the streams of intelligence all the time and were recognizing the very real dangers. We'd had Fort Hood, which didn't involve

Awlaki directing things but did highlight how influential he could be. So after Christmas Day, I think a recognition had built up that we're not going to do this willy-nilly, but there are some dangerous people out there who happen to be American citizens." Leiter said the citizenship issue was thoroughly debated, but no one believed it should be an absolute shield for Awlaki. "The biggest question you are left with is, 'Okay, what's the alternative? Just let this guy keep recruiting people, keep training them, keep telling them things and putting them on airplanes and hope that we keep finding them?'"

If Obama felt a need for reinforcement after making his historic decision, he may have gotten it later that day, when he traveled to CIA headquarters for a memorial service for the seven CIA employees and contractors killed a few weeks earlier when an Al Qaeda double agent had blown himself up at their base in Khost, Afghanistan. Obama praised the work of the CIA officers, who he said were dedicated to "unraveling the dark web of terrorists that threaten us." Addressing an audience that included spouses, children, and parents of those killed, he referred bluntly to the main role of the CIA base at Khost: gathering intelligence to direct drone strikes at militants in nearby Pakistan. "They served in secrecy, but today every American can see their legacy," the president said. Their legacy was written, he said, "in the extremists who no longer threaten our country—because you eliminated them."

With the White House decision, Awlaki, like others placed on the JSOC kill list in Yemen, was assigned a code name picked from a map of Ohio. The CIA didn't bother with code names, but the military insisted on them. Perhaps calling them "objectives" objectified them, helped distance the hunters from the human beings they were trying to kill, the way Middle Eastern males in FBI memos became MEMs, military-age males in Pentagon jargon became MAMs, and dead civilians became "CD," for collateral damage. The military's choice of Ohio was one of the random facts that made Pentagon nomenclature so opaque; perhaps it had been the whim of an anonymous military planner with roots in the state. In Awlaki's case, the name selected was a little town of twenty-five thousand in the west-central part of the state, notable for a collection of houses made from welded steel, product of a 1930s experiment in prefabricated housing. Officials said the name was chosen at random. But it seemed appropriate for an American who had turned against his country and was calling for attacks from within, for it hinted at that mythic symbol of deception and betrayal the Trojan Horse. For JSOC's search team and the spies and eavesdroppers supporting them, Awlaki had become Objective Troy.

The president's decision on Awlaki rested on Barron and Lederman's legal reasoning, which they laid out in writing in a memo dated February 19 and delivered to Attorney General Eric Holder. Oddly, the memo called the proposed drone target "Shaykh Anwar Awlaki," granting him the respectful honorific used by his militant acolytes. Awlaki could legally be targeted by the CIA and the military on the basis of the agency's conclusion that he posed "a continued and imminent threat" to the United States, said the memo, later released with heavy redactions after a lengthy court battle by *The New York Times* and the American Civil Liberties Union. Ordinarily, an "imminent" threat was the kind posed by a gunman pointing a loaded weapon at an innocent person. But Barron and Lederman evidently concluded that terrorists assumed to be plotting in secret qualified as an imminent threat, since requiring the government to wait until they acted would be self-defeating. Because the evidence showed that Awlaki as a leader of AQAP was determined to attack the United States and was working relentlessly toward that goal, there was no requirement that the intelligence agencies know the details and timing of a specific plot. They could assume that an attack was always imminent.

The executive order banning "assassination," dating to the Gerald Ford administration and prompted by the Church Committee's exposure of CIA schemes to kill Fidel Castro and others, did not apply to killings motivated by national self-defense, Barron and Lederman wrote. Nor did the Constitution block Awlaki's killing. The Fifth Amendment dictated that an American could not be deprived of life without "due process of law," which usually meant a criminal trial. But in this case, they decided, no trial was necessary. Citing the Supreme Court's 2004 decision in the case of Yaser Hamdi, an American citizen caught fighting with the Taliban in Afghanistan, Barron and Lederman's analysis said that to decide exactly what "due process of law" was required it was necessary to weigh Awlaki's "private interest" in staying alive against the government's interest in "using an authorized means of force to respond to an imminent threat." Though redactions make it difficult to read this portion of their opinion, clearly they decided that the government's interest took precedence. (Later, in a speech explaining the Justice Department's view, Attorney General Holder would say that adequate "due process" did not necessarily mean court involvement and that careful consideration of evidence inside the executive branch could meet the Fifth Amendment's requirement. "The Constitution guarantees due process, not judicial process," Holder said.)

Nor would the Fourth Amendment, which banned "unreasonable searches and seizures," block targeting Awlaki, Barron and Lederman wrote. They cited a 1985 Supreme Court ruling in *Tennessee v. Garner*, involving a Memphis police officer who had fatally shot a fleeing suspect. The court had ruled that deadly force could be used if there was probable cause to believe the suspect had committed a crime that involved or threatened serious physical harm. The analogy with Awlaki and the Christmas plot was evident, though redactions in the public version of the memo left Barron and Lederman's reasoning riddled with omissions.

But with a deadline pressing, they focused on what they saw as the biggest legal hurdles, leaving what some legal analysts considered to be a gaping hole in their opinion. In April, two months after they completed their memorandum, Kevin Jon Heller, an American law professor teaching in London and Melbourne, wrote a fierce attack on the decision to target Awlaki on the international law blog *Opinio Juris*, beginning with the headline: "Let's Call Killing al-Awlaki What It Is—Murder." Heller had not seen the still-classified legal opinion, but he had read news reports about the addition of Awlaki to the kill list. He based his critique on what was called the foreign-murder statute, 18 USC 1119. On its face, it seemed to apply squarely to the lawfulness of killing Awlaki: it criminalized the act of "a person who, being a national of the United States, kills or attempts to kill a national of the United States while such national is outside the United States but within the jurisdiction of another country." Heller suggested that Obama was matching Bush in legal overreaching: "I have yet to see any reporter ask why Obama believes he has the legal authority to order Americans killed, given that 18 USC 1119 specifically criminalizes such killings," he wrote. He called the Obama administration's presumed override of the foreign-murder statute "deeply problematic—and eerily reminiscent of debates over the Bush administration's authorization of torture."

Such accusations stung, going right to the heart of Barron and Lederman's vulnerability as detractors of the Bush legal record. Having satisfied the urgent demand for a legal ruling with the February opinion, they set out to write a second opinion, completed on July 16, 2010, directly addressing the foreign-murder statute. The law had been passed, they said, to criminalize murders by Americans overseas that might otherwise escape prosecution. But some killings are justified by "public authority"—such as a police officer shooting an armed and threatening criminal. The foreign-murder statute did not apply to such justified killings, they argued, concluding that either military or CIA personnel would be justified in killing a dangerous leader of AQAP who posed an imminent threat to the United States. They conditioned their approval for killing Awlaki on the notion that it was "infeasible" to capture Awlaki alive. But the lawyers left it to the CIA and the Department of Defense to judge whether Awlaki could be captured rather than killed. "Both agencies here have represented that they intend to capture rather than target al-Awlaki if feasible," they wrote, "yet we also understand that an operation by either agency to capture al-Awlaki in Yemen would be infeasible at this time."

More than half the pages of both the February memo and the much longer July memo were blacked out of the copies released to the public, apparently because they summarized the intelligence about Awlaki, his place in AQAP, and the evidence that he was plotting violence. By including the details of the CIA's case against Awlaki—what OLC lawyers called "the factual predicate"—Barron and Lederman seemed to frame their opinion as narrowly as possible. Clearly they hoped that would distinguish their work from the torture memos written by John Yoo, their predecessor in the Bush OLC, who had deliberately tried to stake out a sweeping authorization for presidential power. "In reaching this conclusion," Barron and Lederman wrote in the forty-one-page July memo, "we do not address other cases or circumstances, involving different facts." They did not want to write a blank check to Obama and future presidents to kill Americans vaguely identified as militants or with thin intelligence résumés. In effect, they were attempting to limit their approval to Awlaki himself—whom they argued was at once a leader, an operational planner, and a recruiter for AQAP—avoiding creating any broader precedent.

With their two memos completed, and a green light for the Awlaki hunt, both men left the government—Lederman going to Georgetown University, Barron back to Harvard, where he would remain until Obama named him to an appellate judgeship.

The two OLC opinions were vetted by the so-called lawyers' group at the National Security Council, consisting of the general counsels of the key security agencies and chaired by Mary DeRosa, legal adviser to the NSC. According to two lawyers who attended the meetings, the group recognized the unprecedented nature of the case and discussed it at length, debating the fine points of the law and discussing whether capture might be possible. But in the end, there was no dissent. Inside the government, where the atmosphere was shaped by the constant stream of terror threats, no government lawyer challenged Barron and Lederman's decision that killing Awlaki would be legal and constitutional.

More than once, aides said, Obama remarked on the strength of the evidence against Awlaki, which was highly unusual for a terrorism case. Of course, none of the evidence would be presented in court, subjected to cross-examination, or assessed by a jury of his peers. But Obama and his aides had the firsthand testimony of Abdulmutallab about Awlaki's role in the airliner plot; they had communications intercepted by the NSA that showed Awlaki plotting with other Al Qaeda members; and they had Awlaki's own public declarations that he considered it every Muslim's religious duty to kill Americans. The president considered that more than enough. "This," Obama told aides of the decision to target Awlaki for execution without trial, "is an easy one."

Whether Obama truly found the decision on Awlaki easy—or whether he wrestled with it privately during the late nights he sometimes kept in his small office in the White House family quarters—many other people were troubled. In the larger community of law professors and national security experts, the legal questions surrounding the targeting of Awlaki would provoke debate for years, dividing the community of constitutional scholars. The notion of killing an American troubled the public, too. In my reporting, I asked a range of Americans their view on the question and found an intriguing dichotomy. Once I reminded them who Awlaki was and what he had said and done, most agreed with the decision to put him on the kill list, and some recalled the old adage that the Constitution is not a suicide pact. But if I then followed up and asked, "So you believe that any president should be able to designate an American as a dangerous enemy on the basis of secret intelligence and order them killed?" most people balked. They accepted the specific case of Obama and Awlaki; they rejected the general principle, which sounded scarily un-American.

Later, curious about how the Obama administration's stance was viewed in the academic legal world, I asked Mark Kende, a constitutional law professor at Drake University, to help me organize an informal online survey of his colleagues in the field. Of the thirty-two current and former professors of constitutional law who responded, eleven said they thought killing Awlaki was legal and constitutional; nine said it was not; and twelve said, "It depends" and offered nuanced analyses. In other words, there was no consensus on the question among experts on constitutional law. If Barron and Lederman had hoped to settle the issue, they had failed, perhaps inevitably. Indeed, had the Obama of 2008 been asked whether a president could order the killing of an American, it was easy to imagine that he would have been among the doubters. "I taught constitutional law for ten years," he had said at a town hall meeting in Lancaster, Pennsylvania, during the campaign. "I take the Constitution very seriously. The biggest problems that we're facing right now have to do with George Bush trying to bring more and more power into the executive branch."

The ambivalence, both in the scholarly world and among the general public, was understandable. On the one hand, there was the notion that Awlaki had joined the enemy in a war and that, like German Americans who had fought for the Nazis in World War II, he could expect no immunity based on his citizenship. But the face-off with Al Qaeda bore little resemblance to World War II, or indeed to any war in American history. So there was a bracing alternative analogy: that killing Awlaki would be like a justified police shooting of an armed and threatening criminal. The police shooting parallel was cited by Barron and Lederman and was raised repeatedly by government officials who supported targeting Awlaki. "My view was Anwar al-Awlaki was actively plotting to kill American citizens," said Gerald Feierstein, who was the American ambassador to Yemen during the hunt. "To me, he was like a guy walking down an American street carrying an M-16. The police would take him out." Feierstein agreed with Obama's assessment that the decision was "an easy one."

On the other hand, for decades the United States under both political parties had condemned extrajudicial killing by other countries, notably including Israel, which had pioneered the targeted killing of suspected terrorists. Only since 9/11, under Bush and then under Obama, had the United States openly embraced the practice that it had long condemned. Now that Awlaki's American citizenship added special weight to the decision to kill, elaborate legal justifications, classified as top secret and kept from the public, could not fully counter the sense that the government was acting out of expediency, not principle. It was another mark of how the fear of terrorism had changed the country.

In their effort to sort out the contrary pressures of targeted killing, some ethicists and philosophers revived a concept dating to the Vietnam War called "dirty hands," a phrase used to describe an irresolvable moral quandary. The name was borrowed from the title of a 1948 play by Jean-Paul Sartre about the assassination of a politician. Sometimes, the dirty hands theory argued, an act could be simultaneously morally required and morally forbidden—"the least evil choice available in the circumstances that still leaves an indelible moral stain on the character of the person making the choice," in the words of two scholars. Putting Awlaki on the kill list seemed to me to fit this model: allowing him to operate freely would arguably put at risk the lives of hundreds or thousands of people in a future attack. While AQAP could certainly mount an attack without him, his role in recruiting English-speaking jihadists with access to the United States, and his own focus on the United States as a target, surely magnified the threat. But killing him without a trial could violate some of the country's most cherished principles, setting an alarming precedent for future presidents. Perhaps it was no wonder that the former constitutional law professor who had vowed on taking office to run the most transparent administration in history allowed his administration not just to keep the Barron-Lederman legal opinion classified but to spend years fighting in court to keep it secret.

There would be three more American strikes in Yemen in the months following the cruise missile strike in Al Majala. All would be carried out by JSOC, the secretive American strike force with headquarters at Fort Bragg in North Carolina and the clout to commandeer military assets all over the world. None used drones, because Djibouti still objected; but cruise missiles were also out in view of the massacre of civilians at Al Majala. Instead, they used an array of manned jets, flown from Djibouti and from ships off shore. There was the strike on December 24 in Shabwah that was falsely reported to have killed Awlaki but did kill thirty or more other people, reportedly at an Al Qaeda gathering. On March 15 another strike hit another Al Qaeda site in Abyan, not far from Al Majala.

In approving strikes in Yemen, Obama was completely dependent on the advice of military commanders and intelligence chiefs. When their information was wrong, his decisions would be wrong. After the fourth strike, on May 24, 2010, it swiftly became clear that the intelligence had once again been utterly inadequate. The missiles hit two vehicles in Marib, the same wild tribal province where the CIA had carried out its first drone strike in Yemen back in 2002. Among four or more people killed, according to contradictory reports, were probably two Al Qaeda members. But meeting with them, in an apparent bid for peace, was the popular deputy governor of Marib province, Jabir al-Shabwani. Shabwani was doing his job in a difficult situation, trying to keep his people safe from attacks; like many Yemeni officials, he had a cousin in Al Qaeda, Ayed al-Shabwani, so he had ways to reach out to the terrorist group. JSOC operators learned that they had killed the deputy governor only when infuriated tribesmen attacked a major oil pipeline in the area at the behest of Shabwani's grieving father, Ali, an important tribal leader. The unintended killing of the younger Shabwani, known as a capable and charismatic leader, would alienate the tribes of Marib province from the government in Sanaa for years afterward and make some tribesmen more hospitable to Al Qaeda. It was, in other words, another disastrous mistake.

According to two American officials, the Shabwani blunder was partly a result of JSOC's eagerness to hit Awlaki. Just two days before the botched strike, Awlaki had given an interview to AQAP's media arm, calling on Muslims everywhere to attack the United States. With pressure to find him ratcheted up still more, American intelligence picked up a walkie-talkie signal believed to be associated with Awlaki from the two vehicles in Marib. But walkie-talkies, cell phones, and other items whose signals the Americans routinely tracked could, of course, be passed around. Awlaki was evidently nowhere near the walkie-talkie when the missiles hit.

The strikes of December 17 and May 24 had not involved drones, with their ostensible advantages. But no weapon was better than the intelligence that guided it, and the quality of the intelligence guiding strikes in Yemen seemed to be shockingly poor. Shifting from cruise missiles to drones might make it possible to hit a small target, but if the intelligence was flawed, that wouldn't matter: the precise, drone-fired missile would precisely kill the wrong person. Between the choice of weapons and the abysmal intelligence, by mid-2010, the campaign Obama had started against AQAP in Yemen—his own war, not the one in Pakistan he had inherited from Bush—was looking decidedly like a "dumb war."

Obama, briefed by Brennan on the May 24 strike, was distressed by JSOC's erratic performance in Yemen. He complained sharply to the man some described as the president's favorite general, General James "Hoss" Cartwright, vice-chairman of the Joint Chiefs of Staff. Partly because of protests from President Saleh, and partly because of Obama's displeasure, American strikes in Yemen would be suspended for a year. Had the agencies managed to pinpoint Awlaki's location during the next year, it is likely that the moratorium would have come to a sudden end. In fact, the first strike after the year's hiatus would be aimed at him.

But even as Obama seethed about the mistakes in Yemen, neither he nor his aides offered any public expression of regret to address Yemeni anger at the unintended deaths. As so often occurred in the classified sectors of government, secrecy and compartmentation prevented real accountability for the targeting mistakes. Publicly, Obama spoke only of successful strikes against Al Qaeda in Yemen, and furious Yemenis naturally held him responsible for what had actually been grave blunders. Only privately, in White House meetings, did the president express deep concern about JSOC's record.

For several years, both before and after Anwar's prison term, Nasser al-Awlaki had pleaded with Anwar to tone down his rhetoric, but it did no good. "His father made several attempts to persuade him to stop talking about jihad," recalled Morten Storm, his former Danish follower, who said he had met Nasser al-Awlaki on a couple of occasions. "He told me about this. But he said, 'I respect my dad, but I cannot agree to this because Allah's order, his commandment of jihad, supersedes my obedience to my father.'"

But Dr. Awlaki refused to give up his fight to save his son. The new American reports that Obama had approved the killing of Anwar al-Awlaki, based on leaks from anonymous officials, spurred Nasser al-Awlaki to join a new, more aggressive effort to defend his son. He joined forces with attorneys from two groups that shared his dismay over the Obama administration's decision to target an American citizen for death. The American Civil Liberties Union and the Center for Constitutional Rights made his campaign more than the understandable effort of a father to save his son; now it was a high-profile battle over fundamental rights. Jameel Jaffer and Ben Wizner of the ACLU had traveled to Sanaa in May 2010 to consult with Nasser. They agreed to represent him on July 7, and on July 16 the Treasury Department formally labeled Anwar al-Awlaki as a "Specially Designated Global Terrorist." Government officials insisted that the designation was merely another justified step in the attempt to isolate and neutralize Awlaki. The ACLU lawyers believed that Obama administration officials had made the move to block, or at least delay, their plan to file a lawsuit for Dr. Awlaki on his son's behalf: to represent a designated terrorist might now require a special license from the Treasury's Office of Foreign Asset Control. After a court challenge, Treasury officials agreed to change the rules to permit uncompensated legal representation for people on the terrorist list. On August 30, Nasser al-Awlaki filed suit against the American officials pursuing his son: Barack Obama; Leon E. Panetta, the CIA director; and Robert M. Gates, the defense secretary.

The government was trying to kill an American citizen, the lawsuit alleged, without any criminal charge, without making public its evidence against him, without any trial to weigh whatever evidence it might have. Dr. Awlaki's lawyers essentially argued the opposite of everything that Barron and Lederman had concluded in their still-secret legal opinions. Killing Awlaki, they contended, would flagrantly violate the Fourth Amendment, the Fifth Amendment, and international law. As so-called next friend of his absent son, Nasser al-Awlaki argued that "means other than lethal force could reasonably be employed to neutralize" any threat posed by Awlaki—in other words, capture was feasible.

When the case came to a hearing before District Judge John D. Bates in Washington, Justice Department attorneys advanced three points: the plaintiff lacked standing to bring the claim; the question of whom to kill was a "political question," to be decided solely by the executive and legislative branches; and such matters were in any case far too sensitive to be discussed in open court. (Gates, Panetta, and James Clapper, the director of national intelligence, had all filed statements asserting that a full hearing for the lawsuit would expose important secrets.)

For nearly three hours on a Monday in November 2010, in a Washington courtroom packed with rapt lawyers and law students, the two sides went at it in a case that Judge Bates called "extraordinary and unique." Nasser al-Awlaki's case was laid out by Jameel Jaffer of the ACLU. A Canadian from a Muslim immigrant family, Jaffer, like Obama, had graduated from Harvard Law School. He had joined a Wall Street firm, but after volunteering to represent immigrants detained after 9/11 he had gone to work for the ACLU full time. Now he staked a stark constitutional claim: "If the Fourth and Fifth Amendments mean anything at all, surely they mean there are limits to the circumstances in which the government can use lethal force against one of its own citizens." If that's so, Jaffer said, "the courts have a role to play in delineating those limits and ensuring that they're complied with." Jaffer's cocounsel from the Center for Constitutional Rights, Pardiss Kebriaei, said that the Justice Department's argument that the government could kill an American with absolutely no role for the courts was "terrifying."

Judge Bates put the Justice Department's lawyer, Douglas Letter, through his paces, pressing him to explain one of the commonsense paradoxes the case raised. "How is it that judicial scrutiny is required when the United States decides to target a US citizen overseas for electronic surveillance," Judge Bates asked, "but judicial scrutiny is prohibited, in your view, on the political question doctrine, when the United States decides to target a US citizen overseas for death? How does that all make sense?" In other words, how could a court warrant be required for eavesdropping on Awlaki's cell phone but not for dispatching a drone to kill him?

Letter suggested that the apparent illogic was superficial: In an eavesdropping case, he told the judge, "You're not being asked to stand at the shoulder of the president as the president is trying to decide, is there an imminent threat to the security of US nationals posed by the leader of a highly active terrorist organization?" That role, he argued, is reserved for the commander in chief without court interference.

But perhaps Letter's most telling point, which he said went "to the very strangeness of this suit," hinted at the father-son drama that had unfolded, mostly in private, for years. Anwar al-Awlaki "is urging people to die in an effort to kill Americans, and at the same time is repudiating the power of the US courts," Letter said. "And yet his father is here trying to use the US courts in a way that would allow Al-Awlaki to continue acting as a leader of an organization that is actively engaged in trying to kill Americans."

The contradiction appeared to trouble Judge Bates, too. Anwar al-Awlaki "doesn't respect the US court system," the judge said. "He doesn't think it has any jurisdiction over a Muslim. How can one conclude that he would believe that the US court system should be a vehicle for assessing his rights?"

That question turned out to be decisive when Judge Bates dismissed the lawsuit with an eighty-three-page ruling in December. He did not shy away from the stark questions raised by sending the drones after an American. "Can the Executive order the assassination of a U.S. citizen," Bates wrote, "without first affording him any form of judicial process whatsoever, based on the mere assertion that he is a dangerous member of a terrorist organization?" His answer was yes on two grounds, even as he acknowledged that his conclusion was "somewhat unsettling." First, there was no evidence that Anwar al-Awlaki supported his father's lawsuit and plenty of indirect evidence that he did not. The younger Awlaki had managed to put out jihadist screeds urging the murder of Americans, the judge noted, so he certainly could have smuggled out a statement of support for his father's lawsuit. Under the circumstances, Nasser could not serve as "next friend" in challenging his son's placement on the government's kill list. Second, Bates accepted the government's assertion that, at least in this case, such a targeting decision must be reserved for the executive branch, leaving no place for judicial review. He declined to rule on the government's state secrets claim.

Whether Anwar took note of the lawsuit his father had filed to save his life, or of its dismissal, was unclear.

If there was a sign of trouble regarding Obama's judgment about the targeted killing program—an unsettling hint of how comfortable he had become with the lethal power he was wielding—it had come on Saturday, May 1, 2010, at the White House Correspondents' Association Dinner, a Washington tradition in which reporters donned tuxedoes and invited some of the government officials they covered to a banquet where the president spoke. It was always a lavish scene that made some journalists, including me, uneasy; *The New York Times* management had decided in 2007 that the coziness with officials was unbecoming and banned our participation. In his remarks that night, Obama noted that the Jonas Brothers, the boy band of the moment, were in attendance and offered a conventional protective-dad joke. "Sasha and Malia are huge fans," said the president of the United States, "but boys, don't get any ideas. I have two words for you: Predator drones. You will never see it coming."

In the sixteen months since Obama had taken office, the CIA had carried out more than eighty drone strikes in Pakistan, including five in the previous month, and the pace was increasing. Along with five hundred to seven hundred militants, independent observers counted fifty to two hundred civilians killed on his watch, including as many as two dozen children. American officials, speaking anonymously, claimed that such estimates of the civilian toll were exaggerated, but anger in volatile Pakistan was growing. To joke so casually and publicly about lethal Predator strikes—especially when real strikes were treated by the administration as too sensitive for public discussion—seemed in stunningly bad taste, as some White House officials would later acknowledge. The joke had been written for Obama, of course, but he had apparently not judged it problematic. For a president who had often spoken to aides about the moral burden of drone strikes, it seemed incongruous.

The news from New York City that very Saturday night would underscore the point. About three hours before the president's 10 p.m. remarks in Washington, a Times Square vendor spotted smoke coming from a Nissan Pathfinder parked on the street with the engine running but no one inside. He hailed a mounted police officer, who summoned an explosives team. Some fifty-three hours later, counterterrorism officers stopped a flight on the runway at JFK International Airport and pulled off the plane a Pakistan-born American citizen who had graduated from college in Connecticut, worked as a financial analyst for a cosmetics firm, and married and started a family. Faisal Shahzad, thirty years old at the time of his arrest, would later explain his reasons for attempting the bombing, which he had believed would kill at least forty people. The United States had attacked Islam again and again; he was merely fighting back, he said in remarks at both his guilty plea and his sentencing. He singled out the drones as a big part of his motive. "Until the hour the US . . . stops its drone strikes in Somalia and Yemen and in Pakistan," Shahzad said, "we will be attacking US, and I plead guilty to that." When the judge pressed him about whether his plot might have killed children, he replied: "When the drones hit, they don't see children." Obama had vowed to stop torture and shut Guantanamo because, he said, they had become a recruiting tool for Al Qaeda. Now there was stark evidence that the drones were doing the same thing.

It came as no surprise when Shahzad told FBI agents that he had been inspired to act in part by the online tutelage of Anwar al-Awlaki. "When I watched Anwar Awlaki on video, I thought he was talking to me," he told investigators. If Obama needed a reminder about the deadly serious balancing act he had embarked on with his embrace of the drone, Shahzad would supply a memorable case study. And if the intelligence agencies required an incentive to accelerate their hunt for Awlaki, the Times Square near miss provided that as well.

PART FOUR　　2010–2014

11

THE GUY EVERYONE WANTED TO FIND

In his self-imposed exile in Shabwah, his family's ancestral territory, Awlaki had spent much of his time in 2009 at the mosque in the hamlet of Al Saeed, as a leader of prayers and an informal adviser to the impoverished families trying to scratch a living from an unforgiving land. According to his uncle, Saleh bin Fareed al-Awlaki, who saw him there from time to time, "He'd go five times a day to the mosque. At four o'clock in the morning he'd be at the mosque, at sunrise, then maybe he goes home and again at midday." In addition to preaching, Bin Fareed said, his nephew made himself available for consultation. Awlaki, after all, was an educated man from a prominent family, the kind who ordinarily would live in Sanaa or overseas, far from the deprivations of the village. "He'd sit most of his time in the mosque. People would ask him questions—people would have family problems, children problems, and they would ask him, and he would advise them what to do." His father was supporting him financially, Bin Fareed said, but he seemed to have no long-term career plan. "He was stuck," Awlaki's uncle said.

In fact, while he may not have been confiding in his uncle, he was not at all stuck. Awlaki was reaching out regularly via his blog, Facebook page, and e-mail to Muslims far beyond the Shabwah village where he had sought refuge with his family's tribe. With the help of technically minded allies and the luster added by his imprisonment, he was projecting a steadily more violent message to Muslims across the English-speaking world. To his family, he may have looked like a failure, thwarted in conventional career plans and hounded out of

America, out of England, and finally out of Sanaa. But his modest surroundings did not deter his vision or ambition. In February 2009, he sent the two e-mails to Major Nidal Hasan, who had written him repeatedly, in part to solicit his theological judgment on American soldiers who attacked fellow soldiers to prevent them from fighting Muslims abroad. On March 1, 2009, in a telephone address to an Islamic gathering in Pakistan, he struck a grand, prophetic chord. The world was "on the verge of a Muslim revival," he told his audience. The last caliphate, or transnational Muslim government, had officially ended with the fall of Ottoman Turkey in 1924, he said, and history showed that Islamic awakenings came roughly every one hundred years. Echoing George W. Bush, he declared that "there are forces of good and there are forces of evil and they are conflicting with each other." In effect, Awlaki said, you are either with us or you are with the infidels. Though neither the West nor the hypocritical leaders of Yemen and Pakistan wanted to hear it, he said, the key to the revival was jihad—and not jihad as apologists for the United States were trying to redefine it.

"Forget about those who try to twist the meaning of jihad to exclude fighting," Awlaki told his Pakistani audience. "Forget about those who say this is not the time for jihad because we are weak. Leave them alone and fulfill your duties toward Allah." In the Koran, Allah had addressed "the might of those who disbelieve," and that currently took the form of American soldiers with "their high-tech weaponry and their advanced missiles," he said. "So how can we restrain their might? Is it through negotiations? Is it through giving up? Is it through surrendering?" No, Awlaki said, "Allah gives us the answer in the Koran: Fight in the path of Allah. That is how Allah will restrain the might of those who disbelieve."

By the time of that telephone address to Pakistan in the early spring of 2009, National Security Agency (NSA) eavesdroppers were picking up regular communications between Awlaki and the leaders of the newly formed Al Qaeda in the Arabian Peninsula. How and when they first met is uncertain. Nasser al-Wuhayshi, the former Bin Laden secretary who now was the emir, or leader, of the Yemeni affiliate of the terrorist network, may have recognized in Awlaki an emerging ally and reached out; or Awlaki himself may have initiated contact with the group, whose leaders were hiding nearby in the mountains of Shabwah province or neighboring Marib. Conceivably the initial contacts may have dated back as far as 2006, when Morten Storm, the Danish convert, was surprised when Awlaki referred in conversation to "the brothers," a phrase he believed meant Al Qaeda. Storm said Awlaki later recounted to him that he had met militants of several generations in prison who were admirers of his lectures. His social status in Yemen gave his embrace of jihad particular force, Storm told me. "He came from a rich family," Storm said. "Most of the Yemeni mujahideen are poor—they come from the lower classes of society in Yemen. But this man, his father was rich, and he's an American national, and he speaks English, and he's a scholar." Awlaki, he said, "could reach people that Al Qaeda could not. He would reach out to the foreigners. He was exactly the bridge AQAP needed to reach the West."

However it began, the alliance between Awlaki and Al Qaeda's branch was quite natural. By 2009, Awlaki had evolved to an open embrace of violent jihad, naming in his March 1 talk as its proper targets both the "tyrants" ruling Yemen and other Muslim countries and the "Jews and Christians" of the United States and Europe. His worldview now perfectly matched that of Al Qaeda.

Awlaki's deepening relationship with Al Qaeda may have contributed to another move he made in the summer of 2009—a somber request to his father. His two wives had taken turns staying with him in Shabwah, where he split his time between the provincial capital, Al Ataq, and his family's village of Al Saeed. He had even installed a television in his apartment in Al Ataq so that his teenage second wife could divert herself in this backwater with the Turkish soap operas she loved. (Apparently he had learned to compromise since he had flung his roommate's TV to the floor back at Colorado State in the first flush of his discovery of puritanical Islam nearly two decades earlier.) But now he decided that the hardship and danger, and his increasing absorption with what he saw as the duty of jihad, required a change. "He sent me a message—he said, 'Father, consider my family is your immediate family and take care of them, because I am not able to take care of them under the circumstances,'" Nasser al-Awlaki recalled. Anwar's first wife, after all, had lived with him in Denver, San Diego, Falls Church, and Sanaa, light-years economically and socially from the world of the village. "Things were difficult for his family regarding school and their living conditions," Nasser said, and Anwar "really wanted his family to live under normal conditions, so he asked me that they should stay with me in Sanaa." Anwar's first wife, who was related to Nasser, took their three sons and two daughters and moved into Anwar's apartment inside his father's big house in the capital. The nineteen-year-old second wife, not connected with Nasser by family or tribe, evidently left Shabwah to join her extended family elsewhere in Yemen.

But Anwar was not ready to give up female companionship. Before his pregnant second wife left Shabwah, he mentioned to Morten Storm the possibility of helping him find yet another wife. His first two wives, as traditional Yemeni women, could not be expected to join fully in his cause. But for a third wife, Awlaki imagined, he might find a Western convert who believed in the cause of jihad and would be willing to put up with the isolation and deprivation of the new life he had chosen. Storm didn't know how serious Awlaki was, but the cleric would return again and again to the subject.

By August 1, 2009, Awlaki was publicly taking the side of AQAP in its fight with Yemeni authorities. On his blog, he wrote excitedly about the "humiliating defeat" of government forces by the "mujahideen" in the tribal province of Marib, adjacent to Shabwah. In Awlaki's retelling, which looked for larger meaning in a minor battle, the clash took on an almost miraculous resonance. Three government soldiers had been killed, five had been injured, and five tanks and two armored vehicles had been destroyed, Awlaki wrote, while the Al Qaeda force had grabbed "an entire truck load of weapons" and other gear. "Casualties amongst the ranks of the mujahideen: None. None killed, none injured and no damage to their houses or property either. The first face to face fight between the army and the mujahideen ended in a resounding victory for the mujahideen," he wrote. "May this be the beginning of the greatest Jihad, the Jihad of the Arabian Peninsula that would free the heart of the Islamic world from the tyrants who are deceiving the ummah and standing between us and victory."

The post marked yet another shift. Awlaki's previous public utterances had embraced jihad largely in theory, while avoiding the explicit endorsement of any particular operation. This was different.

Still living more or less openly in Yemen, though far from the capital and on tribal territory where he felt secure, Awlaki was endorsing the bloody insurgency of Al Qaeda against the Yemeni government and military.

Soon after that, he was becoming personally involved in AQAP's plotting. Within weeks of his August blog post, he had approved the eager appeal of Umar Farouk Abdulmutallab to join the jihad, questioning him about his fitness for a mission and sending him to Ibrahim al-Asiri, the bomb maker. By then, some American counterterrorism analysts concluded, Awlaki had formed a small "external operations" cell within AQAP that included the Saudi-born Asiri and Samir Khan, an American who had proselytized for jihad from his parents' North Carolina basement before moving to Yemen. That label may have implied a more formal organization than the loose terrorist gang really had, but its logic was clear: Awlaki and Khan were more focused on "the far enemy" in America than were most of the Yemeni and Saudi operatives in AQAP, who thought first about the fight closer to home. Asiri's sophisticated bomb-design skills, wasted on ordinary IEDs and car bombs for use inside Yemen, were most important for penetrating the formidable security protecting the Saudi monarchy and American and international airports. Indeed, in August 2009, about the time Abdulmutallab was asking around Sanaa for contacts with Awlaki, Asiri fitted his own brother, Abdullah, with a bomb that he could wear either inside or very close to his body and dispatched him to Jiddah, where he claimed to be a repentant jihadi with urgent information about the threat to Saudi Arabia. Remarkably, he managed to talk his way into a personal meeting with Prince Mohammed bin Nayef, the Saudi counterterrorism chief and a name near the top of the list of Al Qaeda's Saudi targets. The bomb made it through metal detectors, and Asiri detonated it when he approached the prince. The force of the explosive suicide blast traveled vertically, however, blowing Abdullah's anatomy into the ceiling while leaving the prince shaken but without serious injury. Ibrahim al-Asiri's handiwork had managed to kill only his brother. But for Mohammed bin Nayef, already a confidant of John Brennan and a close ally of the United States, the fight against AQAP was now a matter of personal survival. Saudi intelligence stepped up its cooperation with the CIA against their mutual enemy.

There were signs that Awlaki, too, was beginning to worry about survival. On September 8, the administrator of his website posted the transcript of an Awlaki lecture about the Guantanamo prisoners, which he had delivered on August 30 by phone to London, with an apologetic note: "I decided to post this on Sheikh Anwar's Blog, even though I can't get in touch with him to get his ok. Hope its ok Sheikh. We all know you are very busy." Awlaki may have been busy trying to stay alive: he knew that using e-mail or a cell phone could make him easy to locate. On September 20, Awlaki's blog wished his readers Eid Mubarak—a mandatory greeting for any imam on the holiday marking the end of the holy month of Ramadan. But the cleric who eight years earlier had so patiently explained Ramadan to non-Muslim Americans in a *Washington Post* video was not available to send the greeting himself. "I am sure that Sh Anwar would have loved to convey his best wishes to everyone, but at this stage he is unable to get to the Internet," the website administrator wrote.

On October 7, Awlaki himself reappeared on the blog with another upbeat account of what he called the "surprising growth" of "the jihad movement" and the military success of the militants in several countries. The post, titled "Could Yemen Be the Next Surprise of the Season?," recounted that "the Jihad of this era started in Palestine, followed by Afghanistan, then Chechnya, then Iraq, then Somalia, then the Maghreb," or North Africa, "and the new front might very well turn out to be Yemen." He noted that the largest bloc of foreign Muslim fighters in the wars in Bosnia, Chechnya, Afghanistan, and Iraq had come from Yemen and Saudi Arabia and that the Arabian Peninsula had been the birthplace of Islam. "When Jihad starts in the Arabian Peninsula, Jihad would be coming back to its home," he wrote. He lambasted the al Saud family ruling Saudi Arabia and called for its destruction, without mentioning the failed suicide attack of Abdullah al-Asiri on the Saudi prince in charge of counterterrorism a few weeks earlier. "They wear cloaks of sheep on hearts of wolfs," he wrote of the Saudi rulers. "There cannot be Islamic rule and a return to khilafah," or a caliphate, a united Muslim state, "without removing them from existence and this is the responsibility of the mujahedeen of the Arabian Peninsula."

And Awlaki's blog post took on Obama directly, trying out the mocking "short leash" line that he would reprise in an audio message the following March:

The American people gave G. W. Bush unanimous backing to fight against the mujahedeen and gave him a blank check to spend as much as needed to fulfill that objective. The result? He failed, and he failed miserably. So if America failed to defeat the mujahedeen when it gave its president unlimited support, how can it win with Obama who is on a short leash? If America failed to win when it was at its pinnacle of economic strength, how can it win today with a recession—if not a depression—at hand? The simple answer is: America cannot and will not win. The tables have turned and there is no rolling back of the worldwide Jihad movement.

By the time Awlaki made this extravagant boast, the Abdulmutallab operation was probably in the planning stages. Awlaki had declared his position on the side of Al Qaeda in its fight against the government in which his father had once served. His wives and children had left Shabwah. Overhead, he was spotting and hearing the Predators cruising over his tribal territory. He knew he might be a target, and according to relatives he feared his presence could endanger the innocent villagers of Al Saeed, many of them his blood relatives. So he decided to leave Al Saeed for more remote hideouts in the Al-Kur Mountains of Shabwah, where his ancestors had lived more than a century earlier and where Al Qaeda's Yemen commanders had already found refuge.

But just one last time, Awlaki took the risk of posting on his blog, which required him either to go online or to use the phone or a courier to deliver his text. After Nidal Hasan carried out his shooting spree at Fort Hood on November 5, some of Awlaki's followers began a debate in comments posted on his website about whether the murder of thirteen people in Texas was religiously justified. The demands for Sheikh Anwar's view of the matter tempted him to take his chances with a final, inflammatory comment. On November 9 he weighed in with what would be his last and most infamous post: "Nidal Hassan Did the Right Thing." There is no evidence that Awlaki realized then that the army major who had yelled "Allahu akbar!" (God is great) and opened fire was the fawning, wife-hunting fan from his former mosque in Virginia with whom he had exchanged e-mails the previous February. But Hasan's shooting spree completely accorded with what Awlaki had written on his blog that July: that any Muslim soldier who killed Muslims on behalf of an infidel nation like the United States was "a heartless beast, bent on evil, who sells his religion for a few dollars."

The next day his website administrator evidently grew concerned that Awlaki's inflammatory declaration that Nidal Hasan was a hero might put him, too, in legal or physical jeopardy. He posted a lengthy disclaimer on the site distancing himself from Awlaki's views: "We hereby declare and make absolute public declaration that the website anwar-alawlaki.com operates under the divine right bestowed by the Creator to freedom of religion and tasteful expression and that in no way, shape or form do we call for war against U.S. civilians." Despite the administrator's newfound concern that Awlaki might have overstepped the boundaries of "tasteful expression," he was back the next day with a chipper promise: "Assaalmu'alaykum all, The website will be back to normal with a few days time." It was not to be. No Internet host any longer felt like giving Awlaki a forum. After a stunningly successful run of less than two years, Sheikh Anwar's blog was history.

By now, in any case, Awlaki was no longer satisfied with blogging about jihad. For better or worse, he had cast his lot with Al Qaeda. In early December, he helped arrange the filming of Abdulmutallab's martyrdom video. A few days later, the young Nigerian was fitted with the underwear bomb, and Awlaki instructed him to wait until he was certain that he was over American soil before detonating it. On December 7, Abdulmutallab flew from Sanaa to Ethiopia, the first leg of several trips designed, as his Al Qaeda instructors had advised him, to put some distance between Yemen and his flight to the United States.

On December 17 came the devastating American strike on the Al Qaeda camp at Al Majala in Abyan province. It cost the terrorist group a dozen or more fighters. But by killing some forty-one civilians, half of them children, this opening strike in the American campaign gave Al Qaeda a huge propaganda opportunity, which it exploited with videos rallying tribesmen for war with the United States. "The Americans just scored a big own goal," Awlaki wrote to

Morten Storm in an encrypted e-mail, using a soccer term for a goal accidentally scored by a team against itself. Then, on December 24, came the second American strike of the month, another volley of cruise missiles hitting a house in Shabwah where US intelligence believed a meeting of Al Qaeda leaders was taking place.

The Yemeni embassy in Washington put out a statement saying that Awlaki was "presumed to be at the site" along with other top AQAP leaders, and early new reports claimed he was among the thirty or so killed. In fact, all of the top leaders had escaped. But if Awlaki had any doubts about the risk he was now running, they were ended in the rubble of the Shabwah house and the speculation about his demise. At the time of the December 24 strike, the Justice Department had not yet written its legal opinion justifying targeting Awlaki, which would be prompted by the Christmas airliner bombing the next day. American officials said that the official targets of the strike were other Saudi and Yemeni leaders of AQAP. But given his role in Al Qaeda, documented by months of intercepted communications, Awlaki was already considered by American authorities a member of the enemy force, not an innocent civilian. Had he been killed, he would have been counted as a combatant.

The eavesdroppers at the NSA, and the counterterrorism analysts at the other agencies who read intercepted communications and wrote reports about them for distribution across the security establishment, got regular legal briefings on privacy protections for American citizens. In most cases, Americans who turned up on the NSA's net were edited out of reports, their names replaced by the anonymizing phrase "US person." Analysts were likewise instructed not to use American names in their searches of classified counterterrorism databases. "But there was a prominent Awlaki exception," said one analyst then assigned to Yemen. "It was written everywhere that anything on him should be pursued." For several years, the Justice Department had kept updating with the Foreign Intelligence Surveillance Court an eavesdropping order on Awlaki, allowing the NSA to scan the ether for his phone calls and e-mails. In the Justice Department's paradoxical legal reasoning, his American citizenship required a court order if the government wanted to intercept his communications—but no court approval was necessary to kill him.

The machinery of American intelligence, from satellites and sur-veillance drones to cell phone intercepts and paid informants, was zooming in on the very territory where American officials believed Awlaki and the rest of AQAP were hiding—the thinly populated ter-ritories of Shabwah and Marib that gradually gave way to the north and east to the vast, legendary desert called the Rub al-Khali, the Empty Quarter. Stretching across Yemen, Saudi Arabia, and Oman, the Empty Quarter consisted of drab gravel plains and red-tinted dunes that stretch for hundreds of miles, all but devoid of oases or of people. Along the western edge of the great desert were arid val-leys and rugged hills like the Al-Kur Mountains that offered endless places to hide. The imagery analysts at the National Geospatial-Intelligence Agency pored over detailed satellite photos and drone footage of the area, but unless the NSA eavesdroppers could pinpoint the location of a cellular call or a walkie-talkie signal, the landscape was barren of real clues.

By now, even the lowliest listeners and linguists in the Ameri-can government knew it: Obama wanted the bomb maker, Asiri, and the leader of AQAP, Wuhayshi, but above all he wanted Awlaki. At the NSA, at the CIA, at the National Counterterrorism Cen-ter, at the Defense Intelligence Agency, at the National Geospatial-Intelligence Agency, the former Yemen analyst said, teams were assigned and spy gear was redirected to track Awlaki. "He was the guy everyone wanted to find. Everyone wanted to get a bullet point on Awlaki into the PDB," the President's Daily Brief, the analyst said. If the evidence that Awlaki was now "operational" made all the difference to the legal analysis, he posed a multifold danger, in the eyes of American officials. He lent to AQAP's targeting of America a sophisticated knowledge of the enemy's ways and thinking. He had the authority to give a religious gloss to attack plans. Perhaps most important, he was the most effective recruiter of English speakers to Al Qaeda's cause, an alluring voice that the agencies, and the White House, wanted to silence.

But that was the problem. Scanning the petabytes of communica-tions scooped up by the NSA was an exercise in frustration. Awlaki's name, even his recorded voice, was everywhere on the web, and al-most everything the computers tripped at turned out to be e-mails containing old quotations of Awlaki's sermons, accolades from his admirers, or forwarded YouTube clips of his myriad lectures. It was like searching the Internet for Jay-Z. The problem was not too little material, but too much—nearly all of it useless. The tiny number of intercepts that seemed to reflect real knowledge of Awlaki's current whereabouts—in calls or e-mails from the tribal areas, for instance—were frustratingly imprecise. Most often, they were mentions of Awlaki, or a "sheikh" or "imam" that sounded like it could be him, reporting that he had been spotted some days earlier in a particular village or heard at a mosque. The reverberations of his travels gave a general sense of where Awlaki might be, but with nothing like the specificity and timeliness required for a capture or kill operation. "We were pretty good at knowing where he was yesterday," said an American official who was briefed regularly on the hunt. "But that didn't help with where he was today."

By now, Awlaki, like other Al Qaeda operatives, was routinely encrypting his e-mails. The NSA would become quite familiar with the militants' favorite encryption program, called Mujahideen Secrets 2, or "MS-2" in agency jargon; Morten Storm, who had become disillusioned with militant Islam and started working with Danish, British, and American intelligence, delivered the software in late 2009 to Western counterterrorism agencies. But the measures Al Qaeda was taking to hide its footsteps made it tough to get real-time information on Awlaki's whereabouts. When Scotland Yard arrested Rajib Karim and got hold of his hard drive, for instance, it took cryptographers nine months to decipher three hundred messages and discover the exchanges between Karim and Awlaki. Karim had used encrypted Word documents that were digitally compressed and uploaded to web hosting sites; the web addresses for the documents, or URLs, were known only to Karim and Awlaki. It was the Internet-age equivalent of a Cold War dead drop, a loose brick in a wall or a rock in the woods where the CIA or KGB could leave secret messages.

But Awlaki was not hiding everything he was writing. In June 2010, with the American hunt for him in high gear, Awlaki doubled down on his message in a way that would resonate for years. He and a young American acolyte named Samir Khan released the first issue of a breathtakingly brazen, English-language AQAP magazine they called simply *Inspire*.

With its breezy style, how-to features, and celebrity promotion, *Inspire* was a dead-on imitation of the American consumer magazine rack, *Maxim* for the jihadi set. But the do-it-yourself articles were about how best to maim, kill, and terrorize non-Muslims in the West, and the celebrities were jihadi heroes—Osama bin Laden, his deputy Ayman al-Zawahri, and most prominently "Shaykh Anwar al-Awlaki," whose name graced the top of the cover.

Some nonplussed American commentators immediately thought of the *Onion* and wondered if *Inspire* might be a sophisticated spoof. After all, would a violent religious fanatic devise the cover story "Make a Bomb in the Kitchen of Your Mom," listing as the author "The AQ Chef"? It seemed too lighthearted, too much like a parody. In fact, Khan and Awlaki were attempting a marketing revolution for their ruthless cause, breaking once and for all with the ponderous, grimly serious style of Bin Laden and Zawahri. If casual observers saw the magazine as a kind of tasteless joke, counterterrorism specialists were shaken by the publication from the beginning. British intelligence attempted a clumsy dirty trick, inserting talk-show host Ellen DeGeneres's favorite cupcake recipes into an early online copy of the first issue of *Inspire*. That odd sabotage became a forgotten footnote, as *Inspire*'s first issue, without the cupcakes, raced around the world, passed from enthusiast to enthusiast and embedded itself ineradicably on the web.

Intelligence analysts believed Awlaki himself was the intellectual force behind the magazine and its sponsor within AQAP, with Samir Khan as the hands-on editor. "It was Awlaki's baby," said a senior American specialist on Yemen who closely tracked the publication. But for anyone who had followed the unlikely career of Samir Khan, *Inspire* arrived with a feeling of déjà vu. Its madcap, attention-deficit-disorder style was almost identical to that of *Jihad Recollections*, a magazine that Khan had produced for four issues from his parents' basement in Charlotte, North Carolina, before departing for Yemen in 2009 to join Awlaki. There was the same odd mix of fundamentalist religion and hip-hop attitude; it was the product one might expect from a talented juvenile at a new-age madrasa.

Two of my colleagues, Michael Moss and Souad Mekhennet, had visited Khan in 2007 in his parents' North Carolina home, where his father was waging an unsuccessful struggle to turn his son away from militancy. His parents, Zafar and Sarah Khan, were Pakistanis who had emigrated to Saudi Arabia, where Samir was born, before moving to the United States in the early 1990s. Samir had gone to high school in Long Island, scandalizing classmates by refusing to recite the Pledge of Allegiance. After moving with his parents to North Carolina, he devoted all his time to creating radical websites. Just twenty-one, he spoke with an arrogant confidence in a *New York Times* video, his bushy beard silhouetted against a window. The death of disbelievers was "no concern of mine," he said, since they were "the people of hellfire." "The American army, the American government, is losing this war. And the Muslims are winning this war," Khan declared. It was hard to know how seriously to take this disaffected kid. He claimed to be doing nothing illegal, just sharing the truth about Islam. "I'm not telling people to build bombs," he said.

With the appearance of *Inspire* three years later, that had changed. Among the most avid readers were the Awlaki trackers at the NSA. Even before the first issue in midsummer 2010, NSA found a way to intercept the copies before they went online—and in some cases to watch as the latest issue was compiled. As a result, American counterterrorism analysts working on Yemen would get each issue two or three weeks before it appeared on militant web forums. They examined the pdf files forensically for electronic clues to Awlaki's location and combed over the substance of each article for hints, intentional or inadvertent, as to what AQAP was planning. But the main effect of each new issue of *Inspire*, according to people in the agencies at the time, was to amp up the hysteria about the threat that terrorists in Yemen posed to America.

At the State Department and the National Counterterrorism Center, some officials thought there should be a formal government response to the magazine. They advanced the familiar argument that the United States was engaged in a battle of ideas and that it should not shy away from the fight or leave the field to Al Qaeda. Others, including Will McCants, a young scholar advising the State Department on radicalization, said that any formal response would simply elevate the magazine and give it greater importance. "*Inspire* magazine really rattled the people inside the government," McCants said. "The thinking was, 'Here is Al Qaeda in English. It's going to mobilize English-speaking Sunni youth to carry out attacks.'" But

McCants argued that there was a danger of overreacting. He countered "the idea that Muslims were automatons who you place inflammatory material before, and they act."

A number of scholars, in fact, consistently argued that Western journalists were exaggerating the importance of both Awlaki and his magazine. They noted that inside Yemen Awlaki was little known beyond small circles of militants, devout foreigners drawn to Yemen, and members of his own extended family and tribe. Considering that just over 1 percent of Yemenis had Internet access and that Awlaki operated almost exclusively in English, he could hardly have reached a broader audience inside the country. The skeptics suggested that Awlaki's rise resulted from a sort of self-fulfilling prophecy by both the foreign media and the Obama administration. By writing about him, the international press raised his profile and drew the attention of impressionable young Muslims to him. By declaring publicly that he was the most dangerous terrorist for the United States, American officials gave him greater status in the AQAP hierarchy and with fellow jihadis.

There was more than a grain of truth in such claims. Western journalists, frustrated that most Al Qaeda ideologists operated in Arabic or other languages they did not know, naturally zeroed in on Awlaki's ubiquitous English-language writings and lectures. The resulting flood of coverage in the West, starting in late 2009, gave him an international spotlight unmatched by any terrorist other than Osama bin Laden. When Wuhayshi, the AQAP leader, proposed in a letter to Bin Laden in August 2010 that Awlaki should take his place as emir of the Al Qaeda branch in Yemen—an unusual moment of self-effacement in the bluster and braggadocio that characterized Al Qaeda—he undoubtedly was trying to capitalize on all the attention Awlaki was getting globally. (Bin Laden, in his secret compound in Pakistan, was not caught up in the Awlaki sensation and may have been a little jealous. He swiftly nixed the idea.)

But the timeline of developments undercuts the notion that Awlaki's significance in the terrorist world was the inadvertent creation of the international media and hysterical bureaucrats. While he was little known to the general public, Awlaki was a star in the English-speaking Islamist world for years before he drew attention from the media. By the time American and European reporters first noticed him, in late November and December 2009 after the Fort Hood attack, he was already a significant figure in AQAP and was in the midst of helping organize its most dangerous plot, the Christmas airliner attack.

Inspire magazine, while brilliantly designed to stir media interest and provoke Americans, reached its target audience of young Western Muslim men without the help of the mainstream media. The cocky, colloquial style and the constant appeals to those in the United States to mount attacks there rattled authorities for a reason. In most cases of US residents charged with terrorist plotting since 2010, investigators have found evidence that the defendants had downloaded and read the magazine. Some of the ideas proposed in the magazine for attacks were ridiculous (spilling oil on roads in hopes of causing cars to slide off, or welding sharp blades to the front of a pickup truck and driving into a crowd). But the basic bomb-making and detonation instructions in *Inspire*, even if presented under a jokey headline, were quite adequate for killing and maiming, as authorities would later discover in the Boston Marathon bombing.

Awlaki's personal contribution to the first issue of *Inspire* was especially dogmatic and vicious, even by his escalating standards. His article focused on the flap over Western cartoonists who had drawn images of the Prophet Muhammad, often derogatory and in any case prohibited by strict Islamic doctrine. In Denmark, where a newspaper had set off a furor by publishing such cartoons, some imams decided to bring groups of young Muslims to Copenhagen for meetings with Danes to promote dialogue and mutual understanding. Awlaki, who in the months after 9/11 had been a regular at interfaith meetings in Washington, now denounced the clerics' efforts as "completely misguided."

"So what is the proper solution to this growing campaign of defamation?" Awlaki asked, and answered: "The medicine prescribed by the Messenger of Allah is the execution of those involved." As usual, he based his case on precedents from the Prophet's life: those who "spoke against" Muhammad in the seventh century, he wrote, had been killed, including "women who sang poetry defaming Muhammad." For him, no dialogue was necessary; examples from fourteen centuries ago settled the matter. He went still further. Killing such cartoonists, he said, was "a golden opportunity" for service to Islam, a greater religious duty even than protecting Muslims by "fighting for Palestine, Afghanistan, or Iraq."

In his previous calls for violence, Awlaki had usually avoided the specific and personal. No more. This time he suggested an appropriate target for murder: "A cartoonist out of Seattle, Washington, named Molly Norris started the 'Everybody Draw Mohammed Day.' This snowball rolled out from between her evil fingers. She should be taken as a prime target of assassination along with others who participated in her campaign." The *Inspire* article was illustrated with a close-up of a handgun, for readers who lacked imagination.

Awlaki was directing his grand jihad at a rather modest target. Norris was a dog lover and part-time cartoonist, barely known even in Seattle, who had been disturbed by the decision in April 2010 of Comedy Central to censor an episode of the irreverent *South Park* show that portrayed Muhammad in a bear costume. On a whim, she drew a satiric poster designating May 20 as "Everybody Draw Mohammed Day" and portraying everyday objects such as a spool of thread and a cup of coffee claiming to be "the real likeness" of Muhammad. The tone was light; she invented a sponsor called "Citizens Against Citizens Against Humor." But her modest attempt at a jocular defense of free speech struck nerves she had never intended, prompting both threats to her and other free-speech advocates from Islamic fundamentalists like Awlaki and bigoted attacks on Islam from others.

"I wasn't savvy," Norris told *City Arts* magazine, the Seattle publication that ran many of her cartoons. "I didn't mean for my satirical poster to be taken seriously. It became kind of an excuse for people to hate or be mean-spirited. I'm not mean-spirited." But it was too late. Norris took down her website and Facebook page and, at the advice of the FBI, adopted a pseudonym, all for fear that someone might carry out what Awlaki described as "the pinnacle of all deeds" by killing an obscure cartoonist and thus sticking up for the Prophet.

As the first issues of *Inspire* stirred excitement in the second half of 2010, the agencies hunting for Awlaki felt even more heat. A pointed question came up repeatedly at the White House and in the congressional intelligence committees: How could this skinny, bespectacled preacher and his sidekicks, hiding in barren mountains, and with the entire American government after them, have the equipment, security, leisure, and self-confidence to put together issue after issue of a slick magazine? It was an embarrassment.

By the time *Inspire* made its debut, there were targeters at both the CIA and the Joint Special Operations Command working exclusively on him. They studied every snippet of signals intelligence, tracked the vague reports of the cleric's travels on large-scale maps of Yemen—and handled a daily barrage of queries from higher-ups, sometimes including the highest-up of all. Obama "was very focused on him," said Ben Rhodes, the deputy national security adviser. "Awlaki and Asiri were seen as irreplaceable figures, Asiri because of his bomb-making skills, Awlaki because of his unique mix of inspirational and operational, and his knowledge of the United States." Questions came from the regular meetings on Yemen at which Obama presided, as well as the Tuesday terrorism meetings in the Situation Room. The Senate and House intelligence committees demanded regular updates on the hunt for Awlaki and the situation in Yemen.

It was a topsy-turvy moment that captured the way terrorism upset the ordinary hierarchies of global power. Perhaps never in American history had a country so insignificant economically and militarily—Yemen's annual gross domestic product was less than Walmart took in each month—attracted so much attention from the top leaders of the United States. But the agencies judged that AQAP, with Awlaki as recruiter and Asiri as master bomb maker, was capable of launching attacks that could penetrate all of America's defenses.

As a spy for Western intelligence inside Al Qaeda, Morten Storm was an infinitely rare creature. During the Cold War, Western spies traditionally had posed as diplomats and, if detected, rarely risked more than expulsion from Moscow or Beijing. Aging CIA veterans boasted of the difficulty of operating by "Moscow rules," under the relentless gaze of Soviet counterintelligence. But Al Qaeda honored no rules at all. Anyone suspected of spying for a Western government would be tortured and executed without hesitation. And instead of trolling for informants at embassy receptions or scientific conferences, a spy penetrating Al Qaeda would have to travel into the wilds of Pakistan's Waziristan or Yemen's Shabwah, often beyond the reach of communications and with no backup to summon in case of emergency.

But as Storm had demonstrated when he switched sides in 2007 and became an informant, Al Qaeda was surprisingly susceptible to infiltration. The terrorist network, after all, invited and accepted volunteers from every country and had no real way to check their credentials. Anyone with a few months of practice at the jargon and dogma of the Salafi-jihadi world could pass as a legitimate Al Qaeda recruit. For Storm, who had met a who's who of militants in Britain, Yemen, and Somalia in his years in the movement, persuading others of his devotion to the Al Qaeda cause posed little difficulty. Awlaki, who had first gotten to know him in the Islamic study circle that Storm had hosted in Sanaa in 2006, seemed to trust him implicitly when he returned to Yemen on several subsequent trips. He had no way of knowing that Storm had switched sides—celebrating his abandonment of Islam in typically outlandish style by ordering a bacon sandwich and a beer with Danish intelligence officers.

Awlaki entrusted to Storm, in fact, a most intimate quest, extremely sensitive from both a personal and an operational standpoint: the search for a Western wife. Having sent away his first two wives, he was pining for female company. Remarkably, at the very time that he was becoming deeply involved in the most sensitive Al Qaeda operations—late 2009 and early 2010—Awlaki was simultaneously angling to import a wife from the West. It is hard not to make a connection with Awlaki's reckless behavior with prostitutes in San Diego and Washington. Then, lust had led him to risk his career as an imam; now he was putting his life in danger by sending e-mails, albeit encrypted, to entice a blond Croatian woman to join him in the mountains of Yemen. The matchmaker was to be Storm, who recounts the yarn in his 2014 memoir *Agent Storm*. Aminah, a pretty thirty-two-year-old Muslim convert, had appeared on Awlaki's Facebook page, responding in November 2009 to Storm's post there seeking "support" for the sheikh. By Storm's account, Aminah, whose real name was Irena Horak, herself suggested that she was prepared to become Awlaki's wife—and was not deterred when informed that he already had two others, not counting the New Zealand woman who had married him and then fled in 2008.

With Storm as the intermediary, the two exchanged encrypted e-mails—Awlaki insisted on a photo—and then personal video messages in which they both sounded like shy teenagers trying out an online dating service. In his e-mails, Awlaki was blunt about his arduous living conditions and other demands. His other two wives had found village life intolerable, he told Aminah, and sometimes he lived in a tent. He made no effort to hide his patriarchal view of marriage: "I do not tolerate disobedience from my wives," and in a disagreement "it must go my way." That sounded like a reflection of the old-fashioned tribal ways to which he had returned, but it was not that simple. After arranged marriages to Yemeni women, the first chosen by his own family and the second by a pair of brothers who were fellow jihadis, Awlaki was clearly looking for something different. In Yemen's conservative, gender-segregated society, women were kept apart from men's work and understandably were often sexually unsophisticated. "I would love a wife that is lightweight and part of my work," he wrote. "Having lived most of my life in the West I would like to be in the company of a Muslim from the West." He was irresistibly drawn to the culture against which he was now trying to wage war. But Aminah was game.

What the technology-enabled lovebirds did not know, of course, was that Storm was working for the CIA, which monitored all the communications and carried out surveillance of Storm's first meeting with Aminah in Vienna. In an interesting reflection of the different ethical assessments of allied spy agencies, British intelligence dropped out of the wedding plans. MI-6, according to Storm, was unwilling to help send an unwitting woman, whose only experience in the Arab world was at a resort in Tunisia, to her possible death in the desert with Awlaki in an American missile strike. Storm's main CIA handler, whom he knew as Jed, a Metallica fan with several children and a Doberman, seemed to have no such qualms; perhaps he was confident that CIA drone operators would be able to catch Awlaki away from his new wife.

But the wariness of Awlaki's associates who met Aminah at the airport in Sanaa foiled the plan to use his Croatian bride to track him down. The gray Samsonite suitcase and the electronic Arabic dictionary Storm had given her—which he understood contained tracking devices—were dumped by those who picked her up. She was directed to repack her clothes in a plastic bag. Awlaki soon e-mailed Storm with his thanks—"She turned out to be better than I expected and than you described"—adding a smiley face that Storm took to be a lascivious reference to her charms.

The scheme had failed. But by then, Storm, who had played his role in the foiled effort with verve and care, had already received $250,000 in CIA cash as his reward. He photographed it in his mother's kitchen—an open attaché case stuffed with packs of hundred-dollar bills. It was becoming obvious that there were few limits on what the agency, under heavy pressure from the White House, would spend or do to find their target.

I n the Hadda neighborhood of Sanaa where Awlaki's parents and now his first wife and five children lived, upscale by Yemeni standards, both FedEx and UPS maintained modest storefronts. There was nothing especially memorable about the young woman who visited both shops on a Wednesday in late October 2010, dressed in black, her face veiled, like virtually every woman in the capital. She showed the ID of a student at Sanaa University and paid in cash to dispatch Hewlett-Packard printers still in their boxes.

If anyone had had time or inclination to get curious, they might have wondered why someone would send a new printer from Yemen, where such things are rare, to Chicago, where they are common. If the tiny Yemeni staff of the UPS store had happened to talk to their FedEx competitors, they might have found it odd that the same woman would split her business and not send both printers from one shop. If anyone at the businesses knew the student whose ID had been stolen, they might have realized, despite the facial veil, that something was amiss.

None of that happened, and two sophisticated bombs, hidden in the printer ink cartridges and rigged to cell phone alarms, were on their way to the United States. Once again, AQAP was hijacking the American air transport system to launch an attack. Passenger airlines had tightened security again in response to the 2009 underwear bomb plot; the terrorist group was changing up, shifting its attention to the cargo system. Perhaps AQAP plotters knew the old adage in counterterrorism, a cliché in the post-9/11 era: the terrorists only had to succeed once, while the security agencies had to succeed every single day.

Once again, however, the Americans got lucky. Just two weeks earlier, a Saudi militant with an intriguing history, Jaber al-Faifi, had contacted Saudi authorities from Abyan province in Yemen to say he was offended by Al Qaeda's use of civilians as human shields and wanted to come home. Faifi, a soccer-loving youth who had drifted into militancy and was caught in Afghanistan after 9/11, had been imprisoned at Guantanamo Bay from 2001 to 2006, when he was turned over to the Saudi government. He completed a rehabilitation program but eventually joined AQAP—this time, it seems, as an infiltrator on behalf of Saudi intelligence. The timing of his return to Saudi Arabia—on a Saudi government jet that picked him up in Sanaa—suggested a decision by him or his handlers that it might be too risky for him to stay in Yemen after the printer plot was foiled. After Faifi alerted them to the cargo plot, Saudi officials were able to get the actual tracking numbers of the two boxes shipped from Sanaa. Since Faifi had left Yemen before the packages were dropped off, he could not have been the source for the numbers; either he managed to get the information from another AQAP contact or he knew enough details of the planned shipments to permit UPS and FedEx to identify the packages.

The day after the packages were shipped, a Thursday, Mohammed bin Nayef, the Saudi prince who had survived an AQAP bombing the previous year, called his old friend in the White House, John Brennan, with the tracking numbers. Bomb squads rushed to East Midlands Airport in central England, where the UPS plane had made a stop, and to Dubai International Airport, to retrieve the second box from the FedEx aircraft. At both locations, initial x-rays and examinations of the printers turned up no explosives, and security experts thought at first the tip might be wrong. Only when they dismantled the ink cartridges did they find that each contained nearly a pound of PETN, four times the amount of the same explosive that Abdulmutallab had carried in his underwear, rigged to a detonator designed to be ignited by a diode connected to a cell-phone alarm. There was no question that the bombs were capable of blowing up the aircraft, killing the pilots, and scattering the wreckage over the land below.

As the aircraft were searched in Dubai and East Midlands, John Brennan visited the president in the White House family quarters at 10:35 p.m. to brief him on yet another near miss. "There was a five-alarm fire in the middle of the night," recalled Rhodes, the deputy national security adviser. The next twenty-four hours were a blur of secure video conference calls as agencies scrambled to make sure no more bombs were on the way. Search teams swarmed planes landing at Philadelphia and Newark that were carrying shipments that had originated in Yemen. Fighter jets escorted an Emirates flight into JFK International in New York.

From his shifting hideouts in the dunes and mountains, Awlaki had, in effect, sent his response to Obama's decision to put him on the kill list.

The bombs had been diabolically well disguised, a signature of Ibrahim al-Asiri. But the addresses on the boxes were erudite inside jokes that intelligence analysts believed to be a product of Awlaki's macabre wit. Chicago—of course!—was Obama's city, whose skyline was featured on page 51 of the second issue of *Inspire* as the cover page for the magazine's section titled "Open Source Jihad," which gave instructions for mounting attacks. The two addresses, evidently taken from outdated online listings, were for Jewish institutions in Chicago. The names of the addressees were notorious anti-Muslim figures from distant European history: Diego Deza, responsible for the torture and death of many Muslims in his role as Grand Inquisitor during the Spanish Inquisition; and Reynald Krak, a French knight during the Second Crusade who had slaughtered Muslim pilgrims and eventually was beheaded by Saladin, the Islamic hero who defeated Western invaders in the twelfth century. The labels were informed by the sense of eternal grievance that Awlaki shared with his fellow militants—that Islam had always been under attack, from the Crusades to the present. The would-be targets combined Awlaki's usual collection of villains: Jews, Christians, and Obama. At the CIA, analysts remembered how Awlaki eight months earlier had quizzed Rajib Karim, the British Airways employee, about ways to evade airline x-ray machines.

Obama was trying to stay focused on the economy and its still-sluggish recovery. The morning after the bombs were discovered, he stuck to his plan to visit Stromberg Sheet Metal, an employee-owned company run by an ex-marine in the suburb of Beltsville, Maryland. He wanted to highlight some steps the administration was taking to support small businesses. Once again, a terrorist plot from Yemen—from Awlaki—had thrown the administration off its stride. "It was just a further indication that AQAP was very committed to homeland plotting, and that Awlaki was at the center of that commitment," said Ben Rhodes. It "certainly ratcheted up" the president's focus on Awlaki, Rhodes said. After returning to the White House from his small-business promotion, Obama appeared in the press room for just four minutes to tell the American people, as he put it, about "a credible terrorist threat to this country." His decision not to take questions, and his somewhat halting recital of the prepared statement, did not project great confidence. The president did not look like a happy man.

After his sleepless night, Brennan then followed the president to the microphone, adding a few details and trying mightily to strike a note of competence and assurance: "I think the American people should feel particularly good that, since 9/11, the US government has built up a very, very capable and robust intelligence, law enforcement, homeland security system. And as a result of the strength of that system, information became available that we were able to act upon very quickly and that we were able to locate these packages." Pressed by reporters for how the information "became available," Brennan demurred: "We were onto this, but I'm not going to get into details about how we knew."

In fact, the bombs had been stopped not by the "robust security system" but only as a result of the Saudi tip, a fact reflected first in an unusual public statement of thanks from Brennan to the Saudi government and then by a call from Obama to Saudi king Abdullah to express his gratitude. Abdulmutallab's bomb had been discovered only after he detonated it and it fizzled. This time the bombs were defused before they could be detonated—but American officials were only too aware of how close AQAP had come to succeeding. Gerald Feierstein, the US ambassador to Yemen, said in an interview with Al Arabiya, the Saudi-owned television channel and online news site, that American authorities believed Awlaki was behind the printer bombs and that American and Yemeni forces were stepping up the hunt for him.

With hindsight, the Americans realized that several packages containing books, CDs, and other items, shipped from Sanaa to erroneous addresses in Chicago in mid-September and monitored by security investigators, had probably been test runs by AQAP. By using the tracking numbers and timing the shipments as they traveled to the United States, Asiri, Awlaki, and their assistants could estimate when to set the timers to explode over American soil. AQAP later claimed it had been responsible for the destruction of an earlier UPS flight, which had caught fire and crashed shortly after leaving Dubai on its way to Germany on September 3, 2010. American intelligence officials believe that Al Qaeda's claim was bogus, but the official investigations of the crash did not come up with a clear cause.

The episode and its reverberations were revealing. Once again, with the printer plot, the Al Qaeda branch that American officials described as the biggest threat, and Awlaki, who some said was the most dangerous terrorist at work against the United States, had failed. They had just barely failed, but they had failed. No one had died. Nothing had blown up. If Abdulmutallab had managed only to scorch his genitals, these printer bombs had merely delayed two cargo planes and inconvenienced a lot of security officials. Indeed, even if the two planes had both blown up with their four pilots and killed a few people on the ground, the death toll would have been smaller than the number killed that day in car wrecks on American roads.

But of course terrorism does not operate that way. The root of the word, the Latin verb *terrere*, means "to cause to tremble." Rarely does that require huge casualties. In both failed attacks, AQAP had demonstrated that it had the capability to penetrate American and international air security systems. With blanket coverage by the American and global media, the terrorists had riveted the attention of their enemies and undermined a sense of security in the West. They had imposed huge disruption on the international air transport system and multiplied the already considerable cost of trying to protect cargo planes.

Al Qaeda had sometimes been described, sardonically but with some justice, as a media organization with a terrorist wing. Never was that truer than with its Yemen branch. AQAP had not killed a single American in years of trying, but it had preoccupied many agencies in the government of a superpower and generated regular headlines and endless cable television chatter. Its swift follow-up in *Inspire* to the foiled cargo plane plot was a case study in transforming defeat into victory. The cover of the third issue of *Inspire*, rushed out three weeks after the event, consisted of an image of a UPS aircraft and a bold-print price: $4,200, which it plausibly claimed was the total cost of what it was now calling "Op Hemorrhage," adopting casual military shorthand. AQAP claimed in a "Letter from the Editor," presumably written by Samir Khan, though some of the syntax sounds like Awlaki, that the scheme had "succeeded in achieving its objectives" and with disarming candor explained the meaning of success. "To bring down America we do not need to strike big. In such an environment of security phobia that is sweeping America, it is more feasible to stage smaller attacks that involve less players and less time to launch and thus we may circumvent the security barriers Americans worked so hard to erect. This strategy of attacking the enemy with smaller, but more frequent operations is what some may refer to as the strategy of a thousand cuts. The aim is to bleed the enemy to death."

In a separate, one-page explanation in the same *Inspire* issue, the unnamed "Head of Foreign Operations" elaborated: With security very tight on passenger airliners, AQAP had made a deliberate decision to target cargo aircraft, he wrote. "Our objective was not to cause maximum casualties but to cause maximum losses to the American economy," he wrote. He claimed that an AQAP bomb had brought down the earlier September 3 flight over Dubai. He explained the choice of addressees from the Inquisition and the Crusades and noted that the synagogue addresses were in "Chicago, Obama's city." Clearly the Head of Foreign Operations wanted to be sure no one missed his cleverness. His punch line, ending the small essay, dropped a big hint about his identity, noting that the plotters had placed a particular English novel in one of the printer boxes: "We were very optimistic about the outcome of this operation. That is why we dropped into one of the boxes a novel titled *Great Expectations*."

Awlaki was being coy. The piece seemed certain to be his handiwork, confirming intelligence reports of his title and role in AQAP. Clearly he intended to be recognized when he harked back to his lengthy discussion on his blog in 2008 of his reading of *Great Expectations* and other Dickens novels while in prison. The grandly named "Foreign Operations" division of AQAP probably consisted of Awlaki, Khan, Asiri, and a few helpers, but it was having an outsized impact.

One consequence of the printer bomb plot was to ratchet up the pressure on the Saleh government to help the Americans neutralize Awlaki. For more than a year, Yemeni officials had been whipsawed by contrary pressures: AQAP certainly threatened the Saleh regime, and the Americans never stopped talking about the danger Awlaki posed. But there was countervailing pressure, too. Anwar's father was a former government minister, his uncle was a powerful tribal leader in the south, and Saleh didn't want to look like an American puppet. In October 2009, when Yemeni authorities sought the help of American intelligence to try to find and arrest Awlaki, the Americans had refused, remarkably, after CIA lawyers decided he was not a threat to Americans. Then, in April 2010, after Awlaki's role in the Christmas bombing was public and Obama had authorized his killing, it was Yemen's turn to call the secretive Americans' bluff. "Anwar al-Awlaki has to us been always looked at as a preacher rather than a terrorist," Yemen's foreign minister, Abu Bakr al-Qirbi, told Yemen's Saba news agency, "and shouldn't be looked at as a terrorist unless the Americans have evidence that he has been involved in terrorism."

Now, with the printer plot in the headlines, Saleh came up with a compromise of sorts. Two days after the plot was foiled, Yemeni prosecutors brought a terrorism case against Awlaki as part of Al Qaeda and immediately began a trial in absentia. Along with a cousin, Othman al-Awlaki, he was charged with "forming an armed group to carry out criminal attacks targeting foreigners." Specifically, they were accused of plotting with a third man, Hesham Mohammed Asem, nineteen, who was charged with fatally shooting a French engineer the previous October at the headquarters of the Austrian oil company OMV in Sanaa.

The chief prosecutor, Ali Al-Sanea'a, tried to use Awlaki's dissolute life in the West against him, describing him as "yesterday a regular visitor of bars and discothèques in America" but now "the catalyst for shedding the blood of foreigners and security forces." He called Awlaki a leader of Al Qaeda and "a figure prone to evil, devoid of any conscience, religion or law." The government put out the prosecutor's diatribe in a public statement to make sure the Americans saw it.

How significant a role Anwar al-Awlaki really played in the French engineer's death, if any, was unclear. But when Obama spoke with the Yemeni president in the wake of the cargo plot, Saleh was able to tell him his government was not sitting idle but had put the cleric on trial just the day before. The State Department spokesman,

Philip J. Crowley, offered a curt public nod: "We've been informed and we completely are supportive of Yemen's announcement today of the indictment of Mr. al-Awlaki." And by pursuing Yemeni criminal charges, Saleh's government was, to outside appearances at least, standing up for Yemeni sovereignty and suggesting that the country could solve its own problems. Saleh, who bragged of dancing on the heads of snakes, may simultaneously have hoped to appease Awlaki's family and tribe by offering an alternative to execution by American drone.

The trial ended with a ten-year sentence for Awlaki. Had the Obama administration trusted Saleh, the Yemeni trial might conceivably have opened a path to Awlaki's arrest and imprisonment, perhaps even his eventual transfer to the United States to face additional charges. But American officials, on the basis of long experience, saw Saleh as an unreliable partner. Nor did they believe that Yemeni authorities were capable of capturing Awlaki. Even if they managed to catch him alive, the record of Al Qaeda jailbreaks gave them no confidence that he would stay behind bars.

The legal opinion justifying Awlaki's killing was premised on the notion that his capture was "infeasible." The word was absolute, but the reality was far more complicated. If American intelligence could find Awlaki in the wilds of Yemen, protected by a handful of bodyguards, it was clearly not inconceivable that a Navy SEAL team could cross the Saudi border in the middle of the night, surprise the encampment, and take Awlaki alive. Indeed, SEAL and Delta Force teams battle-hardened by years of raids in Afghanistan and Iraq might be said to specialize in the "infeasible." But such a mission would be hugely risky to the American commandos, could spark protests in Yemen, and might well end with Awlaki dead anyway, in the gunfight that would likely break out on the ground. "It was an option and it was extensively discussed," said a senior American official who knew Yemen well. "Can you come up with an op to capture? The answer everyone came up with was no. It was beyond Yemeni capabilities. And the blowback from a US operation would be too great." So there was a legitimate case that a capture mission was unwise, if not quite infeasible.

What went unaddressed in the two Justice Department legal opinions was the role of technology in influencing the decision to kill. When Obama and his security aides discussed the feasibility of capture, their thinking was inevitably shaped by the existence of the armed drone, which had already carried out hundreds of lethal strikes. Imagine that Obama, the former constitutional law professor, had decided that, in view of Awlaki's American citizenship and the requirements of the Fifth Amendment, he should be captured alive and brought to the United States for trial. And say that one or more American commandoes were killed in the resulting raid. It is easy to imagine the furious public reaction. Congress and cable television would be aflame with second-guessing: When Obama *knew* Awlaki could be killed with a missile fired from a drone, with no danger to Americans, how could he possibly have insisted on endangering our troops?

The drone, in other words, had enlarged the president's options in some ways, offering an alternative to a large-scale military invasion. But it constrained the president in other ways. It's interesting to speculate about what Obama might have decided had there been no drones. Would he have been willing to order a risky capture mission? Would he have turned up the pressure on Yemen to grab Awlaki? Would he have encouraged Saleh to negotiate with the tribes, which surely had the ability, if not the inclination, to take him into custody and hand him over?

For better or worse, the drone had changed these calculations forever.

12

THE TIME FOR REAPING

When the phone rang it was nearly midnight, and Ammar al-Awlaki was at the end of a long day on a business trip to Vienna—appropriately, as it would turn out, the setting for so many past spy tales in both history and fiction. The American voice on the phone gave an unfamiliar name. He was calling from the hotel lobby, he said, because he had a gift from his own wife for Ammar's wife, who were old acquaintances. It seemed a little odd—he was calling in the middle of the night about this?—but Ammar believed the guy and headed down to the lobby.

It was February 2011. Ammar had completed his education in the United States and Canada and returned home to Yemen in 2009, taking a job with an oil company. He was following the secular, technocratic path that his father had foreseen for Anwar and that Anwar had rejected. Ammar was not religious and had no use for the puritanical Salafi Islam that his brother had preached, let alone Anwar's increasingly open embrace of violence. He had not seen his brother in person, he said, since 2004. Their last contact had come in October 2009: a brotherly phone call from Anwar in Shabwah to the family home in Sanaa, welcoming Ammar back to Yemen. Ammar appreciated the gesture. But the brothers had gone their separate ways.

Entering the lobby, Ammar recalled, "I found this handsome guy, mid-thirties. He's in a navy-colored suit, no tie, and he's saying my name's such and such." But instead of handing over the present, the man asked Ammar if he'd like to get coffee. He realized instantly that the gift story had been a ruse. Several years earlier, while he was an engineering student at Dalhousie University in Halifax, Nova Scotia, he had been questioned several times by Canadian intelligence officers. They had clearly wanted to size him up, but their main task had been to glean information for their American colleagues about Anwar, then imprisoned in Yemen. Now, he realized, the Americans were making a direct approach.

"So I asked him, 'Are you FBI or CIA?,'" Ammar recounted. "He said, 'The latter.'" It was an unusual admission—CIA officers abroad usually mentioned cover jobs or kept their employer vague—and a sign that the conversation would be quite candid. The CIA man said that, as Ammar knew, there was a major American effort to capture or kill Anwar. Capture would be preferable, he said. Ammar immediately interjected that he had no idea where his brother was and no way to assist the hunt, even if he chose to do so. To prove that he was not in touch with Anwar, he said, he would be happy to take a lie detector test.

The CIA man took the opportunity for an awkward segue. In fact, he said, he did have with him almost the equivalent of a polygraph machine. And at that point, in response to the CIA man's signal, a second American walked up and joined the party. Ammar recognized him as a different breed. "This guy who's behind us comes and says hi." He was beefier than the first man and with an ex-military look, "wearing Oakleys and an olive-oil-brown-colored jacket."

The big guy introduced himself as Chris. "I said, 'Was that your name yesterday?', and he laughed and said, 'We try to stick to one name a week.'" Ammar asked if they could prove they were CIA, and one flashed a diplomatic passport, though he pulled it back before Ammar could study it. Ammar joked that the first guy looked like CIA but the other one didn't. He was surprised at his own composure. "For some reason, I did not panic at all," he said. "It was like a friendly conversation, trying to convince me that Anwar would be killed or captured—please help us."

They asked Ammar what he thought would be the best outcome for Anwar—prison in Yemen or prison in the United States—and seemed taken aback when he said Yemen, where Anwar could be visited by his children. The CIA men joked about putting Anwar's children in the witness protection program in the United States. They said they wanted to meet him again, still hoping to persuade him to help. "They said, 'You choose whatever five-star hotel you want, you choose whatever airline you want, and we'll fly you there and spend as much time as you want—but just agree to see us again.'" Ammar demurred.

Finally they offered a brazen pitch—a proposal that, in effect, he sell his brother to the CIA. "They said, 'You've lived in America, you know American culture, you know we're frank people. And there's $5 million for your brother's head. It's better that you guys take it and help put his children through school with that money instead of someone else.'" Ammar still kept his cool. "I was surprisingly calm, because I told them what I knew and I really did not have a way of helping them—even if I thought about it for a split second, which I did not." The two men finally relented but gave him a Hotmail address in case he changed his mind. Occasionally they would check in with him by e-mail, and he would offer the same answer: he had no idea where his brother was.

About the time the CIA caught up with Ammar in Vienna, Michael Leiter, head of the National Counterterrorism Center, was asked at a House hearing whether Awlaki posed as grave a threat as Osama bin Laden. "I actually consider Al Qaeda in the Arabian Peninsula, with al-Awlaki as a leader within that organization, probably the most significant risk to the US homeland," Leiter replied.

A year had passed since the Justice Department lawyers had declared that killing Awlaki would violate neither the law nor the Constitution. For a year, the intelligence agencies had directed their formidable capabilities at a cost-is-no-object hunt for the cleric. The National Security Agency, along with its British counterpart, had thrown an electronic surveillance blanket over the entirety of Yemen. The CIA was paying agents like Morten Storm to help with the hunt and offering a reward of up to $5 million to relatives like Ammar and tribal contacts in return for bringing him in. (American officials offered money privately but did not publicize the reward, apparently because they or their Yemeni counterparts feared it would backfire, exposing anyone who helped the hunt to charges of selling out for foreign cash.) The NGA, the National Geospatial-Intelligence

Agency, was analyzing satellite and drone imagery, watching for Aw-laki whenever they spotted groups of suspected Al Qaeda members moving around Yemen's badlands.

Asked what the government was doing to find Awlaki by then, one person centrally involved in directing the search replied, "Every-thing, right? You're working human sources. You're working signals intelligence. Everything. This is like any other manhunting any-where. You're looking at his associates. You're looking at his family. You're looking at his comms. And you're trying to nail down where he is. And when you get down to the end, you're using overhead as-sets to look for movement."

In March, the State Department weighed in with its own modest contribution: it revoked Awlaki's passport on the grounds that his activities were "causing and/or are likely to cause serious damage to the national security or foreign policy of the United States." Then, as required by federal regulations, the department sent him a letter in-forming him of the revocation. In perhaps an excess of optimism, the cable from Washington instructed the embassy in Sanaa that Awlaki must be contacted and informed that "an important letter" awaited him at the embassy: "Mr. Awlaki will need to appear in person and at that time post will then serve him with revocation letter." The cable declared confidently that "the department has been informed that Anwar Nasser Awlaki is currently located at Rabat St., Sanaa, Yemen"—his father's house. The punctilious compliance with regula-tions about notification, and the passport revocation itself, seemed oddly incongruous from a government that had already asserted the right and intention to kill the passport holder on sight. No one was surprised when Awlaki did not turn up at the embassy.

He may have lost his American passport, but he had sought and received protection from both a new institution and an ancient one: Al Qaeda in the Arabian Peninsula (AQAP), which had networks of watchers and informants across Yemen to send word of any search party that might turn up or any drone spotted overhead; and his fam-ily's Awaliq tribe, in which neither his American birth nor his ter-rorist plotting disqualified him from membership. The Awaliq were fiercely independent, with a celebrated reputation as warriors and a tribal chant that declared, "We are the sparks of hell; he who de-fies us will be burned." Yet some tribal leaders were none too pleased that this American-born cleric was invoking the tribe's protection, aware that if a volley of American missiles came at him, tribesmen and women around him would be endangered. "Even in the Awlaki clan Anwar was controversial," said an American official who kept in touch with Yemen's tribal leaders. "Some said to him, Never show your face in the village. Some felt differently." In an interview with the pan-Arab newspaper *Asharq Al-Awsat*, the governor of Shabwah made the same claim when asked about Awlaki and other Al Qaeda militants, whom he accused of "misleading the people and persuading them that they are mujahedeen in the cause of Allah." The governor, Ali Hasan al-Ahmadi, said the militants were "moving in the mountains and do not settle in any specific place. They are expelled by the citizens wherever they go who refuse to have them remain among them."

The governor was undoubtedly eager to counter the image of his territory as an anything-goes zone for terrorists, and he probably overstated the hostility of villagers to the Al Qaeda fighters—and certainly to Awlaki, whose family had deep and respected roots in Shabwah. The code of tribal hospitality was powerful, with ancient origins in an unforgiving desert and mountain environment where turning away a traveler could be tantamount to killing him. Abdullah al-Jumaili, a tribal sheikh in Al Jawf, near the Saudi border, described the rules to me in astonishing terms. "You've got to accept someone as a guest, even if they killed your son or brother," he said. "Each guest has three days. After that he goes somewhere else."

In his interview with Al Malahem, AQAP's media arm, Awlaki had affected an attitude of unconcern with the American manhunt, basing his confidence mainly on the sympathy of Yemeni tribes. "The concern that I am chased is not true. I go back and forth between the members of my tribe as well as other regions of Yemen, and that is because the people of Yemen hate the Americans and the people of Yemen want justice and the people of justice support the oppressed."

In other words—as both Bush and Awlaki had so often said—you were either with the jihad or you were with America. And America's reputation in Yemen's tribal areas had been seriously undermined by the strike in December 2009 that killed so many women and children and the one in May 2010 that killed the popular deputy governor of Marib province. "I go back and forth between al-Awaliq and I have a base of support in a large section of the people here in Yemen, whether in Obeida, Dahem, Waela, Hashed, Bakil or Kholan, whether in Hadramout, Abyan, Shabwah, Aden or Sanaa [all the names of Yemeni tribes or places]. Praise be to Allah, there are a lot of good people, even though they know they are taking risks and dangers due to America's pursuit of them. Despite that, they graciously and happily come forward and host us with the most refined hospitality."

And Awlaki returned this "most refined hospitality" with his own visible tribute to the tribes. In all his video messages after he fled Sanaa, Awlaki took care to appear with a traditional ceremonial dagger, a *jambiya*, in his belt; to practiced eyes, the hilt of the dagger showed it was made in the style of Shabwah. He wore the *jambiya* in a lengthy video message in November 2010, showing bravado in the face of the American threats. Describing the conflict between the United States and Islam as "the battle of good and evil," he urged his followers to attack Americans wherever and whenever it proved possible. They "should not consult anyone in the matter of killing Americans," he said. "Combating the devil does not require a fatwa, nor consultation, nor does it require prayer to Allah. They are the party of Satan, and fighting them is the obligation of the time." In other portraits from 2010 and 2011, distributed through Al Qaeda's channels and other jihadi forums, the nerdish American sought to project a more martial image, posing in a camouflage jacket with a Kalashnikov rifle or a rocket-propelled grenade launcher. It was unlikely that this bookish intellectual would have been of much use in a real battle, but his pose had a dual appeal—to his jihad-minded followers wherever they might be and, closer to home, to Yemen's well-armed tribes. Any tribesmen who by some unlikely chance happened to see the staged photos of Awlaki brandishing weapons might have smiled at his pretension, but they would also have appreciated his gesture. Now, he was saying, I am one of you.

And to move around safely in the tribal region required a network of helpers, sympathizers, and what might be termed tolerators—those who were happy not to get involved. The main tribal provinces of Shabwah, Marib, and Al Jawf, where he was moving about, had a total population of well over one million people spread over territory nearly the size of North Carolina. Finding a fugitive was not easy even in far more favorable conditions: Eric Rudolph, for instance, who had bombed abortion clinics and the Atlanta Olympics, had evaded an intense manhunt in the mountains of western North Carolina for five years before he was caught in 2003. Awlaki had far more support, and he was hiding in far rougher terrain.

American officials were getting a steady stream of intelligence about Awlaki, but it still fell short of the timeliness or specificity required to plan a strike. "I remember hearing—he's in Shabwah, he's in Marib, he's here, he's there. He's doing this, doing that," said an American counterterrorism official who closely followed the top-secret reports from the manhunt, most of them based on the NSA's intercept of calls and e-mails among Al Qaeda supporters and tribesmen who had glimpsed him. Was Awlaki able to keep plotting while on the run? "I'm not even sure I would agree with the idea that he was on the run," the official said. "He knew that he had to keep his profile down," so he stayed off cell phones and limited his contact with outsiders. "But that doesn't mean they're moving from safe house to safe house every day." After all, he said, a group of men on the move could draw unwanted attention.

As the momentous Arab Spring of 2011 arrived, intelligence agencies were still tracking the plots of AQAP in Yemen. But the ideological appeal of Al Qaeda seemed to many experts to be receding. The menace of fanatics lost the spotlight as thousands of idealistic young Muslims began to rise up against the American-backed dictators who had ruled Arab countries for decades. In Tunisia, Egypt, Libya, and Syria—and finally in Yemen—people were taking to the streets with demands that struck an American ear as reassuringly familiar: they demanded democratic government, freedom from confining traditions, an end to corruption. Not only were the protesters not repeating the sinister demands of Al Qaeda, as people massed in central squares in capital after capital, but there was hardly any mention of Islam at all. When Hosni Mubarak, the Egyptian president, was forced to resign in ignominy on February 11, the canny crowds in the streets had accomplished what Al Qaeda had long dreamed of and had insisted could be accomplished only with violence. Osama bin Laden and the network he had built had been left on the sidelines, seemingly discredited and quite overtaken by events.

President Obama caught the bracing promise of the drama in Cairo in remarks to the nation from the White House in reaction to Mubarak's departure. "There are very few moments in our lives where we have the privilege to witness history taking place," Obama said. "This is one of those moments." There would be "difficult days ahead," the president acknowledged, but "Egyptians have made it clear that nothing less than genuine democracy will carry the day." It was an upbeat, celebratory speech, mentioning Gandhi, quoting Martin Luther King, and comparing the moment to the fall of the Berlin Wall. That combination may have seemed over the top, but it was a heady time. For people accustomed to exclusively bad news from the Middle East, here was a wave of heartening developments that could be understood in the comforting American vocabulary of freedom and democracy. The Muslims of the Middle East were not, it turned out, some alien race, perpetually troubled, obsessively religious, and depressingly prone to violence, as a decade's news coverage had suggested to some Americans. They had the same aspirations as people in the West and the rest of the world.

A couple of weeks after the president spoke, I called a range of experts and found a striking consensus, albeit with some caveats, that Al Qaeda was being bypassed and rendered irrelevant by the rush of events. An old CIA hand, Paul Pillar, told me that "so far—and I emphasize so far—the score card looks pretty terrible for Al Qaeda. Democracy is bad news for terrorists. The more peaceful channels people have to express grievances and pursue their goals, the less likely they are to turn to violence." Brian Fishman, a younger scholar who followed the flood of Internet commentary in the Arab countries, noted that Ayman al-Zawahri, Bin Laden's top deputy and Al Qaeda's No. 2, had once been tortured by Mubarak's government. "Knocking off Mubarak has been Zawahri's goal for more than 20 years, and he was unable to achieve it. Now a nonviolent, nonreligious, pro-democracy movement got rid of him in a matter of weeks. It's a major problem for Al Qaeda."

There were cautionary notes. In my article for the *Times* on Al Qaeda and the Arab awakening, I quoted a few jihadists who claimed to be enthralled with the uprisings and insisted that the revolution was just a stage in their drive for a caliphate ruled by Islamic law. A colleague talked to a veteran Jordanian militant who called himself

Abu Khaled. "There will be many disappointed demonstrators, and that's when they will realize what the only alternative is," he said. "We are certain that this will all play into our hands." The iconoclastic former CIA Bin Laden specialist Michael Scheuer, always good for a contrarian view, sounded the same note. By focusing on westernized, English-speaking students and intellectuals among the Arab demonstrators, Scheuer told me, American journalists and pundits had completely misjudged the moment. Thousands of Islamists had been released from prisons in Egypt alone, he said, and the ouster of secular dictators would revitalize every stripe of Islamism, including that of Al Qaeda and its allies. The terrorist group was highly opportunistic, and with the collapse of the old regimes "we're looking over all at a more geographically widespread, probably numerically bigger and certainly more influential movement than in 2001," Scheuer said.

I quoted him near the bottom of the story, wanting to cover all points of view. But surely, I thought, Scheuer's spoilsport take on the surge of young Muslims demanding democracy and the fall of despots must be wrong.

The upbeat mood certainly extended to the White House. Obama, who was soon to announce his reelection bid, was steering clear of public appearances in Muslim settings. One in five Americans clung to the false belief that he was Muslim, and he would soon release his long-form birth certificate to counter the wacky but widespread belief that he was not an American citizen. But on a Sunday night in early March, he dispatched one of his closest aides, Denis McDonough, to give a highly publicized speech to a Muslim audience at a mosque outside Washington. White House officials stayed away from Awlaki's Dar Al-Hijrah, a conservative institution that was now unfairly tagged on Fox News and in the conservative media with the bogus label of "the 9/11 mosque" because of Awlaki's contacts with the hijackers. Instead they chose a more liberal competitor, the All Dulles Area Muslim Society, better known by its acronym as the ADAMS Center. McDonough, Obama's point man on countering radicalization, spoke to two hundred people gathered in the mosque gym, preceded by an honor guard from the local Boy Scout troop. McDonough's purpose was partly to counter heavily publicized hearings on radicalization being held by a pugnacious Republican congressman, Representative Peter King of Long Island, once an outspoken supporter of the Irish Republican Army but now on a crusade to expose the dangers of Islam. McDonough offered a reassuring message: the administration knew that Muslims were loyal Americans, that few had anything to do with terrorism, that extremist violence was as alien to Islam as to other great religions. He pointed to the revolution in Egypt as a blow to Al Qaeda. "It is the most dramatic change in the Arab world in decades, and al Qaeda had nothing to do with it," McDonough said. "And so President Obama made it a point to commend the Egyptian people and their embrace of 'the moral force of nonviolence—not terrorism, not mindless killing.'"

But McDonough also had something to ask for: cooperation in the battle against extremism. He mentioned Awlaki three times, saying that he and other radicals calling for homegrown terror "have found a miniscule but receptive audience" among American Muslims. Only a partnership between the Muslim community and the government, he said, could prevent young Muslims from going astray. "We will not stigmatize or demonize entire communities because of the actions of a few," he said.

McDonough, one of eleven children from a devout Irish Catholic family, was a surrogate whom no one had accused of being a secret Muslim. But his message was vintage Obama. The president had been adamant that his administration would not conflate Islam and terrorism, and his aides still stayed away from labeling terrorist attacks and plots as "Islamic" or "jihadist," arguing that such terms unintentionally conveyed religious legitimacy to violence. By substituting drone strikes for large-scale American occupations, and by avoiding the religious labeling that many Muslims resented, Obama hoped to put the lie to the claim of Awlaki and others that America was at war with Islam.

A few weeks later, Awlaki offered a confident reply to Obama and all the American officials and commentators who had declared the Arab awakening bad news for Al Qaeda. In late March, the fifth issue of *Inspire* magazine made its appearance on jihadi forums. The cover story was Awlaki's four-page piece called "The Tsunami of Change," and the cover blurb promised clarity: "The unfolding revolution has brought with it a wave of change. Shaykh Anwar explains." The piece made clear that Awlaki's security precautions had not cut him off from news coverage of the Arab uprisings; he accurately quoted

Secretary of State Hillary Clinton, Defense Secretary Robert Gates, the commentator Fareed Zakaria, and the terrorism expert Peter Bergen from late February and early March, fairly reflecting their view that the uprisings were bad news for Al Qaeda. He used his usual cocky American voice, referring to Clinton and Gates as "these guys" and gleefully quoting Malcolm X and his use (made famous by the Spike Lee film) of the word *bamboozled*.

Then Awlaki did his best to dismantle what had become a broad Western consensus. His main point was right in line with Michael Scheuer's view, and it was quite ominous. In fact, he said, while the United States might be spinning the awakening as a welcome development, the fall of authoritarian rulers who had suppressed religious extremists was a big blow to its campaign against terrorism. "The mujahidin around the world are going through a moment of elation," Awlaki wrote, "and I wonder whether the West is aware of the upsurge of mujahidin activity in Egypt, Tunisia, Libya, Yemen, Arabia, Algeria and Morocco? Is the West aware of what is happening or are they asleep with drapes covering their eyes? Or is what is happening too much for the West to handle at the moment and they are just bidding for time while attempting to prop up some new stooges who would return the area to the pre-revolution era?" America, he said, was "an exhausted empire," and the Arab uprisings were opening "great doors of opportunity" for Al Qaeda.

In a sly reference to the Dickens novel included in the printer box in the bomb plot of five months earlier, Awlaki even slipped the phrase "great expectations" into his essay. His article could be dismissed as bravado—the protesters had bypassed the extremists across the Arab world, and now Awlaki was playing spin doctor. It would take a few years to determine who had been right about the true strategic significance of the Arab Spring for Al Qaeda.

In Yemen, the developments of the Arab Spring of 2011 were so disparate that for a while both Western officials and Al Qaeda ideologists could find plenty of evidence to support their theories. On Change Square, in front of Sanaa University, the exuberance of Tunis and Cairo was replicated, as young people gathered with protest signs and bullhorns, demanding democracy. As the weeks passed, there were singing contests, poetry competitions, and sports events to pass the time. The median age in Yemen was an astonishing 18.6 years—in the United States, it was just short of 38—so there was an army of teenagers and twenty-somethings ready to take to the streets.

Among the regulars was a perpetually smiling fifteen-year-old who looked enchantingly goofy in his glasses and dark curls and always seemed to be surrounded by a gang of friends. Abdulrahman al-Awlaki was as skinny as his father had been as a teenager. He and his friends were at an age when they were just becoming fully aware of the political world, its factions and causes, and Sanaa was serving up the most exciting events it had witnessed in years. The sense of freedom and camaraderie on Change Square was like nothing they had ever experienced in their tradition-bound country. Abdulrahman, who had been born in Denver and moved to Yemen with his family at age six, posted with enthusiasm on Facebook, where the only hint of his notorious father was the nickname he'd assigned himself: "Ibn al Shaykh," the son of the sheikh. His subtle boast was not surprising, but his posts had no whiff of jihad. Among his "Favorites," he listed Harry Potter, the Twilight series, Shakira, and Eminem. By all accounts, Abdulrahman was a relaxed, friendly kid, always clowning and mugging for the camera. His life was about schoolwork, video games, rap music, and his teenage pals.

But Ali Abdullah Saleh, the wily survivor of three decades as Yemen's ruler, felt deeply threatened by the demonstrators' persistent calls for his ouster. The regime began to react with violence, and the protests escalated in response. On March 18, government snipers opened fire from the rooftops surrounding the square on the unarmed protesters below, killing fifty-three people and wounding hundreds more. As in other Arab capitals, the protests took on an air of fear and fury. Beyond Change Square, a broader power struggle ensued as Saleh and his son and nephew, who ran different security agencies, squared off against other Yemeni power brokers, each with his own armed militia or loyal military element. The city dissolved into bloody civil strife.

Meanwhile, with security agencies preoccupied with the battle for the capital, Al Qaeda in the Arabian Peninsula took advantage of the chaos to come out of the shadows and seize territory in the group's southern strongholds, especially Abyan province, where the terrible American strike on the village of Al Majala had occurred in 2009.

In scenes that would presage what the world would later see as the so-called Islamic State seized territory in Iraq, AQAP fighters rolled into the cities of Jaar and the Zinjibar, raising the black flag of Al Qaeda over government buildings and setting up provisional rule that would last for months.

American military planners were deeply worried about the advance of AQAP, which also started a trend across the Arab countries by creating a second brand for itself as Ansar al-Shariah, or supporters of Islamic law. In effect, it was saying, if you associate Al Qaeda with brutality, try this kinder, gentler version—we're just a bunch of folks who support Islamic governance. But the Americans were not in a strong position to halt Al Qaeda's advance. After the disastrous strikes of 2009 and 2010, and President Saleh's resistance to a repeat performance, the Obama administration had put strikes on hold in Yemen, and from May 2010 through April 2011 AQAP didn't have to worry about American drones and jets. To complicate matters still more, the Saleh government's escalating violence toward demonstrators, and the breakdown of civil order, led to a temporary cutoff of American security aid. Neither Yemeni nor American authorities were in any position to counter the attempt by AQAP, flush with tens of millions of dollars in revenue from kidnappings, to set up a mini-state in the south.

A story that Anwar al-Awlaki's uncle, Saleh bin Fareed, told me captured poignantly both the government's terrifying loss of control of the country and the underlying reasons for Al Qaeda's strength. As a tribal leader in Shabwah, Bin Fareed traveled regularly from his coastal villa in Aden, the old British port, to his home in the village of Al Saeed, where Awlaki had lived before fleeing to the mountains. It was a drive of four or five hours, and Bin Fareed liked to get an early start, leaving around 4 a.m. in a convoy of three SUVs. One such trip at the height of Al Qaeda's territorial seizures was interrupted half a dozen times at checkpoints set up by the terrorist group. Al Qaeda gunmen would ask the man known as Sheikh Saleh who he was and examine his identification before allowing him to proceed. The militants knew better than to harm him, he said, since that would incur a violent response from his Awaliq tribe. At the third Al Qaeda checkpoint, he said, a teenage guard approached. He was still too young to shave, maybe fifteen or sixteen—just the age of Abdulrahman and his friends, a far more privileged group who were protesting on Change Square in Sanaa two hundred miles to the north. The youth, who Bin Fareed said "was sweating like hell at seven in the morning," was so hapless at his job that he had left his AK rifle lying on a barrel nearby when he came to the car window.

"I didn't know him, but when I looked at his face I could tell what tribe he was and what family," Bin Fareed said. The boy asked how Bin Fareed knew, and he said he could read both tribe and family in the boy's face. "I said, 'What the hell are you doing here?' He said, 'Sheikh Saleh, I have no job, I have no education. My family cannot feed me. The only way for me is to join Al Qaeda.' I told him, 'Do you have any other reason?' He said, 'No—I am starving, that's why I joined Al Qaeda.' I said, 'Okay, jump in the car. I will give you enough money for a year to feed you and your family.'"

Bin Fareed, who had tried to help Anwar al-Awlaki only to see him drift inexorably into militancy, saw an opportunity to save one young tribesman. But it was not to be. The teenager, he said, "smiled and said, 'Sir, if I do it, they will kill me. I wish I could go with you, but if I do it, I will be killed.'" Bin Fareed reluctantly drove on, leaving the boy behind. More than two years after that encounter, he said, the situation had barely improved. Just ten kilometers from Aden, he said, "there is no government existing at all. You drive four hundred kilometers to Shabwa, eight hundred kilometers to Hadramaut, Mukalla, and Al Barra, there is no government existing whatsoever." In the absence of government, he said, Al Qaeda, Ansar al-Shariah, or any other terrorist or criminal group with plenty of cash could thrive.

Obama had always emphasized the fertile ground for terrorist recruiting in impoverished and uneducated populations. He liked to consider underlying causes and debate the nuances of policy. But Anwar al-Awlaki was a different matter. Like many leaders of terrorist movements, from Russian noblemen plotting to kill the tsar in the nineteenth century to Osama bin Laden in the twenty-first, he had come from the most privileged and affluent of backgrounds. And for Obama, any nuance in the Awlaki matter had been settled long ago. The question was how soon he could be found and killed.

The Awlaki hunt through 2010 and early 2011 made regular appearances in the President's Daily Brief as Obama coped with more pressing issues. At home, Obama had to respond to the oil spill in the Gulf, select two new justices to the Supreme Court, manage the auto industry bailout and other measures to spark the economy, and engage in excruciating negotiations with the Republicans over the budget and debt ceiling. Overseas, as the Arab uprisings gathered steam, the administration groped for the proper stance toward the motley forces that were ousting one problematic but familiar leader after another. And framing every action, especially after Republicans swept the 2010 midterms and took control of the House of Representatives, was Obama's approaching campaign for reelection, which he formally announced on April 4, 2011.

White House officials were relieved that the spike in terrorist plotting that had troubled Obama's first year in office, which had concluded with the massacre at Fort Hood and the fizzled bomb above Detroit, was looking like an outlier, not a trend. But no one doubted that a terrorist attack on American soil would undermine his chances for a second term. The entire Republican Party would take up Cheney's soft-on-terror line, ignoring the hundreds of drone strikes. And that message of weakness would resonate, if not with the facts, at least with many Americans' lingering doubts about the first black president, with the odd name and hard-to-remember connection to Islam.

Remarkably, however, the intelligence machinery began to serve up rare victories. First, in mid-April, two weeks after Obama had made his campaign official, American commandos captured a fishing boat shuttling a Somali named Ahmed Abdulkadir Warsame across the Gulf of Aden from Yemen to Somalia. He was a commander for al-Shabab, the Al Qaeda affiliate in Somalia, who had become a liaison between al-Shabab and AQAP. He was taken aboard the USS *Boxer*, a navy amphibious assault ship with a crew of almost two-thousand sailors, where the government's High-Value Detainee Interrogation Group questioned him for two months. The HIG, as it was called, was Obama's alternative to the CIA's brutal interrogations, the waterboarding and wall-slamming that had been dropped years earlier and that Obama had banned for good. Instead of using torture, the HIG used brains. Reprising methods used on high-ranking German and Japanese prisoners during World War II, interrogators learned everything they could about the prisoner and used traditional rapport building and psychological trickery to get them talking. The methods paid off with Warsame, who turned out to have inside knowledge of both Shabab and AQAP—including Awlaki.

Even as Warsame started to talk, a team of veteran SEAL operatives, hardened by the experience of many raids in Afghanistan and Iraq, were practicing for their most important mission. CIA analysts had decided that the tall fellow they had nicknamed "the pacer," who got his exercise walking inside the walls of a mysterious compound in Abbottabad, Pakistan, was indeed Osama bin Laden. In this extraordinary case, Obama rejected the drone option, deciding that physical proof of Bin Laden's capture or, far more likely, his demise, was critical. In a series of Situation Room meetings, Obama pressed each member of his security cabinet to answer the question: Given the CIA's estimate of a 60 percent chance that Bin Laden was in residence, should he order a risky raid? A year after his awkward joke about Predators, his daughters, and the Jonas Brothers, Obama returned as scheduled to the annual White House Correspondents' Association Dinner and joked about footage of his birth in Kenya (with a clip from *The Lion King*), eager to give no hint that he had approved the risky assault into Pakistan for the next day. And late on Sunday night, May 1, as rumors raced around the capital, the president strode along the red carpet in the East Room to the podium and made a historic announcement: "Good evening. Tonight, I can report to the American people and to the world that the United States has conducted an operation . . ."

That opening, in keeping with the importance of the event, avoided any taint of politics by attributing the killing of Bin Laden to the entire country. But deeper into his remarks, Obama asserted his own role in the achievement that had eluded George W. Bush for seven years. He recalled, with satisfaction, the pledge in his maiden national security speech in the presidential campaign that had drawn such scorn and ridicule: "Over the years, I've repeatedly made clear that we would take action within Pakistan if we knew where bin Laden was." In describing the mission, he did not stint on personal pronouns: "Shortly after taking office, I directed Leon Panetta, the director of the CIA, to make the killing or capture of bin Laden the top priority of our war against Al Qaeda. . . . I was briefed on a possible lead to Bin Laden. . . . I met repeatedly with my national security team. . . . And finally, last week, I determined that we had enough intelligence to take action, and authorized an operation to get Osama bin Laden and bring him to justice. Today, at my direction, the United States launched a targeted operation." Even skeptics in security circles had been impressed by Obama's consultations and decision making on the raid. He had made a gutsy decision that had worked out. But even if Obama had not been inclined to emphasize his own central role—the man was a politician, after all—his aides would have insisted. There could be no more potent answer than this operation to the unrelenting criticism for Obama's counterterrorism record from Cheney and the Republicans.

Four days after Bin Laden was killed, on May 5, Obama helicoptered to Manhattan to meet with survivors of the victims of 9/11. He visited a firehouse that had lost fifteen firefighters on the day of the attacks, laid a red, white, and blue wreath at Ground Zero—and made time for an interview with Steve Kroft of *60 Minutes*. A New York Times-CBS poll that morning had reported a bump in Obama's approval rating that cheered his political team: 57 percent of Americans now approved of the president's job performance, up from 46 percent before the raid. But what the president knew, and did not mention as he exchanged hugs and handshakes in New York City, was the true significance of the scattered news reports from Yemen that day about a strike that had killed two Al Qaeda members. What was being reported as a minor blow to AQAP was in fact a major Joint Special Operations Command (JSOC) operation to kill Awlaki, and it had almost succeeded. Only the next day, as Obama and Vice President Joe Biden flew to Fort Campbell, Kentucky, to meet in private with members of the SEAL team who had carried out the Abbottabad raid, did word began to leak of Awlaki's narrow escape.

The JSOC operation in Yemen marked the end of the yearlong moratorium on strikes that had followed the two disastrous American assaults of late 2009 and mid-2010. The vast intelligence net that the United States had cast over Yemen received a reliable report of Awlaki's whereabouts, evidently from tribal informants in the chaotic south. Awlaki was staying in Nisab, a village a short drive west of Al Ataq, the regional capital of Shabwah, where he had first lived after leaving Sanaa. On the night of May 4, learning that

Awlaki would be on the move, JSOC put together an extraordinarily complex array of equipment to catch him on the road, where strikes could be carried out with the least risk of civilian casualties. It was the first American strike in Yemen in a year, against the man now at the very top of Obama's kill list, and military commanders did not want to miss. They organized what Air Force wags called a "drive-by shooting," dispatching at least two Predator drones armed with Hellfire missiles, backed by Harrier jets and a special operations aircraft armed with smaller Griffin missiles.

Using infrared sensors that detected heat signatures and could produce ghostly images even on the darkest night, Predator operators in Nevada spotted a white pickup truck with Awlaki inside. The aircraft shot at least two missiles at it, possibly more. They missed. Though the military and CIA had largely managed to keep the problem under wraps, the performance of laser-guided missiles like the Hellfire and the Griffin against fast-moving targets was not impressive. Because the missile was often aimed from several miles away, the laser "spot" on the ground that guided it could be five or ten feet across, according to a veteran drone pilot. With that imprecision in targeting, and the missile in flight for twenty or thirty seconds, the Hellfires often missed moving vehicles. That shortcoming, in turn, led to a preference for waiting until a vehicle was parked—and that made it harder to avoid collateral casualties, since cars and trucks usually stopped outside buildings. It was a technical issue that had contributed to several bad strikes.

In this case, frustrated pilots saw the white pickup cruise on through the pitted landscape, dodging missile craters, until clouds temporarily blocked their view. Alerted by the booms, Al Qaeda fighters converged on the area, and two brothers, whom Yemeni officials identified as Musad and Abdullah al-Harad, swapped cars with Awlaki. They drove on in Awlaki's pickup, while Awlaki, his driver, and bodyguards piled into the other car and sped away. When the clouds parted a few minutes later, a missile destroyed the pickup. Only later, from cell phone chatter and informants on the ground, did American officials learn that their quarry had escaped.

As it happened, Awlaki would give his own account of the strike to an Al Qaeda member and prison acquaintance, Harith al-Nadari, who later recounted the episode in *Inspire* magazine. While Nadari's story has the tone of wide-eyed hero worship, it roughly accords with American officials' description of events. Nadari recalled being awakened in the night in an Al Qaeda safe house by hearing the sound of distant explosions and feeling the ground shaking. When dawn broke, Awlaki showed up at the house "with a cheerful smile, so we all knew that he was the one targeted." Awlaki recounted that he and his bodyguards had felt a shock wave and seen a flash of light, and that the glass in the truck's windows was shattered—but the cans of gasoline in the back had not ignited. After making his escape in the borrowed SUV, he bedded down temporarily in the hills, hearing the shudder of additional strikes in the distance. At first light he made his way to the safe house, where he learned that the Harad brothers had paid with their lives for their good turn. By Awlaki's account, eleven American missiles had been fired during the night, yet he had survived unscathed. This lucky break seemed to Awlaki a good portent: it "increased my certainty that no human being will die until they complete their livelihood and appointed time."

By now, in fact, from the limited glimpses we have of him in 2011 as he dodged the drones, Awlaki seemed to be increasingly adopting a philosophical tone, playing the fatalist. He betrayed no doubts about the course he had chosen, abandoning his family to plot attacks against faraway strangers. In a lecture years earlier that had become a favorite with his fans, Awlaki had told the story of Ibn Taymiyyah, a puritanical fourteenth-century Islamic scholar who was jailed and persecuted for his views. "What can you do with me?" Awlaki quoted Ibn Taymiyyah as saying. "My *jannah*," or paradise, "is in my heart. If you take me to jail, I'll make *dhikr* of Allah," reciting verses in remembrance of God. "If you exile me out of my land, I will make *tafakur*—contemplate the creation of Allah. If you execute me, I would be a *shaheed*," or martyr. "I am living for *al-akhira*," the afterlife, he quoted Ibn Taymiyyah as saying.

Now, as the Americans closed in, Awlaki, who had turned forty in the spring, seemed to have put aside the cocky defiance of earlier declarations from Shabwah and the gun-slinging pose. His hair was longer and his beard bushier than his style back in the city. In video footage that appears to date from 2011, probably after his narrow escape in May, Awlaki sat in a tent and spoke quietly in Arabic about dying, his face framed in dark curls. "Martyrdom is like a tree—fruits grow on it, the fruits ripen, and then comes the time for reaping those fruits. This happens in specific seasons. This is how Allah's slaves pass through stages, until they reach a stage when it is time for them to be taken as martyrs." Awlaki quoted the Koran and declared: "Hence the tree of martyrdom in the Arabian Peninsula has already got ripe fruits on it, and the time for reaping them has come."

This question of martyrdom had, in fact, started a debate in the United States. Some commentators argued that American officials and media had magnified Awlaki's importance, and now they said that killing him would merely give his message greater authority. No drone strike could kill that message, they argued. Mohamed Elibiary, a young Muslim activist in Texas whom I had consulted from time to time, wrote a piece for FoxNews.com, of all places, under the headline, "It's a Mistake to Assassinate Anwar al-Awlaki." Elibiary called Awlaki "a disingenuous cheerleader in the global jihad who's preying on largely naive or troubled Western-educated youth attempting to form their identities in a global world." But he urged Obama to rescind his kill order. The proper way to counter Awlaki, he wrote, "is not to assassinate the messenger so that he achieves 'martyr' status" but to encourage Islamic clerics, including Salafis, to speak out against Awlaki's "unsound Islamic logic."

"We must ask ourselves whether our public chest thumping in calling for Anwar's head 'dead or alive' is worth the ramifications of having to chase his ghost as a martyr for the next half century, having Al Qaeda's propaganda department embrace Anwar in death to capitalize on his martyrdom, and encourage more Muslim youth to join Al Qaeda's disingenuous jihad to hit the 'tyrannical Americans,'" Elibiary wrote. He understated Awlaki's role in plotting attacks—Awlaki was not just a "messenger"—but he made a strong case. He noted that Egypt's execution in 1966 of Sayyid Qutb, the Islamist writer who had been so horrified by American sexual ways, had helped elevate Qutb to the status of hero-philosopher of jihad, contributing to "the violent radicalization of tens of thousands in a generation that later gave us the leadership of Al Qaeda."

But government officials, and government officials alone, were unable to join the national debate over the kill order on Awlaki. It was part of a growing body of information that might be described as "public but classified." The addition of Awlaki's name to the kill list had been openly reported for months by every news outlet, but it remained against the law for government officials to discuss it. So the people who really mattered—President Obama and top counterterrorism officials—remained silent on the subject. Congress held no hearings on the contentious and critical questions it raised: Was it lawful to kill an American without trial? Was it smart, or might it merely make his message more alluring? As so often in the post-9/11 era, government secrecy rules that were supposed to make the country safer were undermining democratic decision making.

All the American strikes in Yemen since 2009 had been carried out by the military's JSOC, which flew surveillance drones from Djibouti and launched cruise missiles and jets from ships. But as the threat from AQAP seemed to grow more dire in 2010, Obama had acted on the advice of John Brennan and approved the construction of a new, CIA-run drone base to supplement the JSOC operations. On the face of it, duplicating an expensive and complex military capability made little sense. But Obama was not happy with JSOC's performance in Yemen: first, there were the bad strikes that had caused irreparable harm to the image of American counterterrorism efforts there, even among Yemenis who passionately hated Al Qaeda; and second, there was the Awlaki hunt—eighteen months and counting since the order to kill or capture, which really meant kill, and the job was not yet done. True, there had not been an AQAP plot directed at the United States since the printer bombs in October 2010, a likely indication that Awlaki, Asiri the bomb maker, and the rest were distracted from their scheming by the ever-present possibility of a Hellfire missile falling from the sky. But Brennan argued that building a secret drone base over the northern border in Saudi Arabia would make it easier to cover the entirety of Yemen. It would allow some strikes to be carried out as covert actions by the CIA, supposedly never to be acknowledged by the United States— and potentially without the advance approval of the government of Yemen. Most important, it would bring the CIA's Counterterrorism Center, or CTC, with its years of experience carrying out drone strikes in Pakistan, fully to bear on the problem. "I think throughout there was a feeling that the CTC guys were much better—much more precise in their work—than the JSOC guys," said one former high-ranking counterterrorism official who sat through the discussions. Why would CIA officers be better at this military task, I asked, than the military itself?

"Practice," he said.

But there were all kinds of complications in having two agencies both cooperate and compete in Yemen. There was a rivalry between the agencies, even if individual CIA and JSOC officers generally worked well together. There were different legal foundations for strikes by the two agencies, shorthanded as Title 10 of the US Code, the military statute, versus Title 50, which governed CIA operations. Top officials spent multiple meetings discussing whether the official notifications to Congress of American military action overseas, which the White House periodically sent to Capitol Hill under the War Powers Resolution of 1973, could omit strikes carried out by the CIA in Yemen. Officials worried that notifying Congress of JSOC strikes, while omitting the CIA operations, might be misleading. And there was the awkward fact that the Saudis had insisted that the United States keep secret the location of the new base, being built in the harsh desert of the Empty Quarter about twenty-five miles north of the Yemeni border.

As usual, demands for secrecy, whether from CIA lawyers or Saudi diplomats, clashed with a basic fact: drone strikes were never secret, no matter which agency carried them out, because they blew up buildings and cars and killed people. Trying to hide what could not be hidden simply cast a moral shadow over the operations, suggesting that the United States was ashamed of what it was doing. But despite all the tangles, the two-track American war in Yemen proceeded.

Meanwhile, the Americans were losing their on-again, off-again Yemeni ally in the campaign against Al Qaeda. Under intense pressure from both massive popular protests and a brutal power struggle among Yemen's elite, the three-decade rule of Ali Abdullah Saleh was unraveling. By May there was open combat on the streets of the capital, with a death toll rising into the hundreds. In June, after four months of calls for Saleh to step down, an explosion inside the mosque in the presidential palace in Sanaa severely injured him, and he was flown to Saudi Arabia for care. His departure was celebrated by huge crowds, but the festive tone of the early demonstrations on

Change Square, which had so enraptured young Abdulrahman al-Awlaki and his pals, was gone.

Before dawn one morning in early September, after a tumultuous summer, Abdulrahman rose in his grandfather's big house in the capital and scribbled an apologetic note saying that he had taken 9,000 Yemeni rials, currency worth about $45, from his mother's purse. He climbed out a window to keep from waking the rest of the household, made his way to the famous gate to Sanaa's old city, Bab al-Yemen, and caught a bus to Shabwah. He was on his way, he explained in the note, to find his father.

His motives, if hard to be certain about, were easy to imagine. He had turned sixteen on August 26 and was experiencing a rapid political coming of age as he participated in the ferment on the streets. His posts on Facebook in the weeks before he slipped away reflected multiple sides of the teenager: he replaced his profile picture with an image of a muscle-bound anime warrior; he posted his new high scores in a video game called Crazy Cabbie; he put up several snapshots of himself clowning with two friends. But in his last post, on August 20, he wrote in English, instead of his usual Arabic, what appeared to be a comment on the bloodshed in the streets: "When you kill once it's easy to kill again and again."

Abdulrahman was an American citizen by birth and had lived in the United States for his first six years, but his infamous father had joined a war on America. Despite the teenager's public tribute to his absent father with the parenthetical Facebook moniker "Ibn al-Shaykh," son of the sheikh, his posts displayed little interest in Islam. His grandfather, to whom he was very close, had always spoken highly of the United States, recalling fond tales from his life there and telling Abdulrahman that he would study there someday. His Uncle Ammar was a westernized businessman. It must have been a confusing mix. It would be no surprise if Abdulrahman wanted to see his father and talk over all the issues that his family and his country were confronting—and have an adventure at the same time. But according to his family, Anwar had not been in touch for two years, since 2009. Abdulrahman naturally assumed his father was somewhere in Shabwah, the tribal territory, and headed there to ask around about how to find him. When Abdulrahman's mother and grandparents awoke and found him gone, they were frightened for him. The move seemed out of character, though Abdulrahman was clearly growing up. They worried that someone might have put the idea of finding his father in the teenager's head. Given the intensity of the CIA's search for Anwar, in fact, they feared that Abdulrahman might have become an unwitting tool of the American hunt.

In rare public remarks in July, Admiral Eric T. Olson, shortly to step down after four years as head of US Special Operations Command, of which JSOC was part, described Awlaki as a worthy adversary, calling him "charismatic" and crediting him with plots that had gotten far closer to succeeding than most. "He's a savvy guy," Olson said. "He knows how to hide from us pretty well, despite the fact that he's communicating with his own people pretty well. He's publishing a magazine in the English language that's quite frightening. He's a dual passport holder who has lived in the United States. He understands us a lot better than we understand him." It was a tribute that may have masked embarrassment; Olson would be departing the Special Operations Command with the Awlaki hunt, a high-priority assignment to American intelligence and security agencies from the commander in chief, unfinished.

If the US government did not understand Awlaki, it was certainly not because the government had failed to devote adequate resources to him. The NSA, working with the FBI and with the British, Canadian, and Australian intelligence services, had identified hundreds of English speakers abroad who had been in past e-mail contact with him. But persuading them to help entrap him, or spoofing their identities, would no longer work—Awlaki was too wary. NSA eavesdroppers were sitting on many phone numbers in Yemen and abroad of Awlaki's relatives and friends, just in case he called. Saudi intelligence, which made regular payments to many of Yemen's tribal leaders and ran its own eavesdropping and spy operations, were in regular touch with the CIA. The CIA, meanwhile, was paying its own informants directly and through a few trusted Yemeni officials, hoping for word of Awlaki's whereabouts. The Somali Shabab commander who had been held at sea for two months before being moved to a prison in the United States, Ahmed Warsame, was sharing everything he knew about Awlaki's habits and movements. Morten Storm, the Danish former jihadi who had delivered bugged equipment to AQAP for the CIA, had continued to communicate with Awlaki by courier, leaving a thumb drive in Sanaa in August for pickup; he informed the CIA at every step, with the idea that its agents might be able to follow the chain of couriers back to Awlaki's hideout. But none of those channels had paid off. The close call in May had only driven Awlaki further underground.

In the midst of the hunt, there was a major personnel change. The decision of Robert Gates to step down after nearly five years as defense secretary set off musical chairs: Obama asked Leon Panetta to move over from the CIA to the Defense Department and named as CIA director David Petraeus, the favorite general of many Beltway pundits and military journalists. There were mutterings that Obama wanted to eliminate the possibility that Petraeus would decide to challenge him for the presidency in 2012, a plausible notion, though Petraeus had actively sought the CIA job. Petraeus arrived at CIA headquarters in August, dressed in a business suit and leaving behind his entourage of longtime aides; both his retirement from the military and his drastically shrunken retinue were concessions to a civilian intelligence agency wary of Pentagon control. Petraeus, who as commander of US forces in the Middle East had overseen the disastrous cruise missile strike on Yemen in 2009 and had visited Sanaa often, needed no briefings on the significance of AQAP and Awlaki. He had barely learned his way around CIA headquarters when CTC briefers brought him good news: they had fresh word on Awlaki's whereabouts.

Awlaki's relatives had urged him to stay in his family's tribal territory in Shabwah province, where they believed he faced little risk of betrayal. But Awlaki, who had nearly been killed near Shabwah's provincial seat of Al Ataq, evidently decided that Shabwah had become too hot for him. The CIA got word in the second week of September 2011 that he had quietly moved north to Al Jawf, not far from Saudi territory. A little to the west there was a continuing conflict on sectarian lines, with Shia fighters known as Houthis, for the family name of their leader, regularly clashing with religious Sunnis associated with the strict Salafi community at Dammaj, where many foreign Muslims had gone to study Islam. In Al Jawf, Al Qaeda was exploiting the conflict to embed itself, paying Sunni tribesmen and telling them that the Houthis, supported by Iran, posed a grave threat. The chaos and division actually made intelligence easier to gather, generating more electronic chatter for the NSA to pick up and providing cover for paid informants. "People were optimistic that we were getting close," said an American official tracking the hunt from Sanaa. Soon the CIA learned where Awlaki was staying and made plans for a strike—taking control of operations from JSOC for the first time. The sprawling, new CIA drone base in the Empty Quarter of Saudi Arabia, as it happened, had just become operational.

Awlaki had spent half of his forty years in America; he had climbed the mountains of Colorado, loved the deep-sea fishing off San Diego, played with his children in suburban Washington parks. He had, for a time, praised American liberties and described Islam as a religion of peace. Boxed CD sets of his lectures on the Prophet Muhammad and the requirements for a good marriage were in the homes of law-abiding Muslim families all over America. What toxic mix had turned him into an outlaw on the run in a desolate place, notorious for championing mass murder and hunted by his own government? It was plausible to see Awlaki as just one more fanatic preaching an archaic and heartless strain of Islam—the American right's preferred interpretation—or as a political figure radicalized by America's bloody bumbling in Iraq, Afghanistan, Yemen, and other Muslim countries, as some on the left argued. But there were more personal forces at work as well. There was ambition, driving him to find a path to fame after his own peccadilloes and suspicious government officials in Washington and Sanaa blocked conventional success. There may have been a sort of self-loathing, fury at his native country for producing the sinful sexual culture that had so enticed and entangled him. Perhaps, too, he was acting out an Oedipal drama, embracing a point of view at the opposite extreme from his father's wholehearted embrace of America and its values.

Whatever had carried Anwar al-Awlaki on the long road to the war with America, he could not have been terribly surprised when the drones came for him again. He and his small band were sitting outside a large Bedouin-style tent where he had apparently been staying for several days, beside a rough track in Al Jawf, a short drive from Marib to the south and a little farther from the Saudi border to the north. The great ribbed desert of reddish sand swept away to the north and east. It was "Bedouin country," said Abdullah al-Jumaili, a tribal sheikh in Al Jawf. The men were eating a breakfast of dates. With Awlaki were his protégé and *Inspire* magazine colleague, Samir Khan, twenty-five, another American citizen, and two tribesmen who were helping them, later identified by Al Qaeda as Abu Muhsen al-Maribi and Salim al-Marwani. One of them must have heard the distant telltale buzz or caught the glint of morning sun on the fuselage of one of the aircraft.

As in May, the Americans had thrown a lot of hardware into the mission, determined not to miss: a Reaper with multiple Hellfire missiles under each wing, plus two smaller Predators to give the shooters a good view of the ground and two lasers to better "sparkle" the target, as the drone operators liked to say about the guidance procedure. As counterterrorism officials at CIA headquarters watched on their screens, the drone operators at Creech Air Force Base in Nevada drew a bead on their targets from a distance of 8,500 miles. The men on the ground ran for their two vehicles—a Toyota Hilux pickup truck and a Suzuki Vitara SUV, according to someone who saw the aftermath. It might have seemed pointless to flee—they were in open desert, with nowhere to hide. But just a few months before, Awlaki had made a miraculous escape from the Americans. The men jumped in their trucks. This time, Awlaki's fortune had run out. It was, in his own words, his "appointed time." When Abdullah al-Jumaili, the local sheikh, visited the spot a few days later, there were just craters and the burned frames of the trucks.

Never before in history had the US government's awesome power been directed to hunting and killing a single citizen. Filed away in a secret CIA archive, awaiting historians of some distant era, the strike video would have era-defining significance, showing the US government's assault on one of its citizens, an execution without the formalities of indictment, trial, and sentencing. It was simultaneously a triumph of technology, an act of self-defense in the relentless American campaign to eliminate the risk of terrorist attack, and, in the view of some, a challenge to the Constitution and to the legal and ethical standards on which Americans prided themselves. It was a vision of a disquieting future, with the allure of push-button solutions and the erosion of venerable principles, arriving with a jolt.

A few hours later, at a flag-decked retirement ceremony for the nation's top military officer, Admiral Mike Mullen, at Fort Myer in Virginia, the president who had ordered the strike took public note of it. John Brennan had given him the news in an early phone call to the family quarters in the White House. It was, for them, good news for a change. The president had plenty of other business on his mind that week: fund-raisers in Silicon Valley and Hollywood to build a war chest that would help him hang on to the presidency; a decision to seek a fast-track ruling from the Supreme Court that could derail his signature achievement, the expansion of health coverage; the arrest of a would-be jihadi who, in a disturbing turning of tables, had planned to fly remote-control planes loaded with explosives into the Capitol and Pentagon. There was news of massive flooding in the Philippines, a shocking hot spell in the United Kingdom, hundreds of Occupy Wall Street protesters marching on the New York Police Department, and brinksmanship with the Republicans over the budget and debt ceiling. But Anwar al-Awlaki would never again plot an attack. That was something.

As the farewell to Mullen began, Obama spoke in the coy, peeka-boo language customary for official comments on the semisecret drone operations. "Before I begin," he said, "I want to say a few words about some important news. Earlier this morning, Anwar al-Awlaki—a leader of Al Qaeda in the Arabian Peninsula—was killed in Yemen." The president stumbled slightly over the name of the man whose death he had ordered, and he did not say who, exactly, had killed him. The CIA strike was legally a covert action, or in the words of the law, an act "where it is intended that the role of the United States Government will not be apparent or acknowledged publicly." But this supposed secret had topped every morning newscast, and the officers, spooks, and dignitaries gathered on the lawn didn't need to be told. The audience interrupted with applause, prompting Obama to pause.

"The death of Awlaki is a major blow to Al Qaeda's most active operational affiliate," the president resumed, reprising Awlaki's role as AQAP's "leader of external operations" and saying that "he took the lead in planning and directing efforts to murder innocent Americans." The president mentioned the Christmas bombing attempt, the bombs on cargo planes, and Awlaki's recruitment skills. He cast the strike as part of a larger achievement for his administration, saying it "marks another significant milestone in the broader effort to defeat

Al Qaeda and its affiliates." The leaves on the magnolia trees behind him trembled in the breeze. "This success," Obama said, still speaking obliquely, "is a tribute to our intelligence community."

It was a declaration of victory in a quest that Obama had pursued for nearly two years, since his first briefings in Hawaii that had raised the possibility of Awlaki's role in the Christmas bombing attempt. Obama had taken out the terrorist who had nearly derailed his presidency with what would have been the biggest attack since 9/11; who had repeatedly mocked the American president from his desert hideouts; who had addressed the printer bombs to the president's adopted hometown of Chicago. Obama included the usual caveats— that AQAP remained "dangerous, though weakened" and that the United States must be "vigilant." But for a change, as the autumn of 2011 began, the White House security team was feeling decidedly upbeat about the counterterrorism campaign. Bin Laden was gone, and now so was the Bin Laden of the Internet, as some had dubbed Awlaki. Al Qaeda's core in Pakistan had been devastated as its operatives had been picked off, and now the most America-focused members of AQAP, Awlaki and Samir Khan, were dead. The last US combat troops were leaving Iraq, and Obama had set a schedule for getting them out of Afghanistan. The drone was a big part of the story. Obama's strategy for drastically narrowing the campaign against terrorism—*Let's kill the people who are trying to kill us*—seemed to be working, or so many administration officials believed. It was possible, he had demonstrated, to combat the terrorist threat without putting thousands of American soldiers on the ground.

In an interview later on the day Awlaki was killed, Obama spoke enthusiastically with radio host Michael Smerconish about the "incredibly dangerous mission" to kill Bin Laden and then about the death of Awlaki. "Did you give that order?" Smerconish asked. "I can't talk about the operational details, Michael," Obama replied. But he was happy to talk about the significance of the operation. In the two years of the hunt, the president had been notably quiet about Awlaki in public, reluctant to add to the cleric's luster. But now he spoke about the threat he had posed, as plotter and as preacher. "We are very pleased that Mr. Awlaki is no longer going to be in a position to directly threaten the United States homeland as well as our allies around the world." The Christmas bombing and the printer cartridge plot may have failed, but they showed Awlaki's persistence. "This was a guy who was operationally involved in trying to kill Americans, and the fact that he is now no longer around to initiate the kind of propaganda that also was recruiting people all around the world to that murderous cause I think is something that's very good for American security."

Here and there, a few voices expressed anxiety about a president ordering the killing of an American. But they were mostly on the fringe. To many sympathetic observers, Obama was on a roll. On the *Washington Monthly*'s website the day of the Awlaki strike, the liberal blogger Steve Benen hailed what he called "a quiet record of foreign policy successes." There were accolades from commentators for NBC News—the *First Read* blog by correspondent Chuck Todd and his colleagues declared, "No president since George H. W. Bush has had more foreign-policy successes happen under his watch than President Obama," though the column added that he was getting little credit in the polls. At ABC News, Jake Tapper offered a sly tribute to Obama's boldness, listing dead militants and talking about the "terrorist notches" on the president's belt. "Remember when Rudy Giuliani warned that electing Barack Obama would mean that the U.S. played defense, not offense, against the terrorists?" Tapper asked. "If this is defense, what does offense look like?" They were the kind of unrestrained endorsements that a politician running for reelection, even one with Obama's bankroll, just couldn't buy.

The self-congratulatory mood at the White House lasted for exactly two weeks. On the prowl in Shabwah at 9 p.m. on the evening of October 14, 2011, JSOC drone operators believed they had a legitimate Al Qaeda target, the Egyptian-born media chief for AQAP, Ibrahim al-Banna. They fired their missiles at a group of seven men eating by the side of a road. When the smoke cleared and the corpses were identified, word came from Yemeni tribal sources: al-Banna had not been present. Among the dead, along with some rank-and-file militants, were Abdulrahman al-Awlaki and his seventeen-year-old cousin, Ahmed Abdel-Rahman al-Awlaki.

The strike was a catastrophe for Abdulrahman's family, a cruel blow that left them incredulous and inconsolable. For Nasser, the killing of his son, which he had fought to prevent in court, had at least the outlines of logic. He had played down the evidence of Anwar's militancy, plotting, and alliance with Al Qaeda, but he was a rational man who knew that Anwar had called for violent jihad against America and understood the risk he was courting. Abdulrahman, his beloved sixteen-year-old grandson, was a different story. He was a happy kid who had barely begun to live. The strike devastated the grandfather, forcing him to question everything he knew and believed.

"He was a very sweet, very gentle boy," Nasser al-Awlaki later told some American visitors. "He was very slim—he was tall but very slim. He wore eyeglasses, he's nearsighted, and to think that Abdulrahman would be part of Al Qaeda is really ridiculous. . . . He never carried arms in his life. He never learned to use a pistol." Nasser had forced himself to visit the site of his grandson's death, not far from his ancestors' village of Al Saeed, where Anwar had lived before heading for the mountains. He talked to tribesmen who came to the scene immediately after the strike. He was told that Abdulrahman's remains were recognizable only from one intact fragment of his body: the back of his head, with the hair still attached. The missiles, apparently two of them, had so obliterated the bodies that they could not be separated and wrapped in the traditional white burial shroud. Instead, the tribesmen had gathered the pieces of flesh and bone in an empty cement sack, they told Nasser, and buried them with Islamic rites. "Seven people," he said, "in one cement bag."

If the strike was an excruciating tragedy for the Awlaki family, it was also a political and strategic blow to the United States and to the president himself. The strike shattered the confidence at the White House about this unconventional war; JSOC, as they saw it, had managed to snatch defeat from the jaws of victory. Killing Abdulrahman demolished the claim, already battered, that the drone operators had such crisp video of a potential target, and such leisure to study it, that they could know just whom they were killing and strike with precision. If anything, Abdulrahman looked younger than his actual age; no one who glanced at his Facebook page would have imagined him as a legitimate target. When John Brennan gave him the news, Obama was furious, instantly understanding that the killing of a teenager would taint the counterterrorism strikes in Yemen, undermining once again the claim that it was justified

American self-defense or aid for Yemen against Al Qaeda, which most Yemenis despised.

Obama, said one aide who spoke with him shortly afterward, considered the strike "a fuck-up" that was profoundly frustrating. "The nature of his anger was that we'd taken a ton of care around the Awlaki issue—painstaking legal analysis, many, many meetings, very deliberative decision making, to take this action that we recognized was a substantial action"—that is, targeting an American citizen, the aide said. "And none of that was manifested in the other strike." Obama asked for a report on what had gone wrong.

There was an explanation of sorts, if not a full or fully satisfying explanation, for the mistake. At the time of his death, Abdulrahman had been in Shabwah for six weeks. Shabwah was infested with Al Qaeda members and supporters, and until September 30 the teenager would naturally have been asking among them for help and direction in reaching his father. According to multiple Yemeni and American sources, after Abdulrahman heard that an American strike had killed his father two weeks earlier, he was both brokenhearted and angry, and he decided to join AQAP's fight against the Americans. "The son was there specifically to make contact with Al Qaeda," said an American official who read the intelligence reports before and after the strike.

Nasser al-Awlaki refused to believe that his kind-hearted grandson would even contemplate such a move. But the evidence to support the claims that the son had decided to try to avenge the father's death is considerable. First, Abdulrahman had remained in Shabwah for two weeks after learning that his father had been killed. In a phone call a few days before his death, he had promised his grandmother that he would return to Sanaa. While the chaos in southern Yemen certainly made travel difficult, the fact that the teenager had not started the journey home by October 14 suggests that he may have had other plans. Second, it would be both psychologically and socially understandable if Abdulrahman decided to cast his fate with AQAP. In Shabwah, he was surrounded by Awaliq tribesmen for whom revenge of a son for a father's murder would be not just acceptable but mandatory. And in the weeks in September when he was asking after his father, Abdulrahman had probably established contact with AQAP members who undoubtedly after September 30 would have urged him to join their fight. Third, a Yemeni journalist who acknowledges being supportive of AQAP and who is in regular contact with its leaders, Abdul Razzaq al-Jamal, reported that Abdulrahman had decided to cast his lot with Al Qaeda. After hearing of his father's death, Jamal wrote, Abdulrahman told the AQAP leader in the town of Azzan, "I hope to attain martyrdom as my father attained it." AQAP members called Abdulrahman "Usayyid," or lion's cub, a reference to the Arab proverb, "This cub is from that lion," Jamal wrote.

So it is entirely plausible, though the details are difficult to reconstruct, that Abdulrahman and his cousin were with a group that included Al Qaeda members when they were killed. But al-Banna, the Egyptian whom JSOC was purportedly targeting, was not among the dead—the United States would still be offering a reward for information on his location three years later—and the Al Qaeda connections of others killed in the strike remained uncertain. In part that reflects the difficulty of assessing where an individual is on a spectrum of "Al Qaeda ties." In the context of Yemen's tribal provinces, that vague term can include dedicated fighters who have sworn allegiance to the leader of AQAP, but it can also include men with brothers or cousins in Al Qaeda who themselves take no active part.

Abdulrahman, said one administration official who was briefed on the strike, "was certainly with people who we believed to be AQAP." That did not justify the killing of the sixteen-year-old, he said, but it explained how it happened.

A number of initial news reports of the strike, based on interviews with anonymous Yemeni and American officials, mistakenly gave Abdulrahman's age as twenty-one. Outraged, Nasser al-Awlaki countered the false reports by giving reporters copies of Abdulrahman's birth certificate, showing he had been born in Colorado in 1995. The incorrect age raised a possibility that American targeters somehow had bogus information and really believed that Abdulrahman was a twenty-one-year-old Al Qaeda member. But several officials said the incorrect age was either an honest error or a clumsy after-the-fact falsehood intended to minimize the blunder. "That's a 'shit happens' kind of story," said another American official deeply involved in the counterterrorism campaign in Yemen about the strike. "We didn't know he was there."

It was a damning excuse. In two weeks, the United States had killed three Americans in Yemen. By its own account, only one of the killings had been intentional. It undercut claims that the Predators, with their telephoto lenses and high-tech optics, allowed drone operators to examine and identify the faces of those on the ground. They were killing people whose identity they didn't know, often on the basis of sketchy intelligence, hunches, and guesswork.

If there was an explanation for what to most Yemenis looked like the deliberate murder of an innocent teenager, the Obama administration failed to offer it. Instead, officials hid behind the usual shield of secrecy, offering the family no apology and the world no explanation to counter the worst possible assumptions: that the United States had killed Abdulrahman deliberately to eliminate the possibility that he would grow up and take his father's path—a favored theory in tribal Yemen—or that the United States simply didn't care whom it killed. In its official "Report of Death of an American Citizen Abroad," Form DS-2060, the State Department had the gall to say that the cause of Abdulrahman's death was "unknown," a falsehood refuted by thousands of news reports.

The killing of his son and especially his grandson, by his own account, threw Nasser al-Awlaki into months of depression. In an emotional audio statement to British Muslims six weeks after the strike, using religious language that was not typical for him, he called for the spread of Anwar's message, which he suggested was simply a call to Islam. "Anwar was assassinated because of his teachings," he said. "No evidence was ever presented against him." As for Abdulrahman, he "was having dinner with his teenage friends in our homeland, Shabwah province" when he was killed. "He was not traveling with any high-value target, as the Obama administration continues to lie." He called the United States "a state gone mad" and personally attacked "the so-called Nobel Peace Prize laureate" Obama.

"My son Anwar was intelligent, sharp, eloquent, educated, charismatic and brave," he said. "He had qualities and traits that could have taken him places in this world. But he chose this path, and gave it his best—the path of Allah. It is the job of all of us to spread his knowledge and keep it alive."

It was the statement of a father and grandfather blinded by grief;

it belied Nasser's own efforts, over many years, to steer Anwar into a more conventional career and away from militancy. Nasser al-Awlaki was on far more solid ground when he called for the United States to live up to its own principles. Many months later, he explained why he had gone to federal court in the United States for a second time. The first time, he had tried and failed to get Anwar off the kill list. Now, along with Sarah Khan, the mother of Samir Khan, he filed a second federal lawsuit, this time hoping to force the government to publicly acknowledge and explain what it had done and why. He told a story that showed why the American actions were particularly baffling to him. One night about a year before Abdulrahman's death, Nasser said, he and his grandson were talking together by the light of a single candle—Sanaa's power was out, as it so often was. "I told my grandson, 'Look, I don't want you to take any other path except the path of your grandfather. Which means I want you to go to America, and study in America, and come back and serve Yemen, or even stay in America.'" He didn't mention Anwar's choices, but it was clear that he did not want Abdulrahman to follow his father's example. Nasser recalled urging the boy to pay attention. "'Do you listen to me? Please study more English, be as good in English as your father, and I'll take you to America to study after you finish high school.' And he told me yes."

Now he would not be sending Abdulrahman to America or to anywhere else. "I will continue being tormented with questions about why Abdulrahman was killed," Nasser al-Awlaki told me early in 2014, "until the US authorities explain what happened in a court of law." Though his first lawsuit, challenging the placement of Anwar on the kill list had been dismissed, he still believed that the court might give him satisfaction on his second lawsuit. I had covered a hearing on Nasser's second lawsuit where Judge Rosemary Collyer repeatedly pressed Justice Department lawyers to explain why the court should not enforce the constitutional rights of Americans targeted overseas. "Are you saying that a US citizen targeted by the United States in a foreign country has no constitutional rights?" she asked Brian Hauck, a deputy assistant attorney general. "How broadly are you asserting the right of the United States to target an American citizen? Where is the limit to this?" Nasser had read my story about the hearing and taken heart. Most legal authorities still believed the lawsuit was a long shot, but the judge's skeptical stance gave him hope that she would take his side.

A few months later, in April 2014, Judge Collyer dashed that hope. Because Abdulrahman and Samir Khan had not been deliberately targeted, their deaths were unintended and could not be challenged, she said. And as for Anwar al-Awlaki, whom the government admitted deliberately killing, she would not second-guess the executive branch's judgment. "In this delicate area of warmaking, national security, and foreign relations, the judiciary has an exceedingly limited role," she wrote. She called Awlaki "an active and exceedingly dangerous enemy of the United States" and "an AQAP leader who levied war against his birth country, as unambiguously revealed by his role in the Christmas Day bombing, as well as his video and writings."

Nasser al-Awlaki would get no satisfaction from the justice system he had once revered. There would be no judicial condemnation of the strikes, and not even a requirement that the executive branch explain why it had killed his grandson. The lawsuit was dismissed. He felt that the country he had loved, and that had shaped him, had again slammed the courthouse door in his face.

13

A BIGGER BRAND

When Umar Farouk Abdulmutallab entered a federal courtroom in Detroit for sentencing on a chilly afternoon in February 2012, Anwar al-Awlaki had been dead for more than four months. But the young Nigerian, wearing a white prayer cap, stood up and declared that the martyrs of jihad were never dead: Awlaki, like Bin Laden, was "alive and shall be victorious by God's grace," he said.

Now twenty-five, Abdulmutallab had chosen to represent himself, demoting his flustered attorney to legal adviser, and had then flummoxed the attorney and pleased prosecutors by insisting on pleading guilty to all eight counts in the lengthy indictment. His admission of guilt was no reflection of remorse; the underwear bomber had not changed his views. The testimony of five passengers who described their harrowing experience aboard the smoke-filled airliner seemed not to move him. Not even when Shama Chopra, a Canadian passenger, recounted emotionally from the witness stand how Abdulmutallab's parents had called to apologize to her for their son's crime did he seem to take much notice. Abdulmutallab stuck to the position that attempting to blow up Northwest Flight 253 to kill the 289 other people aboard was not just righteous but required by his religion, justified retaliation for the Americans' killing of Muslims in Afghanistan, Iraq, Yemen, and beyond. He knew this, he said, from Awlaki, whom he described in a handwritten statement submitted in court as "my beloved teacher." He did not repeat in court what he had told FBI agents about Awlaki's role in directing the plot, but he declared, "I was greatly inspired to participate in jihad by the lectures of the great and rightly guided mujahideen who is alive, Sheikh Anwar al-Awlaki, may Allah preserve him and his family and give them victory."

The judge gave him the maximum possible sentence, which added up to four life terms plus fifty years. Abdulmutallab had the last word, shouting "Allahu akbar," God is great, as he was led from the courtroom.

It may not have been what he had in mind, but there was something to the Nigerian's insistence that Awlaki lived on. For many Americans, the drone strike in far-off Yemen that killed him was a fleeting good-riddance story—one more terrorist they didn't have to worry about any more. But for Awlaki's target audience, devout, young Muslims searching for a cause, his legacy in the form of lectures, sermons, and interviews preserved on the web was only magnified by his killing, as some Muslim activists had warned. Many fans compiled elaborate tribute videos, which they patched together from the years of material that Awlaki had left behind. Among them was an official video eulogy from AQAP itself, elevating Awlaki to a prophetic martyrdom and further burnishing his credentials—claiming inaccurately, for example, that he had fought Soviet troops in Afghanistan. "The sheikh employed his life, his mind, his wealth, his tongue, and his pen in waging a war against America, which is the leader of war against Islam," said the main eulogist, Ibrahim al-Rubeish, a top AQAP ideologist. Rubeish had a personal motive for his anger at America: he had been imprisoned at Guantanamo for five years before being released to a Saudi rehabilitation program, which in his case had clearly proven ineffective. The thirty-three-minute eulogy video pulled together many threads of the AQAP argument that the United States was occupying Yemen, with clips of General David Petraeus meeting with the soon-to-be-ousted president, Ali Abdullah Saleh; American drones firing missiles; Yemeni demonstrators marching with large banners showing the youthful face of Abdulrahman al-Awlaki; and endless shots of Anwar al-Awlaki, some of them alongside the crumpled remains of his SUV after the missile hit it. Rubeish called on Awlaki's "students in the West" to take revenge for his death and argued that Obama "wants to deceive the American people" by suggesting that killing a few prominent Al Qaeda leaders would end the group's war. In fact, Rubeish said, it was "a war of a whole nation" of Islam, and Awlaki's message was "planted in the hearts of millions of Muslims who had listened to him."

On YouTube alone a search for "Awlaki" turned up tens of thousands of videos, a number that kept climbing in the years after his death. His unobjectionable homilies and stories were mixed randomly with his calls for violent jihad: Awlaki on the Antichrist, Awlaki on why American civilians were legitimate targets, Awlaki on the afterlife, Awlaki on never trusting non-Muslims, Awlaki on early Islamic figures, Awlaki on the American war on Islam, Awlaki on marriage, Awlaki on why American Muslims had a duty to join the jihad. Google, which owned YouTube, had acceded to congressional pressure in November 2010 and agreed to take down Awlaki's inflammatory material. That promise turned out to be meaningless, as I discovered when I did a follow-up story five months later. Awlaki's fans posted material faster than YouTube could take it down, even if the company wanted to try. Anyone who went on the Internet to satisfy his curiosity about Islam and global politics, or the religious legitimacy of terrorism, found Awlaki's face and voice everywhere. "He's a bigger brand now than when he was alive," said Ahmed Younis, the American Muslim activist who had long battled Awlaki's influence.

Some influential Muslims who had raised their voices against Awlaki's calls for violence now denounced his killing. They argued that the drone strike was a betrayal of American values, a self-defeating surrender of the moral high ground. Yasir Qadhi, an American imam who preached a nonviolent variety of Salafi Islam, wrote in *The New York Times* after Awlaki's death that "the accusations against him were very serious, but as a citizen, he deserved a fair trial and the chance to face his accusers in a court of law." Killing Awlaki eroded the government's "moral authority," Qadhi said, since "America routinely criticizes (and justifiably so) such extrajudicial assassinations when they occur at the hands of another government. We most certainly don't approve the regimes of Syria or Iran eliminating those whom they deem to be traitors."

Ed Husain, a British-born writer whose 2007 book *The Islamist* described his own embrace and later rejection of militancy, agreed. "When America kills its own without a trial," he wrote, "it not only demeans itself but it hands over a propaganda victory to its enemies." Far more effective, Husain argued, would have been discrediting

Awlaki by making public the documentation of his hypocritical dallying with prostitutes. Husain had no idea that in 2002 the FBI and Justice Department had actually prepared a criminal case on the prostitution issue before deciding not to pursue it. His argument nine years later underscored the paths the government had not taken.

In May 2012, word leaked to the Associated Press that a second underwear bomber, dispatched from Yemen by AQAP as Abdulmutallab had been with a highly sophisticated explosive device hidden in his clothes, had been thwarted by Western intelligence. It turned out that the would-be airliner bomber was in fact a Saudi-born double agent, working for British, Saudi, and American intelligence, who had infiltrated AQAP and volunteered for a suicide mission blowing up an America-bound plane. The double agent had left Yemen with the device and immediately turned it over to authorities, allowing FBI explosives experts to carry out a thorough assessment of Ibrahim al-Asiri's latest attempt at building a bomb that could pass undetected through airport security. It was quite a coup for counterterrorism, of course, in part because it would fuel crippling paranoia inside the Al Qaeda branch about every new recruit. But in another way, the foiled plot was a troubling sign: it showed that eliminating Awlaki and Samir Khan had not diverted AQAP from its determination to attack the United States.

Nearly a year later came the first of what would be a series of shocking illustrations of Awlaki's lasting influence. Two bombs left in backpacks near the Boston Marathon finish line killed three people and injured more than 260, reviving a sense of vulnerability many Americans had not felt since 9/11. Officials quickly identified the perpetrators as two Chechen immigrant brothers, one killed in a police shootout and the other caught hiding in a trailered boat in a suburban backyard. Within days, investigators learned that the older brother, Tamerlan Tsarnaev, had found his violent ideology in Awlaki's YouTube pronouncements. Tamerlan had helped persuade his younger brother, Dzhokhar, that jihad was their obligation. They knew nothing about explosives, but Awlaki had that covered, too: the Tsarnaev brothers found everything they needed to know in *Inspire* magazine, including step-by-step instructions on turning a pressure cooker into a lethal weapon using the explosive powder found in ordinary fireworks and detonators fashioned from Christmas lights.

There was nothing magical about the videos and magazines that Awlaki had left behind. The Tsarnaev brothers, among the tiny number of Muslims prepared to carry out random murder for their beliefs, might have drawn the same ideology from the writings of Osama bin Laden or Sayyid Qutb and found bomb-making instruction someplace else on the web. But Awlaki, with an assist from Samir Khan, had packaged in accessible, user-friendly form both a vicious interpretation of Islam that glorified mass murder and easy-to-follow directions on how to put it into practice. You could kill the man, but you could not kill his message. Martyrdom, courtesy of a CIA Hellfire missile, had only given Awlaki a more exalted pedestal.

At the time of the marathon bombing, Obama and Ben Rhodes, who worked on most of his national security speeches, were drafting a long-planned speech on terrorism and the country's response to it. Obama had been president for more than four years, and he could speak from visceral experience. He had listened to threat reports at countless meetings in the Oval Office and the Situation Room; he had comforted the families of those gunned down at Fort Hood and blown up in Boston; he had signed off on hundreds of strikes in Pakistan and Yemen. On occasion, he had learned that a strike had gone devastatingly wrong. He had heard the escalating arguments against targeted killings in general—that they killed civilians, that they drew aggrieved people to Al Qaeda, that they made killing too easy by making it risk-free to the drone operators. He had heard the particular arguments about targeting an American like Awlaki, whose advocacy of violence had not stripped him of his constitutional rights.

And on a few occasions Obama had made it clear that he shared some of the doubts, betraying an anxiety about the power to kill that he had exercised with such seeming confidence. Once, on Jon Stewart's *The Daily Show*, of all places, Obama said the country needed a "legal architecture" to make sure that he and future presidents were "reined in" when it came to drone strikes. In an interview with the author Mark Bowden, Obama remarked on the powerful temptation of the drone: "There's a remoteness to it that makes it tempting to think that somehow we can, without any mess on our hands, solve vexing security problems." Obama had often noted that terrorism could not be defeated by military means alone and that the United States must counter jihadist ideology and address economic hopelessness. But those projects were long-term, generational challenges. In the meantime it was a lot easier to put dangerous people on a kill list and then cross them off it. On several occasions, he told aides, with chagrin, that as president he had discovered an unexpected talent. "It turns out," he said, "that I'm really good at killing people."

By 2014, the number of drone strikes in Pakistan had declined drastically from its peak in 2010, and the pace in Yemen was far below the peak there in 2012. The skill of the targeters seemed to be improving: the Bureau of Investigative Journalism in London, which conducted skeptical reviews of every strike, found that the number of civilians killed in Pakistan in 2013 and 2014 was zero or very near zero. In Yemen, with a shorter drone history, the record was poorer. One huge fan, however, was Saleh's replacement as Yemeni president, Abdu Rabbu Mansour Hadi, who said in a Washington visit in 2012 that drones "pinpoint the target" because "the electronic brain's precision is unmatched by the human brain."

But the undeniable fact was that after years of American strikes both Pakistan and Yemen were less stable and their people more hostile to the United States. Yemenis were flabbergasted in September 2014 when Obama said the US strategy in Yemen had proven so successful that it could be a model for battling the Islamic State in Iraq. Pakistan and Yemen were complicated, troubled lands, and the reasons for their problems went way beyond the drones. But even if the strikes had accomplished their narrow goals of reducing the short-term threat of attacks on the United States, political instability and economic distress in both countries raised the possibility of a bigger threat in the future.

When I spoke with the tribal leader who had visited the site of Awlaki's killing in Al Jawf, Abdullah al-Jumaili, he said that support for AQAP in his region had only grown since the death of Awlaki. He didn't quarrel with the American decision to take out an avowed enemy. But he said that the United States should do more to address the root cause of the trouble. "For every missile America launches to kill terrorists, we want five missiles for development," Jumaili said, speaking of the cost of each Hellfire missile, up to $125,000. "Missiles for health. Missiles for schools. It's incredibly important for America to understand this." As a leader pushing development in an impoverished province, Jumaili's comments were perhaps predictable. But in interviews with dozens of Yemenis, from military officers to human rights activists, I found that opposition to American strikes was all but universal. Some were against all such strikes, saying Yemen should be allowed to take care of its own problems. Others criticized the sloppiness with which the American campaign was carried out. If the Americans killed only high-ranking AQAP leaders, I was told, many Yemenis would have been quietly supportive. But too many strikes killed innocent people, they said. Their objection was not necessarily to drone strikes as such, but to incompetent drone strikes.

In February 2013, after years of debilitating and unnecessary secrecy, public debate about drone strikes had burst out in one of the strangest episodes in the modern history of Congress. For years, as the number of strikes climbed, congressional leaders had remained silent about drones, kowtowing to CIA and White House demands for secrecy. But when Obama named John Brennan, who had closely overseen the drone campaign, to head the CIA, the issue came to a boil. Brennan was replacing David Petraeus, the married former general whose sensational resignation after admitting to an affair was a reminder that Awlaki was not the only man on both sides of the terrorism fight to risk his career for sexual gratification. In an ironic twist, Petraeus and his lover, Paula Broadwell, had communicated secretly by saving drafts of notes to a shared e-mail account—a favorite technique of Awlaki and many other terrorists.

Now, required to vote on Brennan's nomination as CIA director, the members of the malleable Senate Intelligence Committee bridled at the fact that even they had not been allowed to read the Justice Department's legal opinions justifying the strikes, especially the killing of an American. The idea that a president could order the extrajudicial execution of a citizen was raising a delayed alarm on both the right and the left. Senator Rand Paul shrewdly spotted an opportunity to address simmering public concern and announced grandly that he would filibuster the nomination of Brennan as CIA chief.

The ambitious eye doctor from Kentucky was perhaps not the ideal drone critic, but he deserved credit for shattering the silence. In a thirteen-hour, stream-of-consciousness performance on the Senate floor in early March, relieved from time to time by fellow senators quite willing to share the spotlight, he tossed out a grab-bag of legitimate issues and libertarian fantasies. "I will speak as long as it takes," Senator Paul began, "until the alarm is sounded from coast to coast that our constitution is important, that your rights to trial by jury are precious, that no American should be killed by a drone on American soil without first being charged with a crime, without first being found to be guilty by a court. That Americans could be killed in a cafe in San Francisco or in a restaurant in Houston or at their home in Bowling Green, Kentucky, is an abomination. It is something that should not and cannot be tolerated in our country." Why wouldn't the president, Paul demanded to know, declare that "no, we won't kill Americans in cafes; no, we won't kill you at home in your bed at night; no, we won't drop bombs on restaurants"?

Of course, no Americans had been killed in drone strikes in the United States, and no such strikes had been proposed. The Senate eventually voted to end the filibuster and confirm Brennan. But the spectacle of Paul's stand at the microphone nonetheless drew a sizable national audience and picked up the support of odd political bedfellows who realized that the Kentucky senator's cri de coeur, however quixotic and hyperbolic, expressed the fear and resentment of many Americans who had never been informed or consulted about the government's aggressive use overseas of this scary new weapon. The next day, the redoubtable leftist Medea Benjamin, cofounder of the peace group Code Pink and not generally a fan of libertarian Republicans, showed up at Rand Paul's Senate office with flowers and candy.

If this was not the way Barack Obama wanted the national debate over drone strikes to begin, he had himself to blame. He had missed many opportunities to open such a discussion. Instead, he had allowed the reflexive secrecy of the intelligence agencies to shape the administration's approach.

Had the president signaled to leaders of the intelligence or armed services committees that he would welcome a series of public, unclassified hearings on targeted killing, they surely would have obliged. Had he taken the initiative to release the classified documents setting the rules for strikes or their legal justification, they would have found an avid audience. In June 2010, after reporting that Awlaki had been added to the kill list, I filed a request under the Freedom of Information Act for all Justice Department legal opinions on targeted killing.

I did not ask for the sensitive intelligence on particular strikes, just for the program's legal basis. The Justice Department summarily rejected my request, and when *The New York Times* and the American Civil Liberties Union sued, the administration took the position that it could neither confirm nor deny the existence of a drone program in Pakistan, though Obama himself had spoken publicly about it. An appeals court finally ruled in our favor nearly four years after my initial request. We got heavily redacted copies of the two 2010 legal opinions by David Barron and Marty Lederman making the case that it was legal and constitutional to kill Awlaki.

Nor did Congress fare much better in peeling back the secrecy. When Senator Dick Durbin, an Illinois Democrat and Obama's friend and former mentor, finally convened the Senate's very first public hearing on drone strikes in April 2013, the White House refused to send a single witness to testify. From a president who had famously promised the most transparent administration in American history, it was another dispiriting performance.

On May 23, 2013, Obama came to the National Defense University in Washington to deliver the big drone speech. This was his chance to make up for years of secrecy and silence, and he indeed spoke more openly and in greater detail about drone strikes than ever before. His speech demonstrated, in fact, that the absurd secrecy surrounding this weapon had never been necessary; he might have given such a speech years earlier without endangering national security.

The speech also reflected Obama's contradictory feelings about the unprecedented role he had taken on, as the first American president to routinely approve individual lethal strikes. "As was true in previous armed conflicts," Obama said, "this new technology raises profound questions—about who is targeted, and why; about civilian casualties, and the risk of creating new enemies; about the legality of such strikes under US and international law; about accountability and morality." He acknowledged civilian casualties as a "hard fact" of US strikes, saying of himself and his aides that "those deaths will haunt us as long as we live." But a decision to order a strike did not occur in isolation, he said. "As commander-in-chief," Obama said, "I must weigh these heartbreaking tragedies against the alternatives." He argued that because most of those killed by Al Qaeda were

civilians—Muslim civilians—killing the terrorists also prevented civilian deaths. He argued that drones killed fewer civilians than other
kinds of strikes and provoked a less intense backlash than even small
numbers of American ground troops.

On the day that Awlaki had been killed, in an awkward nod to
secrecy rules, Obama had avoided explicitly taking responsibility for
the strike. Now he fully embraced it. At the very core of his case for
drones, he defended his decision to order the killing of Awlaki. No
president should deploy armed drones over US soil, he said, and none
should kill an American without due process of law. Then he invoked the police-shooting analogy that had become the administration's shorthand defense of Awlaki's killing. "When a US citizen goes
abroad to wage war against America and is actively plotting to kill
US citizens, and when neither the United States, nor our partners are
in a position to capture him before he carries out a plot," Obama said,
"his citizenship should no more serve as a shield than a sniper shooting down on an innocent crowd should be protected from a SWAT
team." Recounting Awlaki's role in the Christmas bombing and the
printer plot, the president declared that the cleric "was continuously
trying to kill people," leaving the government no real choice. "As
president," Obama said, "I would have been derelict in my duty had I
not authorized the strike that took him out."

Despite the erring intelligence and the targeting mistakes that
had plagued the drone program, despite his worries about the example he was setting for future presidents and for other countries,
despite the growing backlash against strikes in Yemen and Pakistan,
this was Obama's bottom line. As president, he often said, his first
responsibility was to protect the American people. If that required
morally fraught decisions—the doctrine of "dirty hands" that some
moral philosophers had advanced—he did not flinch from them. He
still believed that his use of drones had destroyed the ability of Al
Qaeda's core in Pakistan to mount major plots and had seriously disrupted AQAP, probably averting attacks that might have killed many
Americans. If the strikes also had undesirable effects, so be it. He
would live with the consequences, and with history's judgment.

Remarkably, the gatekeepers at Obama's speech had admitted
along with the crowd of uniformed officers and security officials
none other than Medea Benjamin of Code Pink, who was known for

disrupting congressional hearings and public speeches on disputed security issues. That led to a remarkable scene between Obama and one of his most outspoken critics. Predictably, well into the president's hourlong address, Benjamin stood and began shouting at him from her seat about Guantanamo and drones, mentioning in particular the killing of sixteen-year-old Abdulrahman al-Awlaki. Rather than react angrily, Obama politely asked Benjamin to let him finish talking. Even after she interrupted a second time, Obama was unruffled, departing from his prepared text to defend Benjamin's right to protest. "The voice of that woman is worth paying attention to," the president declared. "Obviously, I do not agree with much of what she said, and obviously she wasn't listening to me in much of what I said. But these are tough issues, and the suggestion that we can gloss over them is wrong." It was an unusual moment in the history of heckling.

Obama's speech made a nuanced case for his record. But to the surprise of no one at the White House, it failed to quiet the growing chorus of detractors. They were mostly on the left and the libertarian right—Cornel West disgustedly denounced Obama as a war criminal and his tenure as "a drone presidency," and fans of Rand Paul echoed his Senate diatribe. More disturbing to Obama's aides were the former security officials, some of whom had themselves overseen targeted killing, who now expressed their doubts in newspaper op-eds or the Sunday morning TV shows. The first was Dennis Blair, but he had been fired as director of national intelligence, so they could dismiss his complaints as sour grapes. But his example was followed by other officials after they stepped down. General Stanley McChrystal, who had built the Joint Special Operations Command into a lethal machine that hunted down targets on the ground and from the air, expressed alarm about the effect of drone strikes on hostility toward America. "They are hated on a visceral level, even by people who've never seen one or seen the effects of one," McChrystal said. Then there was Robert Gates, the former defense secretary, who called himself "a big advocate of drones" but nonetheless expressed concern about the Awlaki killing. "I think this idea of being able to execute, in effect, an American citizen, no matter how awful . . . I think some check on the ability of the president to do this has merit, as we look to the longer term future." Ben Rhodes, Obama's deputy national security adviser, noted that these were second thoughts. "I say this with respect—they tend to express these doubts after they leave government. When you're in government and you have a responsibility to protect the American people, you tend not to ask those questions as much. And look, maybe that's a problem," Rhodes told me.

Even Lee Hamilton, the former congressman and 9/11 Commission vice-chairman who had advised Obama during the 2008 campaign, had deeply mixed feelings. A lawyer by training, Hamilton had been one of the few advisers who supported candidate Obama's decision to say publicly that he would, if necessary, order attacks against terrorists hiding in Pakistan. By 2014, Hamilton was quite anguished, if sympathetic, about Obama's record. In particular, Hamilton told me, he was "deeply disturbed" by the Awlaki strike. "How do you deal with a figure like that? He wants to kill as many Americans as he can. You can't give him due process—I find that awful. But what do you do? The national security adviser comes in and says, 'We've got him in our sights.' What do you do? It's an insoluble dilemma, and I'm very uneasy about it."

These were misgivings from people with deep experience. But perhaps more painful to Obama than his critics were his newly found allies. Among the few prominent voices speaking up for the president's aggressive use of the drone was none other than Dick Cheney, though when Cheney endorsed the Awlaki killing he also demanded an apology. "I think it was a very good strike. I think it was justified," Cheney said on CNN. "I'm waiting for the administration to go back and correct something they said two years ago," when Obama had attacked Bush and Cheney for betraying American values by approving the use of so-called enhanced interrogation techniques.

It was galling, but there was some logic to Cheney's claim. Both Bush and Obama, operating on the basis of secret legal opinions from the Justice Department, had taken steps unprecedented in American history—in Bush's case, approving interrogation methods the United States had long considered torture; in Obama's, ordering the killing of an American citizen without trial. Both presidents defended the extraordinary measures as necessary to meet the terrorist threat. Obama's case was arguably based on a far more solid legal and practical foundation than Bush's; torture is always illegal, while targeted killing can be lawful. But the parallel was undeniable.

It was hard to imagine a comment more humiliating than Cheney's backhanded endorsement, but one eventually came along. Defending his own long-ago record in ordering the secret bombing of Cambodia, Henry Kissinger, ninety-one, reached for an unexpected comparison. "I bet if one did an honest account," he said, "there were fewer civilian casualties in Cambodia than there have been from American drone attacks." His claim was preposterous. Estimates of civilian deaths from the American bombing of Cambodia began at 50,000; many sources put the total at 150,000 or even higher. By comparison, the high-end estimates from the Bureau of Investigative Journalism in London of civilian deaths from drone strikes in Pakistan, Somalia, and Yemen totaled about 1,200 at the time Kissinger spoke. Kissinger's assertion, as misleading and self-serving as it was, capped off the extraordinarily negative turn in the public perception of Obama's drone campaign.

One factor in the dark portrayal of drones was that stories trump facts in the human imagination, and drone strikes produced compelling stories. The outrage that drones often produced was a visceral reaction to the creepiness of flying killer robots and to the arrogance of casually invading another country's airspace. But it was also a matter of scale. Saturation bombing in the style of World War II or Vietnam, or ground invasions of cities like Fallujah in Iraq, produced statistics, not stories; when the number of dead climbed into the thousands, individual tales got lost. Drone strikes, with tolls of two or five or ten, were far easier to grasp and retell as detailed personal accounts. By 2013, survivors of drone strikes began to visit Washington with the support of human rights groups, offering devastating accounts of strikes gone wrong.

Henry Crumpton, a CIA veteran who had been in on the early experiments with armed drones, claimed that the intense focus on civilians killed in drone strikes was, paradoxically, an encouraging sign of human progress. Those who planned the first drone strikes were driven not by humanitarian concerns but by the mission of killing Bin Laden and a few lieutenants, Crumpton admitted: "We never said, 'Let's build a more humane weapon.'" But he argued that the small scale of drone killing was producing growing intolerance for the routine mass slaughter of earlier wars. "Look at the firebombing of Dresden, and compare what we're doing today," Crumpton said. "The public's expectations have been raised dramatically around the world, and that's good news." Drone critics found Crumpton's view

Panglossian; if Dresden was the measure, after all, almost any act of war might look less murderous.

But the numbers did not lie. By comparison with the two big ground wars Obama had inherited, the toll of noncombatants killed in drone strikes was very small—hundreds, versus hundreds of thousands. "I think he understands that you can't eliminate civilian casualties entirely when you're using violence against people," Ben Rhodes told me, as Obama neared the end of his sixth year in office. "But I do think he still believes strongly that this is a very important tool that has been hugely successful, particularly in the effort against the Al Qaeda core in Afghanistan and Pakistan and in disrupting AQAP in Yemen." Obama, Rhodes said, "believes these drones strikes have prevented attacks, and it's impossible to weigh the counterfactual"— that is, to be certain about what might have happened without the drones. "He has very complicated thoughts about all this," Rhodes said. Battered in the press and condemned by many of his progressive political allies, Obama nevertheless steadfastly believed that drones were the least terrible strategy at his disposal to defend the country against terrorism.

Awlaki and Obama would be linked forever, the first American deliberately killed by his own government without a court's judgment, and the president who gave the order. But the third player in their lethal drama, the drone itself, seemed ready to escape its martial origins. True, other countries were imitating the United States and building their own fleets of armed drones, a development that increasingly worried Obama, his aides said. It seemed only a matter of time before Russia used drones to kill, say, Chechen rebels hiding in Georgia, or China sent unmanned aircraft loaded with missiles after Uighur separatists operating from Kazakhstan. Some unlucky State Department spokesman, instructed to condemn the strikes, was going to have the impossible task of distinguishing them from the hundreds already carried out by the United States.

By midway through Obama's second term, however, a growing cast of hobbyists and entrepreneurs were at work finding civilian uses for drones. Some drone evangelists were determined to liberate remotely piloted aircraft from their dark origins in the hands of the CIA and JSOC. One of them, a polymath named Chris Anderson, drew an analogy with the Internet, which had begun life as a Pentagon research project and had grown into a universal servant to humankind with overwhelmingly civilian and benign uses. Anderson had left his job as editor of *Wired* magazine to devote his time to a website he had created, diydrones.com, "The Leading Community for Personal UAVs," and to serve as CEO of a manufacturer of small drones, 3D Robotics. He discovered a huge demand from farmers for small drones with cameras and other sensors, which could survey a huge acreage and report back on the need for water or fertilizer, harvesting, or help for livestock in trouble. "You can literally just toss a drone in the air, and by the time you're done with your breakfast you have great data on the state of your crops," Anderson told me. Power companies were inspecting their lines with drones. Real estate agents were dazzling customers with overhead video of high-end houses. Police departments were studying how they might be used for timely highway accident reporting or to safely survey hostage situations. Amazon and other retailers began to talk about package delivery by drone.

Anderson said 3D Robotics alone was already selling each calendar quarter about as many drones—7,500 or so—as there were in the entire American military fleet. But his craft were much smaller and much cheaper. The same technologies that had made the smart phone possible—GPS, sensors, high-quality miniature cameras—now were being borrowed by the drone industry. If hobbyists' drones struck some people as expensive toys with limited practical value, well, that was what many had said about the earliest personal computers. "People will find new uses, just as we did for the personal computer," Anderson said. "One way or another, the sky's going to be dark with these things. The only question is whether they'll be made by Boeing or by small entrepreneurs."

For anyone who spent his days thinking about terrorists and the agencies that went after them, talking to an upbeat enthusiast like Anderson was a blessed relief. It was possible to imagine a country, and a world, less obsessed by violence and counterviolence, by an alien ideology and the overheated jingoism of the response. In 2011, it seemed quite plausible that Al Qaeda and the era it had defined in American life were finally receding into history. The terrorist network in Pakistan was so reduced that it was incapable of large-scale plotting, and AQAP had distinguished itself mainly by failed attacks. The crowds on the streets of Cairo, Tunis, Sanaa, and other Arab capitals were calling for jobs and elections, not for jihad.

It was nice while it lasted.

By 2013, Awlaki's prediction two years earlier, in his *Inspire* article "The Tsunami of Change," was coming true: the most extreme and violent Islamist organizations were gaining adherents and energy from the Arab awakening, which ended in many places in disillusionment or violent crackdowns. Much of the unrest began to take on a sectarian, Sunni versus Shia cast, or to pit tribes and militias against one another. There was no longer much talk of democracy.

And then, from the chaos and suffering of Syria, arose the monstrous offspring of the Iraq war and the Arab Spring, calling itself at first the Islamic State in Iraq and al-Sham, or Syria. The group broke with Al Qaeda, whose leaders found it disobedient and reckless in its violence. Tasting success, it rebranded itself as simply the Islamic State, claiming to be the core of a new Islamic caliphate that would eventually incorporate all the world's Muslims, and then all the world.

The So-Called Islamic State—the phrase came to serve almost as an official title in the Western media—was medieval in its ideology and brutal in its tactics but up to the technological moment in its propaganda. Bin Laden, recording VHS tapes with Arabic verses and obscure allusions that were couriered to Al Jazeera for broadcast, had been the first generation of jihadi agitprop. Awlaki, with his accessible, colloquial English, fast to take advantage of blogging, Facebook, and YouTube, had represented the second generation. But the Islamic State was online jihad 3.0, I wrote in *The New York Times*. It operated in multiple languages, took full advantage of Twitter, used drones to film its battles from the sky, and produced recruitment videos of frightening sophistication and appeal.

In December 2013, a new, English-language Islamic State video featured a voice familiar to anyone who had followed jihad on the Internet. "Sheikh Anwar al-Awlaki," said the subtitle, and a familiar portrait appeared in the corner of the screen. In the recording, from a lecture he had given by phone in May 2008 to a conference in South Africa, Awlaki hailed the announcement two years earlier of the Islamic State of Iraq, the predecessor of the group now calling itself the

Islamic State. The upstart Islamic State used his words for the jihadi equivalent of a celebrity endorsement. What Awlaki had said then, shortly after his release from prison in Yemen, needed no updating. "Now, whether the state survives to expand into the next Muslim caliphate or is destroyed by the immense conspiracy against the rise of any Islamic state, I believe this to be a monumental event," Awlaki said. "It represents a move of the idea from the theoretical realm to the real world. The idea of establishing the Islamic rule and establishing caliphate on earth now is not anymore talk—it is action!" A Syrian activist group claimed that the Islamic State had created an "Anwar al-Awlaki Battallion" of English-speaking fighters to be dispatched to carry out attacks in the West.

Many of the Westerners who headed to Syria to fight with the jihadists—or were stopped on the way—inevitably turned out to be Awlaki devotees. An American who carried out a suicide bombing for the Al Qaeda affiliate in Syria, Moner Mohammad Abu-Salha, left behind a video interview in which he cited Awlaki twice for giving him the courage to join the jihad. Shannon Conley, a nineteen-year-old Muslim convert from Colorado arrested as she tried to fly to Turkey to join the Islamic State, left behind a pile of CDs and DVDs of Awlaki's lectures. After two French-Algerian brothers burst into the offices of the satirical newspaper *Charlie Hebdo* and murdered a dozen people in January 2015, they repeatedly trumpeted their connection to AQAP and to Awlaki. "I, Chérif Kouachi, was sent by Al Qaeda in Yemen," the younger brother told a television reporter. "I went there, and it was Sheikh Anwar al-Awlaki who financed me." More than three years had passed since Awlaki's death, and the claim at first seemed dubious. But intelligence officials believed it was true. A week after the attack on *Charlie Hebdo*, a twenty-year-old Ohio man was arrested after allegedly scheming with an FBI informant to set off pipe bombs at the US Capitol. He had sent an instant message to his coconspirator, the charging papers said, asserting that "Anwar al-Awlaki before his martyrdom" had given "a thumbs up" to such attacks. The very next day, prosecutors in Florida announced new charges for two Pakistan-born naturalized citizens, also fans of Awlaki, who were accused of studying the bomb-making instruction in *Inspire* magazine and hunting for targets in New York City.

The pile-up of plotters who considered Awlaki their posthumous

mentor was astonishing. But by then the number of YouTube videos accessible via a search of "Awlaki" had climbed to eighty thousand. A study by the New America Foundation in 2014 found that
eighteen people indicted in the United States after Awlaki's death on
terrorism-related charges—and fifty-two since 9/11—either cited his
influence or possessed his materials, a total that kept climbing.

When Awlaki was killed in 2011, it had seemed possible that his
benighted cause was dying as well. But now, with the emergence of
the Islamic State, that cause had blazed up again with new force and
on a much larger scale. The group was flush with cash from oil wells
and kidnappings and armed with American heavy weapons captured
from fleeing Iraqi troops. Awlaki's ideology, and the recruitment
pitch that he had made with such brazen effectiveness, now became
a model for the Islamic State, to disastrous effect. Awlaki's seeming
daydreams about a caliphate returning one hundred years after the
Ottoman Empire's fall were proving, if not real, devastatingly attractive to some young Muslims. In the face of this fresh horror, Obama's
strategy against terrorism faltered.

The American president who had believed he was cutting the
terrorist enemy down to size, freeing the country and the culture to
focus on domestic challenges, now was forced to shift his policy. His
dream of establishing new, positive relations with the Muslim world
lay in tatters. The vaunted precision of the drone was not up to the
task of taking on an army of well-armed fanatics occupying huge
swaths of Syria and Iraq. His reluctance and dismay obvious, Obama
committed the United States to a new, long war in the Middle East.
It began in September 2014 with air strikes and advisers, and it was
hard to say when or how it would end. Surely Awlaki would have
been heartened that the native country he so despised, having given
him the martyrdom he claimed to seek, was being drawn still deeper
into the battles within Islam.

Afterword

A few weeks after the hardcover edition of *Objective Troy* was published, I got an intriguing e-mail.

"My name is Walied Shater," the note began, "and I was a Secret Service agent during 9/11. I was also a case agent on the Anwar al-Awlaki case."

I wasted no time in getting in touch with Shater. I got to know him over the next few months, via e-mail and Skype and then in person, and he recounted his own involvement in the scrutiny of the imam. He had nothing but contempt for a man whom he considered an outrageous hypocrite and a cold-blooded plotter of mass murder. Yet Shater said he had long been disturbed by the possibility that law enforcement pressure, not just on Awlaki but on the Muslim community that he represented, might have inadvertently set him on the path that led to Al Qaeda, a possibility that I already thought quite troubling. I found Shater's unusual dual perspective as a Muslim American and a security professional fresh and provocative. (He is working on a memoir that I think will be a valuable and original read.) His counterterrorism experience and his religious identity meant that he did not fall into the ideological ruts that so often constrain debates over terrorism and what to do about it.

Shater, who grew up in Brooklyn, had joined the Secret Service in 1995 and by 9/11 was working in the agency's elite presidential protection detail. The FBI, suddenly saddled with a mammoth investigation of Al Qaeda, had almost no Arabic speakers. Since he had grown up speaking Arabic with his Egyptian immigrant parents,

Shater was asked to leave his Secret Service duties temporarily to help the bureau chase down thousands of leads flooding in about the 9/11 plot and the possibility of new attacks.

One of his assignments was to help with the investigation of Awlaki, who as we have seen drew FBI attention because some of the 9/11 hijackers had prayed at his mosques. Shater soon learned from the bureau's surveillance teams that Awlaki was regularly visiting prostitutes. More unobtrusively than non-Muslim agents, Shater was able to attend Friday prayers at Dar al-Hijrah outside Washington, blending in with the crowd of worshippers who pressed around the imam with questions afterward.

He found Awlaki a superb speaker, a "rock star," as he put it. This came as no surprise—Shater's own wife, like many other American Muslims, listened to Awlaki's CDs at the time. He remembers in particular a touching sermon on the role of women and wives in Islam. "He said, 'You have a responsibility to treat her well. She has rights over you. You have rights over her.' It was a pro-Muslim-female speech," he said. "I was moved." But at the same time, Shater told me, he was outraged by Awlaki's secret philandering, financed with the unsuspecting congregation's donations. It was all he could do to keep from jumping to his feet mid-sermon to accuse the preacher. "His hypocrisy insulted me, frankly. I would sit and listen to him and want to explode and confront him. But of course I couldn't do that."

Instead, he came up with a plan to give investigators leverage over Awlaki to make sure he was telling all he knew about the hijackers. The agents noticed that Awlaki had a particular fancy for blondes, so Shater asked the Arlington, Virginia, police department to let him know the next time they arrested a blond prostitute. It didn't take long. Shater and his colleagues met the woman and said her charges would be dropped if she helped them. They asked her to enroll in a community college class that Awlaki was taking and casually make his acquaintance. "Then at some point she would cozy on up to him," Shater said, "and the end game was they would get to a hotel, the hotel room would have video surveillance—and we would blackmail him to get him to tell us everything he knew."

The goal, I was surprised to learn, was not to enlist Awlaki as an informant for future cases. In that panicky time, Shater said, the

investigators were focused entirely on the 9/11 plot, hoping to un-
mask any undiscovered coconspirators and thus head off a second attack. The agents did not believe Awlaki had been in on the plot,
but they wanted his help in understanding the milieu in which the
hijackers had hidden and plotted. "He could have provided insight,"
Shater said. "We're looking for clues. What circles they ran in, who
they spoke to, what were some of the challenges. Did they ask you for
help getting a driver's license? We wanted to understand their world."

But the blackmail plan was never carried out, because Awlaki
learned from the manager of an escort service that the FBI was onto
his clandestine sex life. Shater filled in some new details. Agents
questioned a prostitute after one of Awlaki's visits, he recalled. In
a fright, the woman called her madam, who in turn called Anwar
to yell at him for attracting the feds' attention to her business. The
result, as I recount in the book, was unintended but momentous: Awlaki abandoned his blossoming career as a public figure in America
and embarked on the road that would lead to Al Qaeda.

I was struck by Shater's lingering regrets about that outcome. He
said he had been haunted ever since Awlaki emerged as a major figure
in Al Qaeda by the likelihood that the FBI had inadvertently chased
him out of the United States.

"Can you create a terrorist?" Shater asked. "You know, is that possible? Can you alienate someone and push them so far that they turn
against you and against their country?" It was not just the attention
to Awlaki personally, he said. "It was what was happening in society
at that time—the siege mentality" in the Muslim community. "You're
seeing people pulled off planes, you're seeing people arrested, you're
seeing people held on material witness warrants." Shater offered an
analogy with the feelings of African Americans about police mis-
treatment and targeting by race. "It may not have happened to you,
but it happens to your group, so you begin to formulate these opinions," he said. If you are being treated as an enemy of the United
States, in other words, that may make it easier to become an enemy of
the United States.

During the months when I was getting to know Shater, the armed
drone was proliferating, with six countries having carried out strikes
and the number rising. The United Kingdom followed the Awlaki

precedent and used a drone to deliberately target and kill two British citizens, both fighting with the Islamic State in Syria. The fear of terrorism in the West flared again after lethal jihadist attacks in Paris and Brussels, San Bernardino, and Orlando. And in the raucous 2016 Republican presidential primaries, some candidates vied for the most extreme anti-Muslim position. It was a contest that could only alienate American Muslims, playing into the recruiting propaganda of Al Qaeda and ISIS. Al Shabab, the Al Qaeda affiliate in Somalia, actually released a video that combined Donald Trump's call for banning all Muslim immigration with Awlaki's "Call to Jihad." The campaign antics were especially dispiriting for Shater, who had spent years trying to keep America both safe from terrorism and true to its ideals of diversity and tolerance. And it was a reminder of a paradox: only two groups, strange bedfellows, believed that terrorist violence was inseparably connected to Islam—the violent jihadists, and the right-wing Islamophobes. The great mass of people in the middle, Muslim and non-Muslim, were capable of distinguishing a great world religion from the fanatics carrying out mayhem in its name.

One case that made news in federal court in Manhattan in early 2016 suggested that Awlaki had been even more deeply involved in plotting violence for Al Qaeda than previously known. A British citizen of Vietnamese origin, Minh Quang Pham, had converted to Islam and eventually traveled to Yemen in 2010 to join Al Qaeda. While there, he later told investigators, Awlaki personally taught him how to make explosives from household materials. "During the training, AULAQI showed PHAM how to mix chemicals to make an explosive powder," the FBI agents wrote of Pham's account, using the government's spelling of the cleric's name. They tested the powder by setting it off in a tin can, Pham said, adding: "AULAQI had also instructed Pham to tape bolts around the container to act as shrapnel when the device was activated." He then directed his young fan to return to Britain and set off a bomb at Heathrow Airport, telling him to target the arrivals area for flights from the United States and Israel. Pham's lawyer told the court that his client had taken no action to carry out the plot. But the testimony portrayed Awlaki as more of a hands-on terrorist than in any previous case. If Pham was telling the truth, Awlaki had himself learned how to make bombs and had added one more lethal scheme to his résumé.

The 2011 drone strike that killed the cleric had put an end to that kind of plotting.

Yet in 2015 and 2016, it became still more evident that killing Awlaki had also enhanced the power of his message. His myriad videos, still accessible at a click, continued to turn up in new terrorism cases, having coaxed a suspect toward violence, or inspired a decision to try to join the Islamic State. The San Bernardino attack in December 2015 was especially perplexing because the shooters were a husband and wife who left a baby at home before murdering fourteen people. Syed Farook and his wife, Tashfeen Malik, were killed by police. But their neighbor, Enrique Marquez, subsequently recounted to investigators how Farook had introduced him first to Islam and then to Awlaki. The two men had shared and listened to many of Awlaki's lectures, including his series on "The Hereafter" and on an early Islamic hero, Umar ibn al-Khattab.

Both series dated to Awlaki's middle years, between the cleric's early mainstream lectures and his overt calls for violence at the end of his life. "The Hereafter," on the Islamic view of the afterlife, was published in a twenty-two-CD set in 2006 when Awlaki was living with his parents in Sanaa. He does not explicitly call for violence. But "The Hereafter" is a decidedly fundamentalist tract, including references to Islamic prophecy that might be unnerving to non-Muslims, and to any Muslim determined to live in peace with people of other faiths. Awlaki speaks of the future apocalyptic battle between Muslims and people described in scripture as "Romans," whom he interprets as Europeans and Americans. He says that at some future time, there will no *kuffar*, or non-believers. "Islam will rule the world," Awlaki says. "Kuffar will be stamped out." For non-believers, the choice will be "either Islam or death," Awlaki declares.

It is a noxious message that figured in the online education of many jihadists before Farook. For those who fall under Awlaki's spell, it is a crucial way station along the path from "The Life of the Prophet" to "The Call to Jihad." When a troubled man named Omar Mateen carried out the deadliest mass shooting by a single gunman in American history in June 2016, killing forty-nine people at a gay night club in Orlando, I waited for the ghost of Awlaki to make its inevitable appearance. It didn't take long: an older acquaintance from the mosque, it turned out, had called the FBI in 2014 to report his concern after Mateen told him he had been watching Awlaki videos and found them "very powerful."

I saw more clearly than ever that Awlaki's unique power as a radicalizer lay not just in his late screeds calling for attacks, but in the runway that allowed them to take off: his years of mainstream preaching about the history and tenets of his faith. No other jihadist ideologue had built a reputation and a following with traditional preaching before turning to a darker strain of fundamentalism and finally to terrorism. Awlaki's collected works created a confusing conundrum. His earlier work made his later embrace of violence both more authoritative and harder to refute. A teenager listening to Awlaki's explicit endorsement of terrorism in the 2010 "Call to Jihad" may know that his parents have long listened to the same cleric's "Life of the Prophet."

After the San Bernardino attack, in which Farook and Malik were found to have built a stock of pipe bombs following the instructions in Awlaki's *Inspire* magazine, there were new calls for YouTube and other Internet platforms to take down his material, notably from the Counter Extremism Project, an advocacy group led by former government security officials. "His work has inspired countless plots and attacks," Mark D. Wallace, a former diplomat and homeland security official who is the project's chief executive, told me for an article I wrote about the issue for *The New York Times*. "It's hate speech. It should come down, period. Like child porn, it should be expeditiously removed." Wallace said the ban should cover not just violent jihadist material, but even his mainstream recordings, which he said gave credibility to his later calls for attacks. "There are a lot of sources for the teachings of Islam that do not come from a man who became one of the world's most notorious terrorists," he added.

Civil libertarians, and some Muslim activists, objected. Jameel Jaffer of the American Civil Liberties Union said the call to remove all Awlaki videos was "misguided." "People watch these videos for all kinds of entirely legitimate reasons," Jaffer told me. Censoring them, he said, "would certainly make it more difficult for ordinary citizens to learn the motivations, grievances, and worldview of those who call for violence against Americans."

As a writer, I was sympathetic to Jaffer's argument. After all, in researching *Objective Troy*, I had watched many hours of Awlaki's videos and listened to his CDs with the specific goal of trying to understand what made him a terrorist. Moreover, private media companies were clearly loathe to get into the difficult business of judging what was and was not acceptable speech. YouTube, according to its "community guidelines," "strictly prohibits content intended to recruit for terrorist organizations, incite violence, celebrate terrorist attacks or otherwise promote acts of terrorism." Belatedly, in early 2016, YouTube began to remove some of Awlaki's most explicit calls for violence. But the business of policing the Internet is extraordinarily tricky. Does Awlaki's "The Hereafter" cross the company's line? Not explicitly. Yet a series of terrorism cases has shown that its absolutist message and dehumanization of non-Muslims can help prepare an extremist to commit violence.

There is a striking irony in the fact that some of the United States' most innovative and successful companies, with no ill intent, have provided the megaphone that Al Qaeda and ISIS use to reach impressionable young people. Without YouTube, Awlaki would certainly be present on the web, but in far less trafficked corners. Without Twitter, the Islamic State would have had a far more difficult time attracting an army of recruits. Just as the 9/11 plotters hijacked American air travel, their successors are hijacking the Internet.

In an earlier era with different fears, the Supreme Court took up the case of a California woman charged with helping found a Communist group that supposedly advocated the violent overthrow of the government. Justice Louis Brandeis crafted a famous defense of free speech in his 1927 concurring opinion: "If there be time to expose through discussion the falsehood and fallacies, to avert the evil by the processes of education, the remedy to be applied is more speech, not enforced silence. Only an emergency can justify repression."

Does the threat of jihadist violence inside the United States since 9/11 constitute an emergency? Surely not. It has been responsible for a few dozen murders in more than fifteen years, a vanishingly small fraction of the more than 200,000 homicides over that period. So perhaps the remedy for Awlaki on the web is more speech—especially Muslim voices that can persuasively counter his seductive calls for intolerance and attack. His dallying with prostitutes, even as he warned from the pulpit about the sin of fornication, would seem a natural theme for debunkers. Perhaps voices from within the faith, like that of Walied Shater, who all those years ago had to hold his tongue about Awlaki's hypocrisy, can begin to take back the web from its hijackers.

—SCOTT SHANE, MAY 2016

ACKNOWLEDGMENTS

A book is a river with many tributaries. I owe many people, and I will live in fear that they will someday try to collect on the debts. Steve Luxenberg took time from his own book labors to give me useful counsel at every stage and provided invaluable notes on the entire manuscript. With uncommon generosity, Francie Weeks, Suse Shane, Matt Watkins, Rich Krohn, and Robert Schwartz read various drafts, lassoing mistakes and directing improvements. I urge readers with complaints to hunt them down and ask them why, exactly, they couldn't get me to do a better job.

Thanks to Mark Kende, professor of law at Drake University, for helping organize an informal survey of constitutional law professors; J. M. Berger of Intelwire, as well as Judicial Watch, for making public documents obtained under the Freedom of Information Act; Medea Benjamin for sharing her interview with Nasser al-Awlaki; Kristen Wilhelm of the National Archives for helping me break loose a long-secret document from the 9/11 Commission; Rita Katz and Adam Raisman of the SITE Intelligence Group and Steven Emerson of the Investigative Project on Terrorism for helping track down old Awlaki lectures and statements; Susan Schmidt for sharing her documents on Awlaki in 2010; Souad Mekhennet for her superb work interviewing former Awlaki students in London in 2010; my colleague Jo Becker for reporting with me on Obama's counterterrorism record in 2012; Martha Shane for capturing still images from videos; Paul Cruickshank and Morten Storm for sharing photos; Bob Cronan for producing an illuminating Yemen map; Rebecca and Tim More for providing a desk and Wi-Fi at a critical moment. My wonderful in-laws, Bill and Frances Weeks, gave unstinting support, whether I deserved it or not. My sister-in-law, Margie Weeks, contributed a crucial hunt for typos.

Mohammed Albasha, of the Yemeni Embassy in Washington, has been a reliable guide to his fascinating and long-suffering country, and I thank him for supporting my visa request. In Yemen, where I had an unforgettable reporting visit, *shukran* especially to Farea al-Muslimi and Adam Baron for providing accommodations, advice, an introduction to qat-chewing, and help with reporting. Walid Abdulrahman got me places and kept me safe. Shuaib Almosawa and Hamed Sanabani rounded up photos. As readers will recognize, Dr. Nasser al-Awlaki and Ammar al-Awlaki were immensely helpful, both in making sure I got my facts straight and showing me that Anwar ultimately took the path of terror in spite of, not because of, his family.

I'm grateful to Ben Rhodes, the deputy national security adviser, for giving the Obama administration's account of the Awlaki story, and to all the current and former government officials who spoke with me. Many will be relieved I am not thanking them by name. My research for this book has, alas, underscored just how far the federal government has drifted from the openness that is the lifeblood of democracy and that a new president promised in 2009. A central finding of the 9/11 Commission—that excessive secrecy, not excessive transparency, made the country vulnerable to attack—has been forgotten. Reporting on national security has been made more difficult by the Obama administration's unprecedented campaign to imprison officials who share even innocuous classified information with the press. Two former high-ranking officials whose recollections would have been invaluable chose not to talk—understandably, because they were already under FBI investigation for other disclosures. The administration fought to keep secret the legal opinions guiding its use of targeted killing; only after four years of litigation did the courts finally order their partial release. The US Bureau of Prisons blocked my attempts to correspond with Umar Farouk Abdulmutallab and Zachary Chesser. The FBI and CIA declined all interview requests, though both agencies answered a few written questions. In this atmosphere of exaggerated secrecy, many people who talked did so on condition of anonymity.

The New York Times has been a supportive home for the last decade and granted me a year's leave to write this book. Many thanks to Dean Baquet, now the executive editor, who as Washington bureau chief in 2010 first suggested that I take a deeper look at Awlaki, and whose enthusiasm for good stories is infectious; to Rebecca Corbett, assistant managing editor, a mentor and pal at the *Baltimore Sun* and the *Times*, who has spent twenty years teaching me to make every story better; to Bill Hamilton, the national security editor, a wise man who understands the crucial role of humor on deadline; to David McCraw and his assistants, who fought successfully in court to obtain long-secret documents; and to my terrific colleagues on the national security beat and in the bureau, including Mark Mazzetti, Charlie Savage, Helene Cooper, Eric Lichtblau, Eric Schmitt, Thom Shanker, David Sanger, Eric Lipton, Mark Landler, Michael Gordon, Jim Risen, Peter Baker, Michael Schmidt, Matt Apuzzo, Jennifer Steinhauer, Ron Nixon, and Jason DeParle. I've benefited hugely from the Yemen reporting of Bobby Worth and Laura Kasinof. I have learned a lot from several superb books that have covered the United States's battles with terrorism and sometimes with itself, notably Mark Mazzetti's *The Way of the Knife*, Daniel Klaidman's *Kill or Capture*, Eric Schmitt and Thom Shanker's *Counterstrike*, Seth Jones's *Hunting in the Shadows*, Jeremy Scahill's *Dirty Wars*, and Michelle Shephard's *Decade of Fear*. My agent, Larry Weissman, gave me crucial help in honing the idea for this book. At Crown, my first editor, Vanessa Mobley, completed an insightful edit before departing for Little, Brown. Tim Duggan picked up where she left off and has been an enthusiastic champion for the book. Thanks to Claire Potter and Thomas Gebremedhin for patiently explaining the intricacies of publishing, and to Andy Young for giving the book a thorough fact-check.

One dividend of writing this book was the flexibility to spend a little extra time with my wife, Francie Weeks, and our children, Martha, Laura, and Nathan. We shared some memorable adventures in my year away from the newspaper. Francie supported the book and its author in countless ways. While I'm kind of used to that by now, I'm moved by and grateful for her love.

NOTES

A Note on Transliteration

Anwar al-Awlaki initially spelled his surname in English Aulaqi, as most of his family does now. Later, on his CDs and his blog, he switched to Awlaki, and that spelling was picked up by most Western journalists. Various US government agencies have used both of those spellings and other variations, including Awlaqi. For consistency and clarity, and with no disrespect intended to family members who prefer a different spelling, I have stuck to Awlaki throughout. In quoting government documents I have also used Awlaki in the text of the book, but any researcher searching government archives should try Aulaqi and Awlaqi as well. The same goes for Osama bin Laden (Usama bin Ladin in many government documents) and a few other names.

Map

ix US Strikes in Yemen The statistics on the Yemen map are from the count by the New American Foundation, http://securitydata.newamerica.net/drones/yemen/analysis. The sole exception is the count of two American strikes in 2010, which is based on my own reporting.

Prologue

xi Nasser al-Awlaki The information about Nasser al-Awlaki, his years as a graduate student in the United States, and the family's trip to California in 1984 comes from an interview by the author with Dr. al-Awlaki at his home in Sanaa on February 1, 2014; several interviews and e-mail exchanges with his son, Anwar's younger brother, Ammar al-Awlaki; written answers Nasser provided to questions sent by the author in January 2014; and a lengthy interview with Nasser in Sanaa by Medea Benjamin, a peace activist and cofounder of Code Pink, recorded on video in June 2013.

xii Barack Obama in 1984 See, for instance, David Remnick, *The Bridge: The Life and Rise of Barack Obama* (New York: Alfred A. Knopf, 2010), 118–21.

xiii an unseemly whiff of Nazism The columnist Peggy Noonan advised the George W. Bush administration to choose a different name, saying *homeland* "grates on a lot of people, understandably," and quoting a friend as calling it "creepy." Her advice was ignored, and the embrace of the term reflects the sea change in American attitudes in the wake of 9/11. Peggy Noonan, "Rudy's Duty: Plus, Homeland Ain't No American Word," *Wall Street Journal*, June 14, 2002.

xvi **"I have no grudge toward the American people"** Nasser al-Awlaki, interview by Medea Benjamin of Code Pink, June 2013.

EPIGRAPHS

xix **The Prophet beckoned with his hand towards Yemen** *Islamic Hadith (English Translation)* (Hamlet Book Publishers, 2013), Google e-book, no. 5670.

xix **But what is one to say to an act of destructive ferocity** Joseph Conrad, *The Secret Agent: A Simple Tale* (1907), Google e-book, 40.

xix **Perfection of means and confusion of aims** Albert Einstein, message to the London Conference on Science and World Order, quoted in *The Humanities Chart Their Course: Report of the Second Annual Conference Held by the Stanford School of Humanities* (Stanford, CA: Stanford University Press, 1945).

1. MERRY CHRISTMAS

3 **Sheikh Anwar had instructed him** This and other details about Umar Farouk Abdulmutallab's time in Yemen come largely from documents in his criminal case, Case 2:10-cr-20005 in US District Court for the Eastern District of Michigan, especially the opening statement of the lead prosecutor, Assistant US Attorney Jonathan Tukel, on October 11, 2011, and the sentencing memorandum filed by prosecutors on February 10, 2012. Those documents in turn were based on at least eighteen days of FBI interviews with him between December 25, 2009, and April 30, 2010. The FBI refused the author's request for the interview transcripts.

4 **three straight weeks** This and other details come from an interview by Detroit's WXYZ television station with two FBI agents involved with the case. Scott Lewis, "Exclusive: FBI Agents Reveal Underwear Bomber Abdulmutallab Wore Explosive Underwear for Three Weeks," WXYZ Detroit, September 27, 2012, http://www.wxyz.com/news/local-news/investigations/fbi-agents-underwear -bomber-abdulmutallab-wore-underwear-for-3-weeks.

4 **he had seen it, in a visit to Houston for an Islamic conference the previous year** "Terror Suspect Attended 2008 Islamic 'Knowledge Fest' in Houston," CNN, December 30, 2009, http://www.cnn.com/2009/US/12/30/terror.suspect .seminar/.

5 **"I know many of you missed Thanksgiving with your families"** 432nd Air Expeditionary Wing Commander, "From Hunter 1: Thank You and Continue to Press Forward," memo, Creech Air Force Base website, December 2, 2009, http:// www.creech.af.mil/news/story.asp?id=123180301.

5 **the Djibouti government had not yet permitted the United States to load missiles** Two American officials, confidential interviews, 2014.

6 **The Associated Press had called it "Obama's aloha low-key holiday"** Philip Elliott, "Obama's Low-Key Holiday Away from Washington," Associated Press, December 25, 2009.

6 **White House spokesman Bill Burton told the gaggle of reporters aboard Air Force One** "Gaggle by Deputy Press Secretary Bill Burton Aboard Air Force One en Route Honolulu, Hawaii," White House, Briefing Room, December 24, 2009,

http://www.whitehouse.gov/the-press-office/gaggle-deputy-press-secretary-bill
-burton-aboard-air-force-one-en-route-honolulu-ha.

7 remarks to the Turkish parliament in April "Remarks by President Obama
to the Turkish Parliament," Ankara, Turkey, April 6, 2009, White House, Briefing Room, http://www.whitehouse.gov/the_press_office/Remarks-By-President
-Obama-To-The-Turkish-Parliament/. The best source for Obama's public comments
is usually http://www.whitehouse.gov/briefing-room/Speeches-and-Remarks/. The
items are grouped by year and month in the right-hand column.

7 a long-awaited speech at Cairo University "Remarks by the President on a
New Beginning," Cairo University, June 4, 2009, White House, Briefing Room,
http://www.whitehouse.gov/the_press_office/Remarks-by-the-President-at
-Cairo-University-6-04-09.

8 _Onion_ headline _The Onion_, November 5, 2008.

8 2009 had been the rockiest year on the domestic terrorism front See Scott
Shane, "A Year of Terror Plots, Through a Second Prism," _The New York Times_,
January 13, 2010, http://www.nytimes.com/2010/01/13/us/13intel.html.

9 the former president had said that his successor "deserves my silence" On the
different approaches of Bush and Cheney, see Sheryl Gay Stolberg, "Unemployed,
Unapologetic and Unrestrained: It's Cheney Unbound," _The New York Times_,
April 23, 2009, http://www.nytimes.com/2009/04/24/us/24cheney.html.

9 Cheney on Obama's "dithering" Helene Cooper, "Afghan War Is New Topic
of Dispute with Cheney," _The New York Times_, October 23, 2009, http://www
.nytimes.com/2009/10/23/world/asia/23cheney.html.

9 Cheney on "aid and comfort to the enemy" Mike Allen and Jim VandeHei,
"Dick Cheney Slams President Obama for Projecting 'Weakness,'" Politico, December 1, 2009, http://www.politico.com/news/stories/1109/30024.html.

9 Cheney told Sean Hannity "Former Vice President Dick Cheney on
'Hannity,'" interview by Sean Hannity, _Hannity_, December 9, 2009, http://www
.foxnews.com/story/2009/12/09/former-vice-president-dick-cheney-on-hannity/.

9 they were especially loath to link violent attacks explicitly to Islam See, for
example, John O. Brennan's speech at the Center for Strategic and International
Studies, August 6, 2009: "Nor does President Obama see this challenge as a
fight against jihadists. Describing terrorists in this way, using the legitimate term
'jihad,' which means to purify oneself or to wage a holy struggle for a moral goal,
risks giving these murderers the religious legitimacy they desperately seek but in
no way deserve. Worse, it risks reinforcing the idea that the United States is somehow at war with Islam itself. And this is why President Obama has confronted
this perception directly and forcefully in its speeches to Muslim audiences, declaring that America is not and never will be at war with Islam." John O. Brennan, "A New Approach to Safeguarding Americans," August 6, 2009, http://www
.whitehouse.gov/the-press-office/remarks-john-brennan-center-strategic-and
-international-studies.

10 Obama on Fort Hood shootings Obama's public comments on Fort Hood are
excerpted from the White House website's "Briefing Room," under "Speeches and

Remarks," http://www.whitehouse.gov/briefing-room/Speeches-and-Remarks/, for
the month of November 2009.

10 Ralph Peters, a retired Army lieutenant colonel "Obama Can't Be Bothered
by Islamic Terrorism," *New York Post*, November 8, 2009, http://nypost.com/
2009/11/08/obama-cant-be-bothered-by-islamic-terrorism/.

10 "Nidal Hassan Did the Right Thing," Anwar al-Awlaki wrote Awlaki's blog,
http://www.anwar-alawlaki.com/, was taken down not long after his Fort Hood
comments. But this post, dated November 9, 2009, is archived at several locations on the web, including cryptome.org, http://cryptome.org/anwar-alawlaki/
09-1109.htm.

11 Awlaki's two e-mails to Hasan See William H. Webster Commission, *Final
Report of the William H. Webster Commission on the Federal Bureau of Investigation,
Counterterrorism Intelligence, and the Events at Fort Hood, Texas, on November 5,
2009*, http://www.fbi.gov/news/pressrel/press-releases/final-report-of-the-willia
m-h.-webster-commission, 50–51.

11 he had specifically condemned as a "heartless beast" Awlaki's blog post
"Fighting Against Government Armies in the Muslim World," July 14, 2009,
http://www.anwar-alawlaki.com, archived at http://anwar-awlaki.blogspot.com/
2011/10/fighting-against-government-armies-in.html.

12 "The fact that he had an influence" James L. Jones, interview, April 19, 2012.

**12 they had collected multiple, damning pieces of information about the perpe-
trator** See the White House report on the Flight 253 episode, "White House
Review Summary Regarding 12/25/2009 Attempted Terrorist Attack," January 7,
2010, http://www.whitehouse.gov/the-press-office/white-house-review-summary
-regarding-12252009-attempted-terrorist-attack; and the Senate Intelligence Committee report, *Attempted Terrorist Attack on Northwest Airlines Flight 253* (Washington, DC: Government Printing Office, May 24, 2010), http://www.intelligence
.senate.gov/pdfs/111199.pdf.

13 I spoke a few days after Christmas with Tom Kean Scott Shane, "Shadow of
9/11 Is Cast Again," *The New York Times*, December 31, 2009, http://www.ny
times.com/2009/12/31/us/31intel.html.

13 The lives of the 290 people aboard Northwest Flight 253 Details of passengers' and flight attendants' and Abdulmutallab's statements are from the prosecutor's opening statement in Case No. 2:10-cr-20005 in Michigan's Eastern District.

14 *America and the Final Trap* Video released May 26, 2010, accessed on the Internet Archive: https://archive.org/details/AmericaAndTheFinalTrap_918.

15 avid supporter of the Irish Republican Army Scott Shane, "For Lawmaker
Examining Terror, a Pro-I.R.A. Past," *The New York Times*, March 8, 2011, http://
www.nytimes.com/2011/03/09/us/politics/09king.html.

15 "This was an assault on the United States" Rep. Peter T. King quoted in "Air-
line Bombing Suspect Goes Before Judge; Tighter Security Measures at Airports;
New Violence in Iran," CNN, December 26, 2009, http://transcripts.cnn.com/
TRANSCRIPTS/0912/26/cnr.10.html.

15 "We, the United States' political and media culture" A senior White House
official, confidential interview, 2014.

15 the president went before the cameras "The President Addresses the Public on the Attempted Terrorist Attack," *White House Blog*, December 28, 2009, http://www.whitehouse.gov/blog/2009/12/28/president-addresses-public-attempted-terrorist-attack.

15 a brutal statement to Politico Mike Allen, "Dick Cheney: Barack Obama 'Trying to Pretend,'" Politico, December 30, 2009, http://www.politico.com/news/stories/1209/31054.html.

16 Dan Pfeiffer, the White House communications director, fired back Dan Pfeiffer, "The Same Old Washington Blame Game," *White House Blog*, December 30, 2009, http://www.whitehouse.gov/blog/2009/12/30/same-old-washington-blame-game.

17 On January 2, still in Honolulu, Obama used his weekly presidential address "Remarks of President Barack Obama, Weekly Address, January 2, 2010," White House, Briefing Room, http://www.whitehouse.gov/the-press-office/weekly-address-president-obama-outlines-steps-taken-protect-safety-and-security-ame.

17 Every recent president had been ambushed by terrorist acts The Stanford scholar Martha Crenshaw makes this point in an intriguing essay, "Reaction Time: Why Terrorism Derails Every Administration," *Foreign Policy*, November 13, 2012, http://foreignpolicy.com/2012/11/13/reaction-time.

18 He had blown himself up at the CIA base in Khost The bombing in Khost came five days after Abdulmutallab's airliner attack. See Alissa J. Rubin and Mark Mazzetti, "Suicide Bomber Killed C.I.A. Operatives," *The New York Times*, December 30, 2009, http://www.nytimes.com/2009/12/31/world/asia/31khost.html.

19 January 5, 2010, Situation Room meeting This account is based on the recollections of four people who were present, who described it on condition of anonymity.

19 Secretary of State Clinton Confidential interviews with two former Clinton aides, 2012 and 2014.

20 "Part of his point was that the pressure on us would be to do a lot more in Yemen" Ben Rhodes, interview, October 17, 2013.

22 its legal opinions on torture became fodder for news stories The torture opinions, Jay S. Bybee et al., "Standards of Conduct for Interrogation under 18 USC 2340-2340A" and "Interrogation of al Qaeda Operative," August 1, 2002, are available with many other relevant documents at the National Security Archive, http://www.aladin0.wrlc.org/gsdl/collect/torture/torture.shtml.

22 even an hour's research on waterboarding A useful history and other information on waterboarding can be found at the website waterboarding.org.

23 The memos were repudiated by Obama when he took office "Executive Order 13491—Ensuring Lawful Interrogations, January 22, 2009," White House, Briefing Room, http://www.whitehouse.gov/the_press_office/EnsuringLawful Interrogations.

23 a two-part tour de force in the *Harvard Law Review* Martin S. Lederman and David Jeremiah Barron, "The Commander in Chief at the Lowest Ebb," *Harvard Law Review* 121 (2008): 941–1111.

2. You Are Still Unsafe

25 "Phew. Maaaaaan—that was close" The message was sent to Morten Storm, a Danish former Islamic militant who, unbeknownst to Awlaki, had become disillusioned and gone to work for Western intelligence. Morten Storm with Paul Cruickshank and Tim Lister, *Agent Storm: My Life Inside Al Qaeda and the CIA* (New York: Atlantic Monthly Press, 2014), 190. Storm also described to me Awlaki's communication methods.

26 a message from Bin Laden implausibly claimed credit for the plot "'Bin Laden Tape' Warns Obama of More Attacks," BBC News, January 24, 2010, http://news.bbc.co.uk/2/hi/middle_east/8477413.stm.

26 message from Al Qaeda's founder lambasted America for its inaction on climate change Jack Healy, "Bin Laden Adds Climate Change to List of Grievances Against U.S.," *The New York Times*, January 29, 2010, http://www.nytimes.com/2010/01/30/world/middleeast/30binladen.html.

27 twelve-minute "Call to Jihad" in mid-March "Purported al-Awlaki Message Calls for Jihad Against U.S.," CNN, March 17, 2010, http://www.cnn.com/2010/WORLD/europe/03/17/al.awlaki.message. The full transcript of Awlaki's message was obtained from a SITE Intelligence Group report of March 20, 2010.

27 in one of his most popular tracts, Awlaki had offered the sarcastic lament Awlaki made the wisecrack in "44 Ways of Supporting Jihad" (January 5, 2009) in entry no. 42, "Learning Arabic." The entire text of "44 Ways" can be found at http://cryptome.org/anwar-alawlaki/09-0105.htm, copied into the comments section of this blog entry at comment 36. It can be found in many other places on the web as well.

27 Awlaki had first recorded his inflammatory message on video See J. M. Berger's post on his invaluable website Intelwire.com, "Anwar Al-Awlaki Video Release Rehashes 2010 'Message to America,'" December 20, 2011, http://news.intelwire.com/2011/12/new-awlaki-message-in-aqap-video.html.

28 mocking Obama's "short leash" Awlaki had first used this phrase in a written post on his blog: "A Message to the American People," October 13, 2009, http://anwar-awlaki.blogspot.com/2011/10/message-to-american-people, reported by the SITE Intelligence Group on that day. He often recycled passages in a series of messages over many months.

30 as George W. Bush had famously put it "Address to a Joint Session of Congress and to the American People," September 20, 2001, White House Archives, "News and Policies," http://georgewbush-whitehouse.archives.gov/news/releases/2001/09/20010920-8.html.

30 January 21, 2010, Senate Foreign Relations Committee report US Senate Committee on Foreign Relations, *Al Qaeda in Yemen and Somalia: A Ticking Time Bomb*, report, January 21, 2010 (Washington, DC: Government Printing Office, 2010), http://www.foreign.senate.gov/imo/media/doc/Yemen.pdf, 9.

30 Dennis Blair on "specific permission" to kill an American Hearing of the US House Permanent Select Committee on Intelligence, *Annual Threats Assessment,*

Part I, February 3, 2010 (Washington, DC: Government Printing Office, 2010), Federation of American Scientists website, https://www.fas.org/irp/congress/2010_hr/hpsci-threat.pdf.

30 conventional wisdom that Al Qaeda's branch in Yemen was now the most dangerous See, for instance, the January 27, 2010, testimony of Juan Zarate, a top counterterrorism official under Bush, to the House Armed Services Committee. Of various Al Qaeda affiliates, Zarate said, "the outpost in Yemen is the most dangerous because you have seasoned al Qaeda members, long ties to Bin Laden and the core group, directing their attention to the west." Hearing of the US House Committee on Armed Services, *Al Qa'ida in 2010: How Should the U.S. Respond?*, January 27, 2010 (Washington, DC: Government Printing Office, 2010), http://www.gpo.gov/fdsys/pkg/CHRG-111hhrg58293/html/CHRG-111hhrg58293.htm.

31 "They throw grenades at weddings" Confidential interview with a retired American military officer, 2014.

31 famously described his job as "dancing on the heads of snakes" See Victoria Clark, *Yemen: Dancing on the Heads of Snakes* (New Haven, CT: Yale University Press, 2010). Clark's book is an excellent introduction to Yemen's history and politics through the Saleh era.

31 "the Yaman" See, for instance, George Antonius, *The Arab Awakening* (London: Hamish Hamilton, 1938).

32 Per capita income of Saudi Arabia and Yemen The CIA's *World Factbook*, "Country Profiles," https://www.cia.gov/library/publications/the-world-factbook.

32 he told the London-based newspaper *Al-Quds al-Arabi* Combating Terrorism Center at West Point, *A False Foundation? AQAP, Tribes and Ungoverned Spaces in Yemen*, ed. Gabriel Koehler-Derrick (West Point, NY: Combating Terrorism Center at West Point, September 2011), 19.

32 Bin Laden maintained an intense interest in Yemen See, for instance, Nelly Lahoud et al., *Letters from Abbottabad: Bin Laden Sidelined?* (West Point, NY: Combating Terrorism Center at West Point, May 2012), 19, 29–35.

33 Theo Padnos Padnos, "Anwar Awlaki's Blog," *London Review of Books*, January 28, 2010, http://www.lrb.co.uk/v32/n02/theo-padnos/anwar-awlakis-blog. Padnos's books on his time in Yemen, *Light of the Crescent Moon: An Undercover Journey to the Soul of Radical Islam* (New York: Palgrave Macmillan, 2007), and an updated version, *Undercover Muslim: A Journey into Yemen* (London: Bodley Head, 2011), are beautifully written and very helpful in explaining Awlaki's appeal. Padnos, who also uses the name Peter Theo Curtis, was later kidnapped in Syria and was held for two years before being released in August 2014.

33 diplomatic cable sent by the American embassy in Canberra "Visas Viper: Post Recommends 23 Names for No Fly and Selectee Lists," WikiLeaks, January 21, 2010, https://www.wikileaks.org/plusd/cables/10CANBERRA51_a.html. The original uses the spelling "Aulaqi."

34 a Senate report claimed that as many as three dozen American ex-convicts US Senate Committee on Foreign Relations, *Al Qaeda in Yemen*, 1, 4.

34 Abdulhakim Mujahid Muhammad A detailed account of the case, "Abdulhakim Mujahid Muhammad (Carlos Bledsoe): A Case Study in Lone Wolf Terrorism," was written by Daveed Gartenstein-Ross and posted on December 23, 2013, at *Jihadology* (blog), http://jihadology.net/2013/12/23/guest-post-abdulhakim-mujahid-muhammad-carlos-bledsoe-a-case-study-in-lone-wolf-terrorism/. Also revealing are letters Muhammad wrote from jail to reporter Kristina Goetz of *Commercial Appeal*; see Kristina Goetz, "Muslim Who Shot Soldier in Arkansas Says He Wanted to Cause More Death," *Knoxville News Sentinel*, November 13, 2010, http://www.knoxnews.com/news/2010/nov/13/muslim-who-shot-solider-arkansas-says-he-wanted-ca/.

34 "I don't wish to have a trial" See James Dao, "Man Claims Terror Ties in Little Rock Shooting," *The New York Times*, January 22, 2010, http://www.nytimes.com/2010/01/22/us/22littlerock.html. That full letter from Muhammad to Judge Herbert T. Wright Jr., January 12, 2010, is posted at Murderpedia, http://murderpedia.org/male.M/images/muhammad-abdulhakim/muhammad-letter.pdf.

35 "Awlaki," the agents said See Peter Finn's story on Sharif Mobley, "The Post-9-11 Life of an American Charged with Murder," *Washington Post*, September 4, 2010, http://www.washingtonpost.com/wp-dyn/content/article/2010/09/04/AR2010090403328.html.

35 sixteen intelligence agencies and subagencies For a complete list, see "Members of the IC," Office of the Director of National Intelligence, http://www.dni.gov/index.php/intelligence-community/members-of-the-ic.

35 National Reconnaissance Office scandal in 1994 Tim Weiner, "Senate Committee Receives Apology from Spy Agency," *The New York Times*, August 11, 1994.

36 intelligence budget at $80 billion a year Federation of American Scientists, "Intelligence Budget Data," http://www.fas.org/irp/budget/index.html.

36 *Washington Post* on the number of top-secret clearances Dana Priest and William Arkin, "A Hidden World, Growing Beyond Control," *Washington Post*, July 18, 2010.

37 the real total Steven Aftergood, "Number of Security Clearances Soars," Federation of American Scientists, *Secrecy News* (blog), September 20, 2011, http://blogs.fas.org/secrecy/2011/09/clearances/.

37 Obama on Abdulmutallab attack showing "systemic failure" "Statement by the President on Preliminary Information from His Ongoing Consultation About the Detroit Incident," December 29, 2009, at Kaneohe Bay Marine Base, Kaneohe, Hawaii; White House, Briefing Room, http://www.whitehouse.gov/the-press-office/statement-president-preliminary-information-his-ongoing-consultation-about-detroit-.

37 "not acceptable" "Remarks by the President on Security Reviews," January 5, 2010, White House, Briefing Room, http://www.whitehouse.gov/the-press-office/remarks-president-security-reviews.

37 six-page summary of the White House review "White House Review Summary Regarding 12/25/2009 Attempted Terrorist Attack," January 7, 2010, White House, Briefing Room, http://www.whitehouse.gov/the-press-office/white-house-review-summary-regarding-12252009-attempted-terrorist-attack.

38 "After that, as president, it seemed like he felt in his gut the threat" Mike Leiter, interview, February 24, 2012.

38 "He said, 'In the long run, as a country, we cannot be spending billions of dollars'" Ben Rhodes, interview, October 27, 2013.

39 President's Daily Brief, or PDB See Glenn Kessler, "The Bogus Claim That Obama 'Skips' His Intelligence Briefings," *Washington Post*, September 24, 2012; and on different presidents' preferences, Walter Pincus, "Measuring a President's Approach on Foreign Policy," *Washington Post*, January 16, 2012; other details on the PDB are from interviews with former government officials.

39 "Bin Laden Determined to Strike" A copy of the famous April 10, 2004, PDB is posted by the Federation of American Scientists in their Central Intelligence Agency Product Archive, http://www.fas.org/irp/cia/product/pdb080601 .pdf.

39 When Rahm Emanuel, Obama's first chief of staff Former government official, confidential interview, 2012.

40 on the very day of his inauguration as president, January 20, 2009, Saudi and Yemeni militants had announced The name had been used earlier, but it came into common parlance only after the re-formation of the group on that date. On AQAP and its history, see "Al Qaeda in the Arabian Peninsula," Mapping Militant Organizations, Stanford University research project, last updated September 10, 2012, http://web.stanford.edu/group/mappingmilitants/cgi-bin/ groups/view/19.

40 growth of the National Security Council staff See Spencer S. Hsu, "Obama Integrates Security Councils, Adds New Offices," *Washington Post*, May 27, 2009; and I. M. Destler and Ivo H. Daalder, "A New NSC for a New Administration," Brookings Institution, November 2000, Brookings Policy Brief No. 68, http:// www.brookings.edu/research/papers/2000/11/governance-daalder.

40 By 6 a.m., each director Former NSC staff members, confidential interviews, 2014.

41 Dr. Awlaki said he hadn't had any contact with Anwar in eight months Ahmed al-Haj and Donna Abu-Nasr, "US Imam Wanted in Yemen over al-Qaida Suspicions," Associated Press, November 10, 2009.

41 Nasser spoke to a *Washington Post* reporter Sudarsan Raghavan and Michael D. Shear, "Yemen Strikes at al-Qaeda Meeting; U.S.-Aided Attack May Have Killed Cleric Linked to Fort Hood Suspect," *Washington Post*, December 25, 2009, http://www.washingtonpost.com/wp-dyn/content/article/2009/12/24/AR 2009122400536.html.

41 Nasser, who was already caring for Anwar's first wife and five children at his son's request Nasser al-Awlaki, video interview by Medea Benjamin of Code Pink, June 2013, Sanaa.

41 he agreed to speak to CNN reporter Paula Newton in Sanaa Paula Newton, "CNN Exclusive: Al-Awlaki's Father Says Son Is 'Not Osama bin Laden,'" CNN, January 11, 2010, http://www.cnn.com/2010/WORLD/meast/01/10/yemen.al .awlaki.father/.

42 In another Internet statement in the spring of 2010, titled "Western Jihad Is

Here to Stay" The text is available in several locations on the web, including Awlaki's blog, March 19, 2010, http://anwar-awlaki.blogspot.com/2011/10/western -jihad-is-here-to-stay.html.

43 May 2010, AQAP's leader Nasser al-Wuhayshi issued a statement SITE Intelligence Group, "AQAP Leader Speaks in Support of Anwar al-Awlaki," May 16, 2010, http://ent.siteintelgroup.com/Multimedia/site-intel-group-5-16-10 -aqap-leader-audio-awlaki.html.

43 the terrorist group's media arm released a lengthy video interview with Awlaki SITE Intelligence Group, "AQAP Releases Interview with Anwar al-Awlaki," May 23, 2010, https://news.siteintelgroup.com/Multimedia/awlaki52310.html.

43 Senior Yemeni officials had raised such a possibility Margaret Coker and Charles Levinson, "Yemen in Talks for Surrender of Cleric," *Wall Street Journal*, January 15, 2010, http://online.wsj.com/news/articles/SB1000142405274870436 3504575003434023229978.

3. He Had a Beautiful Tongue

47 "I told him" Ghassan Khan, telephone interview, January 3, 2014; all quotations from Ghassan Khan are from this interview.

48 Tablighi Jamaat Ibid.

48 he called his father at home in Sanaa Nasser al-Awlaki, interview, February 1, 2014, Sanaa.

49 Khalid Sheikh Mohammed in Greensboro, North Carolina See, for instance, Terry McDermott, Josh Meyer, and Patrick J. McDonnell, "The Plots and Designs of Al Qaeda's Engineer," *Los Angeles Times*, December 22, 2002.

49 Sayyid Qutb See John Calvert, *Sayyid Qutb and the Origins of Radical Islamism* (New York: Columbia University Press, 2010), 139ff.

49 Qutb's 1951 essay "The America I Have Seen" Kamal Abdel-Malek, ed., *America in an Arab Mirror: Images of America in Arabic Travel Literature: An Anthology* (New York: Palgrave Macmillan, 2000), 9–28.

51 "What happened, happened in America" Remark of Nasser al-Awlaki to a foreign visitor who recounted it to the author, 2010.

51 Aden College For a sense of the atmosphere at the college, which closed in 1967, see their website at http://adencollege.net/body_index.html.

51 "He said, 'If you want to pray'" Ammar al-Awlaki, interview, January 25, 2014, Sanaa.

52 "a cute little boy" This and other quotations and biographical details are from written answers by Nasser al-Awlaki to questions sent by the author, January 2014.

52 their mother repeatedly putting a prayer rug in Anwar's suitcase Ammar al-Awlaki, interview, January 25, 2014.

52 For boys of their generation Walid al-Saqaf, telephone interview, 2010.

53 "That was my first exposure to the field of teaching" Anwar al-Awlaki, "Statement of Purpose," submitted to George Washington University doctoral program, undated but probably about September 2000.

53 Nasser spoke with friends at the US Agency for International Development Nasser al-Awlaki, interview by Medea Benjamin, June 2013, Sanaa; a form completed and signed by a USAID official authorizing Anwar's scholarship lists his birthplace incorrectly as Sanaa.

53 "My father at the time" Anwar al-Awlaki, "Spilling out the Beans: Al Awlaki Revealing His Side of the Story," *Inspire*, no. 9 (May 2012).

53 listed his place of birth as Sanaa "Affidavit of Probable Cause," signed by Steven R. Click, special agent of the Diplomatic Security Service, June 17, 2002.

53 Awlaki's time in the Muslim Student Association Yusuf Siddiqui, telephone interviews, 2010.

54 "I felt like the MSA" Former Colorado State University student, confidential telephone interview, 2010.

55 "I started taking my religion more seriously" Awlaki, "Spilling out the Beans."

55 "We did nothing" Ammar al-Awlaki, interview, January 25, 2014, Sanaa.

55 "I actually only knew about that trip" Nasser al-Awlaki, written answers to questions sent by the author, January 2014.

55 "I spent a winter there" Awlaki, "Spilling out the Beans."

56 "To watch the courageous Afghan freedom fighters" Ronald Reagan, "Message on the Observance of Afghanistan Day," March 21, 1983, American Presidency Project, http://www.presidency.ucsb.edu/ws/?pid=41078.

56 "He said, 'I really need to get an Λ'" Ghassan Khan, telephone interview, January 3, 2014.

56 "Shortly after my scholarship was terminated" Awlaki, "Spilling out the Beans."

57 "You'd have a bunch of Pakistanis" Moin Siddiqui, interview, 2010.

57 "He was very knowledgeable" Mumtaz Hussain, interview, 2010.

57 His choice of courses Awlaki's courses and grades are from his Colorado State University transcript, part of two thousand pages of FBI records released to J. M. Berger of Intelwire under the Freedom of Information Act, available at "Intelwire Releases Awlaki FOIA Files; Hijacker Travel Questions," Intelwire, January 21, 2014, http://news.intelwire.com/2014/01/intelwire-releases-awlaki -foia-files.html.

58 Many years later, on his blog Anwar al-Awlaki, "Book Review 9: English Novels," http://www.anwar-alawlaki.com, August 6, 2008, archived at http://cryptome.org/anwar-alawlaki/08-0806.htm. Awlaki's blog was taken down after reports of his connection to the Fort Hood shooter, Major Nidal Hasan, but it has been archived at cryptome.org.

58 "That would be the topic at the lunch table" Ammar al-Awlaki, interview, January 25, 2014.

58 "I discussed the issue with him" Nasser al-Awlaki, written answers to questions sent by the author, January 2014.

59 Anwar's wealthy uncle, helped play matchmaker Saleh bin Fareed, interview, January 28, 2014.

59 six foot one and 135 pounds From his California driver's license application, August 4, 1997.

59 their first child, a boy they named Abdulrahman Anwar al-Awlaki See

Abdulrahman's birth certificate, posted online by the *Washington Post*, Peter Finn, "Awlaki Family Releases Teen's Birth Certificate," *Checkpoint Washington* (blog), October 18, 2011, http://www.washingtonpost.com/blogs/checkpoint -washington/post/awlaki-family-releases-teens-birth-certificate/2011/10/18/ gIQA9zycuL_blog.html.

59 "He had a beautiful tongue" Palestinian American elder at the Denver Islamic Society, confidential interview, 2010.

61 students who felt the city's main mosque was too liberal Awlaki, "Spilling out the Beans."

61 "He lit up when he was with the youth" Jamal Ali, interview, 2010.

61 Awlaki read lots of books on leadership Ammar al-Awlaki, interview, January 25, 2014.

61 Lincoln W. Higgie III Higgie, telephone interview, 2010.

61 His father spent six months in San Diego Nasser al-Awlaki, written answers to questions sent by the author, January 2014.

62 He "lost everything," Nasser later recalled Nasser al-Awlaki, interview, February 1, 2014.

62 Ammar came for the summer Ammar al-Awlaki, interview, January 25, 2014.

62 San Diego prostitution and loitering charges FBI documents in "Intelwire Releases Awlaki FOIA Files," 229–35.

63 Awlaki incorporated a company "Articles of Incorporation of Al Fahm Inc.," filed with the Nevada Secretary of State, February 18, 2000.

63 "I told him, 'If you come back to Yemen, you'll be just another imam'" Nasser al-Awlaki, telephone interview, October 18, 2014.

63 a scholarship to do a master's degree in educational leadership at San Diego State The status of the degree is a bit of a puzzle. Awlaki later put the master's degree in educational leadership on his résumé and other documents. His transcript shows ten courses completed, all but one with a grade of A or A–, a dramatic improvement on his undergraduate record; the transcript lists thirty "UE," or units earned, and the degree requirement was thirty units. The transcript sent by San Diego State (SDSU) to George Washington University does not show that Awlaki was awarded the master's degree, but a handwritten note by an unnamed George Washington administrator says: "Degree awarded on Aug. 18 [2000]— Grad school 619-594-5213—Called on 12/5/00." Another George Washington University document places an asterisk next to the SDSU master's degree listed on the form and notes: "Not on transcript but SDSU Grad School verified." In addition, Awlaki's application documents include a glowing recommendation for Awlaki from an SDSU official whose name is blacked out in records made public by the FBI but whose title in 2000 was "Coordinator, Postsecondary Education." The writer says Awlaki "was my advisee in our MA in Educational Leadership program and he was a student in a few of my postsecondary education classes." The adviser said Awlaki's "peers in the classes looked to Anwar as a leader," said he would make "an outstanding doctoral student," and predicted a stellar postdoctoral career in Yemen. But SDSU officials, interviewed in 2010 and again in

2014, insisted that they could find no record that the master's degree was officially awarded. They declined to say whether a bureaucratic glitch might be responsible. Certainly the assertion made in some later news reports that Awlaki fraudulently claimed a degree he had not earned is unproven.

64 "The mosque's objective in hiring Anwar" Johari Abdul Malik, interview, February 12, 2014.

65 told his father that he supported George W. Bush Nasser al-Awlaki, interview, February 1, 2014, Sanaa.

4. AN EXQUISITE WEAPON

66 video footage shot from fifteen thousand feet This account of the Afghan Eyes is from interviews with several participants, including the former CIA officials Henry Crumpton in 2012 and Charlie Allen in 2014. In his book *The Art of Intelligence: Lessons from a Life in the CIA's Clandestine Service* (New York: Penguin, 2012), Crumpton described watching Bin Laden on "live video" in September 2000. Allen said that the Predator footage had actually been shot about two weeks before analysts spotted the Bin Laden figure and gave it to senior officials for review.

66 the Predator, a UAV, or an unmanned aerial vehicle reminiscent of a gangly intelligent insect On the development and history of the Predator, see Richard Whittle, "Predator's Big Safari," Mitchell Institute for Airpower Studies, August 2011, Mitchell Paper 7, http://higherlogicdownload.s3.amazonaws.com/ AFA/6379b747-7730-4f82-9b45-a1c80d6c8fdb/UploadedImages/Mitchell% 20Publications/Predator's%20Big%20Safari.pdf.

67 Terrorism barely ranked on the issues that concerned Americans Lydia Saad, "Americans' Fear of Terrorism in U.S. Is Near Low Point," Gallup Politics, September 2, 2011, http://www.gallup.com/poll/149315/americans-fear-terrorism -near-low-point.aspx; detailed results at http://www.gallup.com/file/poll/149318/ Nine_Eleven_Anniv_fear_terror_110902.pdf, 2–3.

67 on April 25, 2000, Richard Clarke, the White House counterterrorism adviser, had sent a memo 9/11 Commission, *The 9/11 Commission Report* (Washington, DC: Government Printing Office, 2004), 189 and 506 n. 112.

67 They saw the man they believed to be Bin Laden a second time Whittle, "Predator's Big Safari," 21.

68 At a meeting in a sixth-floor conference room at CIA headquarters in the spring of 2001 Charlie Allen, interview, October 15, 2013.

68 Clarke was having trouble persuading the new George W. Bush team to take up the Predator issue See Richard Clarke, *Against All Enemies: Inside America's War on Terror* (New York: Simon and Schuster, 2004), 220–21, 237.

69 The first real-world Predator strike Whittle, "Predator's Big Safari," 8.

69 the descendant of generations of unmanned American aircraft Two accounts of the early UAVs—really compilations of oral history—are by William Wagner, *Lightning Bugs and Other Reconnaissance Drones* (Washington, DC: Armed Force Journal International; Fallbrook, CA: Aero Publishers, 1982) and, with William P.

Sloan, *Fireflies and Other UAVs* (Arlington, TX: Aerofax, 1992). Wagner finished
the first book in the early 1970s but could not get the government's permission to
publish it for nearly a decade. A very useful compact account of the pre-Predator
drones is by Kenneth P. Katz, "Before Predator: The Early History of USAF Remotely Piloted Aircraft," 2013, Society of Flight Test Engineers, http://www
.sfte2013.com/files/75234565.pdf.

69 A young lieutenant named Joseph P. Kennedy Jr. "The First Kennedy
Brother," National Naval Aviation Museum, November 22, 2013, http://www
.navalaviationmuseum.org/history-up-close/from-the-cockpit-stories-of-naval
-aviation/first-kennedy-brother/.

**70 Among Radioplane's assembly-line employees was eighteen-year-old
Norma Jeane Dougherty** Michael Beschloss, "Marilyn Monroe's World War II
Drone Program," *The New York Times*, June 3, 2014, http://www.nytimes
.com/2014/06/04/upshot/marilyn-monroes-world-war-ii-drone-program.html.

70 In a project code-named Have Lemon, the Air Force Flight Test Center
Katz, "Before Predator"; a video of the early drone-fired missile tests, *Early Video of
Strike Drone (BGM-34A B)*, is at Military.com, posted March 23, 2012, http://www
.military.com/video/forces/air-force/early-video-of-strike-drone-bgm-34a-b/
1526913903001/.

71 the Association for Unmanned Vehicle Systems was a decade old See "History," on the association's "About" page, http://www.auvsi.org/about (accessed
February 1, 2015).

71 At a press conference, the seventy-three-year-old Teller declared Benjamin F. Schmemmer, foreword to Wagner, *Lightning Bugs,*, xi.

71 his detailed remarks look prescient Edward Teller, "The Unmanned Vehicle
System: The Defense of the United States," speech presented to the Association
for Unmanned Vehicle Systems, Washington, DC, July 21, 1981, reprinted in
Vital Speeches of the Day, November 15, 1981, 94–96.

71 "The Air Force is built around fliers" Schmemmer, foreword, xiii, xiv.

**71 the Air Force would be training more drone pilots than fighter pilots and
bomber pilots** Walter Pincus, "Fine Print: Air Force to Train More Remote Than
Actual Pilots," *Washington Post*, August 11, 2009, quoting Air Force General Stephen R. Lorenz, commander of Air Education and Training Command, http://
www.washingtonpost.com/wp-dyn/content/article/2009/08/10/AR20090810
02712.html.

72 "If you could have cut out a hunk of Iraq's terrain around Baghdad" Matt J.
Martin with Charles W. Sasser, *Predator: The Remote-Control Air War over Iraq
and Afghanistan: A Pilot's Story* (Minneapolis: Zenith Press, 2010), 17.

**73 wingspan of fifty-five feet, nearly twice its length. It weighed, literally, half
a ton** US Air Force, "MQ-1B Predator," Fact Sheet, July 20, 2010, http://www
.af.mil/AboutUs/FactSheets/Display/tabid/224/Article/104469/mq-1b-predator
.aspx.

**73 At Creech, each Predator in the country's growing fleet had a core team of
two** Several former drone pilots, confidential interviews, 2011–14.

74 One intelligence veteran who had spent years high up in the chain of command Former intelligence official, confidential interview, 2013.

75 told me that the armed drone was "an exquisite weapon" Michael Hayden, interview, October 15, 2013.

75 Lieutenant Colonel Matt Martin, for instance, whose book *Predator* makes clear his support Martin and Sasser, *Predator*, 53–54 and 211–12.

76 "Because operators are based thousands of miles away" "UN Special Rapporteur on Extrajudicial Killings Decries 'Playstation' Hits," Reuters, June 4, 2010.

76 Matthew Atkins, an Air Force lieutenant colonel who after long experience believed in the value of drone strikes Lt. Col. Matthew Atkins, "The Personal Nature of War in High Definition," *Lawfare* (blog), January 26, 2014, http://www.lawfareblog.com/2014/01/matthew-atkins-on-the-personal-nature-of-war-in-high-definition/.

77 Brandon Bryant, who had operated drones over Afghanistan "A Drone Warrior's Torment: Ex-Air Force Pilot Brandon Bryant on His Trauma from Remote Killing," *Democracy Now!*, October 25, 2013, http://www.democracynow.org/2013/10/25/a_drone_warriors_torment_ex_air.

78 The target was the head of Al Qaeda in Yemen, Qaed Salim Sinan al-Harithi A detailed account of the Harithi strike is in the most deeply reported study of Al Qaeda in Yemen, Gregory D. Johnsen, *The Last Refuge: Yemen, Al-Qaeda, and America's War in Arabia* (New York: Norton, 2013), 119–23.

78 the American ambassador to Yemen, Edmund Hull, was on his way to Marib that very day Ambassador Edmund J. Hull (Ret.), *High-Value Target: Countering Al Qaeda in Yemen* (Washington, DC: Potomac Books, 2011), 59–62.

79 Associated Press and other news outlets reported accurately John J. Lumpkin, "U.S. Kills Senior al-Qaida Operative in Yemen with Missile Strike," Associated Press, November 4, 2002.

79 Secretary of Defense Donald Rumsfeld hinted gleefully "U.S. missile strike kills al Qaeda chief," CNN, November 5, 2002, http://edition.cnn.com/2002/WORLD/meast/11/05/yemen.blast.

79 The next day the deputy defense secretary, Paul Wolfowitz, made it official "Wolfowitz Hails Success of Missile Strike in Yemen," Agence France Press, November 5, 2002.

79 I called Loch Johnson, who had served as a staffer My article for the *Baltimore Sun*, "Pros, Cons of Assassination: Policy: Killing the Enemy Is Traditional, but the United States Can Expect the Practice to Draw Criticism, Retaliation and Other Complications," appeared on November 8, 2002, http://articles.baltimoresun.com/2002-11-08/news/0211080279_1_qaida-surprise-attacks-political-scientist.

80 one Al Qaeda operative in Harithi's car, Rauf Nassib, had survived Johnsen, *Last Refuge*, 122.

5. WE ARE THE BRIDGE

82 Congress had passed a joint resolution Senate Joint Resolution 23, Authorization for Use of Military Force, September 18, 2001, GovTrack.us, https://www.govtrack.us/congress/bills/107/sjres23/text.

82 President George W. Bush had stopped by Robert D. McFadden, "President, in New York, Offers Resolute Vows Atop the Rubble," *The New York Times*, September 15, 2001, http://www.nytimes.com/2001/09/15/nyregion/15BUSH.html.

82 "I personally think it was horrible" Anwar al-Awlaki, e-mail from his Hotmail account to Ammar al-Awlaki, 12:14 a.m., September 15, 2001, provided by Ammar al-Awlaki.

83 the FBI's written account of the interviews The FBI reports on three interviews with Awlaki, on September 15, 17, and 19, are included in the documents provided to J. M. Berger of Intelwire under the Freedom of Information Act; "Intelwire Releases Awlaki FOIA Files; Hijacker Travel Questions," January 21, 2914, Intelwire, http://news.intelwire.com/2014/01/intelwire-releases-awlaki-foia-files.html. Though several later FBI documents refer to four interviews at this time, I have been unable to locate the notes of a fourth interview. The FBI reports generally use the spelling "Aulaqi."

84 "He was enjoying the limelight" Johari Abdul Malik, interview, 2010.

86 "Most of the questions are, 'How should we react?'" Susan Morse, "First Source of Comfort; When Events Overwhelm, Clergy, Not Doctors, Are on the Front Lines," *Washington Post*, September 18, 2001.

86 attacked by a man with a baseball bat Debbi Wilgoren and Ann O'Hanlon, "Worship and Worry; Fear for Other Muslims Mixes with Support for U.S.," *Washington Post*, September 22, 2001.

86 One neighbor, Patricia Morris Caryle Murphy, "For Muslims, Benevolence Prevails over Backlash," *Washington Post*, October 6, 2001.

86 Awlaki posed for the *Washington Post* smiling alongside Morris Photo by Tracy A. Woodward, *Washington Post*, October 4, 2001, http://www.getty images.com/detail/news-photo/patricia-morris-and-imam-anwar-al-awlaki-photographed-news-photo/97116568.

86 a condemnation of the attacks from a prominent Egyptian-born Islamist scholar, Yusuf al-Qaradawi Qaradawi's statement condemning the 9/11 attacks can be found at "Sheikh Yusuf Al-Qaradawi Condemns Attacks Against Civilians," BeliefNet, September 13, 2001, http://www.beliefnet.com/Faiths/Islam/2002/08/Sheikh-Yusuf-Al-Qaradawi-Condemns-Attacks-Against-Civilians.aspx.

86 "We came here to build" William Branigin, "When Terror Hits Close to Home; Mix of Emotions Sweeps over County Residents," *Washington Post*, September 20, 2001.

87 "at 30 is held up as a new generation of Muslim leader" Laurie Goodstein, "Influential American Muslims Temper Their Tone," *The New York Times*, October 19, 2001.

87 "sees himself as a Muslim leader" Mara Liasson, "Propaganda Wars," *Morn-*

ing Edition, November 1, 2001, NPR, http://www.npr.org/templates/story/story
.php?storyId=1132470.

87 Some have greatness thrust upon them Shakespeare, *Twelfth Night* 2.5.

87 Awlaki—an Internet addict who had rushed to Best Buy Brian Handwerk
and Zain Habboo, "Attack on America: An Islamic Scholar's Perspective," National Geographic News, September 28, 2001.

87 he sat down for questions from Ray Suarez of *NewsHour* on PBS Suarez described the interview in detail in a PBS interview in 2009, after Awlaki resurfaced
in the news: Dave Gustafson, "Ray Suarez: My Post-9/11 Interview with Anwar
al-Awlaki," *PBS NewsHour*, November 11, 2009; http://www.pbs.org/newshour/
updates/religion-july-dec09-alawlaki_11-11/.

87 four bricks and a note threatening Muslims Nick P. Davito, "Muslims in
Virginia Report Backlash a Day After Attacks," Associated Press, September 12,
2001.

87 Suarez later recalled Gustafson, "Ray Suarez."

88 the resulting *NewsHour* segment PBS *NewsHour*, October 30, 2001.

89 Father Gerry Creedon Creedon, telephone interview, May 13, 2014.

89 Simon Amiel Amiel, telephone interview, 2010.

89 Awlaki agreed to star in a sort of Islam-101 film The five-minute edited video,
originally posted at washingtonpost.com, can be found in many places on the web,
including Travis Fox, *From the Archive: Anwar al-Awlaki in "Understanding Ramadan,"* 2001, http://vimeo.com/29837032.

90 "I would not have called Awlaki a moderate" Ahmed Younis, telephone interview, November 19, 2013.

91 Suarez of PBS included a snippet "American Muslim Community Since September 11," video transcript, *PBS NewsHour*, October 30, 2001.

91 Looking back years later, Suarez Gustafson, "Ray Suarez."

92 Awlaki told the *Washington Times* Ralph Z. Hallow and Vaishali Honawar,
"Muslim Students Are Wary of the War; But Islamic Leaders Support Attacks,"
Washington Times, October 11, 2001.

92 online chat with the *Washington Post* "Understanding Ramadan: The Muslim
Month of Fasting," with Imam Anwar Al-Awlaki, November 19, 2001, *Washington Post*, http://www.washingtonpost.com/wp-srv/liveonline/01/nation/ramadan
_awlaki1119.htm.

92 "Either you are with us" George W. Bush, "Address to a Joint Session of
Congress and to the American People," September 20, 2001, White House Archives, "News and Policies," http://georgewbush-whitehouse.archives.gov/news/
releases/2001/s09/20010920-8.html.

93 outtakes of the *Washington Post* video Travis Fox, *From the Archive: Anwar
al-Awlaki (Additional Footage)*, 2001, http://vimeo.com/29838071.

94 Asked by NPR to discuss Liasson, "Propaganda Wars."

94 the religion reporter for *The New York Times* called Goodstein, "Influential
American Muslims."

94 Awlaki's comments on IslamOnline.net "Muslim American Scholars Speak

Out Against Terrorism: Dialogue 4," September 17, 2001, printout by author in 2010; the exchange has since been removed by IslamOnline.net.

96 "Statement of Purpose" in application for doctoral program This document, transcripts of Awlaki's undergraduate and graduate studies, his résumé, his acceptance letter, and other documents submitted to George Washington University were collected by the FBI and provided to J. M. Berger of Intelwire under the Freedom of Information Act, available at Intelwire, "Intelwire Releases Awlaki FOIA Files."

98 "I convinced him that he should have a career in education" Nasser al-Awlaki, telephone interview, October 18, 2014.

98 Umar Lee Umar Lee, telephone interview, February 14, 2014.

98 Hale Smith, a San Francisco attorney Hale Smith, telephone interview, 2010; Smith also provided a trip roster and other documents related to the hajj.

99 He extolled the Prophet Muhammad *Muhammad: Legacy of a Prophet*, PBS documentary film, Unity Productions Foundation and Kikim Media, 2002.

99 a local Islamic institute that helped train Muslim chaplains Glenn Simpson, "A Muslim School Used by Military Has Troubling Ties," *Wall Street Journal*, December 3, 2003.

99 spoke at a conference named "Allah's Final Revelation to Mankind" Online announcement, posted at the newsgroup soc.religion.islam on August 16, 2001, https://groups.google.com/forum/#!topic/soc.religion.islam/wmyoxbx6sqg.

99 he delivered a speech entitled "Tolerance: A Hallmark of Muslim Character" Islamic Society of North America, 2001 conference program, available at http://www.investigativeproject.org/documents/misc/658.pdf.

99 a fund-raiser for Jamil al-Amin and Awlaki's taxi ride from Washington's National Airport Joe Cantlupe and Dana Wilkie, "Former San Diego Islamic Spiritual Leader Defends Mosque," Copley News Service, September 28, 2001.

99 copyright on his lecture series "Lives of the Prophets" On file at the Copyright Catalog, Library of Congress.

100 Al Fahm Inc. and Sam Eulmi "Articles of Incorporation of Al Fahm Inc.," filed with the Nevada Secretary of State, February 18, 2000; Sam Eulmi, interview, 2010.

100 Homaidan al-Turki, who would later go to prison Kieran Nicholson, "Saudi Gets 28 Years to Life in Nanny Abuse," *Denver Post*, September 1, 2006.

100 Awlaki's "Lives of the Prophets" Like other lecture series by Awlaki, they are hard to find on CD but widely available on the Internet; see, for example, "Complete Archive of Sheikh Imam Anwar Al-awlaki Audio (Lectures 2010)," Internet Archive, https://archive.org/details/Anwar.Awlaki.Audio.Archive, and "Lectures, Islam All in One, by Imam Anwar Al-Awlaki" http://www.enjoyislam .com/lectures/AnwarAlAwlaki/lectures.html (accessed February 1, 2015), as well as at YouTube.com.

100 Awlaki was translating and retelling Al Bidayah wa'an-Nihayah Al Basheer Company for Publications and Translations, flier for "Lives of the Prophets," available in FBI documents at Intelwire, "Intelwire Releases Awlaki FOIA Files."

101 "These are the best of stories" Awlaki, "Lives of the Prophets," vol. 1, lecture 1.

101 he got an unusual invitation Catherine Herridge, "Al Qaeda Leader Dined at the Pentagon Just Months After 9/11," Fox News, October 20, 2010, http://www.foxnews.com/us/2010/10/20/al-qaeda-terror-leader-dined-pentagon-months/. Fox News also acquired the Defense Department and FBI documents associated with this event; see Catherine Herridge, Pamela Browne, Cyd Upson, and Gregory Johnsen, "New Details Emerge of Radical Imam's Lunch at the Pentagon," Fox News, May 20, 2011, http://www.foxnews.com/politics/2011/05/19/exclusive-new-details-emerge-al-qaeda-terror-chiefs-lunch-pentagon/.

102 Awlaki's congregants traded stories about insults These details, including the appearance of people with video cameras at Dar Al-Hijrah, are from interviews with multiple worshippers at Dar Al-Hijrah, 2010 and 2014.

103 When Awlaki stepped to the microphone Awlaki, "It's a War Against Islam," audio, available at https://www.youtube.com/watch?v=cVvQ-m9f8b8 and elsewhere on the web.

103 The raids were the culmination of Operation Green Quest See, for instance, Sharon Behn, "US Muslim Community Outraged by Raids on Muslim Offices and Homes," Agence France Press, March 21, 2002; and Josh Gerstein, "A Prosecutor Is Called Relentless," *New York Sun*, July 28, 2008.

103 "the United States is not, and has not been, a substantial source of al Qaeda funding" National Commission on Terrorist Attacks Upon the United States, "Monograph on Terrorist Financing," 4, http://www.9-11commission.gov/staff_statements/911_TerrFin_Monograph.pdf.

6. Totally Planning to Stay

106 Awlaki's December 13, 2001, visit to the Marriott Residence Inn FBI documents obtained by J. M. Berger, "Intelwire Releases Awlaki FOIA Files; Hijacker Travel Questions," Intelwire, January 21, 2014, http://news.intelwire.com/2014/01/intelwire-releases-awlaki-foia-files.html, 400–1. The account of the prostitutes' descriptions of Awlaki is from the same set of documents.

108 "She comes from a poor family" Ibid., 469.

108 he had denounced *zina*, or fornication See Anwar al-Awlaki, "Zina" or Fornication, YouTube, uploaded August 21, 2011, https://www.youtube.com/watch?v=4GQouNwZN7g.

108 twenty-page memorandum to James A. Baker FBI documents, "Intelwire Releases Awlaki FOIA Files," 616–35.

109 studied with concern by both the Congressional Joint Inquiry and the 9/11 Commission Eleanor Hill, staff director of the Congressional Joint Inquiry, and Philip D. Zelikow, executive director of the 9/11 Commission, interviews, 2010.

109 Hazmi and Mihdhar's arrival in California *The 9/11 Commission Report* (Washington, DC: Government Printing Office, 2004), 215ff.

109 Omar al-Bayoumi Ibid., 419.

110 four calls were recorded between Bayoumi's phone and Awlaki's phone FBI agent, name redacted, interview by Raj De of the 9/11 Commission, November 17,

2003, Memorandum for the Record, 9/11 Commission Records, National Archives. The *9/11 Commission Report* mistakenly says that all four calls were on February 4, 2001 (517).

110 lengthy closed-door discussions with the imam *9/11 Commission Report*, 517. It is interesting to note that the San Diego Field Office of the FBI, which had long watched Awlaki, described him as the "spiritual leader" of Hazmi and Mihdhar as early as September 20, 2001, according to a memo in the Intelwire FBI documents, "Intelwire Releases Awlaki FOIA Files," 1739. But the public documents give little idea of what the judgment was based on apart from worshippers who recalled seeing the hijackers with the imam.

110 Hazmi later turned up at Dar Al-Hijrah *9/11 Commission Report*, 221, 229–30.

110 Eyad al-Rababah and Daoud Chehazeh Bob Bukowski, former FBI agent, telephone interview, March 6, 2014.

110 Khaleel, who was vice president of the Denver Islamic Society in the early 1990s Bruce Finley, "War Divides Colorado Arabs," *Denver Post*, January 27, 1991.

110 would later earn a modest footnote in history by purchasing a battery for Osama bin Laden's satellite phone in 1996 The *9/11 Commission Report*, 517, described contact between Awlaki and a "possible procurement agent" for Bin Laden, who a US official later told me was Ziyad Khaleel.

111 Charitable Society of Social Welfare Internal Revenue Service 1998 Form 990-EZ for the Charitable Society for Social Welfare, filed May 13, 1999.

111 an FBI agent later testified Tom Hays, "Charity Eyed in Terror Money Probe," Associated Press, February 26, 2004.

111 FBI counterterrorism investigators, who opened a terrorism investigation on Awlaki *9/11 Commission Report*, 517 n. 33.

111 Awlaki had recently been visited by an associate of Omar Abdel Rahman Congressional Joint Inquiry into 9/11, *Report of the Joint Inquiry into the Terrorist Attacks of September 11, 2001, by the House Permanent Select Committee on Intelligence and the Senate Select Committee on Intelligence*, December 2002, https://www.fas.org/irp/congress/2002_rpt/911rept.pdf, 179.

111 A police search of the apartment in Hamburg, Germany, of Ramzi bin al-Shibh Ibid., 178.

111 a sort of communications hub for the scattered conspirators of 9/11 was a satellite phone in Yemen See James Bamford, *The Shadow Factory: The NSA from 9/11 to the Eavesdropping on America* (New York: Doubleday, 2008), 7ff.

111 Mihdhar was visiting his wife *9/11 Commission Report*, 222.

111 Awlaki was visiting his family in the same city Awlaki family members, interviews, 2014.

111 a plot investigators believed Mihdhar probably knew about in advance Mihdhar and Hazmi had attended a January 2000 Al Qaeda meeting in Kuala Lumpur, Malaysia, where the USS *Cole* plot was likely discussed, before flying to California; see *9/11 Commission Report*, 158; Congressional Joint Inquiry, *Report*, 144.

112 **Awlaki offered a puzzling reply** Lincoln Higgie, interview, 2010.

112 **he considers the Awlaki question "one of the three largest loose ends"** Philip Zelikow, e-mail to author, November 10, 2009.

113 **"Extensive investigation by the FBI"** Beth Lefebvre, FBI Public Affairs, e-mail to author, April 1, 2014.

113 **Heavily redacted FBI documents** FBI documents, "Intelwire Releases Awlaki FOIA Files."

114 **Awlaki himself said later that he had no idea that Hazmi had moved to the Washington area** *Ajras al-khatar* [Bells of danger], documentary by Yosri Fouda for al-Jazeera Television, first broadcast September 14, 2005.

115 **"I think Awlaki had to know"** Former FBI agent Bob Bukowski, telephone interview, March 6, 2014.

116 **One night, Ammar recalled** Ammar al-Awlaki, interview, January 23, 2014, Sanaa.

117 **Neither Anwar nor Ammar knew it, but an FBI surveillance team followed them** The FBI surveillance notes from March 2002 are in the second collection of FBI documents obtained by J. M. Berger of Intelwire, who shared them with me in November 2014. They are not online at the time of this writing, but the surveillance notes for the period of Ammar's visit to Anwar, March 23 to March 31, 2002, are on pages 1806–49.

117 **Ammar asked Anwar lightheartedly** Ammar al-Awlaki, interview, January 25, 2014, Sanaa.

119 **A long-secret document reveals** "Memorandum for the Record: Interview of FBI Special Agent Wade Ammerman," October 16, 2003, 9/11 Commission Records, National Archives. This five-page document was withheld from public release for years at the request of several agencies that considered it sensitive. The author's request to the National Archives in 2014 led to its release with some redactions.

121 **Bin Fareed asked him about the fallout from 9/11** Saleh bin Fareed al-Awlaki, interview, January 28, 2014, Aden.

121 **The mosque prepared a letter** The letter is in the Intelwire FBI documents, "Intelwire Releases Awlaki FOIA Files," 519.

122 **Nussaibah Younis described memorably** Nussaibah Younis, "The Anwar al-Awlaki Who Impressed Me as a Teenager," *Guardian*, November 1, 2010, http://www.theguardian.com/commentisfree/2010/nov/01/anwar-al-awlaki-transformation-political.

123 **They were taken aside for secondary screening** The relevant government documents recording Awlaki's detention at JFK were obtained by Paul Sperry, a researcher on terrorism and author of *Infiltration: How Muslim Spies and Subversives Have Penetrated Washington* (Nashville, TN: Thomas Nelson, 2005). He has posted the documents on his website at http://www.sperryfiles.com/documents.shtml.

123 **Awlaki recalled that customs officials seemed "quite baffled"** Awlaki, "Spilling out the Beans: Al Awlaki Revealing His Side of the Story," *Inspire*, no. 9 (May 2012).

123 **a determined Diplomatic Security Service officer** Ray Fournier, telephone interview, 2010.

124 **warrant was issued for Awlaki's arrest** Warrant for Arrest, issued June 17, 2002, by US Magistrate Judge Michael J. Watanabe, United States District Court, District of Colorado, Case No. 02-1146M.

124 **David Gaouette, ordered the arrest warrant withdrawn** David Gaouette, telephone interview, 2010.

125 **Timimi, an American-born biologist, was later sentenced to life** Jerry Markon, "Muslim Lecturer Sentenced to Life," *Washington Post*, July 14, 2005.

125 **Awlaki showed up at Timimi's house** "Defendant Dr. Ali Al-Timimi's Memorandum in Support of Motion to Compel Discovery," filed July 17, 2003, in Case cr-04-385, United States v. Ali Al-Timimi, United States District Court for the Eastern District of Virginia.

125 **But the bureau flatly denies that Awlaki was cooperating** Beth Lefebvre, FBI Public Affairs, e-mail to author, April 1, 2014.

7. STEALTHY, AGILE, AND LETHAL

126 **Senator Barack Obama stood at the podium** For the text of the speech, see "Obama's Speech at Woodrow Wilson Center," August 1, 2007, Council on Foreign Relations, http://www.cfr.org/elections/obamas-speech-woodrow-wilson-center/p13974. The C-Span video includes the introduction by Lee Hamilton: *Obama Foreign Policy Speech*, http://www.c-span.org/video/?200258-1/obama-foreign-policy -speech.

126 **Five years earlier, at an antiwar rally in Chicago's Federal Plaza, Obama had warned** Just thirteen seconds of the video of Obama's 2002 speech has been preserved: *Obama's 2002 Speech Against the War, Delivered by Supporters*, uploaded October 1, 2007, https://www.youtube.com/watch?v=AUV69LZbCNQ. The full text and audio of his remarks are at "Transcript: Obama's Speech Against the Iraq War," January 20, 2009, NPR, http://www.npr.org/templates/story/story.php ?storyId=99591469.

127 **"greeted as liberators"** Cheney to Tim Russert on NBC's *Meet the Press*, March 16, 2003. Russert first used the word *liberators*, asking the vice president, "If your analysis is not correct, and we're not treated as liberators, but as conquerors, and the Iraqis begin to resist, particularly in Baghdad, do you think the American people are prepared for a long, costly, and bloody battle with significant American casualties?" Cheney replied: "Well, I don't think it's likely to unfold that way, Tim, because I really do believe that we will be greeted as liberators."

127 **burning through some $10 billion a month** These statistics on the Iraq War are from an Associated Press update, "Key Figures About the Iraq War," published on the day of Obama's speech. The day's headlines from Iraq are also from AP stories.

127 **But the sound bites from 2002** Barack Obama, *The Audacity of Hope* (New York: Three Rivers Press, 2006), 292–93.

127 **Mark Mazzetti had reported** Mark Mazzetti, "U.S. Aborted Raid on Qaeda

Chiefs in Pakistan in '05," *The New York Times*, July 8, 2007, http://www.nytimes.com/2007/07/08/washington/08intel.html.

128 I had written about a new National Intelligence Estimate Scott Shane, "6 Years After 9/11, the Same Threat," *The New York Times*, July 18, 2007, http://www.nytimes.com/2007/07/18/washington/18assess.html.

128 Hillary Clinton, who had repeatedly labeled Obama "naive," took him to task for "telegraphing" US moves Dennis Conrad, "Obama: Nukes 'Not on the Table,'" Associated Press, August 1, 2007.

128 in a presidential debate, she spoke scornfully of his remarks February 26, 2008, presidential debate, MSNBC, transcript from "The Democratic Debate in Cleveland," *The New York Times*, February 26, 2008, http://www.nytimes.com/2008/02/26/us/politics/26text-debate.html?pagewanted=all.

128 Christopher Dodd called Obama's comment "irresponsible" Jeff Zeleny and Steven Greenhouse, "War on Terror Takes Focus at Democrats' Debate," *The New York Times*, August 8, 2007, http://www.nytimes.com/2007/08/08/us/politics/08dems.html.

128 "In one week he went from saying he's going to sit down" Mitt Romney in the Republican presidential debate of August 5, 2007, transcript from "The Republican Candidate Debate," *The New York Times*, August 5, 2007, http://www.nytimes.com/2007/08/05/us/politics/05transcript-debate.html.

128 "I find it amusing" Zeleny and Greenhouse, "War on Terror."

131 Obama was talking about the drone Two Obama advisers, confidential interview, 2014.

131 "The drones were coming into sight" Lee Hamilton, telephone interview, May 22, 2014.

132 In *Dreams from My Father*, Obama describes Barack Obama, *Dreams from My Father*, updated ed. (New York: Three Rivers Press, 2004), 78–91.

133 Obama's part-time work teaching constitutional law See David Remnick, *The Bridge: The Life and Rise of Barack Obama* (New York: Knopf, 2010), 261–67; and Jodi Kantor, "Teaching Law, Testing Ideas, Obama Stood Slightly Apart," *The New York Times*, July 30, 2008, http://www.nytimes.com/2008/07/30/us/politics/30law.html.

133 "constitutional-law-professor-president" Jeremy Scahill, interview by Touré, *The Cycle*, MSNBC, June 6, 2013, https://www.youtube.com/watch?v=gLHUelPX8eY.

133 a seminar called "Current Issues in Racism and the Law" The syllabus, for spring term 1994, is posted by *The New York Times* here: http://www.nytimes.com/packages/pdf/politics/2008OBAMA_LAW/Obama_CoursePk.pdf, along with comments by several legal scholars who examined it for *The New York Times* in 2008: Jodi Kantor, "Inside Professor Obama's Classroom," July 30, 2008, http://thecaucus.blogs.nytimes.com/2008/07/30/inside-professor-obamas-classroom/0/.

134 "You rarely got his opinion or his view" Salil Mehra, telephone interview, May 22, 2014.

134 "Is It Right and Wise to Kill a Kidnapper?" This editorial by Frederick

Douglass ran June 2, 1854, in *Frederick Douglass' Paper*, the abolitionist's Rochester-based newspaper, formerly known as the *North Star*. It can be found in Frederick Douglass, *Selected Speeches and Writings* (Chicago: Lawrence Hill Books, 1999), 277–80.

134 a riveting drama that was playing out in 1854 *The Boston Slave Riot and Trial of Anthony Burns* (Boston: William V. Spencer, 1854) is a compilation of contemporary news accounts of the events; it is available online at http://books .google.com/books?id=SNhleTwnWSIC&printsec=frontcover#v=onepage&q& f=false.

135 asked by the *Hyde Park Herald* Remnick quotes the entire statement in *Bridge*, 337.

136 In the unlikely setting of a Barnes & Noble Obama's answer to the question on terrorism is at *Obama on Terrorism in 2004*, uploaded September 19, 2012, https://www.youtube.com/watch?v=SjUI7vM8TrI.

137 He hired Robert Barnett Nicole Ziegler Dizon, "Obama Gets Three-Book Deal Worth $1.9 Million," Associated Press, December 17, 2004.

137 "we have played fast and loose" Obama, *The Audacity of Hope*, 56.

137 "the battle against international terrorism" Ibid., 23.

137 "the growth of militant, fundamentalist Islam" Ibid., 278.

137 "I would argue that we have the right" Ibid., 308–9.

138 Mohammed al-Asaadi, the Yemeni newspaper editor and activist Asaadi, interview, January 30, 2014, Sanaa.

139 Some of the local guests were in tears A person who had been present at the election-day embassy reception, confidential interview, 2010.

139 on December 9, 2008, Obama visited a secure room The description of Obama's December 9, 2009, intelligence briefing is based on confidential interviews in 2012 and 2014 with several of those present.

139 Evidence would later surface that more than one hundred prisoners The Senate Intelligence Committee would count "at least 119" detainees at the black sites, as well as finding a photograph of a waterboard at a CIA site in Afghanistan known as the Salt Pit, though officially no prisoner had been subjected to waterboarding there. Senate Select Committee on Intelligence, *Committee Study of the Central Intelligence Agency's Detention and Interrogation Program*, 106 n. 620, http://www.intelligence.senate.gov/study2014/executive-summary.pdf, 14, 51, n245. Also see Charlie Savage and Scott Shane, "Libyan Alleges Waterboarding by C.I.A., Report Says," *The New York Times*, September 6, 2012, http://www .nytimes.com/2012/09/06/world/middleeast/libyan-alleges-waterboarding-by -cia-human-rights-watch-report-says.html.

139 Obama asked which six techniques were still authorized The Justice Department memo authorizing the six techniques has been declassified. See Stephen G. Bradbury, "Memorandum for John A. Rizzo, Acting General Counsel, Central Intelligence Agency," July 20, 2007, American Civil Liberties Union, https://www.aclu.org/files/torturefoia/released/082409/olc/2007%20OLC%20 opinion%20on%20Interrogation%20Techniques.pdf.

8. That Was the Transformation

145 Awlaki lectures on Ibn Nuhaas and the Book of Jihad Audio of the complete lecture series is posted at the Internet Archive at https://archive.org/details/Mshri and can be found on YouTube as well. I have not been able to determine for certain the location where Awlaki delivered these particular lectures.

145 Salamah Ibn al-Akwa Awlaki's lecture on his early Muslim hero is excerpted at https://www.youtube.com/watch?v=_rCUq6HZLrQ.

147 Among the audience at one of Awlaki's lectures The informant, who had adopted the name Aimen Dean, went public in a series of interviews in 2015. He described one of Awlaki's Book of Jihad lecture series and the presence of the future bombers in *BBC News Magazine* in an April 3, 2015, article by Steve Swann, "A Truly Dangerous Meeting of Minds," http://www.bbc.com/news/magazine-32065132.

147 Shahidur Rahman Rahman and two of his friends, all young Britons with radical views who generally shunned the media, were interviewed in London in 2010 by my *New York Times* colleague Souad Mekhennet. The interviews were used for our profile of Awlaki: "Imam's Path from Condemning Terror to Preaching Jihad," *The New York Times*, May 8, 2010, http://www.nytimes.com/2010/05/09/world/09awlaki.html.

147 dressed in a white *thobe* Videos of Awlaki's Umar lectures at the East London Mosque are available on YouTube and elsewhere on the web: for example, *HD: Introduction to Umar ibn Khattaab—Anwar Al Awlaki*, uploaded June 3, 2011, https://www.youtube.com/watch?v=D0BadunCRls.

147 "Never Ever Trust the Kuffar" See the video of that title, uploaded September 2, 2011, https://www.youtube.com/watch?v=1E38ZSc1fdA.

148 a country that was more than 95 percent non-Muslim "Religion in England and Wales 2011," Office of National Statistics, December 11, 2012. This report includes the statistic for London as well.

149 Ahmed Younis Younis, telephone interview, November 19, 2013.

150 on the Muslim lecture circuit Awlaki's UK appearances in 2002–3 were traced from a number of sources, including searches of Yahoo Groups like "London_Muslim": https://groups.yahoo.com/neo/groups/London_Muslim/search/messages?query=awlaki.

150 Muslim Americans approximately matched the American average in income and education See Pew Research Center, "Muslim Americans: Middle Class and Mostly Mainstream," May 22, 2007, http://pewresearch.org/files/old-assets/pdf/muslim-americans.pdf.

150 In the United Kingdom and the rest of Europe, the picture was quite different See, for instance, Robert S. Leikin, "Europe's Angry Muslims," *Foreign Affairs*, July/August 2005, http://www.foreignaffairs.com/articles/60829/robert-s-leiken/europes-angry-muslims.

150 a series of articles he wrote in 2002 for the *Yemen Observer* Awlaki's articles were photocopied by the author from bound volumes at the *Observer*'s offices in Sanaa: "The Question of Suicide Bombings," May 4, 2002; "Great Successes of the War on Terror," July 27, 2002; "The Next War," August 17, 2002.

152 Al Qaeda had based its declarations of war on America in 1996 and 1998
Gilles Kepel and Jean-Pierre Milelli, *Al Qaeda in Its Own Words* (Cambridge, MA:
Harvard University Press, 2008), 47–50 and 53–56.

153 in Sanaa, he was staying in his father's big house This account of his life at
the family home comes largely from interviews with Nasser al-Awlaki and Ammar
al-Awlaki, 2014.

153 "I encouraged him to complete his PhD in Britain" Nasser al-Awlaki, written answers to questions sent by the author, January 2014.

153 Using his father's money, he invested in real estate These and other details
of Anwar's various plans are from the author's interview with Nasser al-Awlaki,
February 1, 2014, Sanaa.

154 "working within the Muslim community with educated people" Nasser al-
Awlaki, written answers to questions sent by the author, January 2014.

154 Awlaki called one of the FBI counterterrorism agents The FBI memos and
e-mails between the FBI and Awlaki are on pdf pages 1922–60 in a second batch
of FBI documents obtained under the Freedom of Information Act by J. M. Berger
of Intelwire, which he kindly shared with me in November 2014. They are not online at the time of this writing but are likely to be posted eventually at Intelwire
.com. A former American counterterrorism official also described the exchanges
with Awlaki in a confidential interview in 2014.

**154 Ammerman told 9/11 Commission investigators on October 16, 2003, that
he believed Awlaki "may want to return to the US"** "Memorandum for the Record: Interview of FBI Special Agent Wade Ammerman," October 16, 2003, 9/11
Commission Records, National Archives.

155 Ali al-Timimi was expecting indictment Jerry Markon, "Lecturer Expects
Indictment in Va. Jihad Case," *Washington Post*, August 15, 2003.

155 Timimi ultimately would be charged, convicted, and sentenced to life Jerry
Markon, "Muslim Lecturer Sentenced to Life," *Washington Post*, July 14, 2005,
http://www.washingtonpost.com/wp-dyn/content/article/2005/07/13/AR2005
071302169.html.

155 "I think the UK police, Scotland Yard, were looking for him" Mohammed
al-Asaadi, interview, January 30, 2014, Sanaa.

156 "I mean, to see his classmates as high-ranking officers" Saleh bin Fareed al-
Awlaki, interview, January 28, 2014, Aden.

156 he gave a series of lectures on Islam in medieval Spain Sudarsan Raghavan,
"Cleric Linked to Fort Hood Attack Grew More Radicalized in Yemen," *Washington Post*, December 10, 2009.

157 Salman al-Awda Awlaki mentions Awda (using the spelling Salman al-
Odah) in a very interesting blog entry giving an account of his Islamic education: "A Question from a Reader on My Islamic Education," August 12, 2008,
anwar-alawlaki.com, archived at http://cryptome.org/anwar-alawlaki/08-0812
.htm.

157 He moved to the town of Hodeidah on Yemen's west coast Nasser al-Awlaki,
interview, February 1, 2014, Sanaa.

157 "always busy" This phrase and the quotes that follow are from Ammar al-Awlaki, interview, January 25, 2014, Sanaa.

158 Awlaki's name was redacted Details and the FBI's response are in Congressional Joint Inquiry into 9/11, *Report of the Joint Inquiry into the Terrorist Attacks of September 11, 2001, by the House Permanent Select Committee on Intelligence and the Senate Select Committee on Intelligence*, December 2002, https://www.fas.org/irp/congress/2002_rpt/911rept.pdf, 178–79.

158 The *Washington Post* featured Awlaki Susan Schmidt, "9/11 Hijackers San Diego Contacts Detailed by Lawmakers' Report," *Washington Post*, July 23, 2003.

158 a story in *U.S. News & World Report* Chitra Ragavan, "The Imam's Very Curious Story: A Skirt-Chasing Mullah Is Just One More Mystery for the 9/11 Panel," *U.S. News & World Report*, June 13, 2004.

158 "Everyone discussed it politically" This and the quotes that follow are from Ammar al-Awlaki, interview, January 25, 2014, Sanaa.

159 five-hour set of lectures Awlaki's lectures entitled "Constants on the Path of Jihad" are preserved in the Internet Archive, https://archive.org/details/Consta.

159 "the single most influential work" J. M. Berger, "The Enduring Appeal of Al-Awlaqi's 'Constants on the Path of Jihad,'" *CTC Sentinel* (Combating Terrorism Center at West Point), October 31, 2011. Other details are from the same essay and from the lectures themselves.

161 Saeed Ali Obaid Obaid, interview, January 25, 2014, Sanaa.

161 Early in 2006, a young Danish convert living in Sanaa Morten Storm with Paul Cruickshank and Tim Lister, *Agent Storm: My Life Inside Al Qaeda and the CIA* (New York: Atlantic Monthly Press, 2014), 91–99.

162 "Because he did not have a job" Saleh bin Fareed al-Awlaki, interview, January 28, 2014, Aden.

162 "He found listening ears and open hearts" Mohammed al-Asaadi, interview, January 30, 2014, Sanaa.

163 Awlaki stirred up family trouble by announcing that he was taking a second wife Confidential interviews in Sanaa, February 2014. According to Morten Storm, Awlaki later told him that the new bride was a "generous gesture" from the brothers (Storm, *Agent Storm*, 149).

163 London-based Arabic daily *Al-Sharq al-Awsat* reported Jonathan Schanzer, "Basket Catch," *New Republic*, September 1, 2003.

163 "He was telling me, 'I'm not a person who would justify killing'" Mohammed al-Asaadi, interview, January 30, 2014, Sanaa.

164 "I saw someone outside the house chewing qat" Awlaki family neighbor, confidential interview, January 2014, Sanaa.

164 The bureau formally closed its Awlaki investigation in May 2003 William H. Webster Commission, *Final Report of the William H. Webster Commission on the Federal Bureau of Investigation, Counterterrorism Intelligence, and the Events at Fort Hood, Texas, on November 5, 2009*, http://www.fbi.gov/news/pressrel/press-releases/final-report-of-the-william-h.-webster-commission, 34.

164 "ANWAR AWLAKI is no longer in San Diego Division" FBI documents obtained by J. M. Berger, "Intelwire Releases Awlaki FOIA Files; Hijacker Travel Questions," Intelwire, January 21, 2014, http://news.intelwire.com/2014/01/intelwire-releases-awlaki-foia-files.html, 271. The original, like many FBI documents, uses the spelling AULAQI.

164 an FBI source reported that Awlaki had just crossed the border from Canada into Vermont FBI memo dated January 31, 2006, in second collection of FBI documents obtained by J. M. Berger of Intelwire and shared with me, not currently online (dated November 2014), 2471 and 2539; also see William H. Webster Commission, *Final Report*, 34, and first collection of FBI documents obtained by J. M. Berger, "Intelwire Releases Awlaki FOIA Files," 275.

164 when at least twenty-three Al Qaeda operatives escaped from the Political Security Organization's maximum-security prison Bill Roggio, "Al Qaeda Jailbreak in Yemen," *Long War Journal*, February 8, 2006, http://www.longwarjournal.org/archives/2006/02/alqaeda_jailbreak_in.php#.

164 Awlaki was arrested in Sanaa The oft-reported date of the arrest, August 31, 2006, is hard to trace to authoritative sources, and some acquaintances of Anwar al-Awlaki say that he was picked up for questioning more than once before his imprisonment. But the date has been repeated in authoritative reports (for example, Defense Department, *Influencing Violent Extremist Organizations Pilot Report: Focus on Al Qaeda in the Arabian Peninsula (AQAP)*, fall 2011, http://nsiteam.com/scientist/wp-content/uploads/2014/02/SMA_AQAP_Pilot_Integration_Report_-_Final_v21.pdf, 231) and is certainly close to the right date.

165 Awlaki himself later told AQAP's media wing Awlaki's video interview to Al Malahem: SITE Intelligence Group, "AQAP Releases Interview with Anwar al-Awlaki," May 23, 2010, https://news.siteintelgroup.com/Multimedia/awlaki 52310.html.

165 News reports later linked Awlaki, under the pseudonym Abu Atiq Cameron Stewart and Martin Chulov, "Yemen Ties Terror's Loose Ends," *Australian*, November 4, 2006. While the *Australian* does not explicitly identify Abu Atiq as Awlaki, it is clear from details given about Abu Atiq that they are the same person. In addition, an FBI memo from December 1, 2006, identifies Awlaki as "Abu Atiq Anwar Aulaqi." See FBI documents, "Intelwire Releases Awlaki FOIA Files," 788.

165 Yemeni officials told Negroponte American and Yemeni officials, confidential interviews, 2010.

165 "A respected scholar, Imam Anwar Al-Awlaki, has been arrested in Yemen" Cageprisoners statement, posted on Yahoo's London_Muslim newsgroup, November 17, 2006.

166 A legend would later arise The notion that torture was behind a sudden change in Awlaki's views is widespread. It was persuasively refuted by, among others, Shiraz Maher of the International Center for the Study of Radicalization at Kings College London, "Did Anwar al-Awlaki Really Change After His Arrest?," *Harry's Place* (blog), February 9, 2010, http://hurryupharry.org/2010/02/09/did-anwar-al-awlaki-really-change-after-his-arrest/, and J. M. Berger of Intelwire,

"The Myth of Anwar al-Awlaki," *Foreign Policy*, August 10, 2011, http://www
.foreignpolicy.com/articles/2011/08/10/the_myth_of_anwar_al_awlaki.

166 his father said he was never beaten or physically tortured Nasser al-Awlaki,
interview, February 1, 2014, Sanaa.

166 by his own account, he was kept in solitary confinement Awlaki, "Book
Reviews from Behind Bars," June 9, 2008, http://www.anwar-alawlaki.com, archived at http://cryptome.org/anwar-alawlaki/08-0609.htm. Awlaki described
his imprisonment in multiple entries on his blog at http://www.anwar-alawlaki
.com. It was removed from the web in November 2009, but the blog entries are
preserved in a number of places, notably at cryptome.org.

166 His first nine months in prison Ibid.

167 "a Bedouin from Shabwah" Nasser al-Awlaki, interview by Medea Benjamin, June 2013, Sanaa.

167 "Shakespeare was the worst thing" Awlaki, "Book Review 9: English Novels,"
http://www.anwar-alawlaki.com, August 6, 2008, archived at http://cryptome.org/
anwar-alawlaki/08-0806.htm.

168 Ibn Taymiyyah Awlaki, "Book Review 8: Majmu Fatawa Ibn Taymiyyah,"
http://www.anwar-alawlaki.com, August 1, 2008, archived at http://cryptome
.org/anwar-alawlaki/08-0801.htm.

168 Sayyid Qutb Awlaki, "Book Review 3: In the Shade of the Quran by Sayyid
Qutb," http://www.anwar-alawlaki.com, June 22, 2008, archived at http://
cryptome.org/anwar-alawlaki/08-0622.htm.

168 The fellow prisoner, Harith al-Nadari, described his friend Shaykh Harith
Al Nadari, "My Story with Al Awlaki," *Inspire*, no. 9 (May 2012): 12; the issue
can be downloaded at Public Intelligence, https://publicintelligence.net/inspire-al
-qaeda-in-the-arabian-peninsula-magazine-issues-8-and-9-may-2012/.

**169 At different times, they spoke also with the Saudi Prince Bandar bin Sultan
and Abdulwahab al-Hajjri** Nasser al-Awlaki, interview, February 1, 2014, Sanaa.

169 "At the beginning they said" Saleh bin Fareed al-Awlaki, interview, January 28, 2014, Aden.

170 Nasser al-Awlaki persuaded his son to talk to two FBI agents Nasser al-
Awlaki, written answers to questions from the author, January 2014.

171 "He entered the office . . . like a boss" Al Nadari, "My Story," 12.

171 "There was some pressure, which I refused to accept" Awlaki, interview by
Moazzam Begg, December 31, 2007, Cageprisoners, http://old.cageprisoners.com/
articles.php?id=22926.

171 intermittent debate about Awlaki's fate American officials, confidential interviews, 2010 and 2014.

171 "If you have any evidence against him" Saleh bin Fareed al-Awlaki, interview, January 28, 2014, Aden.

172 "AmCit Terror Suspect Released from Yemeni Custody" FBI documents,
"Intelwire Releases Awlaki FOIA Files," 1319.

**172 Heavily redacted e-mail exchanges released by the FBI do not make clear
the nature of the charges** The e-mails are in a second batch of FBI documents

obtained under the Freedom of Information Act by J. M. Berger of Intelwire and provided to me in November 2014. They are not online at the time of this writing, but if and when they are posted, the e-mails about possible charges for Awlaki are on pdf pages 1361–65.

173 Morten Storm, his Danish acolyte Storm, *Agent Storm*, 145–46.

173 Awlaki gave a long-distance interview Awlaki, interview by Moazzam Begg, December 31, 2007, Cageprisoners, http://old.cageprisoners.com/articles .php?id=22926.

173 Awlaki had registered a website, www.anwar-alawlaki.com A check of the registration records in 2010 using DomainTools.com showed the site was first registered on February 27, 2008, by an American company and hosted on a server in California. The site was taken down a few days after Awlaki praised Nidal Hasan's shooting rampage at Fort Hood, Texas, in November 2009. Again, the most accessible copy of the blog, though it is incomplete, is at http://cryptome.org/anwar -alawlaki/anwar-alawlaki.htm.

173 On May 31, 2008, he thanked the unnamed "brothers" Awlaki, "Assalamu Alaykum All," http://www.anwar-alawlaki.com, May 31, 2008, archived at http://cryptome.org/anwar-alawlaki/08-0531.htm.

174 "This prison spell was a gift from Allah" Theo Padnos, "Anwar Awlaki's Blog," *London Review of Books*, January 28, 2010, http://www.lrb.co.uk/v32/n02/ theo-padnos/anwar-awlakis-blog. Padnos was himself briefly jailed in Sanaa and found his own credibility with Yemenis greatly enhanced. See Theo Padnos, *Under cover Muslim: A Journey into Yemen* (London: Bodley Head, 2011), 3–8, 191–205.

174 "After he was allowed out" Saleh bin Fareed al-Awlaki, interview, January 28, 2014, Aden.

9. WWW Jihad

176 a group of young Canadians stood in a snowy Ontario field Michelle Shephard, "The Powerful Online Voice of Jihad," *Toronto Star*, October 18, 2009, http://www.thestar.com/news/world/2009/10/18/the_powerful_online_voice_of _jihad.html.

176 In March 2007, Albanian immigrant brothers Seth Jones, *Hunting in the Shadows: The Pursuit of al Qa'ida Since 9/11* (New York: W. W. Norton, 2012), 289–94.

177 three young PayPal employees were developing YouTube *The History of YouTube*, uploaded May 18, 2007, https://www.youtube.com/watch?v=x2NQiV cdZRY.

177 "He appreciated the power of the Internet" Rita Katz of the SITE Intelligence Group, e-mail to author, December 1, 2014.

177 "Extremists are more and more making extensive use of the internet" "Report of the Official Account of the Bombings in London on 7th July 2005," Home Office, May 11, 2006, http://news.bbc.co.uk/2/shared/bsp/hi/pdfs/11_05 _06_narrative.pdf, 31.

178 a pattern that drew legitimate criticism of the bureau's counterterrorism

tactics The most thoroughly reported and critical account of the bureau's use of informants in terrorism prosecutions is Trevor Aaronson, *The Terror Factory: Inside the FBI's Manufactured War on Terrorism* (Brooklyn, NY: Ig Publishing, 2013).

179 "If you were a second generation Muslim" Alexander Melagrou-Hitchens, e-mail interview, May 30, 2014. Hitchens, the son of the late writer Christopher Hitchens, is especially insightful on the subject of Awlaki's religious evolution in "As American as Apple Pie: How Anwar al-Awlaki Became the Face of Western Jihad," report, International Centre for the Study of Radicalisation and Political Violence, 2011, http://icsr.info/2011/09/as-american-as-apple-pie-how-anwar-al-awlaki-became-the-face-of-western-jihad/.

179 Awlaki's former fellow imam at Dar Al-Hijrah in Virginia, Johari Abdul Malik, began to warn young people away Johari Abdul Malik, interview, February 12, 2014.

180 Philip Mudd The quotations are from my interviews with Mudd in 2010 and 2013; see Scott Shane and Souad Mekhennet, "Imam's Path from Condemning Terror to Preaching Jihad," *The New York Times*, May 8, 2010; and Mark Mazzetti, Charlie Savage, and Scott Shane, "How a U.S. Citizen Came to Be in America's Crosshairs," *The New York Times*, March 9, 2013.

180 An April 2008 FBI memo referred to Awlaki as "a known Al Qaeda facilitator and operative" The memo is included in the second collection of FBI documents obtained by J. M. Berger of Intelwire, who shared them with me in November 2014. They are not online at the time of this writing, but the redacted memo of April 28, 2008, is at pdf page 2026.

180 Charlie Allen, the CIA veteran Senate Committee on Homeland Security and Governmental Affairs, *"A Ticking Time Bomb": Counterterrorism Lessons from the U.S. Government's Failure to Prevent the Fort Hood Attack*, February 3, 2011, http://www.gpo.gov/fdsys/pkg/CHRG-112shrg66620/html/CHRG-112shrg66620.htm, 20.

181 In a much-debated 2007 report, the New York Police Department's Mitchell D. Silber and Arvin Bhatt, *Radicalization in the West: The Homegrown Threat*, New York City Police Department, 2007, http://www.nyc.gov/html/nypd/downloads/pdf/public_information/NYPD_Report-Radicalization_in_the_West.pdf.

181 In early 2009, the group posted on the web its own guide to radicalization See Brian Fishman and Abdullah Warius, "A Jihadist's Course in the Art of Recruitment," *CTC Sentinel* (Combating Terrorism Center at West Point), February 15, 2009, https://www.ctc.usma.edu/posts/a-jihadist%E2%80%99s-course-in-the-art-of-recruitment.

181 Monsignor Lorenzo Albacete, a theologian and physicist Albacete, interview, winter 2002, in PBS documentary *Faith and Doubt at Ground Zero*, 2002, transcript at http://www.pbs.org/wgbh/pages/frontline/shows/faith/interviews/albacete.html.

182 "Within the histories of religious traditions" Mark Juergensmeyer, *Terror in the Mind of God: The Global Rise of Religious Violence*, rev. ed. (Berkeley: University of California Press, 2003), 6.

185 Ibraheim: "May Allah keep Anwar" Comment posted December 5, 2008, on Awlaki's December 1 post "Finding a Balance," http://www.anwar-alawlaki .com, archived at http://cryptome.org/anwar-alawlaki/08-1201.htm.

185 "The sun in that solar system was Awlaki" Will McCants, interview, February 18, 2014.

185 "44 Ways of Supporting Jihad," it drew 737 comments in ten days "44 Ways" is not accessible at http://cryptome.org/anwar-alawlaki/09-0105.htm, but the entire text of Awlaki's tract is copied into the comments section of this blog entry at comment 36.

187 a Virginian named Zachary Chesser The information on Chesser comes from Tara Bahrampour, "Terror Suspect Took His Desire to Belong to the Extreme," *Washington Post*, July 25, 2010; the excerpt from Chesser's high school yearbook at http://www.washingtonpost.com/wp-srv/special/metro/zac-chesser/ docs/document-cloud-chesser-senior.html; and the affidavit of FBI agent Mary Brandt Kinder in *USA v. Zachary Adams Chesser*, July 21, 2010, case 1:10 mj 504, US District Court for the Eastern District of Virginia.

188 In court, he expressed remorse Dana Hedgpeth, "N.Va. Man Sentenced to 25 Years for Threats, Trying to Join Terrorist Group," *Washington Post*, February 24, 2011.

189 listened to more than one hundred hours of lectures by Awlaki Tamer al-Ghobashy, "Recordings Inspired Terrorist," *Wall Street Journal*, April 17, 2012.

189 A former fry cook and Muslim convert in his late twenties, Michael C. Finton, tried to blow up the Federal Building Madeleine Gruen, *Attempt to Attack the Paul Findley Federal Building in Springfield, Illinois*, Nine Eleven Finding Answers (NEFA) Foundation, "Target: America" Report 23, December 2009, https://web .archive.org/web/20120301022613/http://www.nefafoundation.org/miscella neous/FeaturedDocs/nefa_fintontargetamerica.pdf.

189 Roshonara Choudhry British police interview with Choudhry, conducted May 14, 2010, in Vikram Dodd, "Roshonara Choudhry: Police Interview Extracts," *Guardian*, November 3, 2010, http://www.theguardian.com/uk/2010/ nov/03/roshonara-choudhry-police-interview.

189 Paul G. Rockwood Jr. Plea agreement in *USA v. Paul Gene Rockwood Jr.*, filed on July 21, 2010, in US District Court for the District of Alaska, 5, posted at Investigative Project on Terrorism, http://www.investigativeproject.org/documents/ case_docs/1348.pdf.

189 Mohamed Mahmood Alessa and Carlos Eduardo Almonte Criminal Complaint against Mohamed Alessa, filed June 4, 2010, in the US District Court for the District of New Jersey, posted at Investigative Project on Terrorism, http:// www.investigativeproject.org/documents/case_docs/1295.pdf.

189 Barry Bujol Press statement from the US Attorney's Office in the Southern District of Texas, November 14, 2011, posted at Investigative Project on Terrorism, http://www.investigativeproject.org/documents/case_docs/1815.pdf.

190 At a Washington conference in April 2010, Representative Jane Harman Harman spoke at a conference at the Bipartisan Policy Center in Washington,

"The State of Intelligence Reform," on April 7, 2010; transcript available via Federal News Service.

190 At a New York Police Department briefing Judith Miller and David Samuels, "A Glossy Approach to Inciting Terrorism," *Wall Street Journal*, November 27, 2010.

191 Hasan began sending Awlaki messages For the most complete and authoritative account of the e-mail exchanges, see William H. Webster Commission, *Final Report of the William H. Webster Commission on the Federal Bureau of Investigation, Counterterrorism Intelligence, and the Events at Fort Hood, Texas on November 5, 2009*, especially 41ff, http://www.fbi.gov/news/pressrel/press-releases/final -report-of-the-william-h.-webster-commission.

192 Awlaki posted a blistering attack on his website Awlaki, "Fighting Against Government Armies in the Muslim World," http://www.anwar-alawlaki.com, July 14, 2009. This is missing from the Cryptome archive on Awlaki's website but is preserved at http://anwar-awlaki.blogspot.com/2011/10/fighting-against -government-armies-in.html.

193 "this is what Muslims should do, they should stand up to the aggressor" Retired Colonel Terry Lee, a former Fort Hood colleague of Hasan, interview, Fox News, November 5, 2009, http://video.foxnews.com/v/3944018/fight-against-the -aggressor/#sp-show-clips.

193 On November 4, he began to give away his food The details of Hasan's actions before the shootings come from reporting by me and my colleagues; see Scott Shane and James Dao, "Investigators Study Tangle of Clues on Fort Hood Suspect," *The New York Times*, November 14, 2009, http://www.nytimes .com/2009/11/15/us/15hasan.html.

194 "Nidal Hassan is a hero" Awlaki's blog entry "Nidal Hassan Did the Right Thing," http://www.anwar-alawlaki.com, November 9, 2009, http://cryptome.org/ anwar-alawlaki/09-1109.htm.

194 "When a drone is sent into afghanistan" Ibid., comment 21, posted by Abu Mubarak on November 9, 2009, http://cryptome.org/anwar-alawlaki/09-1109.htm.

195 Umar Farouk Abdulmutallab was making his own lethal plans Among the fullest accounts of Abdulmutallab's life are "Umar Farouk Abdulmutallab: One Boy's Journey to Jihad," Sunday *Times*, January 3, 2010; *Delta Christmas Detroit Attempt 25 Dec. 2009*, IntelCenter, Significant Terrorist Event Report, January 6, 2010, http://www.intelcenter.com/icf/STER-DCDA-25Dec2009-V2-8.pdf; and a useful timeline by NBC News, "Timeline: Umar Abdulmutallab," n.d., http:// www.nbcnews.com/id/34713877/ns/us_news-security/t/timeline-umar-abdul mutallab/.

195 Within a few weeks he had connected in Sanaa with a member of Awlaki's underground network "*USA v. Umar Farouk Abdulmutallab*, Government's Sentencing Memorandum," February 10, 2012, 12–14, posted at http://www .washingtonpost.com/wp-srv/world/documents/umar-farouk-abdul-mutallab -sentence-brief.pdf.

196 Abdulmutallab's prolific blog posts Abdulmutallab's writings on the Islamic

Forum at www.gawaher.com are accessible via a search on the site for his screen name "Farouk1986." Also see the links to various posts by Abdulmutallab and a zip file of all his posts here: Noah Shachtman, "Analyze This: The Mind of the Underpants Bomber," *Wired*, December 29, 2009, http://www.wired.com/2009/12/look-inside-the-underpants-bombers-mind/.

197 placed in the computer files, and then essentially ignored Senate Select Committee on Intelligence, *Unclassified Executive Summary of the Committee Report on the Attempted Terrorist Attack on Northwest Flight 253*, May 18, 2010, http://www.intelligence.senate.gov/100518/1225report.pdf.

10. I Face the World as It Is

198 "For those who seek to advance their aims by inducing terror" Obama's first inaugural address, *White House Blog*, January 21, 2009, http://www.whitehouse.gov/blog/inaugural-address.

198 "We intend to win this fight" Scott Shane, "Obama Orders Secret Prisons and Detention Camps Closed," *The New York Times*, January 22, 2009, http://www.nytimes.com/2009/01/23/us/politics/23GITMOCND.html.

199 Michael Hayden, the outgoing CIA chief, went over plans for the latest drone operations The briefing and its aftermath, including the exchange with Rahm Emanuel, were described by two former officials in confidential interviews, 2012 and 2014.

199 Obama would insist on deep personal involvement in the drone program See Jo Becker and Scott Shane, "Secret 'Kill List' Proves a Test of Obama's Principles and Will," *The New York Times*, May 29, 2012, http://www.nytimes.com/2012/05/29/world/obamas-leadership-in-war-on-al-qaeda.html.

200 civilians had been killed in both strikes The most detailed compilation of reports on drone strikes is by the Bureau of Investigative Journalism in London. Though its stories are often openly hostile to the drone program, the bureau has been scrupulous in attempting to fairly collect the full range of reports on each strike. On the strikes of Obama's first week, see the entries for January 23, 2009, at "Get the Data: Drone Wars," Bureau of Investigative Journalism, http://www.thebureauinvestigates.com/2011/08/10/obama-2009-strikes/. On the general difficulty of assessing civilian casualties accurately, see Scott Shane, "C.I.A. Is Disputed on Civilian Toll in Drone Strikes," *The New York Times*, August 11, 2011, and the sidebar, Scott Shane, "Contrasting Reports of Drone Strikes," http://www.nytimes.com/2011/08/12/world/asia/12droneside.html. For an account of those who believe that drones save civilian lives compared to other military approaches, see Scott Shane, "The Moral Case for Drones," *The New York Times*, July 14, 2012, http://www.nytimes.com/2012/07/15/sunday-review/the-moral-case-for-drones.html.

200 "He is determined that he will make these decisions" Tom Donilon, interview, 2012.

200 Eisenhower had suggested at a meeting George Lardner Jr., "Did Ike Authorize a Murder? Memo Says Eisenhower Wanted Congolese Premier Dead," *Washington Post*, August 8, 2000.

200 The CIA station chief would hurl the poisoned toothpaste Scott Shane,

"Memories of a C.I.A. Officer Resonate in a New Era," *The New York Times*, February 24, 2008.

201 **"Non-attribution to the United States for covert operations"** Senate Select Committee to Study Government Operation with Respect to Intelligence Activities, *Alleged Assassination Plots Involving Foreign Leaders*, Report No. 94-465 (Washington, DC: Government Printing Office, 1975), 11.

201 **"Assassination is an extreme measure"** Kate Doyle and Peter Kornbluh, eds., *CIA and Assassinations: The Guatemala 1954 Documents*, National Security Archive Electronic Briefing Book No. 4, document 2, "A Study of Assassination"; a legible transcription of the aging document is at http://www2.gwu.edu/~nsarchiv/NSAEBB/NSAEBB4/ciaguat2.html.

202 **Dick Cheney, who had brought his own sense of history** See Charlie Savage, *Takeover: The Return of the Imperial Presidency and the Subversion of American Democracy* (New York: Little, Brown, 2007), especially chaps. 2 and 3.

202 **Cheney had famously spoken about the need to work "sort of, the dark side"** Cheney speaking to Tim Russert on NBC's *Meet the Press*, September 16, 2001.

202 **When he gave the major national security speech of his early presidency** "Remarks by the President on National Security," delivered at the National Archives, May 21, 2009, White House, Briefing Room, http://www.whitehouse.gov/the_press_office/remarks-president-national-security-5-21-09

203 **"There was complete shock when the new team came in"** Senior counterterrorism official, confidential interview, 2014.

203 **a complex assault on the American embassy in September 2008** For a powerful and detailed account of the strike, see Gregory Johnsen, "The Benghazi That Wasn't: How One Man Saved the American Embassy in Yemen," BuzzFeed, May 23, 2014, http://www.buzzfeed.com/gregorydjohnsen/the-benghazi-that-wasnt-how-one-man-saved-the-american-embas. See also Robert F. Worth, "10 Are Killed in Bombings at Embassy in Yemen," *The New York Times*, September 17, 2008, http://www.nytimes.com/2008/09/18/world/middleeast/18yemen.html. The death toll later rose.

203 **as he received in succession in 2009 a number of senior Americans** The diplomatic cables released by WikiLeaks describe visits from American officials to Yemen: Kappes's visit, 09SANAA1015, May 31, 2009; Seche meeting, 09SANAA1278, July 20, 2009; Petraeus's July visit, 09SANAA1430, August 9, 2009; Brennan's visit, 09SANAA1549, September 15, 2009. All the cables are searchable at Cablegate: http://cablegatesearch.net/.

204 **Special Collection Service** See Scott Shane and Tom Bowman, "Espionage from the Front Lines," *Baltimore Sun*, December 8, 1995.

205 **NSA team studying Yemen's communications** "Yemen Survey," NSA's Texas Special Source Analysis and Discovery Team, August 20, 2009. Obtained by the author from a confidential source.

205 **General Petraeus pushed hard** An official who was present at meetings where the proposed strike was discussed, confidential interview, 2014.

205 **"It was case by case and trying to get some assurances"** General James Jones, interview, April 19, 2012.

206 On the night of December 17, 2009, Petraeus oversaw the strike The most complete account of the strike on Al Majala is in a Human Rights Watch report, *"Between a Drone and Al Qaeda": The Civilian Cost of US Targeted Killings in Yemen*, October 2013, 67–80, http://www.hrw.org/sites/default/files/reports/yemen1013_ForUpload_1.pdf; see also Amnesty International's report on the use of cluster bombs, "Images of Missile and Cluster Munitions Point to US Role in Fatal Attack in Yemen," June 7, 2010, https://www.amnesty.org/en/news-and-updates/yemen-images-missile-and-cluster-munitions-point-us-role-fatal-attack-2010-06-04, and Jeremy Scahill, *Dirty Wars: The World Is a Battlefield* (New York: Nation Books, 2013), 303–13.

206 Djibouti, twenty miles from Yemen across the slender Bab el Mandeb Strait, still would allow only surveillance Predators Two former American counterterrorism officials, interviews, 2014.

206 "We'd been wanting to do strikes forever" Former counterterrorism analyst, confidential interview, March 2014.

206 statement from Yemen's embassy Embassy of the Republic of Yemen, press release, December 17, 2009

206 Yemen announced that Obama had called to congratulate Saleh "Saleh Gets Telephone Call from US President Barrack [*sic*] Obama," Yemen News Agency, December 17, 2009, www.presidentsaleh.gov.ye/shownews.php?Ing=en&_nsid=7958.

206 *The New York Times* wrote that "American firepower" had been involved Thom Shanker and Mark Landler, "U.S. Aids Yemeni Raids on Al Qaeda, Officials Say," *The New York Times*, December 18, 2009, http://www.nytimes.com/2009/12/19/world/middleeast/19yemen.html.

206 ABC News broke the news that US cruise missiles had been used Brian Ross et al., "Obama Ordered U.S. Military Strike on Yemen Terrorists," ABC News, December 18, 2009, http://abcnews.go.com/Blotter/cruise-missiles-strike-yemen/story?id=9375236.

207 on January 2, 2010, Petraeus returned to Sanaa See 10SANAA4, January 4, 2010, at cablegatesearch.net.

207 Human Rights Watch report on Al Majala strike Human Rights Watch, *"Between a Drone and Al Qaeda,"* 67–80.

207 Kazami was dubbed "Objective Akron" Daniel Klaidman, *Kill or Capture: The War on Terror and the Soul of the Obama Presidency* (New York: Houghton Mifflin Harcourt, 2012), 199.

208 Saleh bin Fareed al-Awlaki Bin Fareed, interview, January 28, 2014, Aden.

208 stuffed with 166 yellow cylinders Human Rights Watch, *"Between a Drone and Al Qaeda,"* 72.

208 Convention on Cluster Munitions "The Convention on Cluster Munitions," entered into force August 1, 2010, http://www.clusterconvention.org/.

208 at least four curious children and adults Human Rights Watch, *"Between a Drone and Al Qaeda,"* 72–73.

209 Obama was presiding over a jury-rigged bureaucracy constructed to handle targeted killing Becker and Shane, "Secret 'Kill List.'"

210 Each Tuesday, Obama would descend from the Oval Office to the Situation Room The Tuesday terrorism meetings were described by several participants in confidential interviews in 2012 and 2014.

210 At one Tuesday meeting a few weeks after the underwear bomb episode The meeting was described in confidential interviews in 2012 by two people who had been present.

212 the CIA actually reduced the size of the explosive munition on the Hellfire missile Confidential interviews with one current official in 2012 and one former official in 2014.

212 On July 5, 2001, Secretary of State Colin Powell reiterated the American stance "Cool Reception for Sharon in Europe," BBC News online, July 5, 2001, http://news.bbc.co.uk/2/hi/middle_east/1424911.stm.

212 the State Department spokesman, Richard Boucher Briefing by Richard Boucher, August 27, 2001, US Department of State Archive, http://2001-2009.state .gov/p/nea/rt/4697.htm.

213 "the one thing we didn't anticipate was having to apologize for having won the Nobel Peace Prize" David Remnick, *The Bridge: The Life and Rise of Barack Obama* (New York: Alfred A. Knopf, 2010), 583.

213 Obama asked his speechwriters to dig up readings from Thomas Aquinas White House official, confidential interview, 2012.

213 "I cannot be guided by their examples alone" Barack Obama, "Nobel Lecture: A Just and Lasting Peace," December 10, 2009, http://www.nobelprize.org/ nobel_prizes/peace/laureates/2009/obama-lecture_en.html.

213 John Owen Brennan, whose Jesuit education at Fordham University See Karen DeYoung, "CIA Veteran John Brennan Has Transformed U.S. Counterterrorism Policy," *Washington Post*, October 24, 2012, http://www.washingtonpost .com/world/national-security/cia-veteran-john-brennan-has-transformed-us -counterterrorism-policy/2012/10/24/318b8eec-1c7c-11e2-ad90-ba5920e56eb3 _story.html. There is also a useful compilation of material on Brennan and a sample of his speeches at *The New York Times* Topics page: http://topics.nytimes.com/ top/reference/timestopics/people/b/john_o_brennan/index.html. My description of Obama's view of Brennan is based on multiple confidential interviews with administration officials, mostly in 2012.

214 Brennan won over many of his critics in the human rights world For example, when I called Elisa Massimino, president of Human Rights First, for a story about Brennan's nomination to become CIA director, she offered praise: "During his four years at the White House, he's been clear in backing up the president's insistence that we can't trade our values for security," she said, a remarkable tribute for a man associated closely with the drone campaign.

214 People like Harold Koh, the State Department's legal adviser Koh told me and Jo Becker in 2012, "If John Brennan is the last guy in the room with the president, I'm comfortable, because Brennan is a person of genuine moral rectitude. It's as though you had a priest with extremely strong moral values who was suddenly charged with leading a war." Becker and Shane, "Secret 'Kill List.'"

214 Another notable dissenter was Dennis Blair Two former intelligence officials, confidential interviews, 2012.

215 a swelling tally of foreign militants who had been "removed from the battlefield" See, for instance, Bill Roggio, "Senior al Qaeda and Taliban Leaders Killed in US Airstrikes in Pakistan, 2004–," *Long War Journal*, continuously updated page, http://www.longwarjournal.org/pakistan-strikes-hvts.php, accessed 2014.

215 an interview to a sympathetic Yemeni journalist, Abdulelah Haider Shaye SITE Intelligence Group translation dated February 3, 2010, of interview posted on Al Jazeera's Arabic website on February 2, 2010.

215 Shaye would later be imprisoned in Yemen for three years with the encouragement of the Obama administration Shaye's story is complex; he did some excellent journalistic work, but Yemeni and American officials claimed to have evidence that he had actively collaborated with AQAP. Some human rights activists considered Shaye's conviction in Yemen on terrorism-related charges in 2010 to be payback for his reporting on the Al Majala strike for Al Jazeera, though he was not the first to report the US role or the deaths of women and children there. On February 2, 2011, when a pardon for Shaye was under consideration, Obama spoke with Saleh to express his concern and the pardon was canceled. Shaye was released in July 2013 after serving three years of his five-year term. Six months later, Shaye damaged his reputation with supporters by praising an Al Qaeda attack on a Yemeni Defense Ministry hospital that killed at least fifty-six people, including doctors and nurses. For a sympathetic account of Shaye, see Jeremy Scahill, "Why Is President Obama Keeping a Journalist in Prison in Yemen?" *Nation*, March 13, 2012, http://www.thenation.com/article/166757/why-president-obama-keeping-journalist-prison-yemen.

216 Some civil libertarians argued that See, for instance, several columns for *Salon* by Glenn Greenwald, including "Criminalizing Free Speech," *Salon*, June 1, 2011, where Greenwald takes a different view of the *Brandenburg* case that I discuss below.

216 The Supreme Court's ruling in *Brandenburg v. Ohio* 395 U.S. 444, *Brandenburg v. Ohio* (No. 492), argued February 27, 1969, decided June 9, 1969, Cornell University Law School, Legal Information Institute, http://www.law.cornell.edu/supremecourt/text/395/444#ZO-395_US_444n2ref.

217 Awlaki began exchanging encrypted e-mails with a Bangladeshi man, Rajib Karim I retrieved the original excerpts of the e-mails released by Scotland Yard, but they were subsequently removed from the web. Excerpts with some minor changes in spelling were published on February 28, 2011, by the regional British newspaper the *Northern Echo*: "Excerpts from Rajib Karim Terror Plot Messages," February 28, 2011, http://www.thenorthernecho.co.uk/news/8880903.Excerpts_from_Rajib_Karim_terror_plot_messages/.

217 intercepts of Awlaki's private messages starting in early 2009 Former American intelligence analyst, confidential interview, 2014. A background information sheet on Awlaki given to some reporters when he was killed, and shared with the author, said that Awlaki "has sought to use WMD, specifically poisons including cyanide and ricin to attack Westerners."

218 complete a legal opinion on the legal and constitutional status of a presidential authorization to kill Awlaki This account of Barron and Lederman's work is based on confidential interviews with several government lawyers and counterterrorism officials who participated in discussions of the Awlaki opinion, 2014.

219 "When I saw that he had clearly given an order" Harold Koh, telephone interview, March 7, 2014.

219 On the morning of Friday, February 5, the president and his security cabinet met at the White House Leon Panetta with Jim Newton, *Worthy Fights: A Memoir of Leadership in War and Peace* (New York: Penguin, 2014), 266–67.

219 "If this had happened a year earlier in the administration" Michael Leiter, interview, February 12, 2014.

220 Obama praised the work of the CIA officers "President Obama and CIA Director Panetta Speak at CIA Memorial Service," White House, Briefing Room, February 5, 2010, http://www.whitehouse.gov/the-press-office/president-obama -and-cia-director-panetta-speak-cia-memorial-service.

220 Awlaki was assigned a code name picked from a map of Ohio Two counterterrorism officials described the naming process for the "objectives" on the military kill list in confidential interviews, 2014.

220 notable for a collection of houses made from welded steel See the National Register of Historic Places nomination form for the Hobart Welded Steel Houses, http://pdfhost.focus.nps.gov/docs/NRHP/Text/64000629.pdf.

221 Barron and Lederman's legal reasoning, which they laid out in writing in a memo dated February 19 I had first requested all Office of Legal Counsel opinions on targeted killing under the Freedom of Information Act in June of 2010. After a four-year legal battle by *The New York Times* and the American Civil Liberties Union, the Justice Department lost on appeal and released a heavily redacted copy of the February 19, 2010, legal opinion. The redacted memo can be viewed at Charlie Savage, "First Justice Department Memo on Killing Anwar Al-Awlaki," August 15, 2014, http://www.nytimes.com/interactive/2014/08/16/ us/16firstolcawlakimemo.html.

222 in a speech explaining the Justice Department's view, Attorney General Holder would say that adequate "due process" The text of Holder's speech at Northwestern University School of Law on March 5, 2012, can be found here: "Attorney General Eric Holder Speaks at Northwestern University School of Law, March 5, 2012," US Department of Justice, Briefing Room, http://www.justice .gov/opa/speech/attorney-general-eric-holder-speaks-northwestern-university -school-law.

222 Kevin Jon Heller, an American law professor teaching in London and Melbourne Kevin Jon Heller, "Let's Call Killing al-Awlaki What It Is—Murder," *Opinio Juris* (blog), April 8, 2010, http://opiniojuris.org/2010/04/08/lets-call -killing-al-awlaki-what-it-is-murder/.

223 they set out to write a second opinion, completed on July 16 The second Barron-Lederman memo, dated July 16, 2010, was released in redacted form in

2014 after a federal appeals court ruled in favor of *The New York Times* and the American Civil Liberties Union. The ruling, including the text of the second Awlaki opinion, is usefully annotated by Charlie Savage at "Justice Department Memo Approving Targeted Killing of Anwar Al-Awlaki," *The New York Times*, June 23, 2014, http://www.nytimes.com/interactive/2014/06/23/us/23awlaki -memo.html.

223 "In reaching this conclusion," Barron and Lederman wrote in the forty-one-page July memo Savage, "First Justice Department Memo," 19.

224 "This," Obama told aides of the decision to target Awlaki Two former government officials, confidential interviews, 2012.

225 an informal online survey of his colleagues Professor Mark Kende posted the question on a closed Internet mailing list for professors of constitutional law, conlawprof (http://lists.ucla.edu/cgi-bin/mailman/listinfo/conlawprof). He kindly compiled the results and shared them with me.

225 "I taught constitutional law for ten years" CQ Transcriptions, "Senator Barack Obama Delivers Remarks at a Campaign Event," Lancaster, Pennsylvania, March 31, 2008, retrieved via Nexis.com.

226 "My view was Anwar al-Awlaki was actively plotting to kill American citizens" Ambassador Gerald Feierstein, interview, October 21, 2013.

226 called "dirty hands" Stephen de Wijze, "Targeted Killing: A 'Dirty Hands' Analysis," *Contemporary Politics* 15, no. 3 (2009). The original essay examining this concept and borrowing the name from Sartre was Michael Walzer, "Political Action: The Problem of Dirty Hands," *Philosophy and Public Affairs* 2, no. 2 (1973): 160–80, https://www.sss.ias.edu/files/pdfs/Walzer/Political-action.pdf.

226 "the least evil choice available in the circumstances" Ben Jones and John M. Parrish, "Drones and Dirty Hands," paper presented at the annual meeting of the Western Political Science Association, April 2014, Seattle, WA, http://wpsa .research.pdx.edu/papers/docs/ben%20jones.pdf, which takes issue with the characterization of targeted killing as a "dirty hands" dilemma.

226 who had vowed on taking office to run the most transparent administration in history Obama had promised on his first full day in office that "my Administration is committed to creating an unprecedented level of openness in Government." See "Transparency and Open Government," Memorandum for the Heads of Executive Departments and Agencies, January 21, 2009, http://www.whitehouse.gov/ the_press_office/TransparencyandOpenGovernment. By 2014, most references to the policy found via Google were sarcastic.

227 There would be three more American strikes in Yemen See Scott Shane, Mark Mazzetti, and Robert F. Worth, "Secret Assault on Terrorism Widens on Two Continents," *The New York Times*, August 14, 2010, http://www.nytimes .com/2010/08/15/world/15shadowwar.html.

228 American intelligence picked up a walkie-talkie signal believed to be associated with Awlaki Two former counterterrorism officials, confidential interviews, 2014. Other examples of the hazard of relying on the signatures of cell phones and other electronic devices for targeting strikes are discussed in Jeremy Scahill and

Glenn Greenwald, "The NSA's Secret Role in the U.S. Assassination Program," *Intercept*, February 10, 2014, https://firstlook.org/theintercept/2014/02/10/the -nsas-secret-role/.

228 He complained sharply to the man some described as the president's favorite general, General James "Hoss" Cartwright Senior Obama administration official, confidential interview, 2014.

229 "His father made several attempts to persuade him to stop talking about jihad" Morten Storm, telephone interview, August 31, 2014.

229 on July 16 the Treasury Department formally labeled Anwar al-Awlaki as a "Specially Designated Global Terrorist" Treasury Department, "Treasury Designates Anwar Al-Aulaqi, Key Leader of Al-Qa'ida in the Arabian Peninsula," press release, July 16, 2010, http://www.treasury.gov/press-center/press-releases/ Pages/tg779.aspx.

229 The ACLU lawyers believed See Case 1:10-cv-01303-JDB, *AMERICAN CIVIL LIBERTIES UNION et al. v. GEITHNER et al.*, US District Court for the District of Columbia.

229 Nasser al-Awlaki filed suit Case 1:10-cv-01469-JDB, *AL-AULAQI v. OBAMA et al.*, US District Court for the District of Columbia. All documents, including a full transcript of the November 8, 2010, hearing before Judge Bates, are available on the Pacer electronic records system.

230 A Canadian from a Muslim immigrant family For more on Jameel Jaffer, see Michelle Shephard, "How a Lawyer from Canada Became a Leading Critic of U.S. National Security Policies," *Toronto Star*, January 15, 2013, http://www.thestar .com/news/world/2013/01/15/how_a_lawyer_from_canada_became_a_leading _critic_of_us_national_security_policies.html.

232 *The New York Times* management decided in 2007 Michael Calderone, "Times Withdraws from Chummy Galas, Leaving Rove Dateless," *New York Observer*, May 2, 2007, http://observer.com/2007/05/itimesi-withdraws-from -chummy-galas-leaving-rove-dateless/.

232 "Sasha and Malia are huge fans" *Remarks by the President at the White House Correspondents Association Dinner*, video, May 1, 2011, White House, http://www .whitehouse.gov/photos-and-video/video/president-obama-and-jay-leno-white -house-correspondents-dinner#transcript.

232 the CIA had carried out more than eighty drone strikes in Pakistan Several organizations compiled data on press reports of strikes in Pakistan, and though counts of civilian casualties varied, they were invariably higher than those American officials offered on background. Among the counts were those by the Bureau of Investigative Journalism in London, "Get the Data: Drone Wars," http://www .thebureauinvestigates.com/category/projects/drones/drones-graphs/; the New American Foundation, "Drone Wars, Pakistan: Analysis," http://securitydata .newamerica.net/drones/pakistan/analysis; and *Long War Journal*, "Charting the Data for US Airstrikes in Pakistan, 2004–," http://www.longwarjournal.org/ pakistan-strikes.php.

233 Faisal Shahzad Scott Shane and Mark Mazzetti, "Times Sq. Bomb Suspect

Is Linked to Militant Cleric," *The New York Times*, May 6, 2010, http://www
.nytimes.com/2010/05/07/world/middleeast/07awlaki-.html; also see Richard
Esposito, Chris Vlasto, and Chris Cuomo, "Sources: Shahzad Had Contact with
Awlaki, Taliban Chief, and Mumbai Massacre Mastermind," ABC News, May 6,
2010, and Alexander Melagrou-Hitchens, "Anwar al-Awlaqi's Disciples: Three
Case Studies," Combating Terrorism Center at West Point, post, July 1, 2011,
https://www.ctc.usma.edu/posts/anwar-al-awlaqi's-disciples-three-case-studies.

233 which he had believed would kill at least forty people "Government's Memorandum in Connection with the Sentencing of Faisal Shahzad," filed September 29, 2010, in *US v. Faisal Shahzad*, Case 1:10-cr-00541 in the US District
Court for the Southern District of New York.

**233 "When I watched Anwar Awlaki on video, I thought he was talking to
me"** John Miller, "Inside the Plans of Capitol Bomb Suspect," CBS News, February 18, 2012, http://www.cbsnews.com/news/inside-the-plans-of-capitol-bomb
-suspect/. Miller, a former FBI official, worked in the office of the Director of
National Intelligence at the time of the Times Square bombing attempt.

11. The Guy Everyone Wanted to Find

237 "He'd go five times a day to the mosque" Saleh bin Fareed, interview, January 28, 2014, Aden.

**238 On March 1, 2009, in a telephone address to an Islamic gathering in Pak-
istan** The audio of Awlaki's talk to the Pakistanis, often under the title "State of
the Ummah," is available on YouTube, for instance at https://www.youtube.com/
watch?v=itXhos7yEhc.

239 the initial contacts may have dated back as far as 2006 Morten Storm, *Agent
Storm: My Life Inside Al Qaeda and the CIA* (New York: Atlantic Monthly Press,
2014), 102–3.

239 "He came from a rich family," Storm said Morten Storm, telephone interview, August 31, 2014.

239 He had even installed a television in his apartment in Al Ataq This and
some other details on Awlaki's relationship with his first two wives are from Storm,
Agent Storm, 148–51, and Morten Storm, telephone interview, August 31, 2014.

**239 "He sent me a message—he said, 'Father, consider my family is your imme-
diate family'"** Nasser al-Awlaki, video interview by Medea Benjamin, June 2013,
Sanaa.

240 Anwar "really wanted his family to live under normal conditions" Nasser
al-Awlaki, written answers to questions sent by the author, January 2014.

**240 he mentioned to Morten Storm the possibility of helping him find yet an-
other wife** Storm, *Agent Storm*, 151.

240 By August 1, 2009, Awlaki was publicly taking the side of AQAP Awlaki's
blog entry "The Army of Yemen Confronts the Mujahideen," http://www.anwar
-alawlaki.com, August 1, 2009, archived at Cryptome.org: http://cryptome.org/
anwar-alawlaki/09-0801.htm.

**241 he had approved the eager appeal of Umar Farouk Abdulmutallab to join the
jihad** "*USA v. Umar Farouk Abdulmutallab*," Case: 2-10 cr. 20005 in the Eastern

District of Michigan, Government's Sentencing Memorandum," February 10, 2012, posted at http://www.washingtonpost.com/wp-srv/world/documents/umar -farouk-abdul-mutallab-sentence-brief.pdf, 13. Some commentators have understandably been confused by the seeming overlap between Awlaki and the person Abdulmutallab described as "Abu Tarak" in his initial FBI interview. According to an American official familiar with the thinking of FBI agents and prosecutors, Abdulmutallab later acknowledged that "Abu Tarak" did not exist but was a sort of composite of Awlaki and others who had helped him. An AQAP video released in late 2014 suggested that Qaid al-Dhahab, an Al Qaeda operative whose sister was Awlaki's second wife, had met Abdulmutallab in Sanaa and may have connected him with Awlaki. (See: Site Intelligence Group, "AQAP Releases First Part in Video Documentary on Dhahab Brothers," December 26, 2014, https://news.site intelgroup.com/Jihadist-News/aqap-releases-first-part-in-video-documentary -on-dhahab-brothers.html. This video includes previously unreleased footage of Awlaki with Abdulmutallab and Nasser al-Wuhayshi, the leader of AQAP, underscoring Awlaki's role in both the airliner plot and the Al Qaeda branch.) The point is that "Abu Tarak" was not a pseudonym for Awlaki and that not everything Abdulmutallab said about the made-up character was true of Awlaki. For instance, Abdulmutallab said "Abu Tarak" lived in Sanaa in 2009, while Awlaki lived in Shabwah. Because of an agreement with the defense that prosecutors would not use Abdulmutallab's later FBI interviews in his trial, the lead prosecutor, Jonathan Tukel, used only the statements about "Abu Tarak" in his opening statement at trial. Later, after Abdulmutallab pleaded guilty, the judge permitted prosecutors to use Abdulmutallab's later statements about Awlaki in their sentencing memorandum (Justice Department official, confidential telephone interview, 2014).

241 Awlaki had formed a small "external operations" cell This notion was proposed by the Norwegian terrorism expert Thomas Hegghammer in an e-mail to a State Department official in November 2010 that Hegghammer provided to the author. In the e-mail, Hegghammer wrote: "My working hypothesis is that Awlaki, Khan and Asiri are core members of a cell that specializes in international ops and that keeps mostly to itself (though not necessarily in a single location). They need assistants, but not too many (for security reasons), hence the 5–20 estimate." Analysts at the CIA and other agencies had reached basically the same conclusion by late 2009, in part on the basis of intercepted Al Qaeda communications (multiple government officials, confidential interviews, 2013 and 2014). As explained later in this chapter, the US intelligence identification of Awlaki as head of AQAP's "external operations"—those directed at the United States and other targets outside Yemen—appeared to be corroborated by an essay entitled "The Objectives of Operation Hemorrhage" in a special issue of *Inspire* (November 2010) that was almost certainly by Awlaki and whose author was identified as "The Head of Foreign Operations."

241 Asiri fitted his own brother, Abdullah, with a bomb that he could wear either inside or very close to his body Many news accounts suggested that the bomb fit inside Abdullah al-Asiri's rectum, but the terrorism expert Peter Bergen reported that Saudi investigators concluded that it was actually hidden in his underwear.

Peter Bergen, "Saudi Investigation: Would-Be Assassin Hid Bomb in Underwear," CNN, September 30, 2009, http://www.cnn.com/2009/WORLD/meast/09/30/saudi.arabia.attack/index.html.

242 On September 8, the administrator of his website posted the transcript This and some other later posts on Awlaki's blog are archived in a single page at cryptome.org, a snapshot of Google's cache of http://www.anwar-awlaki.com/?feed=rss2 as it appeared on November 9, 2009: http://cryptome.org/anwar-al awlaki/09-1109-2.htm.

242 On September 20, Awlaki's blog wished his readers Eid Mubarak Ibid.

242 On October 7, Awlaki himself reappeared on the blog This post, "Could Yemen Be the Next Surprise of the Season?" is missing from the archive at cryptome.org but is preserved in several other places, including here: http://azelin .files.wordpress.com/2010/08/anwar-al-awlaki-could-yemen-be-the-next -surprise-of-the-season.pdf.

243 he was spotting and hearing the Predators cruising over his tribal territory Saleh bin Fareed al-Awlaki, interview, January 28, 2014, Aden.

243 So he decided to leave Al Saeed for more remote hideouts in the Al-Kur Mountains Nasser al-Awlaki, interview, February 1, 2014, Sanaa.

243 some of Awlaki's followers began a debate in comments posted on his website See comments at the bottom of the post "Response to Abdullaah bin Abdur-Rahmaan al-Jarboo," October 11, 2009, http://www.anwar-alawlaki.com, archived at http://cryptome.org/anwar-alawlaki/09-1011.htm.

243 On November 9 he weighed in with what would be his last and most infamous post "Nidal Hassan Did the Right Thing," http://www.anwar-alawlaki .com, archived at http://cryptome.org/anwar-alawlaki/09-1109.htm.

244 "a heartless beast, bent on evil, who sells his religion for a few dollars" Blog entry by Awlaki, "Fighting Against Government Armies in the Muslim World," http://www.anwar-alawlaki.com, July 14, 2009. This is missing from the Cryptome archive on Awlaki's website but is preserved at http://anwar-awlaki.blogspot .com/2011/10/fighting-against-government-armies-in.html.

244 He posted a lengthy disclaimer on the site distancing himself from Awlaki's views See http://cryptome.org/anwar-alawlaki/anwar-alawlaki.htm.

244 he was back the next day with a chipper promise "Website Coming Back Online," http://www.anwar-alawlaki.com, November 11, 2009, archived at http://cryptome.org/anwar-alawlaki/09-1111.htm.

244 In early December, he helped arrange the filming of Abdulmutallab's martyrdom video "USA v. Umar Farouk Abdulmutallab, Government's Sentencing Memorandum," February 10, 2012, posted at http://www.washingtonpost.com/wp-srv/world/documents/umar-farouk-abdul-mutallab-sentence-brief.pdf, 14.

244 "The Americans just scored a big own goal," Awlaki wrote to Morten Storm Storm, *Agent Storm*, 190. While Storm preserved many of his exchanges with Awlaki, this message is from his recollection.

245 The Yemeni embassy in Washington put out a statement Statement from the Embassy of the Republic of Yemen, December 24, 2009.

245 "But there was a prominent Awlaki exception," said one analyst then assigned to Yemen Former US intelligence analyst, confidential interview, 2014.

247 "We were pretty good at knowing where he was yesterday" American official, confidential interview, 2013.

247 Morten Storm, who had become disillusioned with militant Islam Storm, *Agent Storm*, 182–84.

247 it took cryptographers nine months to decipher three hundred messages London Metropolitan Police Service, statement, February 28, 2011.

247 Karim had used encrypted Word documents that were digitally compressed Paul Cruickshank, "Did NSA Leaks Help al Qaeda?," CNN, June 25, 2013, http://security.blogs.cnn.com/2013/06/25/did-nsa-leaks-help-al-qaeda/.

247 the first issue of a breathtakingly brazen, English-language AQAP https://archive.org/stream/inspr1to10/Inspire_1. All of the issues of *Inspire* are available at the Internet Archive, archive.org.

248 British intelligence attempted a clumsy dirty trick Paisley Dodds, "British Spies to Terrorists: Make Cupcakes Not War," Associated Press, June 3, 2011; Duncan Gardham, "MI6 Attacks al-Qaeda in 'Operation Cupcake,'" June 2, 2011, *Telegraph*, http://www.telegraph.co.uk/news/uknews/terrorism-in-the-uk/8553366/MI6-attacks-al-Qaeda-in-Operation-Cupcake.html.

248 "It was Awlaki's baby" American official, confidential interview, 2013.

248 for anyone who had followed the unlikely career of Samir Khan See Michael Moss and Souad Mekhennet, "An Internet Jihad Aims at U.S. Viewers," *The New York Times*, October 15, 2007, http://www.nytimes.com/2007/10/15/us/15net.html, and the accompanying video; and J. M. Berger, *Jihad Joe: Americans Who Go to War in the Name of Islam* (Washington, DC: Potomac Books, 2011), 190–92. *Jihad Recollections* magazine is available at https://archive.org/details/EnglishJihadMagazine1stEdition.

249 NSA found a way to intercept the copies before they went online Two former counterterrorism officials, confidential interviews, 2014.

249 "*Inspire* magazine really rattled the people inside the government" Will McCants, interview, February 18, 2014.

250 A number of scholars, in fact, consistently argued that Western journalists were exaggerating See, for instance, Gregory Johnsen's essay in *The New York Times* on November 19, 2011: "A False Target in Yemen," http://www.nytimes.com/2010/11/20/opinion/20johnsen.html., as well as Thomas Hegghammer's reply in *Foreign Policy* four days later: "The Case for Chasing al-Awlaki," http://foreignpolicy.com/2010/11/24/the-case-for-chasing-al-awlaki/.

250 When Wuhayshi, the AQAP leader, proposed in a letter to Bin Laden *Letters from Abbottabad: Bin Laden Sidelined?* (West Point, NY: Combating Terrorism Center at West Point, May 2012), 19.

251 Awlaki's personal contribution to the very first issue of *Inspire* Shaykh Anwar al-Awlaki, "May Our Souls Be Sacrificed for You!," *Inspire*, no. 1 (January 2010): 26–28.

252 she drew a satiric poster designating May 20 as "Everybody Draw Moham-

med Day" The poster is preserved on Wikipedia: http://en.wikipedia.org/wiki/ File:Everybody_Draw_Mohammed_Day.jpg.

252 "I wasn't savvy," Norris told *City Arts* **magazine** Patrick Oppmann, "FBI Warns Seattle Cartoonist About Threats from Radical Cleric," CNN, July 14, 2010.

253 Obama "was very focused on him" Ben Rhodes, interview, October 15, 2014.

254 Storm, who recounts the yarn in his 2014 memoir *Agent Storm* Storm, *Agent Storm*, 195–221.

256 She showed the stolen ID of a student at Sanaa University Mark Mazzetti, Robert F. Worth and Eric Lipton, "Bomb Plot Shows Key Role Played by Intelligence," *The New York Times*, October 31, 2010, http://www.nytimes .com/2010/11/01/world/01terror.html.

256 a Saudi militant with an intriguing history, Jaber al- Faifi "Wanted Terror Suspect Surrenders," *Saudi Gazette*, October 16, 2010, http://www.saudigazette .com.sa/index.cfm?method=home.PrintContent&action=Print&contentID= 0000000085421; "Second Terror Surrender Announcement Soon," *Saudi Gazette*, October 18, 2010, http://www.saudigazette.com.sa/index.cfm?method=home .regcon&contentID=2010101885580; and Hamza Hendawi and Ahmed Al-Haj, "Yemen: Al-Qaeda Insider Told Saudis of Bomb Plot," Associated Press, November 1, 2010.

257 John Brennan visited the president in the White House family quarters at 10:35 p.m. Press Briefing by Press Secretary Robert Gibbs and Assistant to the President for Homeland Security and Counterterrorism John Brennan, October 29, 2010, White House, Briefing Room, http://www.whitehouse.gov/the-press -office/2010/10/29/press-briefing-press-secretary-robert-gibbs-and-assistant s-president-home.

257 "There was a five-alarm fire in the middle of the night" Ben Rhodes, interview, October 27, 2013.

258 The names of the addressees were notorious anti-Muslim figures Mark Mazzetti and Scott Shane, "In Parcel Bomb Plot, 2 Dark Inside Jokes," *The New York Times*, November 2, 2010, http://www.nytimes.com/2010/11/03/ world/03terror.html.

258 "It was just a further indication that AQAP was very committed to homeland plotting" Ben Rhodes, interview, October 15, 2014.

259 Obama appeared in the press room for just four minutes Statement by the President, October 29, 2010, White House, Briefing Room, http://www.white house.gov/the-press-office/2010/10/29/statement-president.

259 Gerald Feierstein, the US ambassador to Yemen, said in an interview with Al Arabiya "Yemeni Radical Cleric Behind Parcel Bombs: U.S. Ambassador," Xinhua, November 26, 2010.

259 With hindsight, the Americans realized that several packages containing books, CDs, and other items Scott Shane and Robert F. Worth, "Earlier Flight May Have Been Dry Run for Plotters," *The New York Times*, November 1, 2010, http://www.nytimes.com/2010/11/02/world/02terror.html.

260 AQAP later claimed it had been responsible for the destruction of an earlier

UPS flight *Inspire*, no. 3 (November 2010): 4. Two detailed reports on the accident are Federal Aviation Administration, "Freighter Airplane Cargo Fire Risk Model," September 2011, http://www.fire.tc.faa.gov/pdf/11-18.pdf; and General Civil Aviation Authority of the United Arab Emirates, "Air Accident Investigation Interim Report," Accident Reference: 13-2010, Dubai, United Arab Emirates, Boeing 747-44AF, September 3, 2010.

260 The root of the word, the Latin verb *terrere*, means "to cause to tremble" Douglas Kellner, entry for "Terrorism," *Blackwell Encyclopedia of Sociology Online*.

261 "Letter from the Editor," presumably written by Samir Khan *Inspire*, no. 3 (November 2010): 3.

261 in the same *Inspire* issue, the unnamed "Head of Foreign Operations" elaborated *Inspire*, no. 3 (November 2010): 7.

261 his lengthy discussion on his blog in 2008 of his reading of *Great Expectations* "Book Review 9: English Novels," http://www.anwar-alawlaki.com, August 6, 2008, http://cryptome.org/anwar-alawlaki/08-0806.htm.

262 In October 2009, when Yemeni authorities sought the help of American intelligence David Ignatius, "For Lack of Hard Evidence, a Terrorist Evaded Capture," *Washington Post*, March 26, 2010, http://www.washingtonpost.com/wp-dyn/content/article/2010/03/25/AR2010032503634.html.

262 "Anwar al-Awlaki has to us been always looked at as a preacher" Dale Gavlak, "Yemen Not Going After Radical US-Born Cleric," Associated Press, April 10, 2010.

262 Yemeni prosecutors brought a terrorism case accusing Awlaki Mazzetti and Shane, "In Parcel Bomb Plot."

262 The State Department spokesman, Philip J. Crowley, offered a curt public nod Assistant Secretary Philip J. Crowley, Daily Press Briefing, November 2, 2010, US State Department, http://m.state.gov/md150291.htm.

263 "It was an option and it was extensively discussed" Senior American official, confidential interview, 2013.

12. The Time for Reaping

265 Ammar al-Awlaki was at the end of a long day Ammar al-Awlaki, interview, January 25, 2014, Sanaa.

267 "I actually consider Al Qaeda in the Arabian Peninsula" Michael Leiter, testimony to the House Homeland Security Committee, February 9, 2011, *Understanding the Homeland Threat Landscape: Considerations for the 112th Congress*, http://www.gpo.gov/fdsys/pkg/CHRG-112hhrg72212/pdf/CHRG-112hhrg72212.pdf, page 26.

267 American officials offered money privately but did not publicize the reward To the surprise of many people following the hunt for Awlaki, no reward appeared on the Rewards for Justice website, http://www.rewardsforjustice.net/, operated by the State Department to attract tips on tracking down wanted terrorists. Nor did the FBI add Awlaki to its "Most Wanted Terrorists" list, http://www.fbi.gov/wanted/wanted_terrorists. This was not unprecedented, and in a traditional, tribal society like Yemen, publicizing a reward might have generated a backlash that could intimidate tipsters. CIA officers, however, spoke of a $5 million reward to Morten Storm, Ammar al-Awlaki, and others.

268 one person centrally involved in directing the search replied, "Everything, right?" Senior American official, confidential interview, 2014.

268 the State Department weighed in with its own modest contribution State Department cable to US embassy in Sanaa, March 24, 2011; the cable was obtained by Judicial Watch in response to a Freedom of Information Act request and can be seen at Politico, http://images.politico.com/global/2012/11/28/binder1.html.

268 tribal chant that declared, "We are the sparks of hell" Patrick Cockburn, "Threats to Yemen Prove America Hasn't Learned the Lesson of History," *The Independent,* December 31, 2009, http://www.independent.co.uk/voices/commentators /patrick-cockburn-threats-to-yemen-prove-america-hasnt-learned-the-lesson-of -history-1853847.html.

269 "Even in the Awlaki clan Anwar was controversial" American official who worked on Yemen policy, confidential interview, 2013.

269 In an interview with the pan-Arab newspaper *Asharq Al-Awsat* "Q & A with Shabwa Governor Ali Hasan al-Ahmadi," interview by Abdulsattar Hatitah, *Asharq Al-Awsat,* December 1, 2010, http://www.aawsat.net/2010/01/article5525 2195.

269 Abdullah al-Jumaili, a tribal sheikh in Al Jawf Abdullah al-Jumaili, interview, January 28, 2014, Sanaa.

269 In his interview with Al Malahem, AQAP's media arm SITE Intelligence Group, "AQAP Releases Interview with Anwar al-Awlaki," May 23, 2010, https:// news.siteintelgroup.com/Multimedia/awlaki52310.html.

270 He wore the *jambiya* in a lengthy video message in November 2010 SITE Intelligence Group, "Awlaki Urges Support of Mujahideen, Killing of Americans," November 8, 2010, https://news.siteintelgroup.com/Multimedia/awlaki-urges -support-of-mujahideen-killing-of-americans.html.

270 the nerdish American sought to project a more martial image A Google image search for "Awlaki" turns up a selection of portraits, including those in which he is wearing a *jambiya*, holding a ceremonial dagger, or holding a weapon.

271 "I remember hearing—he's in Shabwah" American counterterrorism official, confidential interview, 2014.

272 President Obama caught the bracing promise "Remarks by the President on Egypt," February 11, 2011, White House, Briefing Room, http://www.whitehouse .gov/the-press-office/2011/02/11/remarks-president-egypt.

272 I called a range of experts All the remarks that follow are from my article on expert views of the Arab Spring and Al Qaeda at *The New York Times,* "Al Qaeda Finds Itself at a Crossroads," http://www.nytimes.com/2011/02/28/world/ middleeast/28qaeda.html.

273 One in five Americans clung to the false belief that he was Muslim Jon Cohen and Michael D. Shear, "Poll Shows More Americans Think Obama Is a Muslim," *Washington Post,* August 19, 2010, http://www.washingtonpost.com/ wp-dyn/content/article/2010/08/18/AR2010081806913.html.

273 **he dispatched one of his closest aides, Denis McDonough** "Remarks of Denis McDonough Deputy National Security Advisor to the President, ADAMS Center, Sterling, Virginia," March 6, 2011, White House, Briefing Room, http://www.whitehouse.gov/the-press-office/2011/03/06/remarks-denis-mcdonough-deputy-national-security-advisor-president-prepa.

274 **The cover story was Awlaki's four-page piece called "The Tsunami of Change"** *Inspire*, no. 5 (March 2011): 50–53, https://ia801603.us.archive.org/6/items/inspr1to10/Inspire_5.pdf.

275 **On Change Square, in front of Sanaa University** A Yemeni account is Samar Al-Ariqi, "How Change Square Became the Birthplace of an Uprising," *Yemen Times*, February 11, 2014, http://www.yementimes.com/en/1754/report/3465/How-Change-Square-became-the-birthplace-of-an-uprising.htm.

275 **The median age in Yemen was an astonishing 18.6 years** Yemen Demographics Profile 2014, Index Mundi, Factbook, http://www.indexmundi.com/yemen/demographics_profile.html; the US median is at "United States Median Age," Index Mundi, Factbook, http://www.indexmundi.com/united_states/median_age.html.

276 **Abdulrahman, who had been born in Denver and moved to Yemen with his family at age six, posted with enthusiasm on Facebook** I viewed Abdulrahman's Facebook page at https://www.facebook.com/abdulrahman.alawlaki multiple times in 2013 and 2014, but it was taken down by early 2015. This account is also based on interviews with several family members and friends of the teenager.

276 **On March 18, government snipers opened fire from the rooftops** Laura Kasinof and Robert F. Worth, "Dozens Are Killed in Yemen, but Protesters Stand Ground," *The New York Times*, March 19, 2011; the total of reported deaths rose as severely wounded demonstrators died. For a gripping personal account of the sniper attack and Yemen's Arab Spring, see Laura Kasinof, *Don't Be Afraid of the Bullets: An Accidental War Correspondent in Yemen* (New York: Arcade, 2014).

277 **A story that Anwar al-Awlaki's uncle, Saleh bin Fareed** Saleh Bin Fareed al-Awlaki, interview, January 28, 2014, Aden.

279 **American commandos captured a fishing boat shuttling a Somali named Ahmed Abdulkadir Warsame** Charlie Savage, "U.S. Tests New Approach to Terrorism Cases on Somali Suspect," *The New York Times*, July 6, 2011, http://www.nytimes.com/2011/07/07/world/africa/07detain.html.

280 **The methods paid off with Warsame, who turned out to have inside knowledge** Benjamin Weiser, "Terrorist Has Cooperated with U.S. Since Secret Guilty Plea in 2011, Papers Show," *The New York Times*, March 25, 2013, http://www.nytimes.com/2013/03/26/nyregion/since-2011-guilty-plea-somali-terrorist-has-cooperated-with-authorities.html.

280 **Obama returned as scheduled to the annual White House Correspondents' Association Dinner** "Remarks by the President at the White House Correspondents Association Dinner," posted May 1, 2011, White House, Briefing Room, http://www.whitehouse.gov/the-press-office/2011/05/01/remarks-president-white-house-correspondents-association-dinner.

280 **the president strode along the red carpet in the East Room to the podium**

"Remarks by the President on Osama Bin Laden," posted May 2, 2011, White House, Briefing Room, http://www.whitehouse.gov/the-press-office/2011/05/02/remarks-president-osama-bin-laden.

281 A New York Times-CBS poll that morning had reported a bump in Obama's approval rating James Dao and Dalia Sussman, "For Obama, Big Rise in Poll Numbers After Bin Laden Raid," *The New York Times*, May 4, 2011, http://www.nytimes.com/2011/05/05/us/politics/05poll.html.

281 JSOC put together an extraordinarily complex array of equipment to catch him on the road This account of the May 5 strike is based on confidential interviews with three counterterrorism officials in 2014. See Mark Mazzetti, "Drone Strike in Yemen Was Aimed at Awlaki," *The New York Times*, May 6, 2011, http://www.nytimes.com/2011/05/07/world/middleeast/07yemen.html, and Martha Raddatz, "U.S. Missiles Missed Awlaki by Inches in Yemen," ABC News, July 19, 2011, http://abcnews.go.com/Blotter/us-missed-awlaki-inches-yemen/story?id=s14108686.

282 the performance of laser-guided missiles like the Hellfire and the Griffin against fast-moving targets was not impressive Former American drone pilot, confidential interview, 2014.

282 Harith al-Nadari, who later recounted the episode in *Inspire* magazine Shaykh Harith Al Nadari, "My Story with Al Awlaki," *Inspire* no. 9 (May 2012): 9–13; the issue can be downloaded from Public Intelligence, https://publicintelligence.net/inspire-al-qaeda-in-the-arabian-peninsula-magazine-issues-8-and-9-may-2012/.

283 "What can you do with me?" Awlaki quoted Ibn Taymiyyah as saying The passage from the early lecture is at 10:28 in a memorial video posted on YouTube: *[New] Tribute to Imam Anwar Al Awlaki (RA)*, March 29, 2012, https://www.youtube.com/watch?v=OQXFd3NXsoI.

283 "Martyrdom is like a tree" Awlaki's remarks about martyrdom are included at 11:30 in the memorial video. Ibid.

284 Mohamed Elibiary, a young Muslim activist in Texas whom I had consulted Mohamed Elibiary, "It's a Mistake to Assassinate Anwar al-Awlaki," FoxNews.com, April 16, 2010, http://www.foxnews.com/opinion/2010/04/16/mohamed-elibiary-alawlaki-assassinate-muslims-war-terror-nsc/.

285 "I think throughout there was a feeling that the CTC guys were much better" Former counterterrorism official, confidential interview, 2014.

286 the Saudis had insisted that the United States keep secret the location of the new base *The New York Times* and other news organizations initially agreed on a deadline to the Obama administration's request that the location of the base in Saudi Arabia not be revealed; officials said that Saudi Arabia might stop letting the Americans use it if the country was named in the media. Instead, we used the formula "on the Arabian Peninsula." Later, finding that the Saudi location was mentioned in several reports on the web, *Times* editors decided to reverse course and we began reporting the location. See the discussion by Margaret Sullivan, the *Times*'s public editor: "The *Times* Was Right to Report—at Last—on

a Secret Drone Base," February 6, 2013, http://publiceditor.blogs.nytimes
.com/2013/02/06/the-times-was-right-to-report-at-last-on-a-secret-drone-base/.

**287 Abdulrahman rose in his grandfather's big house in the capital and scrib-
bled an apologetic note** Nasser al-Awlaki, interview by Medea Benjamin of Code
Pink, June 2013, Sanaa.

288 In rare public remarks in July, Admiral Eric T. Olson Video of Olson's
remarks at the Aspen Security Forum on July 29, 2011, is posted on YouTube:
ASF2011: In Conversation with Admiral Eric Olson, https://www.youtube.com/
watch?vz=rd0CNWfI-8c.

**288 Morten Storm, the Danish former jihadi who had delivered bugged equip-
ment to AQAP** Morten Storm with Paul Cruickshank and Tim Lister, *Agent
Storm: My Life Inside Al Qaeda and the CIA* (New York: Atlantic Monthly Press,
2014), 258.

289 The CIA got word in the second week of September 2011 An NSA budget
document released by the former NSA contractor Edward Snowden stated that "the
CIA tracked Aulaqi for three weeks before a joint operation with the U.S. military
killed Aulaqi." The document called the strike "another integrated CIA and military success in the counterterrorism fight." Jeremy Scahill and Glenn Greenwald,
"The NSA's Secret Role in the U.S. Assassination Program," *Intercept,* February 10,
2014, https://firstlook.org/theintercept/2014/02/10/the-nsas-secret-role/.

289 "People were optimistic that we were getting close" American official, confidential interview, 2013.

290 He and his small band were sitting outside a large Bedouin-style tent
This account of Awlaki's death is based on confidential interviews with multiple
American counterterrorism officials, 2014.

290 It was "Bedouin country," said Abdullah al-Jumaili Abdullah al-Jumaili,
interview, January 27, 2014, Sanaa.

291 "Before I begin," he said, "I want to say a few words" "Remarks by the President at the 'Change of Office' Chairman of the Joint Chiefs of Staff Ceremony,"
September 30, 2011, White House, Briefing Room, http://www.whitehouse.gov/
the-press-office/2011/09/30/remarks-president-change-office-chairman-joint
-chiefs-staff-ceremony.

**291 an act "where it is intended that the role of the United States Government
will not be apparent or acknowledged publicly"** Definition of *covert action* at 50
USC 3093e, Cornell University Law School, Legal Information Institute, http://
www.law.cornell.edu/uscode/text/50/3093.

292 Obama spoke enthusiastically with radio host Michael Smerconish Obama,
interview by Michael Smerconish, October 26, 2012, *Smerconish,* CNN, http://
smerconish.com/michael-smerconish-interviews-president-obama/.

294 On the *Washington Monthly*'s website the day of the Awlaki strike Steve
Benen, "A Quiet Record of Foreign Policy Successes," *Washington Monthly,* September 30, 2011, http://www.washingtonmonthly.com/political-animal/2011_09/a
_quiet_record_of_foreign_poli032532.php.

294 There were accolades from commentators for NBC News "First Thoughts:

Needing a Boost," *First Read* (blog), September 30, 2011, NBC News, http://first read.nbcnews.com/_news/2011/09/30/8058456-first-thoughts-needing-a-boost.

294 At ABC News, Jake Tapper offered a sly tribute Jake Tapper, "The Terrorist Notches on Obama's Belt," ABCNews.com, September 30, 2011, http://abcnews .go.com/blogs/politics/2011/09/the-terrorist-notches-on-obamas-belt/.

294 They fired their missiles at a group of seven men eating at the side of a road Obama administration and military officials have never given a public account of the October 14 strike, and officials who have spoken on background have given somewhat inconsistent accounts. This account is based on both confidential interviews with multiple American officials and interviews with Yemenis, including Nasser al-Awlaki, in January and February 2014, as well as Nasser's interview with Medea Benjamin of Code Pink in Sanaa, June 2013.

295 "He was a very sweet, very gentle boy" Nasser al-Awlaki, interview by Medea Benjamin of Code Pink, June 2013, Sanaa.

296 "The nature of his anger was that we'd taken a ton of care around the Awlaki issue" Obama aide, confidential interview, 2013.

296 "The son was there specifically to make contact with Al Qaeda" Senior American official involved with Yemen policy, confidential interview, 2013.

296 Abdul Razzaq al-Jamal, reported that Abdulrahman Bill Roggio, "Anwar al Awlaki's Son Hoped 'to Attain Martyrdom as My Father Attained It,'" *Long War Journal*, December 8, 2011, quoting from a jihadist forum as translated by the SITE Intelligence Group, http://www.longwarjournal.org/archives/2011/12/ anwar_al_awlakis_son.php.

297 the United States would still be offering a reward Statement from the State Department, "Reward Offers for Information on Al-Qaida in the Arabian Peninsula (AQAP) Leaders," October 14, 2014, listing Ibrahim al-Banna.

297 "was certainly with people who we believed to be AQAP" Senior Obama administration official, confidential interview, 2014.

297 Nasser al-Awlaki countered the false reports by giving reporters copies of Abdulrahman's birth certificate "Abdulrahman al-Awlaki's Birth Certificate," http://www.washingtonpost.com/wp-srv/world/documents/abdulrahman-al -awlaki-birth-certificate.html.

297 "That's a 'shit happens' kind of story" American official briefed in detail on strikes in Yemen, confidential interview, 2013.

298 In its official "Report of Death of an American Citizen Abroad," Form DS-2060 The document, dated December 20, 2011, is page 60 in a larger collection of documents related to Abdulrahman al-Awlaki obtained from the State Department under the Freedom of Information Act by Judicial Watch, "Abdulrahman al-Aulaqi Docs Combined," November 27, 2012, https://www.scribd.com/ doc/114624884/Abdulrahman-al-Aulaqi-docs-combined.

298 In an emotional audio statement to British Muslims Nasser al-Awlaki's statement is on YouTube: *Message from Dr Nassar Al-Awlaki to Muslims of UK*, uploaded December 2, 2011, https://www.youtube.com/watch?v=0AIywZqHjIE.

299 "I told my grandson, 'Look, I don't want you to take any other path except

the path of your grandfather'" Nasser al Awlaki, interview by Medea Benjamin of Code Pink, June 2013, Sanaa.

299 "I will continue being tormented with questions about why Abdulrahman was killed" Nasser al-Awlaki, written answers to questions from the author, January 2014.

299 Nasser had read my story about the hearing Scott Shane, "Judge Challenges White House Claims on Authority in Drone Killings," *The New York Times*, July 19, 2013, http://www.nytimes.com/2013/07/20/us/politics/judge-challenges -white-house-claims-on-authority-in-drone-killings.html.

299 A few months later, in April 2014, Judge Collyer dashed that hope Opinion of Judge Rosemary M. Collyer in *Aulaqi et al. v. Panetta et al.*, Civil Action No. 12-1192, US District Court for the District of Columbia, available at Center for Constitutional Rights website, http://ccrjustice.org/files/2014-04-04_Al -Aulaqiv.Panetta_OpinionDismissingCase.pdf.

13. A Bigger Brand

301 When Umar Farouk Abdulmutallab entered a federal courtroom in Detroit for sentencing The transcript of Abdulmutallab's sentencing on February 16, 2012, before Judge Nancy G. Edmunds is part of the online case file, *US v. Abdulmutallab*, Case No. 10-CR-20005.

302 Many fans compiled elaborate tribute videos See, for instance, *[New] Tribute to Imam Anwar al Awlaki (RA)*, uploaded March 29, 2012, https://www .youtube.com/watch?v=OQXFd3NXsoI.

302 Among them was an official video eulogy from AQAP itself The transcript can be found in "AQAP Releases Video Focused on Anwar al-Awlaki," SITE Intelligence Group, December 20, 2011, https://news.siteintelgroup.com/ Jihadist-News/aqap-releases-video-focused-on-anwar-al-awlaki.html; the video itself is preserved in many places on the Internet, including the Internet Archive: *Al Malaheem: The Martyr of Dawaah*, https://archive.org/details/AlMalaheem -TheMartyrOfDawaah.

302 Rubeish had a personal motive for his anger at America Ibrahim al-Rubeish was known by several names and spellings, including Ibrahim al-Rubaish and Ibrahim Arbaysh; see *The New York Times*'s Guantanamo Docket, "Ibrahim Sulayman Muhammad Arbaysh," http://projects.nytimes.com/guantanamo/detainees/192 -ibrahim-sulayman-muhammad-arbaysh, and Murad Batal al-Shishani, "Ibrahim al-Rubaish: New Religious Ideologue of al-Qaeda in Saudi Arabia Calls for Revival of Assassination Tactic," Jamestown Foundation, November 25, 2009, http:// www.jamestown.org/single/?no_cache=1&tx_ttnews%5Btt_news%5D=35771# .VFFG9It4rut.

303 On YouTube alone a search for "Awlaki" turned up tens of thousands of videos, a number that kept climbing Author's observation from YouTube searches, 2009–14; a search on YouTube for "Awlaki" in October 2014, for example, produced "about 98,800 results," according to the count by YouTube.

303 That promise turned out to be meaningless, as I discovered when I did a

follow-up story Scott Shane, "Radical Cleric Still Speaks on YouTube," *The New York Times*, March 4, 2011, http://www.nytimes.com/2011/03/05/world/middleeast/05youtube.html.

303 "He's a bigger brand now than when he was alive" Ahmed Younis, telephone interview, November 19, 2013.

303 Yasir Qadhi, an American imam who preached a nonviolent variety of Salafi Islam Yasir Qadhi, "An Illegal and Counterproductive Assassination," *The New York Times*, October 1, 2011, http://www.nytimes.com/2011/10/02/opinion/sunday/assassinating-al-awlaki-was-counterproductive.html.

303 "When America kills its own without a trial," he wrote Ed Husain, "U.S. Shouldn't Have Killed al-Awlaki," CNN, September 30, 2011, http://edition.cnn.com/2011/09/30/opinion/husain-awlaki-killing/.

304 It turned out that the would-be airliner bomber was in fact a Saudi-born double agent Scott Shane and Eric Schmitt, "Double Agent Disrupted Bombing Plot, U.S. Says," *The New York Times*, May 8, 2012, http://www.nytimes.com/2012/05/09/world/middleeast/suicide-mission-volunteer-was-double-agent-officials-say.html.

304 the older brother, Tamerlan Tsarnaev, had found his violent ideology in Awlaki's YouTube pronouncements Scott Shane, "A Homemade Style of Terror: Jihadists Push New Tactics," *The New York Times*, May 5, 2013, http://www.nytimes.com/2013/05/06/us/terrorists-find-online-education-for-attacks.html.

305 Once, on Jon Stewart's *The Daily Show* "Barack Obama Pt. 2," *The Daily Show*, October 18, 2012, http://thedailyshow.cc.com/videos/g36uvc/barack-obama-pt—2.

305 In an interview with the author Mark Bowden Mark Bowden, *The Finish: The Killing of Osama Bin Laden* (New York: Grove Press, 2012), 262.

306 "It turns out," he said, "that I'm really good at killing people" A version of this comment was first reported by Mark Helprin and John Heilemann in *Double Down: Game Change 2012* (New York: Penguin, 2013). An administration official told me that he had heard the president make similar remarks on several occasions.

306 the number of civilians killed in Pakistan in 2013 and 2014 was zero or very near zero The data collected by the Bureau of Investigative Journalism can be found at "Get the Data: Drone Wars," http://www.thebureauinvestigates.com/category/projects/drones/drones-graphs/.

306 One huge fan, however, was Saleh's replacement as Yemeni president, Abdu Rabbu Mansour Hadi Scott Shane, "Yemen's Leader Praises U.S. Drone Strikes," *The New York Times*, September 29, 2012, http://www.nytimes.com/2012/09/29/world/middleeast/yemens-leader-president-hadi-praises-us-drone-strikes.html.

306 Yemenis were flabbergasted in September 2014 when Obama said the US strategy in Yemen had proven so successful "Statement by the President on ISIL," September 10, 2014, White House, Briefing Room, http://www.whitehouse.gov/the-press-office/2014/09/10/statement-president-isil-1.

306 "For every missile America launches to kill terrorists, we want five missiles for development" Abdullah al-Jumaili, interview, January 28, 2014, Sanaa.

307 Petraeus and his lover, Paula Broadwell, had communicated secretly by saving drafts of notes to a shared e-mail account Kimberly Dozier and Pete Yost, "Petraeus Said to Be Shocked by Girlfriend's Emails," Associated Press, November 13, 2012, http://bigstory.ap.org/article/info-emerges-about-2nd-woman-petraeus-case.

307 In a thirteen-hour, stream-of-consciousness performance on the Senate floor *Senator Rand Paul (R-KY) Filibuster*, March 7, 2013, http://www.c-span.org/video/?c4373357/senator-rand-paul-filibuster.

309 An appeals court finally ruled in our favor nearly four years after my initial request Charlie Savage, "Court Releases Large Parts of Memo Approving Killing of American in Yemen," *The New York Times*, June 23, 2014, http://www.nytimes.com/2014/06/24/us/justice-department-found-it-lawful-to-target-anwar-al-awlaki.html.

309 the Senate's very first public hearing on drone strikes in April 2013 Hearing of the Subcommittee on the Constitution, Civil Rights and Human Rights of the Senate Judiciary Committee, "Drone Wars: The Constitutional and Counterterrorism Implications of Targeted Killing," April 23, 2013, https://www.ccrjustice.org/files/HOOD,_Alkarama,_CCR_SJC_Submission.pdf.

309 On May 23, 2013, Obama came to the National Defense University "Remarks by the President at the National Defense University," May 23, 2013, White House, Briefing Room, http://www.whitehouse.gov/the-press-office/2013/05/23/remarks-president-national-defense-university. The interruption by Medea Benjamin and the president's reply are included in the transcript.

311 Cornel West disgustedly denounced Obama as a war criminal and his tenure as "a drone presidency" "Hear Cornel West on Obama: 'A Drone Presidency,'" *Time*, October 6, 2014, http://time.com/3475306/hear-cornel-west-on-obama-a-drone-presidency/.

311 The first was Dennis Blair See, for instance, Dennis C. Blair, "Drones Alone Are Not the Answer," *The New York Times*, August 14, 2011, http://www.nytimes.com/2011/08/15/opinion/drones-alone-are-not-the-answer.html.

311 "They are hated on a visceral level" Stanley McChrystal, quoted in David Alexander, "Retired General Cautions Against Overuse of 'Hated' Drones," Reuters, January 7, 2013, http://www.reuters.com/article/2013/01/07/us-usa-afghanistan-mcchrystal-idUSBRE90608O20130107.

311 Then there was Robert Gates, the former defense secretary, who called himself "a big advocate of drones" Robert Gates on CNN, State of the Union with Candy Crowley, February 10, 2013, http://edition.cnn.com/TRANSCRIPTS/1302/10/sotu.01.html.

312 "I say this with respect—they tend to express these doubts after they leave government" Ben Rhodes, interview, October 15, 2014.

312 By 2014, Hamilton was quite anguished, if sympathetic, about Obama's record Lee Hamilton, telephone interview, May 22, 2014.

312 "I think it was a very good strike. I think it was justified" Dick Cheney on State of the Union with Candy Crowley, CNN, October 2, 2011, http://transcripts.cnn.com/TRANSCRIPTS/1110/02/sotu.01.html.

313 Henry Kissinger reached for an unexpected comparison Henry Kissinger, NPR interview, "Henry Kissinger's Thoughts on the Islamic State, Ukraine and 'World Order,'" September 6, 2014, http://www.npr.org/2014/09/06/346114326/henry-kissingers-thoughts-on-the-islamic-state-ukraine-and-world-order.

313 Estimates of civilian deaths from the American bombing of Cambodia began at 50,000 See, for example, Ben Kieman, *How Pol Pot Came to Power: Colonialism, Nationalism, and Communism in Cambodia, 1930–1975* (New Haven, CT: Yale University Press, 2004), xxiii.

313 By comparison, the high-end estimates from the Bureau of Investigative Journalism in London of civilian deaths "Get the Data: Drone Wars," http://www.thebureauinvestigates.com/category/projects/drones/drones-graphs/.

313 Crumpton admitted: "We never said, 'Let's build a more humane weapon'" Henry Crumpton, interview, 2012.

313 "I think he understands that you can't eliminate civilian casualties entirely" Ben Rhodes, interview, October 15, 2014.

314 One of them, a polymath named Chris Anderson, drew an analogy with the Internet Chris Anderson, telephone interview, 2013.

316 But the Islamic State was online jihad 3.0, I wrote in *The New York Times* Scott Shane and Ben Hubbard, "ISIS Displaying a Deft Command of Varied Media," *The New York Times*, August 30, 2014, http://www.nytimes.com/2014/08/31/world/middleeast/isis-displaying-a-deft-command-of-varied-media.html.

316 In December 2013, a new, English-language Islamic State video "ISIL Video Features Posthumous Clip of Awlaki Promoting Islamic State," SITE Intelligence Group, December 10, 2013, https://news.siteintelgroup.com/Jihadist-News/isil-video-features-posthumous-clip-of-awlaki-promoting-islamic-state.html. The audio came from Awlaki's lecture "The Battle of Hearts and Minds," delivered by phone on May 11, 2008, to the South African conference, called "Holding on to Hot Coals: Surviving as a Muslim in the West." A transcript of the entire talk is at http://archive.org/stream/BattleOfTheHeartsAndMinds/BattleOfTheHeartsAndMinds_djvu.txt.

317 A Syrian activist group opposed to the Islamic State "Jihadist John Expands to Europe," news release from the Syrian group called Raqqa Is Being Slaughtered Silently, January 21, 2015, , http://www.raqqa-sl.com/en/?p=338.

317 An American who carried out a suicide bombing for the Al Qaeda affiliate "American Suicide Bomber Moner Mohammad Abu-Salha Discusses Immigration to Syria in First Part of Posthumous Interview," SITE Intelligence Group, August 27, 2014, https://news.siteintelgroup.com/Jihadist-News/american-suicide-bomber-moner-mohammad-abu-salha-discusses-immigration-to-syria-in-first-part-of-posthumous-interview.html.

317 Shannon Conley, a nineteen-year-old Muslim convert from Colorado Kirk Mitchell, "Arvada Teen Jihadist 'Wannabe' Pleads Guilty to Terror Charge," *Denver Post*, September 10, 2014, http://www.denverpost.com/news/ci_26504683/arvada-jihadist-wannabe-set-plead-guilty-terror-charge.

317 After two French-Algerian brothers burst into the offices Scott Shane, "In

New Era of Terrorism, Voice From Yemen Echoes," *The New York Times*, January 10, 2015, http://www.nytimes.com/2015/01/11/world/middleeast/paris-attacks-anwar-al-awlaki.html.

317 A week after the attack on *Charlie Hebdo*, a twenty-year-old Ohio man Criminal Complaint, *USA vs. Christopher Lee Cornell*, Case No. 1:15-cr-00012, US District Court for the Southern District of Ohio, 3.

317 The very next day, prosecutors in Florida announced News Release, "Qazi Brothers Charged with Additional Terrorism Violations and Attempted Murder of Two Deputy U.S. Marshals," US Attoney's Office, Southern District of Florida, January 15, 2015, http://www.fbi.gov/miami/press-releases/2015/qazi-brothers-charged-with-additional-terrorism-violations-and-attempted-murder-of-two-deputy-u.s.-marshals. See also Lizette Alvarez, "Details Are Revealed in Brothers' Terror Case," *The New York Times*, December 18, 2012, http://www.nytimes.com/2012/12/19/us/details-are-revealed-in-brothers-terror-case.html.

318 A study by the New America Foundation in 2014 found that eighteen people indicted in the United States Peter Bergen and David Sterman, "The Man Who Inspired the Boston Bombings," April 11, 2014, http://www.cnn.com/2014/04/11/opinion/bergen-boston-bombing-awlaki-jihadists.

INDEX

ABOUT THE AUTHOR

Scott Shane is a national security reporter for *The New York Times* based in Washington, DC, where he has worked for over a decade.